Dedication

I would like to dedicate this book to my family, especially to my brother, Faisal Hoque, and to my sister-in-law, Chris. I really owe a lot to them for their continuing support and help. Thanks for being there for me for all these years! Any time you need a shoulder of support, I will be there.

Acknowledgments

This book is a collaboration of many people's effort and help. I hope to mention all of their names here but if I forget any, please know that I thank you from the bottom of my heart.

First, I would like to thank my publisher for working so hard to publish this book. Ann Lush, my editor was a big help with this project. Thanks for your support and inspiration throughout the whole project.

Next, I would like to thank Louis Schumacher for the tremendous enthusiasm he's had for this project from the very beginning. From reviewing my proposal to writing two of the most important chapters, Louis has had a significant impact on this book.

Next, I would like to thank Edward Sfreddo and Piroz Mohseni for contributing some chapters to this book. Darryl Stoflet wrote many of the examples that were presented in this book and the CD. He is a very bright young man and I thank him for all his work.

The people I worked with at FGIC Public Sourcing Services also get a big thanks from me. Their encouragement and support was admirable and greatly appreciated! Ephrem Bartolomeos, Terrence Curley, Gavind Rao and Tarun Sharma deserve a big round of applause. Thanks to Terrence for fixing the computers and to Gavind and Tarun, I would like to mention that without your help, I would not be able to write those chapters!

My web hosting service OLM.NET is a great service and George did a great job helping me setup my site.

Thanks to all those who have contributed their code and software to the book and the CD. Jeremy Black from Infohiway.com contributed the most JavaScript examples to the CD and I am grateful for his generosity. Also thanks to Pioneer Joel for the VRML tutorial.

My special appreciation goes to those who helped me promote the book. Mitch Wright at tradepub.com and Harold Carey from ibic.com were very helpful providing me with the web space for the mirror sites for JavaScript Resouces a 2 z.

Best wishes go to Doctors Earl and Harriet Kaylor and to my friends Kathy Roamierz, Eddy Zhang, Harsha Kumar, Neaz Khan, and Chris Plam for giving me moral support throughout the whole project.

Now, I would like to send my special thanks to my family who have been a tremendous help and showed extreme patience with this project. My brother and my sister-in-law were like angels who stood by me for the journey. Their continuous help and encouragement have been most beneficial to the end product.

Last but not least, I would like to thank the Mighty One for the power he/she has given me. Thanks to him/her for making me understand, "Fate is what you create."

About the Contributing Authors

Louis Schumacher

Louis Schumacher is a software developer and project manager with 20 years of computer industry experience. He has worked for several software tool vendors and some of corporate America's largest companies. Louis is proficient in C, PowerBuilder, shell scripting, Assembler, and UNIX system administration. His last project was with FGIC Public Sourcing Services (a GE Capital Company).

Louis would like to dedicate the Java and LiveConnect chapters (Chapters 14 and 15) to his lovely wife, Bridget. He would like to tell Bridget, "Thanks for always being there for me through thick and thin."

Edward Sfreddo

Edward Sfreddo currently Director of Professional Services for EC³ (www.eccubed.com), a software development firm which specializes in building communities on the web. He has worn many different hats during his 12 years of experience including project manager, product developer, and corporate MIS developer. His background in developing commercial database applications includes database engines such as Sybase, DB2, SQL/DS, SQLBase, and SQL Anywhere. Edward spent the past year creating a commercial electronic commerce Web site using the Netscape suite of products.

Edward would like to dedicate his LiveWire section (Chapters 16–18) of the book to his wife, Gracine, their daughter, Hannah, and their dog Marley. He would like to tell Gracine, "I truly appreciate your love and support during this project. And yes, now I'll fix the kitchen chairs and take you for those long rides you enjoy so much."

Piroz Mohseni

Piroz Mohseni works at Lucent Technologies as a software consultant. He is involved in a variety of Web and database projects. He was formerly an assistant scientist at Ames Laboratory in Iowa. Piroz received a B.S. in Computer Engineering from Iowa State University in May of 1995. His professional interests include the Internet, Java, and databases. He wrote Chapter 13, " LiveConnect."

PRACTICAL JAVASCRIPT PROGRAMMING

M&T BOOKS

Henry Holt & Company, Inc. New York

M&T Books
A Division of MIS:Press, Inc.
A Subsidiary of Henry Holt and Company, Inc.
115 West 18th Street
New York, New York 10011
http://www.mispress.com

First Edition—1997

ISBN 1-55851-513-5

Associate Publisher: *Paul Farrell*

Managing Editor: *Shari Chappell*	**Production Editor:** *Anthony Washington*
Editor: *Ann C. Lush*	**Technical Editor:** *Simon St. Laurent*
Copy Edit Manager: *Shari Chappell*	**Copy Editor:** *Betsy Hardinger*

CONTENTS

Part One
Getting Started

Part Two
JavaScript Examples

Part Three
Using LiveConnect

Part Four
Using LiveWire

Part Five
The End?

PART ONE

GETTING STARTED

INTRODUCTION

If it seems to you that the World Wide Web is everywhere, you're not alone. Almost every announcement or advertisement you see on television, in newspapers, and in magazines includes a Web address where viewers and readers can get more information. Not long ago, few people knew what those funny letters stood for. The rate of growth in Web recognition has been dramatic.

As part of the Web hype, you've probably also heard of Java, CGI, VRML, and VBScript, all of them are tools that can help make a Web site more interactive. As interest in the Web has grown, so have people's expectations of the kind of interaction they will have at a Web site. Plain HTML isn't good enough any more, and many companies are evaluating tools to help them add interactive features. You may be asking yourself, "Which tool should I use? How much time and money do I have to spend to learn how to use any of these tools?" This book will explain how you can take advantage of JavaScript's chief benefits—simplicity and ease of use—to enhance your Web site with popular features.

Why JavaScript?

JavaScript has come a long way since Netscape released the Navigator 2.0 Web browser. Now JavaScript is supported not only by Netscape but also by Microsoft Internet Explorer and other browsers. You can use JavaScript to create many sophisticated applications that formerly could be created only with

3

Java or CGI. The chief benefit of JavaScript is its quick learning curve, which means that your company does not need to spend much cash to start programming. To write scripts in JavaScript, all you need is a text editor and a compatible browser. On the other hand, to program in Java you need a full-blown development environment, which can cost as much as $250–$300, and you must have a core C++ background to master the language. But how about VBScript or a CGI language such as Perl? Perl is very difficult to master, and VBScript is not supported by Netscape. Because Netscape enjoys almost 80 percent of the browser market, you might want to think twice about using VBScript.

What can JavaScript do for you? JavaScript-based pages can save your Web visitors time, because it is run on the client side. JavaScript code resides in your HTML page, so once the page is loaded, the script is ready to run. So you can forget about waiting for scripts to load, as with Java applets, and you can dispense with the server requests required with CGI. JavaScript can also be used to control your Web page content, unlike many other languages such as Java. Among other things, JavaScript can also be used to create custom forms, detect the client's browsers, communicate with other tools such as Java, ActiveX, and VRML, and connect with databases to display dynamic data on the fly. These JavaScript functions are based on Netscape 3.0, the version available at the time of this writing. As Netscape works to enhance this powerful scripting language, JavaScript functionality will likewise be improved.

Why This Book?

Within three months after the release of JavaScript, the bookstores were swamped with books on the subject. What I found interesting was that many authors discussed at length the history of the language and the language syntax. As a Web developer, I felt that these authors did not realize that many of us do not have time to learn every detail about new technologies such as JavaScript. Descriptions of JavaScript and redundant information about other technologies such as VBScript or ActiveX were interesting, but I felt that there was a need for an application-based JavaScript book. I wanted a book that would quickly teach readers how to program in JavaScript, focusing on how to create practical JavaScript scripts. I couldn't find such a book, so I decided to write one.

Because this book focuses solely on JavaScript, it lets us explore the language in depth. It covers, for example, LiveConnect (JavaScript communicating with plug-ins and Java) and LiveWire (a tool that can connect with databases using server-side JavaScript). These aspects of the book are intended to serve as a useful resource for someone who wants to program like a professional.

The accompanying CD-ROM includes almost more than 100 code examples that you can cut and paste as well as scripts that will put your Web site in business overnight. Many of these scripts were donated by companies and individuals who are using the scripts regularly. The decision to include the scripts as examples was a joint one, and I hope you will find the examples useful.

Who Should Read This Book

This book is for you if you fall into any of these categories:

- You are a Web developer who knows HTML and you want to learn how to use a fairly easy but effective interactive Web-page creation tool.
- You don't have much time to learn Java or other difficult languages, but you still want to create killer apps.
- You are a student or a teacher who is interested in Web development and want to expand your knowledge beyond HTML.
- You are simply a programmer who wants a step-by-step walkthrough of examples that will show you how the JavaScript technology works.

The book is not only for someone who wants to develop client-side applications but also for those who want to learn how to access a database via the World Wide Web. Here you will find out how to use your existing database knowledge and create fast and cost-effective Web databases.

If you are a Java programmer and want to tie together plug-ins, JavaScript, and Java, this book will show you how. The LiveConnect part of the book will show you how to create Java applets that will talk to plug-ins and JavaScript, something that many programmers can only dream about.

How This Book Is Organized

Part One is dedicated to JavaScript syntax. You will get a jump-start on the syntax you need to know to start scripting overnight. I've tried to make sure that all the essential concepts are explained in as much detail as necessary. If you feel that you need more explanation of a certain area, please visit the Netscape JavaScript Handbook site at: http://home.netscape.com/eng/mozilla/3.0/handbook/javascript/index.html.

Part Two will give you a step-by-step explanation of useful scripts that will make your Web site come alive. I start with a simple example chapter, Chapter 5, and then graduate to more-sophisticated scripts such as a JavaScript painter, JavaScript calendar, and so on.

Part Three is for those who want to learn about LiveConnect technology, which lets you use Java, JavaScript, and plug-ins together. The chapters are set up so that you first get a flavor of what LiveConnect is. Then you learn a little about Java, and finally you walk through some of the industry-standard LiveConnect examples.

Part Four will talk about LiveWire, which can be used to access databases using JavaScript. The chapters are structured just as they are in Part Three. First, we talk about what LiveWire is, then we give you a quick SQL course, and later we explain a full LiveWire application.

Part Five, the last part of the book, is where I talk about JavaScript working with ActiveX, VRML, JavaScript bugs, and describe what is on the accompanying CD-ROM.

Icons Used

Two icons are used in the book.

This icon is used to point out concepts or code that may need a closer look. Many times these notes were used as tips for certain code or concepts.

NOTE

This icon is used to warn you about what will happen if you do not follow certain instructions.

WARNING

CHAPTER ONE

JavaScript Basics

Since the end of 1994, there have been significant changes to the traditional flat homepages of the World Wide Web. With different tools and languages, a client-side scripting language called JavaScript was born. In addition to being easier to use than many other Web languages, such as CGI, JavaScript is a great tool to make the visitors to your homepage feel that they are interacting more with your page. It also saves the visitors time, because JavaScript does not use a server to run its code (except for server-side JavaScript). JavaScript's immediate recognition and response to user events have made JavaScript programmers more confident in creating user-friendly applications using the language.

This chapter covers:

- What JavaScript is
- What JavaScript can do
- What JavaScript's limitations are
- Embedding JavaScript in documents
- JavaScript reserved words
- Declaring variables
- JavaScript operators

What Is JavaScript?

JavaScript is a World Wide Web scripting language that is understood by the browser when it is between <SCRIPT> ... </SCRIPT> tags. JavaScript was developed by Netscape Communications and Sun Microsystems. First named LiveScript, it draws much of its roots from the Java programming language, which was developed by Sun. It is closely related to HyperText Markup Language (HTML). Although both Java and JavaScript are a subset of C++, there are quite a few differences between these two languages. Java is object-oriented and platform-independent at run time, whereas JavaScript is totally platform-independent and can be fully executed by a JavaScript compatible browser (Figure 1.1). Any platform running this browser can run a JavaScript application without problems. Java programs called *applets* are also capable of creating standalone applications that can be implemented in a Web page. Java is compiled into byte code, which is difficult to compile and program if you don't have previous programming experience. JavaScript, on the other hand, can be implemented as an HTML page easily and does not need to be compiled (except for server-side JavaScript).

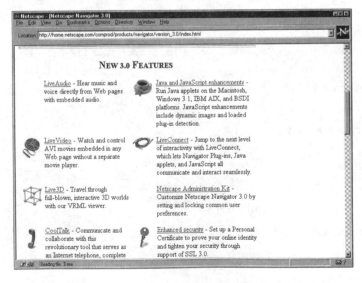

Figure 1.1 Netscape Navigator compiles JavaScript.

What Can JavaScript be Used For?

Creating Forms

The most efficient use of JavaScript is to handle client-side forms (Figure 1.2), which traditionally has been done with CGI. CGI takes a great deal of time to send back the user's response, and if the user makes a mistake and goes back to the CGI form, the data on the form is lost. With JavaScript, the user's valuable time can be saved, and the data will not be lost. It is even possible to perform calculations (e.g., create a tax calculator) in a standalone manner.

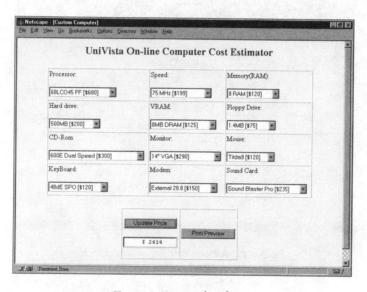

Figure 1.2 An on-line form.

Input Validation

When a user inputs data in a text field of a form, he or she traditionally has had to submit the data to a server and wait to find out if he or she made any mistakes. With JavaScript, you can check the type of the data as users keep fill out each field.

Object Manipulation

JavaScript has many built-in functions and predefined objects. It is possible to create an on-line clock (Figure 1.3) using the time function, which once could be programmed only with a complicated language like Perl. JavaScript lets you manipulate the document of an HTML page so that the user can change the background, text, or link color. You can also manipulate the browser by manipulating the toolbar, location, status bars, and so on.

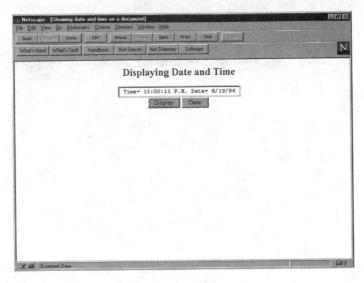

Figure 1.3 A clock created in JavaScript.

Graphics Manipulation

With Netscape Navigator 3.0 or later versions, you can change graphics on the fly. This means that you can create a JavaScript animation using graphics files. Although it's probably not the fastest way to do graphics animation, JavaScript gives you the functionality you need to work with graphics.

Handling Events

JavaScript is mostly event-driven. An event such as onLoad, for example, lets you play an **.au** sound file when a user loads your HTML document. Other event handlers, such as onClick, onSubmit, and onSelect, let even inexperienced programmers create button-driven, frame- or window-based Web pages easily (Figure 1.4).

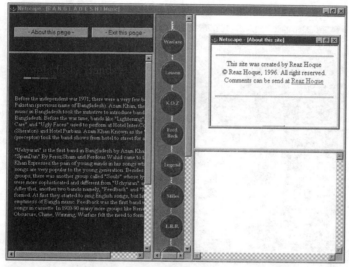

Figure 1.4 An example frame-based Web page.

Communicating with Java and Plug-Ins

With Netscape Navigator 3.0 or later versions, JavaScript can be used to communicate using Java and *plug-ins*. Called LiveConnect, this technology lets programmers call preprogrammed Java applets using a JavaScript function. JavaScript can easily detect whether the user's browser has the plug-in required by your HTML document. For more information on LiveConnect, see Chapter 13.

Accessing Databases

With server-side JavaScript and Netscape's latest tool, called LiveWire, you can access ODBC-compliant data from a database (Figure 1.5). This functionality has made light-weight JavaScript more useful than ever. Now you can create an on-line shopping mall and store all the data in your server-side database using JavaScript. For more information on LiveWire and server-side JavaScript, please see Chapter 16.

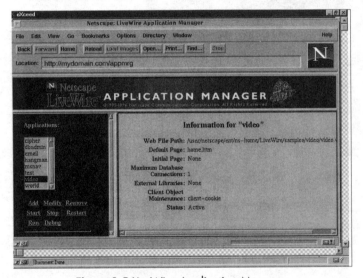

Figure 1.5 LiveWire Application Manager.

Limitations of JavaScript

As with any language, there are some limitations to what JavaScript can do. It is not designed to do extensive programming. It is considered an extension of HTML and an easy-to-learn scripting language that can be used to create simple client-side applications. For this reason, JavaScript is not as extensive as Java is. The JavaScript object model is limited to a predefined object and its properties and methods.

JavaScript cannot talk directly to the server without the help of a tool such as LiveWire. JavaScript can only invoke, analyze, and build URLs.

Unlike CGI, client-side JavaScript cannot write a file to the Web server's disk. This limitation is strictly for security purposes and is aimed at reducing electronic vandalism. Another limitation of JavaScript is that only the Netscape Navigator browser can run all of its syntax. Even though Microsoft Explorer 3.0 supports JavaScript, Explorer does not support many of the JavaScript features.

Embedding JavaScript in a Document

When a JavaScript script is written, it is embedded in HTML within a SCRIPT tag:

```
<SCRIPT>
//Code goes here
</SCRIPT>
```

The language is specified in the following manner:

```
<SCRIPT LANGUAGE="JavaScript">
//Code goes here
</SCRIPT>
```

Unless the SRC attribute is present to specify the script language, the LANGUAGE attribute is mandatory. Here is another way to specify the language:

```
<SCRIPT SRC="http://test.js">
```

The SRC attribute (optional) specifies a URL that loads the text of a script. (This option was not available in Netscape 2.0, but is available in Netscape 3.0.) This external JavaScript file contains functions that can be shared with many different HTML files. This is a useful feature of JavaScript because you can use the same set of functions over and over. Such files, however, cannot contain any HTML tags; they can contain only JavaScript statements and function definitions.

```
<SCRIPT LANGUAGE="language" SRC="http://rhoque.com/test.js">
```

You should put your <SCRIPT LANGUAGE="JavaScript"> .. </SCRIPT> code within the <HEAD>. This location is recommended because it forces the script to be loaded into the browser's memory first; then the tags are evaluated after the page loads. Errors might occur if you put the code somewhere else in the page, because the user might click on a link or button before the code is fully loaded. Listing 1.1 shows what it should look like.

Listing 1.1 Sample JavaScript Code

```
<HTML>
<HEAD>
<TITLE>SAMPLE</TITLE>
<SCRIPT LANGUAGE="JavaScript">
myfirstfunction(){
alert("Hello World");
}
</SCRIPT>
</HEAD>
<BODY body=ffffff onLoad='myfirstfunction()'>
<h2>Hello World</h2>
</BODY>
</HTML>
```

You don't need to ponder the code in Listing 1.1 at this time. Its purpose is to show you what a fully functional JavaScript script looks like. Just note that except for string literals, JavaScript is case-insensitive and treats all letters as lowercase.

TIP

Some quick rules of thumb:

- SRC URL should be used with an **.js** extension.
- A function should be called using JavaScript event handler from an HTML page.
- To make sure that the script is not visible from browsers that don't support JavaScript, the following style should be used after

```
<SCRIPT LANGUAGE="JavaScript">:
```

```
<SCRIPT LANGUAGE="JavaScript">
<!—hiding from old browser
//Script Goes Here
//—done hiding>
</SCRIPT>
```

In the following sections, we will discuss in more detail the JavaScript syntax and basics. Let's start with JavaScript reserved words.

TIP The following section will give you the information you need to get started with JavaScript scripting. If you want to learn more information about any of the following areas, please refer to http://home.netscape.com/eng/mozilla/ 3.0/handbook/javascript/index.html.

JavaScript Reserved Words

The reserved words in JavaScript have special meanings and cannot be used as JavaScript variable, function, method, or object names. Table 1.1 lists all the JavaScript reserved words.

Table 1.1 JavaScript Reserved Words

abstract			
boolean			
break			
byte	extends	native	this
byvalue	false	new	threadsafe
case	final	null	throw
catch	finally	package	transient
char	float	private	true
class	goto	protected	try
const	implements	public	var
continue	import	return	void
default	in	short	while
delete	instanceof	static	with
do	int	super	
double	interface	switch	
else	long	synchronized	

Declaring Variables

A variable name can be any legal identifier, and its value can be any legal expression. Remember that variables should begin with a letter (it cannot be a number) or an underscore. You cannot use a space within a variable name, and variable names are case-sensitive. To define a variable, just name it:

```
num1=0;
```

You can also use the reserved word var to declare a variable and optionally initialize it to a value. It is a good programming practice to use var to declare a variable. Note: if you intend to declare the variable to be local, you must use var before it. Here is an example:

```
var num1=0;
```

To make sure that a variable is global, declare it at the top of the functions; to use the variable as local, declare it within a function. Let's see an example:

```
var glob_num=0;     //global variable
function x(){
var loc_var=0;      //local variable
    }
```

JavaScript Operators

An operator lets you manipulate variables. For example:

```
var ans=num1 + num2;
```

Here you are manipulating ans by adding num1 and num2. The left element of the operation is called the *left operand* (or *first operand*), and the right element is called the *right operand* (or *second operand*). JavaScript operators can be divided into seven types. We'll look at each type next.

Assignment Operators

Table 1.2 shows the assignment operations in JavaScript. The table examples use num1 and num2, which have the values 2 and 5. The table shows the calculated result of `num1` after each operator is applied. Please note that for each operator, `num1` and `num2` have been given the same value: 2 and 5.

Table 1.2 Assignment Operators

Operator	Description	Example
=	Assigns first operand's value to the second operand.	`num1 = num2;` `//Now num1 holds the value 5`
+=	Adds both the operands and assigns the value to the first operand.	`num1 += num2;` `//Now num1 holds the value 7`
-=	Subtracts the first operand from the second and assigns the value to the first operand.	`num1 -= num2;` `//Now num1 holds the value -3`
*=	Multiplies both the operands and assigns the value to the first operand.	`num1 *= num2;` `//Now num1 holds the value 10`
/=	Divides the first operand by the second operand and assigns the value to the first operand.	`num1 /= num2;` `//Now num1 holds the value 2`
%=	Divides the first operand by the second operand and assigns the remainder to the first operand.	`num1 %= num2;` `//Now num1 holds the value 1`

Arithmetic Operators

Table 1.3 shows all the JavaScript arithmetic operators. Again, I have used `num1` and `num2` and have given them the values 5 and 2. This time, I stored the resulting value in another variable, called `ans`. Each time, `ans` has been calculated independently. After each calculation, I show the value of `ans`. Let `num1=2`, `num2=5`, and `ans=0` for each operation.

Table 1.3 Arithmetic Operators

Operator	Description	Example
+	Adds both operands.	`ans=num1+num2; //ans= 7`
–	Subtracts the second operand from the first operand.	`ans=num1-num2; //ans= -3`
*	Multiplies the two operands.	`ans=num1*num2; //ans= 10`
/	Divides the first operand by the second operand.	`ans=num1/num2; //ans= 2`
%	Divides the first operand by the second operand and evaluates to the remainder.	`ans=num1%num2; //ans= 1`
++	Increments the operand by 1 (can be used before or after the operand).	`ans++; //ans=1`
–	Decrements the operand by 1 (can be used before or after the operand).	`ans=–; //ans=-1`
–	Changes the sign of the operand.	`(-)ans=num1-num2; //ans=3`

Logical Operators

Logical operators take Boolean operands and return either a true or false valve. Table 1.4 lists the operators.

Table 1.4 Logical Operators in JavaScript

Operator	Description	Example
&&	If both the operands are true, logical and returns true; otherwise, it returns false.	`if (x=2) && (y=1)` `{      //do something }`
||	If one of the operands is true, logical or returns true. It returns false when both operands are false.	`if (x=2) || (y=1)` `{      //do something }`
!	If the operand is false, logical not returns true; otherwise, it returns false.	`if(!value_true)` `{   //do something}`

Comparison Operators

In a comparison operation, a true or false value is returned after the operation compares its operands. Table 1.5 lists all the comparison operators in JavaScript.

Table 1.5 Comparison Operators in JavaScript

Operator	Description	Example
= =	Returns true if the operands are equal; otherwise, it returns false.	`if (num1= = num2)` `{ //do something}`
!=	Returns true if the operands are not equal; otherwise, it returns false.	`if (num1!= num2)` `{ //do something}`
>	Returns true if the first operand is greater than the second operand; otherwise, it returns false.	`if (num1> num2)` `{ //do something}`
<	Returns true if the first operand is less than the second operand; otherwise, it returns false.	`if (num1< num2)` `{ //do something}`
>=	Returns true if the first operand is greater than or equal to the second operand; otherwise, it returns false.	`if (num1>= num2)` `{ //do something}`
<=	Returns true if the first operand is less than or equal to the second operand; otherwise, it returns false.	`if (num1<= num2)` `{ //do something}`

Bitwise Operators

A bitwise operator uses 0 and 1 to represent its operands. Thus, 5 would have the binary representation 101. For the most part, you will not need to know much about this operator.

In JavaScript, bitwise operators can be divided into two types: logical operators and shift operators. Table 1.6 shows the logical operators in JavaScript.

Table 1.6 Bitwise Logical Operators in JavaScript

Operator	Description
AND (or &)	If both the operands are true, bitwise and returns a 1; otherwise, it returns a 0.
OR (or |)	If one of the operands is true, bitwise or returns a 1. It returns a 0 when both operands are false.
XOR (or ^)	If either operand is true, bitwise xor returns a 1. It returns a 0 for any other combination.

Table 1.7 shows the shift operators in JavaScript. Note that bitwise shift operators take two operands: the first operand is shifted by the position number specified by the second.

Table 1.7 Bitwise Shift Operators in JavaScript

Operator	Description
Left shift (<<)	Shifts the first operand to the left. Note that zero bits are not shifted to the left; they are shifted to the right.
Zero-fill right shift (>>>)	Shifts the first operand to the right.
Sign-propagating right shift (>>)	Shifts the first operand to the right. Note that excess bits that are shifted off to the right are discarded.

Conditional Operators

A conditional expression can be either true or false based on a condition stated. A conditional expression takes this form:

```
(condition) ? num1 : num2
```

If condition is true, the expression evaluates to num1; otherwise, it evaluates to num2.

String Operators

The concatenation operator (+) is one of two string operators. It evaluates to a string that combines the left and right operands. The concatenation assignment operator (+=) is also available. In the following example, ans will hold the value JavaScript.

```
var str1="Java"
var str2="Script"
var ans=str1 + str2;
```

Operator Precedence

Figure 1.6 shows the operator precedence for JavaScript (from lowest (top) to highest (bottom) precedence).

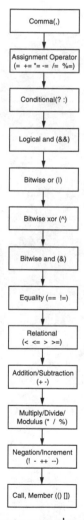

Figure 1.6 Operator precedence in JavaScript.

CHAPTER TWO

JavaScript Event Handlers

Although JavaScript is similar to C++ in many ways, JavaScript is quite different when it comes to event handlers. The JavaScript event handlers can be compared to the Visual Basic language. JavaScript has some of the same event handlers (`onClick`, `onSelect`, and so on) as Visual Basic.

The way to understand event handlers is to take an example from our everyday lives. We do certain things every day, but events may change the way we do things. For example, say you are driving to an interview when your car breaks down. Now your planned way of going to the interview will be changed in response to that event. Similarly, when you create a Web page with certain JavaScript event handlers, the page will act a certain way in response to events triggered by the user's interaction with the page.

This chapter covers:

- HTML form elements
- Event handlers

HTML Form Elements

Before we discuss JavaScript event handlers, we need become familiar with forms, because most of the event handlers work with forms. In brief, a form is a page where the user fills out a number of fields using checkboxes, fill-in blanks, and so on and submits the page for action by the form (Figure 2.1).

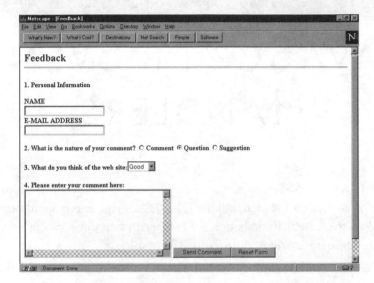

Figure 2.1 A simple feedback form in HTML.

Now let's look at the various elements in a form.

Text Element

A text element lets you fill in a single text line (Figure 2.2).

Figure 2.2 A text element.

Textarea Element

A textarea is similar to a text element except that a textarea gives you the option of entering multiple lines of text. If your text has multiple columns, textarea provides a scrolling option that lets you scroll through the columns and rows (Figure 2.3).

Figure 2.3 A textarea element.

SELECT Element

A select element lets you choose an option from a list of items. Here, you can choose only one item (Figure 2.4).

Figure 2.4 A select element.

Checkbox Element

A checkbox element lets you make multiple selections at a time (Figure 2.5).

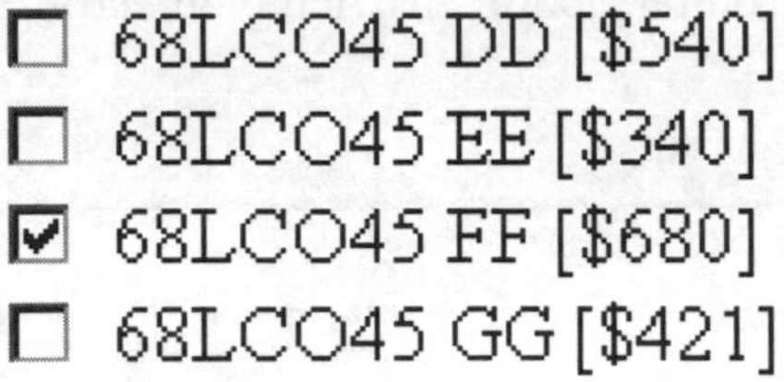

☐ 68LCO45 DD [$540]
☐ 68LCO45 EE [$340]
☑ 68LCO45 FF [$680]
☐ 68LCO45 GG [$421]

Figure 2.5 A checkbox element.

Radio Element

A radio element (Figure 2.6) lets you choose only one option without letting you scroll through the list of options. In other words, a radio element displays all the options on the page, whereas in a select element you get a drop box option.

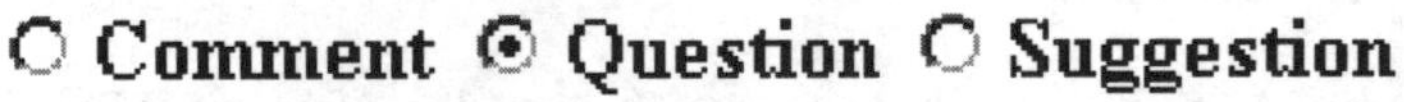

○ Comment ⊙ Question ○ Suggestion

Figure 2.6 A radio element.

Button Element

You click a button element to make certain requests of the form (Figure 2.7).

Send Comment

Figure 2.7 A button element.

Reset Element

A reset element (Figure 2.8) is a button that lets you reset the whole form to its default value. This button is useful when the user makes a mistake while entering data in the form.

Figure 2.8 A reset element.

Submit Element

A submit element (Figure 2.9) submits the whole form to the URL specified in the form via the POST or GET method.

Figure 2.9 A submit button.

Event Handlers

An event handler executes a segment of code based on certain events, such as onLoad and onClick, occurring within the application. JavaScript event handers can be divided into two types: interactive event handlers and non-interactive event handlers. An *interactive* event handler depends on user interaction with the form or document. For example, onMouseOver is an interactive event handler, because it depends on the user's action with the mouse. On the other hand, onLoad is a *non-interactive* event handler, because it automatically executes JavaScript code without the user's interaction. Table 2.1 lists the event handlers in JavaScript.

Table 2.1 JavaScript Event Handlers

Name	Used In
onAbort	image
onBlur	select, text, text area
onChange	select, text, textarea
onClick	button, checkbox, radio, link, reset, submit, area
onError	image
onFocus	select, text, textarea
onLoad	window, image
onMouseOver	link, area
onMouseOut	link, area
onReset	form
onSelect	text, textarea
onSubmit	form
onUnload	window

onAbort

An onAbort event handler executes JavaScript code when the user aborts loading an image. Listing 2.1 shows an example of onAbort.

Listing 2.1 Example of the onAbort Event Handler

```
<HTML>
<TITLE> Example of onAbort Event Handler </TITLE>
<HEAD>
</HEAD>

<BODY bgcolor="ffffff" >
<H3> Example of onAbort Event Handler: </H3>
<b>Stop the loading of this image and see what happens:</b><br><br>
<IMG  SRC="http://rhoque.com/rhoque.jpg"   onAbort="alert('You stopped the load
    ing the image!')">
</body>
</HTML>
```

Here, an alert() method is called via onAbort if the user aborts the loading of the image (Figure 2.10).

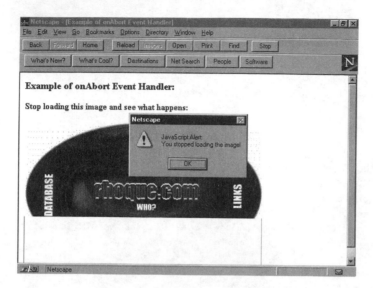

Figure 2.10 Output of Listing 2.1.

onBlur

An onBlur event handler executes JavaScript code when input focus leaves the field of a text, textarea, or select. For windows, frames, and framesets, the event handler executes JavaScript code when the window loses focus. In Windows, you need to specify the event handler in the <BODY> attribute. For example:

```
<BODY BGCOLOR='#ffffff' onBlur="document.bgcolor='#000000'">
```

On the Windows platform, the onBlur event does not work with <FRAMESET>. More information on frames can be found in Chapter 6.

WARNING

Listing 2.2 Example of onBlur Event Handler

```
<HTML>
<TITLE> Example of onBlur Event Handler </TITLE>
<HEAD>
```

```
<SCRIPT LANGUAGE="JavaScript">
function valid(form){
var input=0;
input=document.myform.data.value;
      if (input<0){
alert("Please input a value that is more than 0");
}
}
</SCRIPT>
</HEAD>
<BODY BGCOLOR="FFFFFF" TEXT="000000">
<H3> Example of onBlur Event Handler: </H3>
Try inputting a value less than zero:<br>
<form name="myform">
 <input type="text" name="data" value="" size=10 onBlur='valid(this.form)'>
</form>
</BODY>
</HTML>
```

In this example, data is a text field. When a user attempts to leave the field, the onBlur event handler calls the valid() function to confirm that data has a legal value (Figure 2.11). Note that the keyword this is used to refer to the current object.

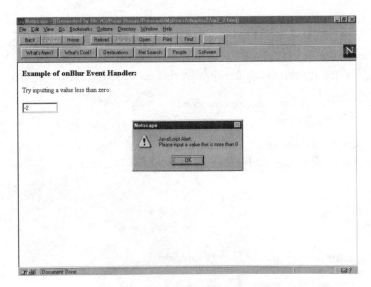

Figure 2.11 Output of Listing 2.2.

onChange

The onChange event handler executes JavaScript code when input focus exits the field after the user modifies its text (Listing 2.3). For example, when a user changes an option from a list of selection options, this event handler will execute JavaScript code.

Listing 2.3 Example of onChange Event Handler

```
<HTML>
<TITLE> Example of onChange Event Handler </TITLE>
<HEAD>
<SCRIPT LANGUAGE="JavaScript">
function valid(form){
var input=0;
input=document.myform.data.value;
alert("You have changed the value from 10 to " + input );
}
</SCRIPT>
</HEAD>
<BODY BGCOLOR="FFFFFF" TEXT="000000">
<H3> Example of onChange Event Handler </H3>
Try changing the value from 10 to something else:<br>
<form name="myform">
<input type="text" name="data" value="10" size=10 onBlur='valid(this.form)'>
</form>
</BODY>
</HTML>
```

In this example, data is a text field. When a user attempts to leave the field after changing the original value, the onChange event handler calls the valid() function, which tells the user which value has been entered (Figure 2.12).

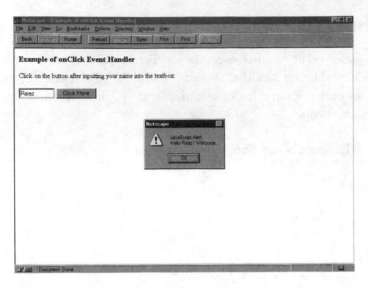

Figure 2.12 Output of Listing 2.3.

onClick

In an onClick event handler, a JavaScript function is called when an object in a button (regular, radio, reset, and submit) is clicked, a link is pressed, a checkbox is checked, or an image map area is selected. Except in the case of the regular button and the area, the onClick event handler can return false to cancel the action. For example:

```
<INPUT TYPE="submit" NAME="mysubmit" VALUE="Submit"
    onClick="return confirm('Are you sure you want to submit the form?')"
```

On the Windows platform, the onClick event handler does not work with reset buttons.

WARNING

Listing 2.4 shows an example of the onClick event handler.

Listing 2.4 Example of onClick Event Handler

```
<HTML>
<TITLE> Example of onClick Event Handler</TITLE>
<HEAD>
<SCRIPT LANGUAGE="JavaScript">
function valid(form){
var input=0;
input=document.myform.data.value;
alert("Hello " + input + " ! Welcome...");
}
</SCRIPT>
</HEAD>
<BODY BGCOLOR="FFFFFF" TEXT="000000">
<H3> Example of onClick Event Handler </H3>
Click on the button after inputting your name into the textbox:<br>
<form name="myform">
 <input type="text" name="data" value="" size=10>
<INPUT TYPE="button" VALUE="Click Here" onClick="valid(this.form)">
</form>
</BODY>
</HTML>
```

In Listing 2.4, when the user clicks the button **Click Here**, the `onClick` event handler calls the function `valid()` (Figure 2.13).

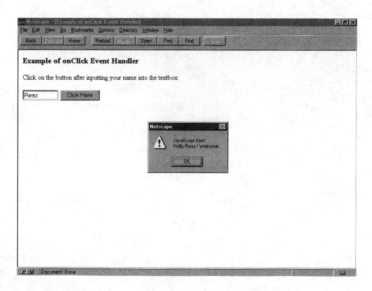

Figure 2.13 Output of Listing 2.4.

onError

An onError event handler executes JavaScript code when an error occurs while a document or image is being loaded. Using the onError event, you can turn off the standard JavaScript error messages and have your own function that will trace all the errors in the script. To disable all the standard JavaScript errors, all you need to do is set window.onerror=null. To call a function when an error occurs, use this code:

```
onError="myerrorfunction()"
```

Listing 2.5 shows how you can display your own error tracing.

Listing 2.5 Example of onError Event Handler

```
<HTML>
<TITLE> Example of onError event handler </TITLE>
<HEAD>
<SCRIPT Language="JavaScript">
window.onError = ErrorSetting

var e_msg="";
var e_file="";
var e_line="";

document.form[8].value="myButton"; //This is the error

function ErrorSetting(msg, file_loc, line_no) {
      e_msg=msg;
      e_file=file_loc;
      e_line=line_no;
      return true;
}

function display() {
      var    error_d = "Error in file: " + e_file +
                          "number:" + e_line +
                            ":" + e_msg;
      alert("Error Window:"+error_d);

}

</SCRIPT>
</HEAD>

<BODY bgcolor="ffffff" text="000000">
<h3> Example of onError event handler </h3>
```

```
<form>
<!input type="text" name="mytext" value="" size=50>
<input type="button" value="Show the error" onClick="display()"></form>
</body>
</HTML>
```

Notice that the function `ErrorSetting()` takes three arguments: the message text, the URL, and the line number where the error occurred. We invoke the function when an error occurs and set these values to three different variables. Then we display the values via an `alert` method (Figure 2.14).

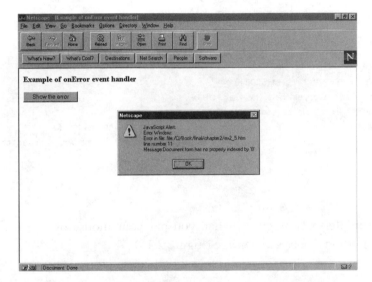

Figure 2.14 Output of Listing 2.5.

If you set `ErrorSetting()` to `False`, the standard dialog will be displayed.

NOTE

onFocus

An `onFocus` event handler executes JavaScript code when a field receives input focus by the user's tabbing in or by clicking but not selecting in the field. For windows, frames, and framesets, the event handler executes JavaScript code when the window gets focus. In Windows, you need to specify the event handler in the <BODY> attribute. For example:

```
<BODY BGCOLOR='#ffffff' onFocus="document.bgcolor='#000000'">
```

On the Windows platform, the onFocus event handler does not work with <FRAMESET>.

WARNING

Listing 2.6 Example of onFocus Event Handler

```
<HTML>
<TITLE> Example of onFocus Event Handler </TITLE>
<HEAD></HEAD>
<BODY BGCOLOR="FFFFFF" TEXT="000000">
<H3> Example of onFocus Event Handler </H3>
Put your mouse into the textbox:<br>
<form name="myform">
 <input type="text" name="data" value="" size=10 onFocus='alert("You focused the
textbox!")'>
</form>
</BODY>
</HTML>
```

In the example in Listing 2.6, when you put your mouse on the textbox, an alert() method displays a message (Figure 2.15).

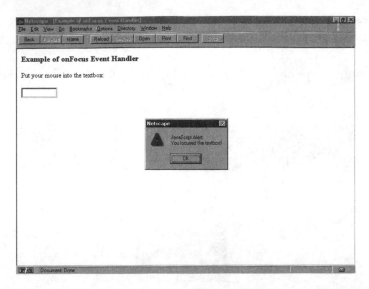

Figure 2.15 Output of Listing 2.6.

onLoad

An onLoad event occurs when a window or image finishes loading. For Windows, this event handler is specified in the <BODY> attribute of the window. For an image, the event handler executes handler text when the image is loaded. For example:

```
<IMG  NAME="myimage" SRC="http://rhoque.com/ad_rh.jpg" onLoad="alert('You loaded myim-
age')">
```

Listing 2.7 shows an example of an onLoad event handler.

Listing 2.7 Example of onLoad Event Handler

```
<HTML>
<TITLE> Example of onLoad Event Handler </TITLE>
<HEAD>
<SCRIPT LANGUAGE="JavaScript">
function hello(){
     alert("Hello there...This is an example of onLoad.");
     }
</SCRIPT>
</HEAD>
<BODY BGCOLOR="FFFFFF" TEXT="000000" onLoad="hello()">
```

```
<H3> Example of onLoad Event Handler </H3>
</BODY>
</HTML>
```

The example shows how the function `hello()` is called by using `onLoad` (Figure 2.16).

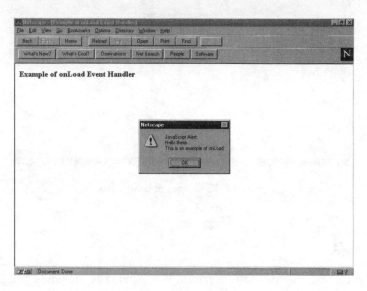

Figure 2.16 Output of Listing 2.7.

onMouseOver

When using the `onMouseOver` event handler, JavaScript code is called from outside an object or area when the mouse is over a specific link, object, or area. For an area object, the event handler is specified using the `<AREA>` tag. For example:

```
<MAP NAME="mymap">
<AREA NAME="FirstArea" COORDS="0,0,49,25" HREF="mylink.html"
     onMouseOver="self.status='This will take you to mylink.html'; return true">
</MAP>
```

Listing 2.8 shows an example of an `onMouseOver` event handler.

Listing 2.8 Example of onMouseOver Event Handler

```
<HTML>
<TITLE> Example of onMouseOver Event Handler </TITLE>
<HEAD>
</HEAD>
<BODY BGCOLOR="FFFFFF" TEXT="000000">
<H3> Example of onMouseOver Event Handler </H3>
Put your mouse over <A HREF="" onMouseOver="window.status='Hello! How are you?' ;
return true;"> here</a> and look at the status bar.
</BODY>
</HTML>
```

In this example, when you point your mouse to the link, the text "Hello! How are you?" appears on your window's status bar (Figure 2.17).

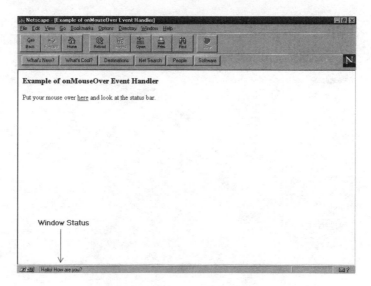

Figure 2.17 Output of Listing 2.8.

onMouseOut

JavaScript code is called from outside an object or area when the mouse leaves a specific link, an object, or area. For area objects, the event handler is specified with the <AREA> tag. Listing 2.9 shows an example.

Listing 2.9 Example of onMouseOut Event Handler

```
<HTML>
<TITLE> Example of onMouseOut Event Handler </TITLE>
<HEAD>
</HEAD>
<BODY BGCOLOR="FFFFFF" TEXT="000000">
<H3> Example of onMouseOut Event Handler </H3>
Put your mouse over <A HREF="" onMouseOut="window.status='You left the link!' ; return
true;"> here</a> and then take the mouse pointer away.
</BODY>
</HTML>
```

In this example, after you point your mouse and leave the link , the text "You left the link!" appears on your window's status bar (Figure 2.18).

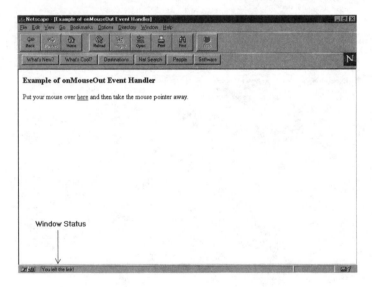

Figure 2.18 Output of Listing 2.9.

There is a problem with the `onMouseOver` and `onMouseOut` event handlers. Whenever the user points the mouse to the link (or leaves the link), the status bar doesn't erase the text. Chapter 5 will give you a solution to this problem.

T I P

onReset

An onReset event handler executes JavaScript code when the user resets a form by clicking on the **Reset** button. Listing 2.10 shows an example.

Listing 2.10 Example of onReset Event Handler

```
<HTML>
<TITLE> Example of onReset Event Handler </TITLE>
<HEAD></HEAD>
<BODY BGCOLOR="FFFFFF" TEXT="000000">
<H3> Example of onReset Event Handler </H3>
Please type something in the textbox and press the reset button:<br>
<form name="myform" onReset="alert('This will reset the form!')">
 <input type="text" name="data" value="Select This" size=20 value="" >
<input type="reset" Value="Reset Form" name="myreset">
</form>
</BODY>
</HTML>
```

In this example, when you press **Reset Form** after typing something, the alert method displays the message, "This will reset the form!" (Figure 2.19).

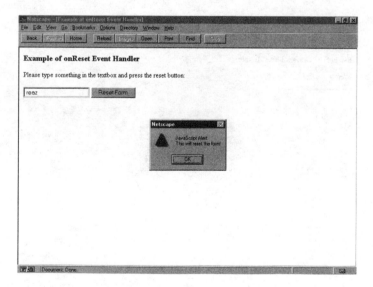

Figure 2.19 Output of Listing 2.10.

onSelect

An `onSelect` event handler executes JavaScript code when the user selects some of the text within a text or textarea field. Listing 2.11 shows an example.

Listing 2.11 Example of onSelect Event Handler

```
<HTML>
<TITLE> Example of onSelect Event Handler </TITLE>
<HEAD></HEAD>
<BODY BGCOLOR="FFFFFF" TEXT="000000">
<H3> Example of onSelect Event Handler</H3>
Select the text from the textbox:<br>
<form name="myform">
 <input type="text" name="data" value="Select This" size=20 onSelect='alert("This is an
example of onSelect!!")'>
</form>
</BODY>
</HTML>
```

In this example, when you try to select the text or part of the text, the `alert` method displays the message, "This is an example of onSelect!!" (Figure 2.20).

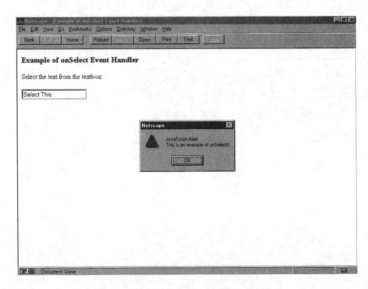

Figure 2.20 Output of Listing 2.11.

onSubmit

An onSubmit event handler calls JavaScript code when the form is submitted. Listing 2.12 shows an example.

Listing 2.12 Example of onSubmit Event Handler

```
<HTML>
<TITLE> Example of onSubmit Event Handler </TITLE>
<HEAD>
</HEAD>
<BODY BGCOLOR="FFFFFF" TEXT="000000">
<H3> Example of onSubmit Event Handler </H3>
Type your name and press the button<br>
<form name="myform" onSubmit='alert("Thank you " + myform.data.value +"!")'>
<input type="text" name="data">
<input type="submit" name ="submit" value="Submit this form">
</form>
</BODY>
</HTML>
```

In this example, the onSubmit event handler calls an alert() method when the button **Submit this form** is pressed. The listing produces the output shown in Figure 2.21.

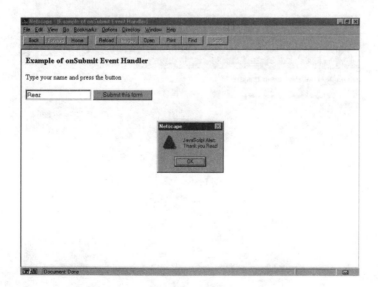

Figure 2.21 Output of Listing 2.12.

onUnload

An onUnload event handler calls JavaScript code when a document is exited. Listing 2.13 shows an example.

Listing 2.13 Example of onUnload Event Handler

```
<HTML>
<TITLE> Example of onUnload Event Handler </TITLE>
<HEAD>
<SCRIPT LANGUGE="JavaScript">
function goodbye(){
     alert("Thanks for Visiting!");
     }
</SCRIPT>
</HEAD>
<BODY BGCOLOR="FFFFFF" TEXT="000000" onUnload="goodbye()">
<H3> Example of onUnload Event Handler </H3>
Look what happens when you try to leave this page...
</BODY>
</HTML>
```

In this example, the onUnload event handler calls the Goodbye() function as a user exits a document (Figure 2.22).

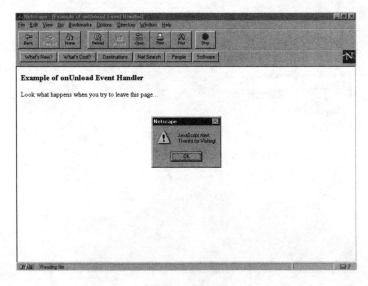

Figure 2.22 Output of Listing 2.13.

You can also call JavaScript code via explicit event handler calls. For example, say you have a function called `myfunction()`. You could call it like this:

```
document.form.mybutton.onclick=myfunction
```

N O T E   Notice that you don't need to put `()` after the function. Also, the event handler must be spelled out in lowercase.

CHAPTER THREE

STATEMENTS AND FUNCTIONS

JavaScript statements and functions are the same as those in many other languages, such as C/C++. JavaScript statements cannot be used as variable names and are used for specific tasks within the script. In brief, a JavaScript *statement* is similar to an English language statement in that it brings expressions together. A *function*, on the other hand, is an independent entity that performs a specific task.

This chapter covers:

- JavaScript statements
- JavaScript functions

JavaScript Statements

In Chapter 2, we learned how to define variables by using the keyword var. In this section, we will focus on the following sets of statements: comments, conditional statements, loop statements, and object manipulation statements.

Comments

A *comment* is used to make JavaScript code more readable. Netscape Navigator ignores comments. There are two ways to comment your code: forward slashes (//) and a combination of forward slashes and asterisks (/* ... */). Forward slashes are used for single-line comments. For example:

```
var myname=0; //myname is used to hold the name of the person
```

The other type is used to comment multiple lines. Multiple lines of comments are useful when you need to explain a lot of code. For example:

```
var myname=0; /* Notice that we used this variable to make sure the person's name is
              passed correctly to our next function */
```

Conditional Statements

Conditional statements are performed based on the logic of the code. There is only one conditional statement in JavaScript:

```
if...else
```

In an `if ... else`, when the `if` statement is true, the statements within the `if` statement are executed; otherwise, the statements within the `else` statement are executed. Here is an example:

```
function feedback()
{
if(ans==num2){      //assuming ans and num2 were declared  variables
alert("Sorry, can't have both values the same!");
}else{
alert("Thanks for your input!");
    }
}
```

Here, if `ans` is equal to `num2`, we see a JavaScript `alert` that displays the message, "Sorry, can't have both values the same!" Otherwise, you will see a JavaScript `alert` that displays the message, "Thanks for your input!"

Loop Statements

As the name suggests, a loop is used to perform a set of code statements repeatedly. In this way, you need not type the same code over and over to perform the same task. You use a loop to perform the repeated task instead. Let's look at the two kinds of loop statements.

While Loops

A `while` statement is executed when the expression condition is true and repeats the process until the condition is false. When the condition becomes false, the next statement after the loop is executed. For example:

```
function test()
{
var ans=0;
var j=0;
while (j<3){
    j++;
    ans=j+ans;
    }
var num=ans;
}
```

After the first pass, `j=1` and `ans=1`. After the second pass, `j=2` and `ans=3`, and after the third pass, `j=3` and `ans=6`. After the third pass, the `while` loop condition becomes false. The next statement, `num=ans`, executes, and `num` holds the value 6.

For Loops

A `for` statement is quite straightforward. You execute the `for` loop as many times as needed by using the following instructions:

1. Define the initial expression.
2. Set a condition.
3. Update the expression.
4, Define the statements within the loop.

For example, let's convert our `while` loop into a `for` loop:

```
function test()
{
var ans=0;          //initialize ans to zero
for(var j=0; j<=3;){
    ans=ans+j;
    j++;
        }
}
```

Here, `ans` is our addition value and `j` is our counter. Inside the `for`, we set the initial value of `j` equal to 0 and set a condition for the loop to iterate until `j` is less than or equal to 3. Finally, we update `j` by 1. Let's see what happens after each pass.

The first thing the loop does is to check the condition. Is `j` (which contains 0) less than or equal to 3? It's yes, so we continue.

1. First pass: `ans=0+0=0` (notice that we have initialized `ans` to zero) and `j=1`. Is `j` (which contains 1) less than or equal to 3? Yes, so continue.

2. Second pass: `ans=0+1=1`, `j=2`. Is `j` (which contains 2) less than or equal to 3? Yes, so continue.

3. Third pass: `ans=1+2=3`, `j=3`. Is `j` (which contains 3) less than or equal to 3? Yes, so continue.

4. Fourth pass (the final pass): `ans=3+3=6`, `j=4`. Is `j` (which contains 4) less than or equal to 3? No, so stop.

Notice that in the `for` loop the iteration is one more than in the `while` loop, making the value of `ans` equal to 6.

Break Statements

The `break` statement terminates a `for` or `while` loop and executes the statement following the loop. For example:

```
function compute(num){
    for(var j=0;j<=num;j++){
        if (j==8){
```

```
        break;
    }
alert('Access Denied!');
}
```

In this example, when the variable j becomes 8, the for loop will terminate and you will see an alert message saying "Access Denied!"

Continue Statements

The concept of a continue statement is the same as the break statement except that a continue statement jumps back to the condition (for a while loop) or jumps to the update expression (for a for loop). For example:

```
function compute(num){
    for(var j=0;j<=num;j++){
        if (j==8){
            continue;
        }
alert('Accessing new data!');
}
```

When the variable j becomes 8, the alert message pops up with the text, "Accessing new data!"

Object Manipulation Statements

There are four object manipulation statements in JavaScript. Let's look at each of them.

For ... in Statements

The for ... in statement is used to iterate within an object using its properties. This statement lets you loop through the properties of the object without testing for a condition or initializing or updating a counter. The statement loops through an object from the first property to the last. The syntax for this loop looks like this:

```
    for (counter in objectname)
{statements}
```

New Statement

A new statement creates an instance of an object. For example, the following is a user-defined object type called book. The book object has the properties type, page, and price:

```
function book(type, page, name){
    this.type=type;
    this.page=page;
    this.name=name;
}
```

To create an object called mybook, we do the following:

```
mybook= new book("internet", 400, "Practical JavaScript Programming");
```

This code creates the object mybook with the properties specified within the parentheses.

This Statement

The this statement specifies the current object. For example:

```
<FORM>
<input type=button name="mybutton" value="Press Here" onClick="myfunction(this.form)">
</FORM>
```

In the preceding example, the onClick event handler calls the function myfunction() when the button is clicked, and this.form identifies the current form.

With Statement

A with statement identifies the current object. For example, let's take the mybook object from our new statement. The properties of mybook could be declared using the with statement:

```
with (mybook){
type="internet";
page=400;
name="Practical JavaScript Programming";
}
```

JavaScript Functions

One of the most important concepts you need to understand about JavaScript is functions. A function is basically a segment of code that is called via, say, an event handler or called from another function. To understand functions, think of an example from your daily life. Say you want to buy a car. Buying a car is a function for you. To make that function work, you need some parameters: money and the type of car you want to buy. The same concept works in JavaScript. When you call or write a function, you need to define parameters for it. For functions, we need to know two things: how to create a function and how to call it.

Some of the JavaScript functions (mostly mathematical functions) are treated as methods. They will be discussed in Chapter 4.

NOTE

Creating a Function

To create a function, you specify the name of the function followed by the parameter name in parentheses and any additional code inside curly open and close brackets. Let's see an example:

```
function myfunction(myname, myvalue)
{
if (myname=myvalue){
        alert("Hello world!");
    }
}
```

As you can see, we're using a parameter name and value, which are passed into the function and used inside the function. Some functions return a value, and others do not. When you create a function that returns a value, you don't need to do anything special; just use the reserved word return at the end of the function.

The `return` statement returns a value from a function. For example:

```
function myfunction(num){
If (num>4)
return true;
else
      return false;
}
```

In this example, the function returns `true` if the value of `num` is more than 4; otherwise, the function returns `false`.

Calling a Function

In JavaScript, there are many different ways you can call a function. For example, you can have a variable, a function, or an event handler call a function. When you call a function, make sure that any parameters are defined correctly. Remember that the parameters of a function need not contain the same variable name. If you have a function called `myfunction(myname, myvalue)` and you call it somewhere, the function could have a parameter such as `myfunction(hisname, hisvalue)`.

You need to be careful about the order of the parameters. Suppose you define your first parameter as a string and the second parameter as an integer. If you call this function and reverse the order of the parameters, you will get an error when compiling the code.

Now let's examine how you can call functions. Here are three examples:

```
//Example 1
var myvariable=myfunction(hisname, hisvalue, theirname);

//Example 2
if (!myvalue(hisname, hisvalue)){
      //do something
}

//Example 3
onLoad = "myfunction(hisname, hisvalue)";
```

Built-In JavaScript Functions

JavaScript has three built-in functions: `eval`, `parseInt`, and `parseFloat`. These functions are known as the *top-level* functions. Why have built-in functions when you can create functions of your own? Although you need to create your own functions, these built-in functions are ready to perform specific tasks. For example, if you wanted to evaluate an expression you might want to use the built-in function `eval` rather than create a function of your own.

Eval Function

The `eval` function takes a string and evaluates it as an expression. The expression might be any string, including variables and properties of existing objects, statements, or sequences of statements. For example:

```
function mycompute(num1, num2, num3{
global_var = eval("num1+num2)/num3");
}
```

In this example, the function passes three values: `num1`, `num2`, and `num3`. When the function is called, these three values are evaluated by `eval` and the result is assigned to the variable called `global_var`. So if `num1` passes 3, `num2` passes 1, and `num3` passes 2, `global_var` will hold 2.

ParseInt Function

The `parseInt` function takes a string argument and returns an integer. The integer that is returned depends on a specified radix, or base. For example, a radix of 8 yields integers that are converted to octal, and base 16 values are converted to hexadecimal. If the values are greater than base 10, they are represented via A–Z letters rather than numbers. When the string is a floating-point number, `parseInt` truncates everything to the left, including the decimal point. Listing 3.1 shows an example. The resulting output appears in Figure 3.1.

Listing 3.1 An Example of parseInt

```
<HTML>
<TITLE> Example of parseInt </TITLE>
```

```
<HEAD>
<script>
function compute(form){
    form.data2.value=parseInt(form.data.value);
}
</script>
</HEAD>
<BODY BGCOLOR="FFFFFF" TEXT="000000">
<H3> Example of parseInt</H3>
Put a value in the text box and press the button:<br>
<form>
<input type="text" name="data" value="" size=20 >
<input type="button" Value="Check" name="myreset" onClick="compute(this.form)">
<input type="text" name="data2" value="" size=20 >
</form>
</BODY>
</HTML>
```

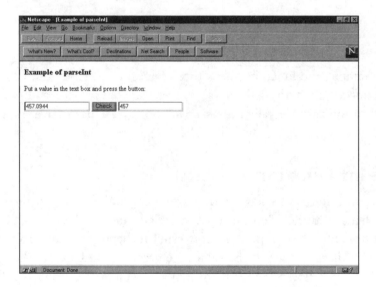

Figure 3.1 Output of Listing 3.1.

ParseFloat Function

A parseFloat takes a string argument and returns a floating-point number as long as the first character is "+," "-," ".," an exponent, or a number. When parseFloat finds any other character, it returns the floating-point number up to the unrecognized character. If the string is not recognized at all, it returns NaN. Listing 3.2 shows an example, and Figure 3.2 shows the output.

Listing 3.2 An Example of parseFloat

```
<HTML>
<TITLE> Example of parseFloat </TITLE>
<HEAD>
<script>
function compute(form){
     form.data2.value=parseFloat(form.data.value);
}
</script>
</HEAD>
<BODY BGCOLOR="FFFFFF" TEXT="000000">
<H3> Example of parseFloat </H3>
Put a value in the text box and press the button:<br>
<form>
<input type="text" name="data" value="" size=20 >
<input type="button" Value="Check" name="myreset" onClick="compute(this.form)">
<input type="text" name="data2" value="" size=20 >
</form>
</BODY>
</HTML>
```

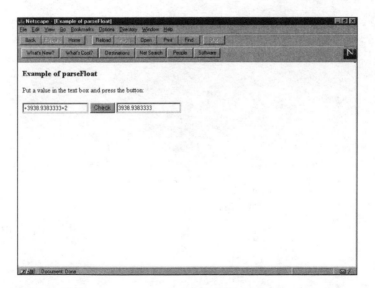

Figure 3.2 Output of Listing 3.2.

CHAPTER FOUR

OBJECTS AT A GLANCE

In this chapter, we talk about objects, the central concept of object-oriented programming. In other languages such as C, objects are referred to as library functions. To understand the concept of *object*, imagine a car. A car has certain variables, such as color, size, and type. These variables are known in JavaScript as object *properties*. The car can also perform some functionality, such as acceleration, braking, and so on. These functions are known as object *methods*. So, for example, if we wanted to use the properties (the variables) of the car, we would use the following instructions:

```
car.color
car.size
car.type
```

The same goes for the methods:

```
car.brake()
car. accelerate()
```

JavaScript follows the same rules. To use the object's properties and methods in JavaScript, you use the following instructions:

```
Objectname.Property
Objectname.Method(parameters)
```

Many of the JavaScript objects can also be a part of other objects. For example, imagine a person being an object. This person can be a part of a group, culture, or nationality. If the person is a part of a youth foundation, for example, he or she would be referred to as a property of that foundation. Similarly, the built-in JavaScript objects, such as string, math, and date, use many of the objects as their properties. In addition to the built-in functions, users can create new objects using the keyword new, which we have discussed before. This chapter will cover the changes in objects for Navigator 3.0 as well as the new objects that have been added.

 In JavaScript, many properties and methods behave the same for different objects. For that reason, we will explain all the methods and properties at the end of the chapter.

N O T E

This chapter covers:

- JavaScript objects
- Object properties
- Object methods

JavaScript Objects

Anchor Object (Anchors Array)

In an HTML page, you can include hyperlinks that let users travel from one position to another in the document. Hyperlinks are implemented using something called an *anchor*. You can define the anchor objects as items in an anchors array. Why would you want to do this? If there are many anchors, it will be easier for you to refer to them as arrays rather than call them by name. For example, you can refer to anchors as document.anchors[0], document.anchors[1], and so on. To find out the exact number of anchors in a document, you use the length property of the array: document.anchors.length. An anchor object is a property of the document object.

HTML Syntax

```
<A      [HREF=locationOrURL]
    NAME="anchorName"
    [TARGET="windowName"]>
    anchorText
</A>
```

Here, `HREF=locationOrURL` defines the link where the anchor or URL exists, `NAME="anchorName"` specifies the hypertext tag within the current document, `TARGET="windowName"` specifies the window that the link should be loaded into, and `anchorText` is the text that should be displayed as the anchor.

Properties

`length`

Methods

There are no methods for the `anchor` object.

Event Handlers

There are no event handlers for the `anchor` object.

Applet Object

The `applet` object specifies a Java applet in the page. If you have more than one applet in the page, you can access the applet via an array: for example, `document.applets[0]`, `document.applets[1]`, and so forth. Remember that the elements in the applets array are read-only. The `applet` object is a property of the `document` object.

HTML Syntax

```
<APPLET
   CODE=NameOfClassFile
   HEIGHT=height
   WIDTH=width
   MAYSCRIPT
   [NAME=NamepfApplet]
   [CODEBASE=DirectoryOfClassFile]
   [ALT=alternateText]
   [ALIGN="left"|"right"|
      "top"|"absmiddle"|"absbottom"|
```

```
        "texttop"|"middle"|"baseline"|"bottom"]
    [HSPACE=spaceInPixels]
    [VSPACE=spaceInPixels]>
    [<PARAM NAME= NameOfParameter VALUE = ValueOfParameter>]
    [ ... <PARAM>]
</APPLET>
```

Here, CODE=NameOfClassFile indicates the name of the **.class** file (Java applet), and HEIGHT=height indicates the height of the applet in the page (in pixels). WIDTH=width indicates the width of the applet in the page (in pixels), MAYSCRIPT gives permission to the applet to access JavaScript code, and NAME=NamepfApplet indicates the applet name. CODEBASE=DirectoryOfClassFile indicates the directory where the **.class** file is located (this is different from the directory of the HTML page). ALT=alternateText specifies the text that will be displayed for a browser not supported by Java. ALIGN indicates where the applet should be aligned in the page, HSPACE=spaceInPixels indicates the horizontal margin for the applet, and VSPACE=spaceInPixels indicates the vertical margin for the applet. PARAM defines the applet parameter, NAME specifies the parameter name, and VALUE specifies the parameter value.

Properties

name

Methods

There are no methods for this object.

Event Handlers

There are no event handlers for this object.

Area Object

Area lets you define an image map. In brief, an image map lets you create hyperlinks from the different parts of the image. The area object is a property of the document object.

HTML Syntax

```
<MAP NAME="NameofMap">
    <AREA
        [NAME="NameofArea"]
        COORDS="x1,y1,x2,y2,..."|"x-center,y-center,radius"
        HREF="location"
```

```
        [SHAPE="rect"|"poly"|"circle"|"default"]
        [TARGET="NameofWindow"]
        [onMouseOut="handlerText"]
        [onMouseOver="handlerText"]>
</MAP>
```

Here, MAP NAME="NameofMap" indicates the name of the map, AREA is the image area used as an image map, and NAME="NameofArea" indicates the area object name (referring to an area object by name is not allowed). HREF="location" indicates the URL that should be loaded for a specific map area, SHAPE indicates what type of shape the map should have, and TARGET="NameofWindow" defines the window the URL should be loaded into.

Properties

hash

host

hostname

href

pathname

port

protocol

search

target

Methods

There are no method for the Area object.

Event Handlers

onClick

onMouseOut

onMouseOver

Array Object

This object lets you create and manipulate arrays. An array is an object with a list of properties: for example, myarray[0], myarray[1], and so on.

Properties

length

Methods

join

reverse

sort

Event Handlers

There are no event handles for the `array` object.

Button Object

A button is used to let the user interact more with a homepage. When a button is clicked, it lets the program execute a certain segment of the JavaScript code. The `button` object is a property of the `form` object.

HTML Syntax

```
<input
TYPE="button"
NAME=Nameofbutton"
VALUE="buttonText"
[onClick="hndlerText"]>
```

`TYPE="button"` defines the `TYPE` attribute for the button, `NAME=Nameofbutton` defines a specific name for the button, and `VALUE="buttonText"` defines the value of the button that is visible from the Web page.

Properties

name

value

type

Methods

click

Event Handlers

onClick

Checkbox Object

A checkbox is used when there are multiple options to choose from in a form. The checkbox object is a property of the form object.

HTML Syntax

```
<INPUT
   TYPE="checkbox"
   NAME="checkboxName"
   VALUE="ValueofCheckbox"
   [CHECKED]
   [onClick="handlerText"]>
   textToDisplay
```

Here, TYPE="checkbox" defines the TYPE attribute for the checkbox, NAME="checkboxName" defines a specific name for the checkbox object, VALUE="ValueofCheckbox" specifies a specific value (if selected) to the server when the form is submitted, CHECKED indicates whether the checkbox is selected, and textToDisplay indicates the checkbox caption.

Properties

checked

defaultChecked

name

value

type

Methods

click

Event Handlers

onClick

Date Object

The date object lets the user create a date and time. The date object is a built-in object in JavaScript.

JavaScript Syntax

```
dateObjectName = new Date()
dateObjectName = new Date("month day, year hours:minutes:seconds")
dateObjectName = new Date(year, month, day)
dateObjectName = new Date(year, month, day, hours, minutes, seconds)
```

Here, `dateObjectName` could be the name of a new object or the property of an existing object. Notice that the second style is used for returning a string value, and the third and fourth are used for returning integer values. A full script using date and time is shown in Chapter 5.

Properties

prototype

Methods

getDate

getDay

getHours

getMinutes

getMonth

getSeconds

getTime

getTimeZoneOffset

getYear

setDate

setHours

setMinutes

setMonth

setSeconds

setTime

parse

setYear

toGMTString

toLocaleString

UTC

Event Handlers

There are no event handlers for this object.

Document Object

The document object contains information for the current document. It is a built-in object in JavaScript.

HTML Syntax

```
<BODY
    BACKGROUND="backgroundImage"
    BGCOLOR="backgroundColor"
    TEXT="TextColor"
    LINK="unfollowedLinkColor"
    ALINK="activatedLinkColor"
    VLINK="followedLinkColor"
    [onLoad="handlerText"]
    [onUnload="handlerText"]>
</BODY>
```

BACKGROUND="backgroundImage" specifies the background image that should work as a wallpaper, BGCOLOR="backgroundColor" specifies the background color, and TEXT="TextColor" specifies the color of the text. LINK="unfollowedLinkColor" specifies the color for unfollowed links, ALINK="activatedLinkColor" specifies the color for the activated link ,and VLINK="followedLinkColor" specifies the color for the visited link.

Properties

title

location

lastmodified

referrer

bgColor

fgColor

images

linkColor

vlink

Methods

There are no methods for the document object.

Event Handlers

There are no event handlers for the document object.

Element Array

The element array lets you refer to form elements (a button, text box, and so on) using an array. For example, you could refer to the form element like this: myform.elements[0], myform.elements[1], and so on. Referring to form elements using the element array saves you from referring to the elements by name. The element array object is a property of the form object.

Properties

length

Methods

There are no methods for the element array.

Event Handlers

There are no event handlers for the element array.

FileUpload Object

The FileUpload object lets the user upload a file as an input in an HTML form. This object is a property of the form object.

HTML Syntax

```
<INPUT
   TYPE="file"
   NAME="NameoffileUpload">
```

Here, TYPE="file" indicates the TYPE attribute for the file, and NAME="NameoffileUpload" indicates the FileUpload object name. Note that NAME does not reflect the name of the file to upload.

Properties

name

value

Methods

This object has no methods.

Event Handlers

This object has no event handlers.

Form Object (Forms Array)

In Chapter 2, we covered forms. An HTML form is an on-line document in which the user can input using radio buttons, checkboxes, selection lists, or text boxes. The `form` object reflects the HTML form in JavaScript. Please note that each HTML form in JavaScript is referred to as a unique object. You can refer to the `form` object using the `forms` array: for example, `document.form[0]`, `document.form[1]`, and so on. The `form` object is a property of the `document` object.

HTML Syntax

```
<FORM
    NAME="NameofForm"
    TARGET="NameofWindow"
    ACTION="serverURL"
    METHOD=GET | POST
    ENCTYPE="encodingType"
    [onSubmit="handlerText"]>
</FORM>
```

Here, `NAME="NameofForm"` indicates a specific name for the form object, and `TARGET="NameofWindow"` specifies the window the form should be submitted into. `ACTION="serverURL"` specifies the CGI URL that should handle the form request, and `METHOD=GET | POST` indicates the method the form should use to send the information to the server. `ENCTYPE="encodingType"` specifies which mime encoding (`"application/x-www-form-urlencoded"` (the default) or `"multipart/form-data"`) should be used to send the data.

Properties

name

target

action

method

enctype

Methods

submit

reset

Event Handlers

OnSubmit

onReset

Frame Object (Frames Array)

A frame splits a window into several parts. Each part of the frame can work as an individual page. You can refer to the frame object using the frames array: for example, parent.frame[0], parent.form[1], and so on. The frame object is a property of the window, and the frames array is a property of both the frame and the window.

HTML Syntax

```
<FRAMESET
    ROWS="rowHeightList"
    COLS="columnWidthList"
    [onLoad="handlerText"]
    [onUnload="handlerText"]>
    [<FRAME SRC="locationOrURL" NAME="NameofFrame">]
</FRAMESET>
```

Here, ROWS="rowHeightList" defines the height of frame rows (separated by a comma), and COLS="columnWidthList" defines the width of frame columns (separated by a comma). <FRAME> specifies a frame, SRC="locationOrURL" indicates the URL of the page for the frame, and NAME="NameofFrame" indicates the name of the frame that is used as a target of a hyperjump.

Properties

```
frames
parent
self
top
window
```

Methods

```
alert
close
confirm
prompt
SetTimeout
clearTimeout
```

Event Handlers

```
onBlur
onFocus
```

Function Object

We talked about functions in Chapter 3. In a `function` object, you can have segments of JavaScript code act as a function. To define a new function, you use the keyword `new`. For example:

```
myvar = new Function("num1", "num2", "return num1+num2");
```

To call this `function` object, you call `myvar` as if it were a function:

```
document.myform.mybutton.onclick= myvar(10,12);
```

Properties

```
arguments
prototype
```

Methods

There are no methods for the `function` object.

Event Handlers

There are no event handlers for the function object.

Hidden Object

The hidden object reflects a hidden field from an HTML form. This a property of the form object.

HTML Syntax

```
<INPUT
    TYPE="hidden"
    NAME="NameofHidden"
    [VALUE="textValue"]>
```

Here, TYPE="hidden" defines the TYPE attribute for the hidden object, NAME="NameofHidden" defines a specific name of the object, and VALUE="buttonText" defines the value of the hidden object.

Properties

name

value

type

Methods

There are no methods for the hidden object.

Event Handlers

There are no event handlers for this object.

History Object

The history object allows a script to work with the Navigator browser's history list. For security and privacy reasons, the contents of the list are not displayed to the user. This is a property of the document object.

Properties

length

Methods

back

forward

go

Event Handlers

There are no event handlers for this object.

Image Object

The `image` object works in an HTML form. This is a property of the `document` object.

HTML Syntax

```
<IMG
   [NAME="NameofImage"]
   SRC="Location"
   [LOWSRC="Location"]
   [HEIGHT="Pixels"|"Value"%]
   [WIDTH="Pixels"|"Value"%]
   [HSPACE="Pixels"]
   [VSPACE="Pixels"]
   [BORDER="Pixels"]
   [ALIGN="left"|"right"|
      "top"|"absmiddle"|"absbottom"|
      "texttop"|"middle"|"baseline"|"bottom"]
   [ISMAP]
   [USEMAP="Location#MapName"]
   [onAbort="handlerText"]
   [onError="handlerText"]
   [onLoad="handlerText"]>
```

Here, `NAME="NameofImage"` defines a specific name for the `image` object. `SRC="Location"` indicates the image source, and `LOWSRC="Location"` indicates the location of the low-resolution version of the image. `HEIGHT="Pixels"|"Value"%` indicates the height of the image either in pixels or in percentage, and `WIDTH="Pixels"|"Value"%` indicates the width of the image either in pixels or in percentage. `HSPACE="Pixels"` defines the left and right margin space around the image, `VSPACE="Pixels"` defines the top and bottom margin space around the image, and BORDER="Pixels" indicates a border of the image. ALIGN defines the alignment of the image as left, right, center, bottom, or top, ISMAP defines a server-side image map for the image, and USEMAP="Location#MapName" ISMAP defines a client-side image map for the image.

JavaScript Syntax

To create an image object, use the following syntax:

```
imageName= new Image([width, height])
```

To use an image object's properties, use the following syntax:

```
1. imageName.propertyName
2. formName.elements[index].propertyName
```

If you want to use a number of images as an array, use the following syntax:

```
1. document.images [index]
2. document.images.length
```

In the preceding syntax, imageName is the name of the image object or a property of an existing object. width is the width (in pixels) of the image, and height is the height (in pixels) of the image. formName is the name of the form, index is an integer that represents the image in a form, propertyName is the property of the object, methodName is the method of the object, and length is the number of images in a document.

Properties

border

complete

height

hspace

lowsrc

name

src

vspace

width

length

Methods

There are no methods for this object.

Event Handlers

`onAbort`

`onError`

`onLoad`

Link Object (Links Array)

The `link` object lets the user browse from one location to another. It reflects a hypertext link. For example:

```
<a href="javascript:history.go(-1)">Back</a>
```

If you want JavaScript not to go anywhere (for example, for the `onMouseOver` event handler), you can type the following statement:

```
<A HREF="javascript:void(0)">This will take you nowhere</A>
```

The `link` object is a property of the `document` object. You can reference the `link` objects using the `links` array: for example, `document.links[0]`, `document.links[1]`, and so on. Table 4.1 lists the most common URLs.

Table 4.1 Common URLs

URL Type	Protocol	Example
File	file://	file://intro.html
FTP	ftp://	ftp://ftp.yoursite.com/intro.zip
JavaScript Code	javascript	javascript:history.go(+1)
Mailto	mailto://	mailto:you@ask.com
Gopher	gopher://	gopher.yoursite.com
World Wide Web	http://	http://www.yoursite.com

HTML Syntax

```
<A HREF=locationOrURL
    [NAME="NameofAnchor"]
    [TARGET="NameofWindow"]
    [onClick="handlerText"]
```

```
    [onMouseOver="handlerText"]>
    linkText
</A>
```

Here, HREF=locationOrURL specifies the location of the link, NAME="NameofAnchor" specifies the object as an anchor object, and TARGET="NameofWindow" indicates which window the link should be reflected into.

Properties

hash

host

hostname

href

pathname

port

protocol

search

target

The links array has the following property:

length

Methods

There are no methods for this object.

Event Handlers

onClick

onMouseOver

onMouseOut

Location Object

The location object indicates the current URL. For example, http://www.somedomain.com/index.html is a location object. This is a property of the window object.

Properties

href

protocol

host

hostname

port

path

search

hash

Methods

reload

replace

Event Handlers

There are no event handlers for the location object.

Math Object

The math object provides properties and methods for advanced mathematical calculations. It is a built-in object in JavaScript.

Properties

E

LN10

LN2

PI

SQRT2

SQRT1_2

Methods

abs

acos

asin

```
atan

atan2

ceil

cos

exp

floor

log

max

min

pow

random

round

sin

sqrt

tan
```

Event Handlers

There are no event handlers for this object.

MimeTypes

mimeTypes is an array of MIME types that are supported by the browser. The MIME type can be supported by the browser either internally or via helper apps or plug-ins. For example, the audio MIME type for **.wav** files would be audio/x-wav. This is a property of the document object.

Properties

```
type

description

enabledPlugin

suffixes
```

Methods

There are no methods for this object.

Event Handlers

There are no event handlers for this object.

Navigator Object

The `navigator` object reflects information about the version of Netscape Navigator being used. This is a built-in object in JavaScript.

Properties

appCodeName

appName

appVersion

versionNumber

userAgent

mimeType

plugins

Methods

javaEnabled

Event Handlers

There are no event handlers for this object.

Option Object

The `option` object is created using the keyword `new`. For example:

```
var myoption = new Option("option1", "option2")
```

The `option` object works side by side with the `selection` object. Once the `option` object is created and you want to add it to the `selection` object, you must add the statement `history.go(0)` to the end of your function.

JavaScript Syntax

To create an `option` to add to an existing `Select` object:

`optionName = new Option([optionText, optionValue, defaultSelected, selected])`

To add the new `option` to an existing `select` object:

`selectName.options[index]=optionName`

To delete an `option` from a `Select` object:

`selectName.options[index] = null`

Here, `optionName` refers to the old option name or the new one we have cre-ated. `optionText` reflects the selection list text, and `optionValue` specifies a spe-cific value (if selected) to the server when the form is submitted. `defaultSelected` indicates (with `true` or `false`) whether the selection is selected by default, and `selected` reflects (with `true` or `false`) whether an option is selected. `selectName` is the current `Select` object name, and `index` represents (as an integer) an `option` in the object. This is a property of the `form` object.

NOTE Suppose you have three options—`option[0]=option1`, `option[1]=option2`, and `option[2]=option3`—and you delete `option1`. In this case, `option2` will become `option[0]`, and `option3` will become `option[1]`.

Properties

`defaultSelected`

`index`

`prototype`

`selected`

`text`

`value`

Methods

There are no methods for this object.

Event Handlers

There are no event handlers for this object.

Password Object

The `password` object reflects a password text field from an HTML form in JavaScript. This is a property of the form object.

HTML Syntax

```
<INPUT
   TYPE="password"
   NAME="NameofPassword"
   [VALUE="textValue"]
   SIZE=integer>
```

Here, `TYPE="password"` defines the `TYPE` attribute for the `password` object, and `NAME="NameofPassword"` defines a specific name of the object. `VALUE="buttonText"` defines the value of the `password` object, and `SIZE=integer` indicates how many characters the user can input in the password box.

Properties

defaultValue

name

type

value

Methods

focus

blur

select

Event Handlers

There are no event handlers for this object.

Plug-in Object

The `plug-in` object displays the plug-in file in a Web browser. This is a property of the `document` object.

HTML Syntax

```
<EMBED
   SRC=source
   NAME=appletName
   HEIGHT=height
   WIDTH=width>
   [<PARAM NAME=parameterName VALUE=ValueofParameter>]
   [ ... <PARAM>]
</EMBED>
```

Here, `SRC=source` indicates the source for the plug-in file, and `NAME=appletName` indicates the embedded object name. `HEIGHT=height` defines the applet height (in pixels) inside the document, and `WIDTH=width` defines the applet width (in pixels) inside the document. `<PARAM>` indicates the embedded object parameter, `NAME=parameterName` indicates the parameter name, and `VALUE=ValueofParameter` indicates the value of the parameter.

Properties

There are no properties for this object.

Methods

There are no methods for this object.

Event Handlers

There are no event handlers for this object.

Plug-in Array

The `plug-in` array (not to be confused with the `plug-in` object) enables you to find out whether your Web visitor has a particular plug-in installed. Now with JavaScript you can find out whether the client is capable of displaying that plug-in. You can have it set up so that when the client is not capable of displaying the plug-in, you could substitute text or an image for the embedded plug-in.

Part 3 of the book talks more about plug-ins.

NOTE

Properties

There are no properties for this object.

Methods

There are no methods for this object.

Event Handlers

There are no event handlers for this object.

Radio Button Object

The radio button object reflects a set of radio buttons from an HTML form in JavaScript. To access individual radio buttons, use numeric indexes starting at zero. For instance, individual buttons in a set of radio buttons named testRadio could be referenced by testRadio[0], testRadio[1], and so on. This is a property of the form object.

HTML Syntax

```
<INPUT
   TYPE="radio"
   NAME="NameofRadio"
   VALUE="ValueofButton"
   [CHECKED]
   [onClick="handlerText"]>
   textToDisplay
```

Here, TYPE="radio" indicates the TYPE attribute for the radio object, NAME="NameofRadio" defines a specific name for the object, VALUE="ValueofButton" specifies a specific value (if selected) to the server when the form is submitted, CHECKED identifies whether the radio button is selected, and textToDisplay defines the text around the radio button.

Properties

checked

defaultChecked

length

name

type

value

Methods

click

Event Handlers

onClick

Reset Object

The reset object reflects a **Reset** button of an HTML form in JavaScript. This is a property of the form object.

HTML Syntax

```
<INPUT
    TYPE="reset"
    NAME="NameofReset"
    VALUE="buttonText"
    [onClick="handlerText"]>
```

Here, TYPE="reset" indicates the TYPE attribute for the button, NAME="NameofReset" indicates a specific name for the reset object, and VALUE="buttonText" defines the value of the button that is visible from the browser.

Properties

name

value

type

Methods

click

Event Handlers

onClick

Select Object (Options Array)

The select object is a selection list with the option of one or more items in an HTML form. This is a property of the form object.

HTML Syntax

```
<SELECT
    NAME="NameofSelect"
    [SIZE="integer"]
    [MULTIPLE]
    [onBlur="handlerText"]
    [onChange="handlerText"]
    [onFocus="handlerText"]>
    <OPTION VALUE="optionValue" [SELECTED]> textToDisplay [ ... <OPTION>
textToDisplay]
</SELECT>
```

Here, NAME="NameofSelect" indicates a specific name for the select object, and SIZE="integer" indicates how many options will be displayed at a time on the Web page. MULTIPLE indicates whether multiple options can be chosen, OPTION indicates an element in the option list, and VALUE="optionValue" specifies a specific value (if selected) to the server when the form is submitted. SELECTED indicates whether the option is selected by default, and textToDisplay indicates the text for the element.

Properties

length

name

options

defaultSelected

index

```
selected

text

value

selectedIndex
```

Methods

There are no methods for this object.

Event Handlers

```
onBlur

onFocus

onChange
```

String Object

The string object provides properties and methods for working with string literals and variables. This is a built-in object in JavaScript.

Syntax

To create a new string, you must use the following syntax:

```
stringObjectName = new String(string)
```

stringObjectName is a specific name for the string object, and string represents the string.

Properties

```
length
```

Methods

```
anchor

big

blink

old

charAt

fixed
```

```
fontcolor

fontsize

indexOf

italics

lastIndexOf

link

small

strike

split

sub

substring

sup

toLowerCase

toUpperCase
```

Submit Object

The `submit` object reflects a **Submit** button from an HTML form in JavaScript. This is property of the `form` object.

HTML Syntax

```
<INPUT
    TYPE="submit"
    NAME="NameofSubmit"
    VALUE="buttonText"
    [onClick="handlerText"]>
```

Here, `TYPE="submit"` indicates the `TYPE` attribute for the button, `NAME="NameofSubmit"` indicates a specific name for the `submit` object, and `VALUE="buttonText"` indicates the text that is visible on the button from the Web page.

Properties

```
name

value
```

Methods

click

Event Handlers

onClick

Text Object

The text object reflects a text field from an HTML form in JavaScript. This is a property of the form object.

HTML Syntax

```
<INPUT
    TYPE="text"
    NAME="NameofText"
    VALUE="textValue"
    SIZE=integer
    [onBlur="handlerText"]
    [onChange="handlerText"]
    [onFocus="handlerText"]
    [onSelect="handlerText"]>
```

Here, TYPE="text" indicates the TYPE attribute for the text object, NAME="NameofText" defines a specific name, VALUE="textValue" indicates a pretyped text in the text box, and SIZE=integer specifies the exact text box size for users to input text.

Properties

defaultValue

name

value

Methods

focus

blur

select

Event Handlers

```
onBlur

onChange

onFocus

onSelect
```

Textarea Object

The `textarea` object reflects a multiline text field from an HTML form in JavaScript. This is a property of the `form` object.

HTML Syntax

```
<TEXTAREA
   NAME="NameofTextarea"
   ROWS="integer"
   COLS="integer"
   WRAP="off|virtual|physical"
   [onBlur="handlerText"]
   [onChange="handlerText"]
   [onFocus="handlerText"]
   [onSelect="handlerText"]>
   textToDisplay
</TEXTAREA>
```

Here, `NAME="NameofTextarea"` indicates the name of the textarea, `ROWS="integer"` indicates how many rows the textarea should have, and `COLS="integer"` indicates how many columns the textarea should have. `textToDisplay` indicates the pretyped text in the `textarea` object, and `WRAP="off|virtual|physical"` indicates the word-wrapping control inside the textarea.

Properties

```
defaultValue

name

value
```

Methods

focus

blur

select

Event Handlers

onBlur

onChange

onFocus

onSelect

Window Object

A `window` object is basically the browser window. It is the top level for each window or frame and is also the parent object for the `document`, `location`, and `history` objects. This is a built-in object in JavaScript.

JavaScript Syntax

The following syntax is used to create a new window:

```
windowVar = window.open("URL",  "NameofWindow", ["windowFeatures"])
```

Here, `windowVar` is the name of the new window that is used to refer to a window's properties, methods, and containership. URL is the name of the URL to be opened, `NameofWindow` is the name of the window to target (as in frames), and `windowFeatures` is the specification of the browser options as well as the window size, resize, scroll, and so on.

Properties

The properties of the `window` object are the same as those of the `frame` object in addition to the following ones:

defaultStatus

opener

Methods

Like the properties, the window methods are the same as those of the `frame` object in addition to the following methods, which exist only for the `window` object:

`blur`

`focus`

`scroll`

WARNING

For security purposes, only when you open a window using the `open()` method will the `close()` method work. Otherwise, you will get an error message.

Event Handlers

`onBlur`

`onFocus`

`onLoad`

`onUnload`

`onError`

JavaScript Properties

Now that you have seen all the objects and have seen that most of them have a number of properties, let us see what these properties are.

action: sends the input to (if specified) a URL address or "mailto." Basically used for sending data to a specific server, such as a CGI application.

alinkColor: indicates the active link color of a document.

anchors: indicates the array of anchor names in the document.

appCodeName: specifies the code name of the client (such as "Mozilla" for Netscape Navigator).

appName: refers to the name of the client (such as "Netscape" for Netscape Navigator).

appVersion: refers to the version information for the client in the form.

border: indicates the border of the image.

bgColor: refers to the background color of the document (in RGB value).

checked: indicates (with `true` or `false`) whether an object (checkbox and radio) is selected.

complete: indicates (with `true` or `false`) whether an image has finished loading.

cookie: a string of values that is stored in the navigator to maintain state.

defaultChecked: indicates (with `true` or `false`) whether a form element (checkbox and radio) is checked by default.

defaultSelected: indicates (with `true` or `false`) whether an option was selected by default (reflects the SELECTED attribute).

defaultStatus: contains the default value displayed in the window status bar.

defaultValue: specifies a default value for the object.

description: indicates the type of `mimeType` for a plug-in.

E: returns the value of Euler's constant (roughly 2.718).

elements: indicates the array of form elements in the document.

encoding: indicates MIME encoding for a form.

fgColor: refers to the foreground color or text of the document (in RGB value).

filename: indicates the filename for a plug-in.

forms: indicates all the forms (in an array) in the document.

frames: indicates all the frames (in an array) in the document.

hash: indicates the URL anchor name. For example, in http://www.mydomain.com/~me/myypage.html#one, the "#" is the hash.

height: indicates the height of an object in percentage or in pixels.

host: indicates either the host and domain name or the IP address of a network. For example, in http://204.56.76.252:80/mypage.html, the "204.56.76.252:80" is the host.

hostname: indicates the port portion of the URL (the host). For example, in http://www.mydomain.com, the hostname is www.mydomain.com.

href: indicates the entire URL address used as a JavaScript string. For example: http://www.rhoque.com/index.html.

hspace: indicates the hspace of the object.

index: an integer value reflecting the index of an option.

lastModified: refers to the last modification date of a document.

length: returns the number of elements in the document.

linkColor: refers to the color of hyperlinks (in RGB value).

links: indicates all the link objects (in an array) in the document.

LN2: returns the value of the natural logarithm of 2 (roughly 0.693).

LN10: returns the value of the natural logarithm of 10 (roughly 2.302).

LOG2E: returns the value of base 2 logarithm of E (approximately 1.442).

LOG10E: returns the value of base 10 logarithm of E (approximately 0.434).

lowsrc: indicates the low resolution source of the image.

method: defines which method (GET or POST) should be used for the input to be sent.

name: returns a specific name for the object.

opener: when you're opening a window with the open() method, this property specifies the window name.

options: reflects in an array each of the options in the selection list (in order).

parent: returns the name of the window whose frameset is the current frame.

path: indicates the path of the location of the document. For example, in http://www.mydomain.com/~me/index.html, the path is "/~me/index.html."

PI: returns the value of PI (roughly 3.1415).

port: indicates the server port number, if any; otherwise, "". For example, in http://www.mydomain.com:80, the port is 80.

protocol: indicates the leftmost portion of the URL up to and including the first colon. For example, in http://rhoque.com, the http: part is the protocol.

prototype: enables you to add properties to an object.

referrer: refers to the URL address that called the current document.

search: indicates a search query. For example, in http://www.mydomain.com/~find/something?JavaScript, the "?JavaScript" is the search.

selected: indicates in Boolean if an option of a `select` object is selected.

selectedIndex: reflects the index of the currently selected option in the selection list.

self: specifies the current window.

SQRT1_2: specifies the value of the square root of one-half (roughly 0.707).

SQRT2: returns the value of the square root of 2 (roughly 1.414).

src: indicates the source of the object.

status: indicates the status bar for the window. You can display text on the window's status bar.

suffixes: indicates the file extension for the MIME type. For example: wav, au, and so on.

target: indicates the target of the frame.

text: indicates the text that is displayed in the selection list for a particular option.

title: refers to the title of the document.

top: indicates the topmost window.

type: indicates the HTML form TYPE object.

URL: indicates the full URL address for the document.

userAgent: specifies a value to identify the client (such as Mozilla/3.0b7 (Win32; I)).

value: indicates a string value for the object.

vlinkColor: indicates the color of the visited links (in RGB value).

vspace: indicates the vspace of the object.

width: indicates the width of the object.

window: specifies the current window.

JavaScript Methods

Now that we have covered all the properties of JavaScript objects, here are the descriptions of all the current JavaScript methods:

abs: takes a number and returns its absolute value.

acos: takes a number and returns its arc cosine value.

alert: displays a message box with an **OK** button.

anchor: lets you create or display an anchor in the document.

asin: takes a number and returns its arc sine value in radians.

atan: takes a number and returns its arc tangent value in radians.

atan2: takes two numbers and returns the angle of polar coordinates.

back: takes you back to the previous document in the history list.

big: takes a string and makes the font size big, as in the <BIG> tag.

blink: takes a string and makes it blink, as in the <BLINK> tag.

blur: loses the focus of an object.

bold: takes a string and makes it bold, as in the <BOLD> tag.

ceil: takes a number and returns the next integer greater than the number. For example, −89.98 becomes −89; on the other hand, 89.98 becomes 90.

charAt: takes a position index (as an integer) for a string and returns that character for that index.

clearTimeout: clears the time out that was set earlier.

click: performs a selection for the form element (button, checkbox, radio, reset, and submit). For example, if you call this method for a radio element, the element will be selected.

close(document): closes a stream that was opened by `document.open()` and displays the stream on the window.

close(window): closes a window that was opened by `window.open()`.

confirm: displays a message box with **OK** and **Cancel** buttons.

cos: takes a number and returns the cosine value in radians.

escape: takes a string and returns the ASCII encoding in the ISO Latin-1 character set.

exp: takes an argument and returns a Euler's constant to the power of the argument in the base of natural logarithms.

fixed: takes a string and displays the text as in a `<TT>` tag.

floor: takes a number and returns the next integer less than the number. For example, –89.98 becomes –90; on the other hand, 89.98 becomes 89.

focus: puts focus on the object.

fontColor: takes a string and sets the color as in the `<FONT COLOR=color>` tag.

fontSize: takes a string and sets the font size as in the `<FONTSIZE=size>` tag.

forward: takes you to the next document in the history list.

getDate: returns the day of the month for the current month as an integer (ranges from 1 to 31).

getDay: returns the day of the week for a `date` object as an integer (the returned integer ranges from 0 to 6, where 0 is Sunday and 6 Saturday).

getHours: returns the hour for a `date` object as an integer (the returned integer ranges from 0 to 23).

getMinutes: returns the minutes for a `date` object as an integer (the returned integer ranges from 0 to 59).

getMonth: returns the month in a `date` object as an integer (the returned integer ranges from 0 to 11, where 0 is January and 11 is December).

getSeconds: returns the seconds in the current time as an integer (the returned integer ranges from 0 to 59).

getTime: takes a specific date string and returns a value in milliseconds.

GetTimeZoneOffset: displays the time zone difference in minutes for the current local time and GMT.

getYear: returns the year in the `date` object as a two-digit integer representing the year less 1900.

go: takes you the specified URL in the history list.

indexOf: takes two parameters in order: searched string and starting string (optional; if not specified, takes the first position of the string) and returns the index of their first occurrence. For example, the following variable `myposition` holds 2:

```
var myString="JavaScript"
var myposition= myString.indexOf("a");
```

isNan: takes an argument and evaluates whether the argument is not a number (in the UNIX platform only).

italic: takes a string and makes the font italic as in the `<I>` tag.

javaEnabled: determines whether Java is enabled for the browser.

join: makes a string that takes all the array elements.

lastIndexOf: takes two parameters in order: searched string and starting index (this is optional; if no value is provided, it takes the last character in the string) and returns the index of the last occurrence of finding string. For example, the following variable `myposition` holds 4:

```
var myString="JavaScript"
var myposition= myString.lastIndexOf("a");
```

link: creates a hyperlink, as in `<a href="LocationURL">LinkText</a>`.

log: takes a number and returns the natural logarithm value.

max: takes two numbers and returns the greater of the two.

min: takes two numbers and returns the smaller of the two.

open(document): takes the output of the `write` or `writeln` method and opens a stream to display it.

open(window): opens a new Web browser.

parse: takes a date string and returns the numbers of milliseconds between January 1, 1970, at 00:00:00 and the date specified.

pow: takes two numbers and returns the value of the first number to the power of the second number.

prompt: displays a message box with **OK** and **Cancel** buttons.

random: returns a random number between zero and 1.

reload: refreshes the document.

replace: replaces the current history entry and loads the specified URL. When you use this method, you cannot navigate to the previous URL by using Navigator's **Back** button.

reset: resets a form without specifying a **Reset** button.

reverse: changes the order of the array element.

round: takes a number and returns the closest integer.

scroll: takes two parameters (x-coordinate and y-coordinate) and scrolls the document according to the coordinates.

select: selects the input from the text box, textarea, or password object.

setDate: takes an integer (between 1 and 31) and sets the day of the month. For example, the following variable `mydate` holds Jun 2, 1996, after this method is emulated:

```
var mydate="Jun 11, 1996 13:00:00";
mydate.setDate(2);
```

setHours: takes an integer (between 0 and 23) and sets the hour.

setMinutes: takes an integer (between 0 and 59) and sets the minutes.

setMonth: takes an integer (between 0 and 11) and sets the month.

setSeconds: takes an integer (between 0 and 59) and sets the seconds.

setTimeout: takes two parameters in order—an argument and an integer—and evaluates the expression after using the integer as milliseconds. For example, the following function `myfunction()` will be called after 10 seconds of the document load:

```
<Body onLoad="timerID=setTimeout('myfunction()',10000)">
```

setTime: assigns the date and time to other date functions. For example:

```
mydate = new Date("Jan 1, 1996")
mydate2 = new Date()
mydate2.setTime(mydate.getTime())
```

setYear: sets the year for a date object.

sin: takes a number and returns the sine of the number, where the number represents an angle in radians.

small: takes a string and displays its font small, as in the <SMALL> tag.

sort: sorts the elements of the array.

split: splits a string into array elements.

sqrt: takes a number and returns its square root.

strike: takes a string and displays as struck out text, as in the <STRIKE> tag.

sub: takes a string and displays it as subscript, as in the <SUB> tag.

submit: submits a form without the need to have a **Submit** button in the form.

substring: takes two parameters (not in order)—first index and last index—and returns a subset corresponding to the parameters. For example, the following variable `findsub` holds the string "my."

```
var str="oh my"
var findsub= str.substring(3,4);
```

sup: takes a string and displays it as superscript, as in a <SUP> tag.

tan: takes a number and returns the tangent value, where the number represents an angle in radians.

toGMTString: takes a `date` object and converts it into a GMT string.

toLocaleString: takes a `date` object and converts it into the current local time.

toLowerCase: takes a string and converts it to lowercase.

toString: takes an object and converts it into a string.

toUpperCase: takes a string and converts it to uppercase.

unescape: takes a string and converts it into ASCII.

UTC: takes date parameters (year, month, day [, hrs] [, min] [, sec]) and returns the number of milliseconds since January 1, 1970, at 00:00:00 GMT.

write: writes a string or HTML expression on a document.

writeln: writes a string or HTML expression on a document and returns a new line.

PART TWO

JavaScript Examples

CHAPTER FIVE

SIMPLE JAVASCRIPT SCRIPTS

Now that you have a good background in JavaScript, I would like to encourage you to try some of the simple JavaScript snippets you will see in this chapter. This chapter will introduce some neat little programs that you can use in your homepage and surprise others who are not familiar with this language. Just by cutting and pasting some of the code, you can make your homepage better-looking than ever.

This chapter covers:

- Your first JavaScript program: outputting text
- Displaying messages
- Using the date and time functions
- Measuring a user's time spent on a page
- Detecting the proper browser
- Playing on-demand sound
- A scrolling banner
- A solution to the onMouseOver and onMouseOut problem

Your First JavaScript Program

In any program, the programmer needs to find out how to output text in a document. To output text in JavaScript, you must use write() or writeln(). Listing 5.1 shows an example, and Figure 5.1 shows the output.

Listing 5.1 Writing Text on a Document

```
<HTML>
<HEAD>
<TITLE> Writing text on a document</TITLE>
</HEAD>
<BODY>
<SCRIPT LANGUAGE="JAVASCRIPT">
<!— Hiding the code
document.write("Welcome to Applications in JavaScript!");
// done hiding —>
</SCRIPT>
</BODY>
</HTML>
```

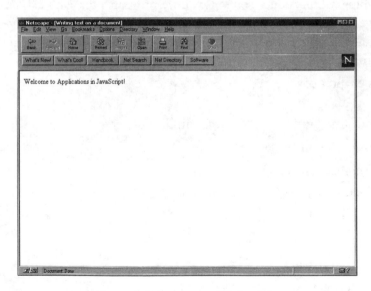

Figure 5.1 The output of Listing 5.1.

You will recognize most of the syntax from the first part of the book. Notice that we included the code between <SCRIPT> and </SCRIPT>. We also made sure that the document object write is in lowercase, because JavaScript is case-sensitive.

You might be wondering what the difference is between write and writeln. The write method outputs text, and writeln outputs a line feed after the text output. For example:

```
<SCRIPT>
document.writeln("Hello 1...");
document.write("Hello 2 +");
document writeln("Hello 3...");
</SCRIPT>
```

The preceding code outputs the following:

```
Hello1...
Hello 2 +Hello 3...
```

With write and writeln, you could use some special characters to display your output. Table 5.1 shows all the special characters in JavaScript for strings.

Table 5.1 Special Characters in JavaScript

Character	Description	Example
\b	Backspace	document.write("Hello\b");
\f	Form feed	document.write("Hello\f");
\n	New line	document.write("Hello\n");
\r	Carriage return	document.write("Hello\r");
\t	Tab	document.write("Hello\t");

What if you want to display the text in bold or italic? As with HTML, you can include <B> and </B> or <I> and </I> to manipulate the text output. Let's see what happens using different HTML tags in an example. Listing 5.2 shows the code, and Figure 5.2 shows the output.

Listing 5.2 Writing Text on a Document Using Special HTML Tags

```
<HTML>
<HEAD>
<TITLE> Writing text on a document: 2</TITLE>
```

```
</HEAD>
<BODY>
<SCRIPT LANGUAGE="JAVASCRIPT">
<!- Hiding the code
 document.write("<b>Welcome</b>");
 document.write(" <h2>to</h2>");
 document.write(" <font size=-1>Applications</font>");
 document.write(" <i>in</i>");
 document.write(" <pre>JavaScript!</pre>");
// done hiding ->
</SCRIPT>
</BODY>
</HTML>
```

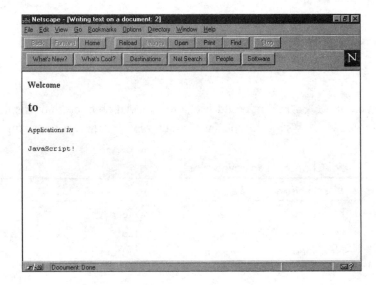

Figure 5.2 The output of Listing 5.2.

To display an image on the screen, you again use `write` or `writeln`. For example:

```
document.write('<IMG SRC="Hello.gif">');
```

Notice the usage of single quotes (' ') outside the tag and the double quotes (" ") for calling the image file.

Displaying a Message

Suppose you create a program in which you want to make sure that the user enters the correct input. If the user enters a number greater than 10, you want to alert the user by saying something like, "That's illegal!" There are three ways to implement such a display, as listed in Table 5.2. Figures 5.3, 5.4, and 5.5 show the message boxes.

Table 5.2 JavaScript Display Box Commands

Command	Description	Example
alert()	Displays text with **OK** option.	alert("Welcome to Applications in JavaScript!");
confirm()	Displays text with **OK** and **Cancel** options. If the user chooses **OK**, the function returns true; otherwise, it returns false.	confirm("Welcome to Applications in JavaScript!");
prompt()	Displays text with single input field and with **OK** and **Cancel** options. If the user chooses **OK**, the function returns true; otherwise, it returns false.	prompt("Welcome to applications in JavaScript!\n");

Figure 5.3 An alert().

Figure 5.4 A `confirm()`.

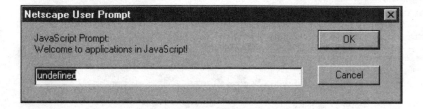

Figure 5.5 A `prompt()`.

Date and Time

As you read in Chapter 4, there are two built-in functions in JavaScript that let you display date and time. The example in Listing 5.3 displays the current time and date in a text box with an option to stop the time.

Listing 5.3 Showing Date and Time on a Document

```
<HTML>
<HEAD>
<TITLE> Showing date and time on a document</TITLE>
<SCRIPT LANGUAGE="JAVASCRIPT">
<!--Hiding the code
var show_time=false;
var timerID=null;
function stop(){
    if (show_time){
        clearTimeout(timerID);
```

```
            document.clock.date_time.value=" ";
    }
    show_time=false;
}
function start(form){
var today=new Date();
var display_value =" Time= " + today.getHours()
if(today.getMinutes() < 10){
    display_value+=":0" + today.getMinutes();
    }
else{
    display_value+=":" + today.getMinutes();
    }
if (today.getSeconds() < 10){
    display_value+=":0" + today.getSeconds();
    }
else{
    display_value+=":" + today.getSeconds();
    }
if(today.getHours()>=12){
    display_value+=" P.M."
    }
else{
    display_value+=" A.M."
    }
        display_value += " Date= " + (today.getMonth()+1) + "/"  +
        today.getDate() + "/" + today.getYear();
document.clock.date_time.value=display_value;
timerID=setTimeout("start()",100);
show_time=true;
}
//done hiding-->
</SCRIPT>
</HEAD>
<BODY BGCOLOR=white Text=Red Link=Green onLoad=stop()>
<center>
<H2>Displaying Date and Time</H2>
<FORM name=clock>
<INPUT type="text" name="date_time" size=35 value=" "><br>
<INPUT type="button" name="show_now" value="Display" onClick=start()>
<INPUT type="button" name="clear_now" value=" Clear " onClick=stop()>
</center>
</FORM>
</BODY>
</HTML>
```

This program has two functions (stop() and start()) for the two buttons **Display** and **Clear**. When the **Display** button is pressed, the start() function is called, and when the **Clear** button is pressed the stop() function is called. Both functions are called via the onClick event handler.

The stop() function simply clears the setTimeout method that is used in the start function. This function also clears the text box that displays the time and date. Finally, the function puts a false value in the Boolean variable show_time.

In the start() function, a new instance of the date is created using the statement new. Then the variable display_value is defined so that we can later export the date and time value in the text box. Remember that we are using the display_value as a string variable. Then we must make sure that if the second or minute value is less than 10, it is displayed as a single digit. The if..else statement is used for that purpose. To display A.M. or P.M., another if..else statement is used to check for a value greater than or equal to 12. If the time value is more than 12, display_value will hold "P.M." Otherwise, it will hold "A.M." Then the value of the day, month, and year is added into the variable. Now it's time to display the data in the text box:

```
document.clock.date_time.value=display_value;
```

The preceding code takes the value of display_value and puts it in the property called value of the text box named date_time. The word document is used to ensure the current document. Next, the variable timerID is set and show_time is set to true. Notice that timeID uses the setTimeOut() function with the parameters start() and 100. We use 100 to call the function start() within one-tenth of a second (Figure 5.6).

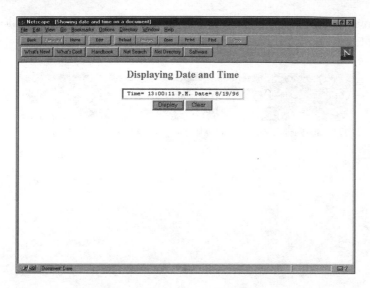

Figure 5.6 The output of Listing 5.3.

Displaying Automatic Page Update Information

Suppose you have a homepage and you update it quite frequently. Every time you change your homepage, wouldn't it be nice to see the last update date so that you know when you last changed the page? Listing 5.4 shows how you can do that.

Listing 5.4 Displaying Automatic Page Update Information

```
<HTML>
<HEAD></HEAD>
<TITLE> Displaying Update Info</TITLE>
<BODY bgcolor=ffffff>
<script language="JavaScript">
<!--hide script from old browsers
 document.write("<h2>This page has been updated: " + document.lastModified +
    "</h2>")
 // end hiding -->
</BODY>
</HTML>
```

All you need to do here is to use the `lastModified` property of the document. That's all! Figure 5.7 shows the output.

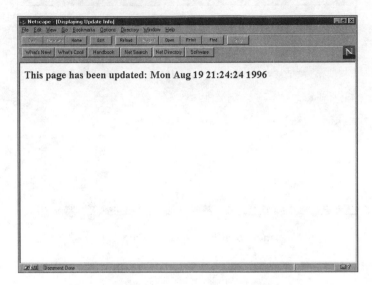

Figure 5.7 The output of Listing 5.4.

Measuring a User's Time on a Page

The next little script can be very useful. This program tells visitors how much time they have spent on your page. First, we create a function, called `person_in()`, that creates a new date instance that is called via the `onLoad()` event handler. We then create another function, `person_out()`, that is called via the `onUnload()` event handler. This function also creates a new date instance. We then take the difference between the two date instances, divide the result by 1000, and round the result. We divide the result by 1000 to convert the visit time from milliseconds into seconds. The result is then displayed via an `alert()` method (Listing 5.5). Figure 5.8 shows the output.

Listing 5.5 Measuring a User's Time on a Page

```
<HTML>
<HEAD>
<TITLE>Detecting a User's Time on a Page</TITLE>
<SCRIPT LANGUAGE="JavaScript">
function person_in() {
      enter=new Date();
        }
function person_out() {
        exit=new Date();
        time_dif=(exit.getTime()-enter.getTime())/1000;
        time_dif=Math.round(time_dif);
        alert ("You've only been here for: " + time_dif + " seconds!!")
    }
</SCRIPT>
</HEAD>
<BODY bgcolor=ffffff onLoad='person_in()' onUnLoad='person_out()'>
</BODY>
</HTML>
```

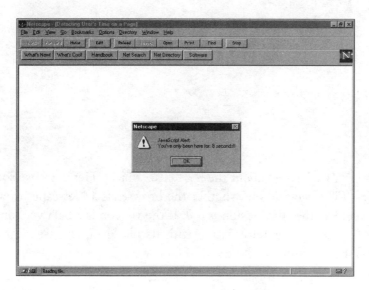

Figure 5.8 The output of Listing 5.5.

Detecting a Particular Browser

Our next example shows you how to detect a particular browser. This is a useful script if your page supports JavaScript for only Netscape 3.0 and you want to exclude visitors who don't have Netscape 3.0. Listing 5.6 shows the code.

Listing 5.6 Detecting the Appropriate Browser

```
<HTML>
<HEAD>
<TITLE>DETECTING USER'S BROWSER</TITLE></HEAD>
<BODY BGCOLOR=FFFFFF>
<SCRIPT LANGUAGE="JAVASCRIPT">
IF (NAVIGATOR.APPNAME == "NETSCAPE"){
       IF (NAVIGATOR.APPVERSION.SUBSTRING(0, 3) == "3.0"){
             IF (NAVIGATOR.APPVERSION.SUBSTRING(3, 4) == "B"){
                   ALERT('YOU ARE USING :' + NAVIGATOR.APPNAME + ' (' + NAVIGATOR.APPCODENAME
                         + ') ' + NAVIGATOR.APPVERSION + '\NSORRY! YOU ARE NOT USING NETSCAPE
                         3.0+');
                   HISTORY.BACK();
             }
       }
}
ELSE {
      ALERT('SORRY! YOU ARE NOT USING NETSCAPE 3.0+');
      }
</SCRIPT>
</BODY>
</HTML>
```

In Chapter 4, we learned about the `navigator` object. Here, we use some of its properties. First, we find out whether the browser is a Netscape browser; if it is, we detect whether the version is 3.0. If the version is a beta version, we display the whole browser information with its platform, and we alert the user that he or she is not using a Netscape 3.0 browser.

Notice that before we close the `if` statement, we use the `history.back()` statement. When users press **OK** on the alert message box, the document automatically takes them to the previous page. This arrangement is useful, because if you run JavaScript 1.1 with the Netscape browser 2.0 or less, the browser may crash. Our technique will prevent users from crashing their browsers.

NOTE

You could also send the user to a different page if the browser is not Netscape 3.0 browser. Instead of the `history.back()` statement, you need to type the following statement:

`window.location="mypage.html"`

Also note that this script will work only on browsers that can handle JavaScript syntax, such as Netscape 2.0+ or Microsoft Explorer 3.0.

If the browser is not a Netscape browser, we alert users that they are not using a Netscape 3.0 browser. Figure 5.9 shows the output of Listing 5.6.

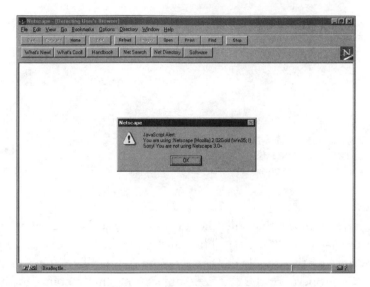

Figure 5.9 The output of Listing 5.6.

WARNING

The `else` statement will not be effective unless you use a JavaScript-enabled browser other than Netscape, such as Microsoft's Explorer 3.0.

Playing On-Demand Sound

A page with sound can be especially appealing to visitors. With JavaScript, you can play sound when the document is loaded or exited or when the user pushes a link. Listing 5.7 shows how to use an image as a link for playing on-demand sound.

Listing 5.7 Playing On-Demand Sound

```
<HTML>
<HEAD>
<TITLE>Playing on-demand sound</TITLE>
<SCRIPT LANGUAGE="JavaScript">
  function play(){
          window.location = "sample.au"
          }
</SCRIPT>
</HEAD>
<body bgcolor=ffffff>
<h2>Playing on-demand sound:</h2>
<b>Please click on the image below</b><br>
<a href="javascript:play()"><img src="sound.jpg" border=0></a>
</body>
</HTML>
```

First, we have an image that calls the function `play()`. Notice the way we link the function: `javascript:play()`. This function makes sure that this hyperlink is a JavaScript link that should call the function `play()`. The `play` function uses the `location` property of the `document` object and simply points to the sound file. Figure 5.10 shows the output of Listing 5.7.

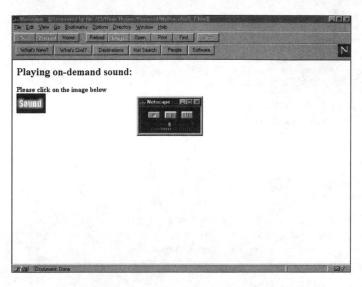

Figure 5.10 The output of Listing 5.7.

 If you want to play other files, such as a Shockwave file, all you need to do is replace **sample.au** with a Shockwave file (such as **sample.dcr**).

T I P

A Scrolling Banner

The next example shows you how to create a scrolling banner that will display the text, in your Windows status bar. In this example you can stop, pause, or or manipulate the banner speed. Listing 5.8 shows the script.

Listing 5.8 Scrolling Banner

```
<HTML><HEAD>
<SCRIPT LANGUAGE="JavaScript">

var b_speed=8; //defines banner speed
var banner_id=10;
var b_pause=0;//to pause the banner
var b_pos=0;
```

```
function stop() {

  if(!b_pause) {
                clearTimeout(banner_id);
                b_pause=1;
      }

        else {
                banner_main();
                b_pause=0;
      }

  }

function banner_main() {
        msg="W e l c o m e   t o   J a v a S c r i p t!"
        +" JavaScript can do some really"
        +" Cool stuff.  Check out http://rhoque.com"
        +" for more examples..."

        var k=(40/msg.length)+1;
        for(var j=0;j<=k;j++) msg+="        "+msg;

        window.status=msg.substring(b_pos,b_pos+120);
        if(b_pos++==msg.length){
            b_pos=0;
        }

        banner_id=setTimeout("banner_main()",1000/b_speed);
    }
</script>
</head>

<TITLE>Banner</TITLE>
</HEAD><BODY BGCOLOR="ffffff">
<H2> Example 5.8:</h2>
<P ALIGN=Center>
<FORM name="form1" action="">
<P ALIGN=Center>
<input type="button" value="Start"
onclick='{
    clearTimeout(banner_id);
    b_pos=0;
    banner_main()
    }'>
<input type="button" value="Slower" onclick="
{
if (b_speed<3){
```

```
alert("Does not get any slower!");
}
else b_speed=b_speed-1;
}
<input type="button" value="Faster" onclick="
{
if (b_speed>18){
alert("Does not get any faster!");
}
else b_speed=b_speed+2;
}
<input type="button" value="Pause" onclick='stop()'>
<input type="button" value="Reset" onclick='b_speed=8;'>
</FORM>
</BODY></HTML>
```

The output appears in Figure 5.11.

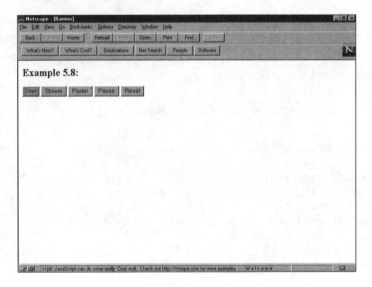

Figure 5.11 The output of Listing 5.8.

The program is simple to create. The stop() function is used to pause the scrolling text. First, we check whether the banner is paused. If it is not, we use the clearTimeout() method to pause the banner and make the b_pause variable true. When the user clicks on the **Pause** button again, the function calls the banner_main() function and makes the b_pause variable false.

In our `banner_main()` function, first a value is assigned to the variable `msg`. Then we take the length of `msg`, divide that by 40, and add 1 to the result. This value is assigned to `k`. Now a loop is used from `j` to `k` to add blanks to the value of `msg` . Next, we display the banner in the window's status bar by taking the substring of `msg` from 0 to 120. Later, we see whether the `b_pos` becomes as long as the `msg` length, and then we set the `b_pos` equal to 0 again.

To make the banner go faster, we just increase the value of `b_speed`. To make it go slower, we decrease the value of `b_speed`.

A Solution to the onMouseOver and onMouseOut Problem

In Chapter 2, we noticed a problem with `onMouseOver` and `onMouseOut`. When you have an `onMouseOver` (or `onMouseOut`) link that displays text on your status bar, the existing text never disappears. The solution to this problem is simple, as you can see in Listing 5.9.

Listing 5.9 Solution to the onMouseOver Problem

```
<HTML>
<TITLE>Solution to onMouseOver and onMouseOut Problem</TITLE>
<HEAD>
<SCRIPT LANGUAGE="JavaScript">
function show_status(stat_txt){
    window.status=stat_txt;
    setTimeout("show_null()",2000);//2000+ will keep the text longer
}
function show_null(){
    window.status="";
}
</SCRIPT>
</HEAD>
<BODY bgcolor=ffffff>
<h2>Example 5.9:</h2>
<B><A HREF="" onMouseOver='show_status("This is onMouseOver text"); return true;'
    onMouseOut='show_status("This is onMouseOut text"); return true;'>CLICK HERE</A>
</B></BODY>
</HTML>
```

When the user puts the mouse over the Hello link, the onMouseOver (and onMouseOut) event handler calls the function show_status(). Notice that the parameter ("This is onMouseOver text" for onMouseOver) of show_status() is passed to stat_txt. Inside the function, stat_txt is assigned to window.status, which displays the text on the status bar. Next, the function show_null() is called using setTimeOut. This function makes sure that the status bar displays NULL after one-half second.

CHAPTER SIX

A WINDOW AND FRAME-BASED HOMEPAGE

A nice feature of JavaScript is the ability it gives you to create your own windows. This means that you can create a window that will pop up when a user presses the appropriate button or link. Suppose you want a site map for your page. When a visitor clicks a link or button, you can render a small, stay-on-top window that works something like a remote control, letting users navigate the site easily. When you create a new window, you can define its dimensions and manipulate its look and feel. You can, for example, choose not to display a toolbar.

Another useful Web page option is frames. Almost every homepage uses frames to divide an HTML page into several independent subpages, each of which can have its own look and feel. Frames are useful for navigation. With JavaScript, you can communicate within frames. You can update multiple frames by clicking a single link or button, or you can use a button to manipulate text or graphics in another frame.

This chapter covers:

- Creating windows
- JavaScript and frames
- A window- and frame-based math game

Creating Windows

JavaScript has a method called open( ). To create a new window, we use the window method open( ). This method follows this syntax:

```
[windowVar = ][window].open("URL", "windowName", ["windowFeatures"])
```

Here, windowVar defines the name of the new window, URL is the URL location that will be opened, and windowName is the window name that is used in the TARGET attribute for the <FORM> or <A> tag. Remember that this name is a value that contains only alphanumeric or underscore (_) characters. Finally, windowFeatures is a comma-separated list that uses only the following options:

```
toolbar[=yes|no]|[=1|0]
location[=yes|no]|[=1|0]
directories[=yes|no]|[=1|0]
status[=yes|no]|[=1|0]
menubar[=yes|no]|[=1|0]
scrollbars[=yes|no]|[=1|0]
resizable[=yes|no]|[=1|0]
width=pixels
height=pixels
```

When you're creating a new window, make sure that you define the height and width for all the images in the page that will open a new window as well as for any window that might have an image. JavaScript seems to have problems opening windows when you don't have the height and width defined in the page. Listing 6.1 shows how to customize and open a new window based on the syntax shown previously.

Listing 6.1 Window Control Script

```
<HTML><HEAD>

<TITLE>Window Creation Page</TITLE>
```

```
<SCRIPT LANGUAGE="JAVASCRIPT">
<!- hide

function customize(form) {

    var address = document.form1.url.value;
    var op_tool  = (document.form1.tool.checked== true)  ? 1 : 0;
    var op_loc_box  = (document.form1.loc_box.checked == true)  ? 1 : 0;
    var op_dir  = (document.form1.dir.checked == true)  ? 1 : 0;
    var op_stat  = (document.form1.stat.checked == true)  ? 1 : 0;
    var op_menu  = (document.form1.menu.checked == true)  ? 1 : 0;
    var op_scroll  = (document.form1.scroll.checked == true)  ? 1 : 0;
    var op_resize  = (document.form1.resize.checked == true)  ? 1 : 0;

    var op_wid  = document.form1.wid.value;
    var op_heigh = document.form1.heigh.value;

    var option = "toolbar=" + op_tool + ",location=" + op_loc_box + ",directo
      ries="
        + op_dir + ",status=" + op_stat + ",menubar=" + op_menu + ",scroll
      bars="
        + op_scroll + ",resizable="  + op_resize + ",width=" + op_wid +
      ",height="
        + op_heigh;

    var new_win = window.open(address, "NewWindow", option );

}

function clear(form){

    document.form1.wid.value="";

    document.form1.heigh.value="";

}

// done hiding ->

</SCRIPT>

</HEAD>

<BODY BGCOLOR="#FFFFFF">

<CENTER><font color=blue size=+2>

Customized window

</font>
<br>
<b>Please choose from the following <br>selections to customize your window</b>

<br>
```

```
<TABLE cellpadding=5 border><TR><TD>
<PRE><FORM name=form1  ACTION="javascript:" METHOD="POST">
<INPUT TYPE="text" NAME="url" value="http://rhoque.com" >: URL
<INPUT TYPE="checkbox" NAME="tool">: Toolbar
<INPUT TYPE="checkbox" NAME="loc_box">: Location
<INPUT TYPE="checkbox" NAME="dir">: Directories
<INPUT TYPE="checkbox" NAME="stat">: Status
<INPUT TYPE="checkbox" NAME="menu">: Menubar
<INPUT TYPE="checkbox" NAME="scroll">: Scrollbars
<INPUT TYPE="checkbox" NAME="resize">: Resizable
<INPUT TYPE="text"   NAME="wid" value= >: Width
<INPUT TYPE="text"   NAME="heigh" value=>: Height
<BR><CENTER>
<INPUT TYPE="button" VALUE="=ENTER=" OnClick="customize(this.form)">
<INPUT TYPE="reset" VALUE="=RESET=" onClick="clear(this.form)">
</PRE></TD></TR></TABLE>

</FORM></center>

</body>
</HTML>
```

Figure 6.1 shows the output of Listing 6.1.

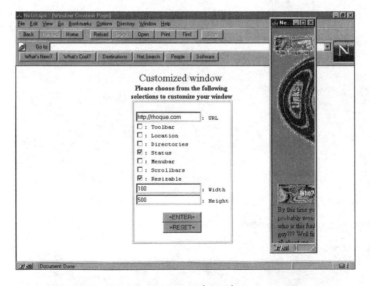

Figure 6.1 Customized window script.

We first created a form with check boxes to display the window options. We set a default URL, http://rhoque.com, that will be loaded when users click **Enter**. The button calls the customize() function. This function has variables that take the new window options from the user's input and put all the options in the variable option. We then use the open() method and follow the syntax described previously. The clear() function simply clears the form if **Reset** is clicked.

NOTE

If you want to know more about HTML form elements, please read Chapter 2 or Chapter 8 for more detail.

JavaScript and Frames

In Chapter 4, we showed you the HTML syntax for frames. In Listing 6.2, we define a set of frames that is used in our math game.

Listing 6.2 HTML Syntax for Creating Frames

```
<html><head></head>
<title>Simple Frame</title>
<FRAMESET FRAMEBORDER="0" border="0" FRAMESPACING="0" ROWS="72 ,*">
    <FRAME MARGINWIDTH="0" MARGINHEIGHT="0" SRC="title.htm" NAME="top" NORESIZE
SCROLLING="auto">
    <FRAMESET FRAMEBORDER="0" border="0" FRAMESPACING="0" COLS="310,*">
        <FRAME MARGINWIDTH="10" MARGINHEIGHT="5" SRC="control.htm" NAME="left"
scrolling="no">
        <FRAME MARGINWIDTH="2" MARGINHEIGHT="0" SRC="math.htm" NAME="right" NORESIZE
SCROLLING="auto">
    </FRAMESET>
</FRAMESET>
<noframe>
<BODY>
You need Netscape 2.0+ to visit this site...
</BODY>
</noframe>
</html>
```

Here, we create a top frame and two frames below it. We use the <FRAMESET> tag to create the columns and rows for the frames. The tag <FRAMESET col=>

creates column divisions, and `<FRAMESET rows=>` creates row divisions. Inside these tags we also define the frame border, frame spacing, and the width of the rows and columns. To define the width of columns and rows, the "*" reserves the remaining space.

The `<FRAME>` tag lets you indicate the source for the frame as well as define other specifications, such as margin width, margin height, and the name of the frame. Keep in mind, when creating frames, that you should always specify a name for each frame. This technique will help you target a hyperlink to a specific frame.

The scrolling option of a frame is defined using the word `scrolling` inside the `<FRAME>` tag. You can give your frame the option to scroll or not to scroll or even let the frame scroll automatically depending on the browser size. You define the scrolling option by setting `yes`, `no`, or `auto` equal to the word `scrolling`.

To accommodate browsers that don't support frames, you use the `<noframe>` tag. Any text that you placed inside this tag will be visible to browsers that don't support frames. If you don't use this tag or place text inside it, these browsers will display a blank page.

Now let's look at the relationships among the five frames on the math page. As you can see in Figure 6.2, the *parent* frameset contains the remaining frames in a tree hierarchy. We use the term *frameset* to refer to any frame that acts as a parent to one or more other frames. Our parent frameset has two *child* frames, one of which acts as a frameset and contains two *grandchild* frames.

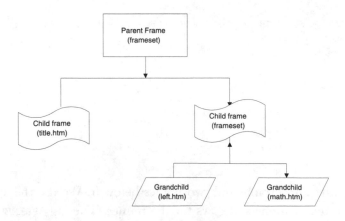

Figure 6.2 Interrelation between frames.

Suppose you create a function called myfunction() in **control.htm** and you want to access it from **math.htm**. To do that, you can use either type of the following syntax:

```
parent.left.myfunction()
parents.frames[1].myfunction
```

As we mentioned in Chapter 4, frames can be used as arrays and are arranged in the order they are defined in. For example, if there are two frames, you refer to them as Frames[0] and Frames[1]. Many times it can be messy to work with array references to frames. I suggest you stick with frame names to refer to your frames.

The following section describes a useful tool developed by Bill Dortch of hIdaho Design. This tool lets you access functions across frames without mentioning any location. It is known as the hIdaho Frameset.

The hIdaho Frameset

The following documentation is provided by Bill Dortch of hIdaho Design.

The hIdaho Frameset is a set of functions that provide a global function registration and calling mechanism for multiple-frame JavaScript applications. The hIdaho Frameset also provides a means for synchronizing the activity of JavaScript functions across multiple frames, although this functionality is incidental to the Frameset's primary function.

The hIdaho Frameset is useful primarily in applications in which functionality is spread across multiple frames, and especially, across multiple framesets within a tree of framesets. By eliminating the requirement that functions in one frame know the specific locations of other functions within the frameset hierarchy, the hIdaho Frameset simplifies the task of building larger JavaScript applications, promotes reusability of components, and reduces the time required for maintenance and the likelihood of bugs being introduced in the process.

Note that the hIdaho Frameset is of little or no value in simple JavaScript applications involving code in one or two frames within the same frameset. The hIdaho Frameset consists of five main functions: Register, UnRegister,

UnRegisterFrame, IsRegistered, and Exec. The Register function registers a function's name and its location within the frameset tree. The frameName parameter specifies the name of the caller's frame. Notably, this name does not need to be hard-coded but can be obtained at run time from the self.name property. The Register function (as with the other Frameset functions) is called in the immediate parent frame (in other words, parent.Register (self.name, "myFunction")). The call is passed up the frameset tree to the topmost frameset, where the function name is stored. If successful, Register returns true; if not (because the function name is already registered or the name table is full), it returns false.

The UnRegister function unregisters a function's name. The frame name need not be specified, because all registered function names must be unique. (We have, in effect, a global name space.) The UnRegisterFrame function unregisters all functions registered for the specified frame. This function is most useful when called from an onUnload event handler. The IsRegistered function returns true if the specified function has been registered; otherwise, it returns false. The Exec function locates and calls the specified function, passing it any parameters given. The Exec function returns the value returned by the specified function. If the function specified is not registered, Exec returns null.

One incidental benefit of using Exec is that it is not generally harmful to call a function that is not currently registered, or even loaded, as long as a return value of null is checked for. No JavaScript alert will be generated. However, a better practice would be to call IsRegistered before Exec or at least to call IsRegistered for one function in a frame containing a group of "public" functions, at the start of any block of code that Execs one or more of those functions. In this manner, you can use IsRegistered to synchronize frames during the loading process, especially in a timer loop. For example:

```
function initialize () {
  if (!parent.IsRegistered ("functionInAnotherFrame"){
    setTimeout ("initialize()", 250);  // try again in .25 seconds
    return;
  }
  [...]
  var retval = parent.Exec ("functionInAnotherFrame", "param1", "param2");
  [...]
}
[...]
<body onload="initialize()">
```

Listing 6.3 shows the hIdaho Frameset code. Note that this code is copyright 1996, Bill Dortch, hIdaho Design. You are free to use and modify the hIdaho Frameset code as you see fit, provided you retain the copyright notice at the top. A discussion of implementation follows the code.

Listing 6.3 hIdaho Frameset

```
<script language="JavaScript">
<!- begin script
// **********************************************************************
// The hIdaho Frameset. Copyright (C) 1996 Bill Dortch, hIdaho Design.
// Permission is granted to use and modify the hIdaho Frameset code,
// provided this notice is retained.
// **********************************************************************
var debug = false;
var amTopFrameset = false; // set this to true for the topmost frameset
var thisFrame = (amTopFrameset) ? null : self.name;
var maxFuncs = 32;
function makeArray (size) {
  this.length = size;
  for (var i = 1; i <= size; i++)
    this[i] = null;
  return this;
}
var funcs = new makeArray ((amTopFrameset) ? maxFuncs : 0);
function makeFunc (frame, func) {
  this.frame = frame;
  this.func = func;
  return this;
}
function addFunction (frame, func) {
  for (var i = 1; i <= funcs.length; i++)
    if (funcs[i] == null) {
      funcs[i] = new makeFunc (frame, func);
      return true;
    }
  return false;
}
function findFunction (func) {
  for (var i = 1; i <= funcs.length; i++)
    if (funcs[i] != null)
      if (funcs[i].func == func)
        return funcs[i];
  return null;
}
```

```
function Register (frame, func) {
  if (debug) alert (thisFrame + ": Register(" + frame + "," + func + ")");
  if (Register.arguments.length < 2)
    return false;
  if (!amTopFrameset)
    return parent.Register (thisFrame + "." + frame, func);
  if (findFunction (func) != null)
    return false;
  return addFunction (frame, func);
}
function UnRegister (func) {
  if (debug) alert (thisFrame + ": UnRegister(" + func + ")");
  if (UnRegister.arguments.length == 0)
    return false;
  if (!amTopFrameset)
    return parent.UnRegister (func);
  for (var i = 1; i <= funcs.length; i++)
    if (funcs[i] != null)
      if (funcs[i].func == func) {
        funcs[i] = null;
        return true;
      }
  return false;
}
function UnRegisterFrame (frame) {
  if (debug) alert (thisFrame + ": UnRegisterFrame(" + frame + ")");
  if (UnRegisterFrame.arguments.length == 0)
    return false;
  if (!amTopFrameset)
    return parent.UnRegisterFrame (thisFrame + "." + frame);
  for (var i = 1; i <= funcs.length; i++)
    if (funcs[i] != null)
      if (funcs[i].frame == frame) {
        funcs[i] = null;
      }
  return true;
}
function IsRegistered (func) {
  if (debug) alert (thisFrame + ": IsRegistered(" + func + ")");
  if (IsRegistered.arguments.length == 0)
    return false;
  if (!amTopFrameset)
    return parent.IsRegistered (func);
  if (findFunction (func) == null)
    return false;
  return true;
```

```
}
function Exec (func) {
  if (debug) alert (thisFrame + ": Exec(" + func + ")");
  var argv = Exec.arguments;
  if (argv.length == 0)
    return null;
  var arglist = new makeArray(argv.length);
  for (var i = 0; i < argv.length; i++)
    arglist[i+1] = argv[i];
  var argstr = "";
  for (i = ((amTopFrameset) ? 2 : 1); i <= argv.length; i++)
    argstr += "arglist[" + i + "]" + ((i < argv.length) ? "," : "");
  if (!amTopFrameset)
    return eval ("parent.Exec(" + argstr + ")");
  var funcobj = findFunction (func);
  if (funcobj == null)
    return null;
  return eval ("self." + ((funcobj.frame == null) ? "" : (funcobj.frame + "."))+
    funcobj.func + "(" + argstr + ")");
}
// ************************************************************************
// End of hIdaho Frameset code.
// ************************************************************************
// end script -->
</script>
```

The hIdaho Frameset is implemented by including the preceding code in each frameset-level document. For example:

```
<html>
<head>
<title>My Application</title>
<script language="JavaScript">
[...]
[hIdaho Frameset code goes here]
[...]
</script>
</head>
<frameset rows="*,*">
  <frame name="frameA" src="frameA.html">
  <frame name="frameB" src="frameB.html">
</frameset>
</html>
```

The only change that needs to be made is that the `amTopFrameset` switch must be set to `true` for the topmost frameset. It should be set to `false` for lower-level framesets.

Although the overhead imposed by the hIdaho Frameset is small, some of the functions are not called by lower-level framesets and can be omitted in them to achieve a slight reduction in memory and bandwidth use. However, for maximum reusability I recommend that you use the full frameset in each frameset-level document. (A "stripped" version of the frameset is included later.)

You may have noticed that the hIdaho Frameset provides access only to functions and not to data. It would be easy to provide additional functions to do this (and you can write your own if you are determined), but I have omitted them in favor of encouraging access to the data of other documents' by function call. This technique promotes encapsulation of data with its corresponding functions and hiding of the internal representation of data from "outside" documents. Although this approach involves a slight amount of additional work at the outset, in the long run it will save work in maintenance and debugging time.

Bill Dortch's ColorCenter application uses the hIdaho Frameset extensively. ColorCenter can be found at: http://www.hidaho.com/c2/cc.html. In addition to the top-level **cc.html**, you will find useful examples in the following subdocuments. (Warning: these files will generate JavaScript alerts when you load them.)

- http://www.hidaho.com/c2/ccglobal.html
- http://www.hidaho.com/c2/ccpbody.html
- http://www.hidaho.com/c2/ccpvtool.html
- http://www.hidaho.com/c2/ccptext.html

Please bear in mind that Dortch retains full copyrights on all code except for that marked as the hIdaho Frameset.

Listing 6.4 shows the stripped version of the hIdaho Frameset (for use in lower-level framesets).

Listing 6.4 Stripped Version of hIdaho Frameset

```
// ***********************************************************************
// The hIdaho Frameset. Copyright (C) 1996 Bill Dortch, hIdaho Design.
// Permission is granted to use and modify the hIdaho Frameset code ONLY,
// provided this notice is retained.
//
// *** NOTE: Stripped Version ***
//
var debug = false;
var amTopFrameset = false; // This MUST be false for stripped version
var thisFrame = (amTopFrameset) ? null : self.name;
function makeArray (size) {
  this.length = size;
  for (var i = 1; i <= size; i++)
    this[i] = null;
  return this;
}
function Register (frame, func) {
  if (debug) alert (thisFrame + ": Register(" + frame + "," + func + ")");
  if (Register.arguments.length < 2)
    return false;
  return parent.Register (thisFrame + "." + frame, func);
}
function UnRegister (func) {
  if (debug) alert (thisFrame + ": UnRegister(" + func + ")");
  if (UnRegister.arguments.length == 0)
    return false;
  return parent.UnRegister (func);
}
function UnRegisterFrame (frame) {
  if (debug) alert (thisFrame + ": UnRegisterFrame(" + frame + ")");
  if (UnRegisterFrame.arguments.length == 0)
    return false;
  return parent.UnRegisterFrame (thisFrame + "." + frame);
}
function IsRegistered (func) {
  if (debug) alert (thisFrame + ": IsRegistered(" + func + ")");
  if (IsRegistered.arguments.length == 0)
    return false;
  return parent.IsRegistered (func);
}
function Exec (func) {
  if (debug) alert (thisFrame + ": Exec(" + func + ")");
  var argv = Exec.arguments;
  if (argv.length == 0)
```

```
   return null;
 var arglist = new makeArray(argv.length);
 for (var i = 0; i < argv.length; i++)
   arglist[i+1] = argv[i];
 var argstr = "";
 for (i = ((amTopFrameset) ? 2 : 1); i <= argv.length; i++)
   argstr += "arglist[" + i + "]" + ((i < argv.length) ? "," : "");
 return eval ("parent.Exec(" + argstr + ")");
}
// ************************************************************************
// End of hIdaho Frameset code.
// ************************************************************************
```

A Window- and Frame-Based Math Game

The next example shows how to build a full-blown window- and frame-based page that uses JavaScript. In this example, users test their math skills by answering random math questions that are presented to them. They answer all the questions and then find out how they did. This game has three levels. The first level has simple addition and subtraction problems and no negatives. The second level has addition and subtraction problems with negatives, and the third level includes simple multiplication and division. This script was written in part by Ed Zhang from Cornell University (ezh1@cornell.edu).

Creating the Front End

As shown in Listing 6.1, we have created three frames. The first, or top, frame holds the banner for the game. The left-hand frame, the control panel, has links to the different levels, a color control option, and navigation buttons. The right-hand frame displays the math questions as well as the instructions for the game. Figure 6.3 shows the math game homepage.

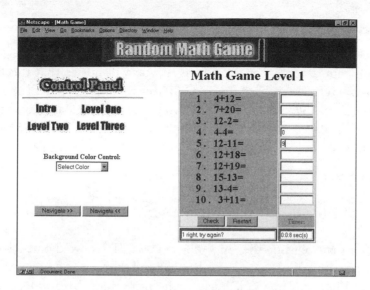

Figure 6.3 Math game in action.

The control panel has four graphical links to the three levels and the instruction frame. A list option box holds the color options that the user can choose from. Once you choose any of these options, the right-hand frame displays that background color. Two **Navigate** buttons take the user back and forth between the frames.

The right-hand frame first displays the introduction page, where we explain how this math game works. Three HTML pages display 10 questions each. The questions vary with the level chosen. Each page has 12 text boxes. Ten of them are used to input answers to the math questions, one displays the time that is spent on the page, and the other one shows how many answers were right. The **Check** button is used to check the answers, and **Restart** is used to start the game. Once a user clicks on **Check**, a window pops up with the answers.

Creating the Back End

Now, let us take a look at the JavaScript code from our two files: **control.htm** (the control panel) and **choice3.htm** (math level 3). All the levels have the same script on the back end, so we will show you the code from only one page.

The control.htm File

There are four images that link to the three levels and to the intro page. If you point your mouse to any of these images, you will notice that the link gets highlighted. Here, we've used the image object we discussed in Chapter 4. We have two images: one that is displayed when the page is loaded and a second one that is displayed when the user points to it with the mouse. Here is the code for the first link:

```
<a href="math.htm"  onMouseover = 'show0.src="m_intro.jpg"'
    onMouseout = 'show0.src="intro.jpg"' target=right>
<img name="show0" src="intro.jpg" border=0 width=120 height=36></a>
```

Notice first that we name the image object show0. Then we define a source for this object in the onMouseover event handler and the onMouseout event handler. That's it! When this image is clicked, the page **math.htm** is loaded in the frame called right (our right-hand frame) via the TARGET attribute.

Next, we deal with the options list that is used to control the background color of this frame. We create a function called change_bg() that handles the chosen options. Remember, in JavaScript, array indexing starts at 0, so we have our first selection (or the 0th selection) as "Select This". That is why we worry only about the preceding selections. For the selection, say "aliceblue", we use the following syntax:

```
if (form.bg_color[1].selected)
    parent.frames[2].document.bgColor="aliceblue";
```

When this second selection is chosen, we take the third frame array and set the background color property to aliceblue. Note that the function change_bg() is called via the event handler onChange from our selection option list.

Finally, we have two buttons that let you go back and forth between the frames. Here we have used the back and forward methods of the history object. This is the syntax for the forward button:

```
<input type="button" value="Navigate >>" onClick="parent.frames[2].history.for
    ward()">
```

The final listing for the control panel is shown in Listing 6.5.

Listing 6.5 control.htm

```
<html><title>control for Math</title>
<head>
<script>
window.onerror=null;
function change_bg(form){
if (form.bg_color[1].selected)
    parent.frames[2].document.bgColor="aliceblue";
else if (form.bg_color[2].selected)
    parent.frames[2].document.bgColor="antiquewhite";
else if (form.bg_color[3].selected)
    parent.frames[2].document.bgColor="aqua";
else if (form.bg_color[4].selected)
    parent.frames[2].document.bgColor="aquamarine";
else if (form.bg_color[5].selected)
    parent.frames[2].document.bgColor="azure";
else if (form.bg_color[6].selected)
    parent.frames[2].document.bgColor="beige";
else if (form.bg_color[7].selected)
    parent.frames[2].document.bgColor="darkgreen";
else if (form.bg_color[8].selected)
    parent.frames[2].document.bgColor="darkkhaki";
else if (form.bg_color[9].selected)
    parent.frames[2].document.bgColor="darkmagenta";
else if (form.bg_color[10].selected)
    parent.frames[2].document.bgColor="darkolivegreen";
else if (form.bg_color[11].selected)
    parent.frames[2].document.bgColor="darkorange";
else if (form.bg_color[12].selected)
    parent.frames[2].document.bgColor="darkorchid";
}
</script>
</head>
<body bgcolor=white><br>
<img src="control.jpg" width=300 height=40><br>
<hr>
<a href="math.htm"  onMouseover = 'show0.src="m_intro.jpg"'
    onMouseout = 'show0.src="intro.jpg"' target=right>
<img name="show0" src="intro.jpg" border=0 width=120 height=36></a>
<a href="choice1.htm" onMouseover = 'show1.src="m_level1.jpg"'
    onMouseout = 'show1.src="level1.jpg"' target=right>
<img name="show1" src="level1.jpg" border=0 width=120 height=36></a>
<br>
<a href="choice2.htm" onMouseover = 'show2.src="m_level2.jpg"'
    onMouseout = 'show2.src="level2.jpg"' target=right>
```

```
<img name="show2" src="level2.jpg" border=0 width=120 height=36></a>
<a href="choice3.htm" onMouseover = 'show3.src="m_level3.jpg"'
    onMouseout = 'show3.src="level3.jpg"' target=right>
<img name="show3" src="level3.jpg" border=0 width=120 height=36></a>
<form><br>
<b><center>Background Color Control:</b><br>
<select name="bg_color" onChange="change_bg(this.form)">
<option selected>Select Color
<option>aliceblue
<option>antiquewhite
<option>aqua
<option>aquamarine
<option>azure
<option>beige
<option> darkgreen
<option>darkkhaki
<option>darkmagenta
<option>darkolivegreen
<option>darkorange
<option>darkorchid
</select><p><br><br><br>
<input type="button" value="Navigate >>" onClick="parent.frames[2].history.for
    ward()">
<right>
<input type="button" value="Navigate <<" onClick="parent.frames[2].history.back()">
</form>
</body>
```

The choice3.htm File

Because this is a very simple script, we will only give you an overview of the code. This page uses the following functions:

- showtime() creates a timer using three counters—hours, minutes, and seconds—and displays it in the text box called **Timer**.

- stopClock() stops the clock.

- startClock() calls showtime() and stopClock().

- createnum() creates random numbers. Note that the lowest number is 0. We have added 1 so that we don't have to worry about 0.

- `initArray()` creates and initializes the array.

- `getsol()` places the user input in the array.

- `check()` checks how many answers were correct.

- `correctsol()` creates a solution list and displays it in a pop-up window. Notice that we have created a variable called `temp` where we store the HTML tags as we would do to create a new HTML page. Then we store all the answers in the variable. Note that here we are taking advantage of creating dynamic HTML using JavaScript. Next, we use our `open()` method to create a blank window and display the value of `temp` using the `write()` method.

- `start_again()` resets the form and reloads the documents when called.

To print the random questions, we use a loop and the `document.write()` method. As we display the questions, we keep track of our own calculation of the equations so that later we can check the user's input (Figure 6.4).

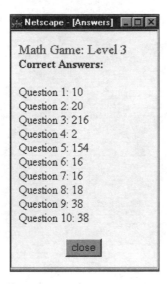

Figure 6.4 Math game answers in a pop-up window.

Listing 6.6 displays the full script of the level 3 frame of the math game.

Listing 6.6 The choice3.htm Page

```
<HEAD>
<TITLE>Math Game Level 3</TITLE>
<script language="JavaScript">
<!— begin game

    var TimerId = null;
    var TimerRunning = false;

    Seconds = 0
    Minutes = 0
    Hours = 0

function showtime()
    {
      if(Seconds >= 59)
      {
        Seconds = 0
        if(Minutes >= 59)
    {
      Minutes = 0
        if(Hours >= 23)
      {
        Seconds = 0
        Minutes = 0
        Hours = 0
      }
      else {
        ++Hours
        }
        }
      else {
        ++Minutes
    }
      }
      else {
    ++Seconds
      }
      document.results.timer.value = (Hours+':'+Minutes+':'+Seconds+' sec(s)');
      TimerId = setTimeout("showtime()", 1000);
      TimerRunning = true;
    }

    var TimerId = null;
    var TimerRunning = false;

    function stopClock() {
```

```
      if(TimerRunning)
   clearTimeout(TimerId);
      TimerRunning = false;
    }

    function startClock() {
      stopClock();
      showtime();
    }

function createnum(i) {
    number=Math.round(Math.random()*i)
    return number+1; //+1 will display numbers from 1
                //as we don't want to deal with 0s
}

//inits the array

function initArray() {
  x = initArray.arguments.length;
  for (var i=0; i<x; i++)
  {
      this[i+1] = initArray.arguments[i];
  }
}

var solutions= new initArray();

function getsol() {

    solutions[0]=document.results.solution0.value;
    solutions[1]=document.results.solution1.value;
    solutions[2]=document.results.solution2.value;
    solutions[3]=document.results.solution3.value;
    solutions[4]=document.results.solution4.value;
    solutions[5]=document.results.solution5.value;
    solutions[6]=document.results.solution6.value;
    solutions[7]=document.results.solution7.value;
    solutions[8]=document.results.solution8.value;
    solutions[9]=document.results.solution9.value;

    check();
     stopClock();
     correctsol();
}

function check(){
var correct=0;
for(i=0;i<10;i++){
  if (solutions[i]==parseInt(answers[i])){
```

```
        correct++;
    }
}
if (correct<5)document.results.conclude.value=(correct+" right, try again?");

else document.results.conclude.value=(correct+" right! You are way too smart for
    us!");

}

function correctsol(){
    var temp=       '<html><body
    bgcolor=ffffff><title>Answers</title><head></head>'
        + '<font color=red size=+1>Math Game: Level 3</font><br><b>Correct
    Answers:<p></b>'
        + 'Question 1: '+answers[0]+'<br>Question 2: '+answers[1]+'<br>Question 3:
'+answers[2]+'<br>Question 4: '+answers[3]+'<br>Question 5: '+answers[4]+'<br>Question
6: '+answers[5]+'<br>Question 7: '+answers[6]+ '<br>Question 8:
'+answers[7]+'<br>Question 9: '+answers[8]+'<br>Question 10: '+answers[9]+' '
        +'<form><center><input type=button value=close
    onClick=self.close()></center></body></html>';


msgWindow=window.open("","displayWindow","toolbar=no,width=200,height=320,direc
    tories=no,status=no,scrollbars=no,resize=no,menubar=no")
                msgWindow.document.write(temp)
                msgWindow.document.close()
}

function start_again(){
    document.results.solution0.value="";
    document.results.solution1.value="";
    document.results.solution2.value="";
    document.results.solution3.value="";
    document.results.solution4.value="";
    document.results.solution5.value="";
    document.results.solution6.value="";
    document.results.solution7.value="";
    document.results.solution8.value="";
    document.results.solution9.value="";
    window.location.reload();
    correct=0;
}
// end -->
</script>
</head>
<body bgcolor=white text="#000000" link="red" vlink="blue" onLoad="startClock()">
<center><h1>Math Game Level 3</h1>
```

```
<table border=1 width=300>
<tr><td width=200 bgcolor=indigo align=left><font color=#c0c0c0>

<h2>
<SCRIPT LANGUAGE="JavaScript">
var z=10;
var answers=" ";
var ans=" "
//answers = new initArray();
answers= new Array(10)
for(j=0;j<10;j++){
     answers[j]=" ";
}

for(i=0;i<10;i++)
{
  num1=createnum(20);
  num2=createnum(20);
  count=i+1;
  if (num1<num2)
  {
    document.write("      " + count + " .   " +
    num1 + "*" + num2 +"= ");
    ans=num1*num2;
  }
  else
    {
         temp=num1*num2;
         document.write("      " + count + " .   "
    +temp+"/"+num2+"= ");
         ans=num1;
    }
  document.write("<br clear=left>");
  answers[i]=ans;
}
//- ->
</SCRIPT>
</font>
</h2></td><td bgcolor=darkkhaki width=100 valign=top align=right>
<form name=results>
<input type=text name=solution0 size=10><br clear=left>
<input type=text name=solution1 size=10><br clear=left>
<input type=text name=solution2 size=10><br clear=left>
<input type=text name=solution3 size=10><br clear=left>
<input type=text name=solution4 size=10><br clear=left>
<input type=text name=solution5 size=10><br clear=left>
<input type=text name=solution6 size=10><br clear=left>
```

```
<input type=text name=solution7 size=10><br clear=left>
<input type=text name=solution8 size=10><br clear=left>
<input type=text name=solution9 size=10>
</td></tr>
<tr><td width=300 bgcolor=darkkhaki>
<center>
<input type=button value=" Check " onclick="getsol()">
<input type=button value=" Restart " onclick="start_again()">
</center>
</td><td align=center bgcolor=crimson>
<center><table bgcolor=indigo border=0 width=80><tr><td>
<center><font color=white><b>Timer:</b></td></tr></font></center>

</tr></td></table></center>

<tr bgcolor=cyan><td width=300>
<input type=text name=conclude size=30>
</td>
<td><INPUT TYPE="text" NAME="timer" SIZE=10></td>
</tr>
</table></center></form>
</body>
</HTML>
```

CHAPTER SEVEN

A HOMEPAGE BUILDER

In this chapter, we will show you how to create an application in which a user can create homepages without writing a single line of HTML code. The front end of the application is basically an HTML form where the user fills out several blank fields. After the form is submitted, the user sees a new HTML document right on the screen. Creating homepages over the net has never been this easy!

After the page is created, the user saves it using the Navigator **Save as** option and uses it instantly. You can customize this form as necessary. The script was written by Kevin Gorsline from http://homedirections.com.

This chapter covers:

- Creating the front end for the homepage builder
- Creating the back end for the homepage builder
- Putting the script together for the homepage builder

Creating the Front End for the Homepage Builder

The HTML form is divided into four sections. When the user opens the application, the first three sections are fully visible (Figure 7.1). The top section holds the user's name and e-mail address along with the name of the homepage. The second section asks users to specify the color of five things: the page's background, text, hot links, active links and visited links. The third section holds hot links to the HTML page. The bottom section, which becomes visible as the user scrolls, holds the first 25 lines of the page (Figure 7.2).

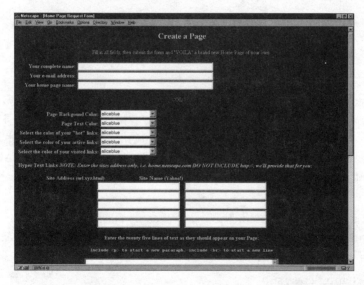

Figure 7.1 The first half of the homepage builder form.

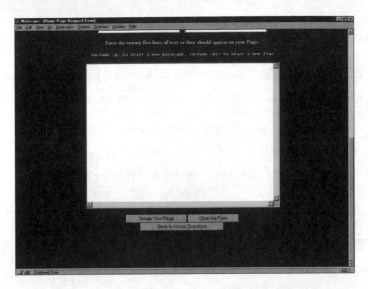

Figure 7.2 The second half of the homepage builder form.

First, let us concentrate on the first section. Listing 7.1 shows the HTML code to create the three text fields.

Listing 7.1 User Name, E-mail, and Homepage Name

```
<b>Your complete name:</b> <INPUT
name="uname" SIZE=50 onFocus="window.status='Enter your full name, First Name
then Last Name'; return true"><br>

<b>Your e-mail address:</b> <INPUT
    name="email" SIZE=50 onFocus="window.status='Enter your e-mail address, i.e.,
    yourname@isp.com'; return true"><br>

<b>Your homepage name:</b> <INPUT
name="pgename" SIZE=50 onFocus="window.status='This will appear in the title and the
first line of your page, i.e., Kevin's First Page'; return true"
    onBlur="window.status='
    '; return true"><p>
```

Notice that we used the same HTML code to create all the text fields. We named each field by using `name` and defined the size of the field by using `size`. You will also notice that we have used two event handlers: `onFocus` and `onBlur`. The `onFocus` shows text on the browser's status bar when the user focuses on the field. The `onBlur` event handler makes sure that the text is cleared from the status bar when the field loses focus.

The second section is based on some list box options. Listing 7.2 shows the HTML code to create these sections.

Listing 7.2 Background, Text, Link, Active, and Visited Link Fields

```
<b>Select Your Page Background Color:</b> <SELECT name="Backgrnd" >
<OPTION>aliceblue <OPTION>antiquewhite <OPTION>aqua <OPTION>aquamarine
<OPTION>azure <OPTION>beige <OPTION>bisque <OPTION>black </select><br>

<b>Select Your Page Text Color:  </b> <SELECT name="textclr" >

<OPTION>aliceblue <OPTION>antiquewhite <OPTION>aqua <OPTION>aquamarine
<OPTION>azure <OPTION>beige <OPTION>bisque <OPTION>black

<OPTION>yellow    <OPTION>yellowgreen </select><br>
<b>Select the color of your "hot" links:</b>
<SELECT name="links" >
<OPTION>aliceblue <OPTION>antiquewhite <OPTION>aqua <OPTION>aquamarine
<OPTION>azure <OPTION>beige <OPTION>bisque <OPTION>black
<OPTION>yellow    <OPTION>yellowgreen
</select><br>

<b>Select the color of your active links:</b> <SELECT name="alinks" >
<OPTION>aliceblue <OPTION>antiquewhite <OPTION>aqua <OPTION>aquamarine
</select><br>

<b>Select the color of your visited links:</b> <SELECT name="vlinks" >
<OPTION>aliceblue <OPTION>antiquewhite <OPTION>aqua <OPTION>aquamarine
<OPTION>azure <OPTION>beige <OPTION>bisque <OPTION>black
 </select><p>
```

As you can see, for the list box options, we define the fields by using the keywords `<SELECT >`...`</SELECT>` and give specific names for each selection by using the keyword `name`. To create options, we use the keyword `<OPTION>`.

The third section is based on the exact same text fields as the first section. We use the HTML code in Listing 7.3 to create this section.

Listing 7.3 Hot Links

```
<b>Hypertext Links <i>NOTE: Enter the site's address only, i.e., home.netscape.com. DO
NOT
INCLUDE http://. We'll provide that for you:</i><p>
Site Address (url.xyz.html)<IMG Site Name (Yahoo!)</b><br><center>
<INPUT name="hypertext1" SIZE=30><INPUT name="hyperdescr1" SIZE=30><br>
<INPUT name="hypertext2" SIZE=30><INPUT name="hyperdescr2" SIZE=30><br>
<INPUT name="hypertext3" SIZE=30><INPUT name="hyperdescr3" SIZE=30><br>
<INPUT name="hypertext4" SIZE=30><INPUT name="hyperdescr4" SIZE=30><br>
<INPUT name="hypertext5" SIZE=30><INPUT name="hyperdescr5" SIZE=30><p>
```

As you can see, we created a number of text fields with unique names and sized each field to hold as many as 30 characters. If you like, you could assign your own names and sizes for each of the text fields.

The last section is a textarea with 25 rows and 70 columns. We have named the textarea `textline`. The following HTML code was used to create this section:

```
<TEXTAREA name="textline" ROWS=25 COLS=70></TEXTAREA><br>
```

We also created three buttons. The first button submits the form (which calls a function called `drawPage()`), the second button resets the form, and the third button closes the window. (If you come to this page from homedirections.com, you will notice that this page opens a new window. To go back to the index.html page, you need only close the new window. That is why the button says **Back to Home Directions**.) Listing 7.4 shows the HTML code to create these buttons.

Listing 7.4 Creating Buttons

```
<INPUT TYPE ="submit" Value=" Create Your Page " onClick=drawPage()>
<INPUT TYPE ="reset" Value=" Clear the Form "><br>
<INPUT TYPE ="button" Value=" Back to Home Directions " onClick=ConfirmClose()>
```

Creating the Back End for the Homepage Builder

To handle the entire form, it takes only three functions: `drawPage()`, `doText()`, and `ConfirmClose()`. The `drawPage()` function creates a new page with all the information from the user, and `doText()` handles all the information submitted from the form. `ConfirmClose()` confirms whether the browser window is to be closed by the user.

drawPage()

This function opens a new document with the specification of text or HTML. It then calls the function `doText()` and puts it in a variable called `result`.

Finally, the data from doText() is passed to this document. Listing 7.5 shows the code for drawPage().

Listing 7.5 drawPage()

```
function drawPage() {
    document.open ("text/html");
    var result=doText();
    document.write (result)
    document.close();
}
```

doText()

When creating a new HTML page, the first thing we need to do is to make sure we use the user-specified color in the <BODY> attribute for the background, text, hot link, active link, and visited link. First, the doText() function takes the selectedIndex properties for all the list box options and puts them into the variables bgSelIndex, txSelIndex, lnSelIndex, vlSelIndex, and alSelIndex. You may have noticed that we gave a specific name to the form and the list boxes. For this reason, every time we refer to any object from the form we must mention both the form name and its object's name. The order goes like this: current document (document), form name (for this script, hp), list box option name (Backgrnd, textclr, links, vlinks, or alinks).

We then assign a variable named result, which holds all the information from the text fields and option list boxes. Next we put the familiar header tags, such as <HTML>, <HEAD>, and <TITLE>.

 When assigning a string that includes double quotes, you need to use single quotes (") around the string. When you assign another variable to result, you don't need to use quotes.

NOTE

Remember that we asked the user for the HTML page name. We assign this value to result. The += after result means that we will add more data to the existing data that the variable holds.

NOTE

We have declared the `result` variable in `drawPage()` as well, but in both functions the variable is used locally.

Next, we assign the background color by using the following code:

```
result+='<BODY BGCOLOR='
result+=document.hp.Backgrnd.options[bgSelIndex].text
```

You must be wondering about the second line. When you look at it carefully you will see that we refer to the text of the option list (using the array index) using the list name `Backgrnd`, which is located in the form `hp` of the current document. We then assign the link, text, active, and visited link color the same way.

We then center the user-defined HTML page name in the document. This name is displayed in a header 1 font size. The textarea field is displayed next, and later we put the list of hot links. Because we asked the user not to input **http://** when entering the hot links, we take care of that when processing the information (see Listing 7.6).

Listing 7.6 Handling Hot Links

```
result+='<A HREF="http://'+document.hp.hypertext1.value+'">'
result+=document.hp.hyperdescr1.value+'</a><br>'
result+='<A HREF="http://'+document.hp.hypertext2.value+'">'
result+=document.hp.hyperdescr2.value+'</a><br>'
result+='<A HREF="http://'+document.hp.hypertext3.value+'">'
result+=document.hp.hyperdescr3.value+'</a><br>'
result+='<A HREF="http://'+document.hp.hypertext4.value+'">'
result+=document.hp.hyperdescr4.value+'</a><br>'
result+='<A HREF="http://'+document.hp.hypertext5.value+'">'
result+=document.hp.hyperdescr5.value+'</a><br>'
result+='</BLOCKQUOTE></BLOCKQUOTE><CENTER>'
```

NOTE

Note that `<HR>` displays a horizontal line on the document and `<br>` displays a line feed.

Then we set up three hyperlinks: one to the e-mail address of the user, another to the initial form, and a third one to the Home Directions main page. We use the code in Listing 7.7.

Listing 7.7 Handling the Page Footer

```
result+='<HR>Send me mail at: <A HREF="mailto:'
result+=document.hp.email.value+'"> '+document.hp.uname.value+'</a>'
result+='<br><A HREF="http://homedirections.com/homecre.html">Back'
result+=' to Creator Page</a>'
result+='<br>Created by &copy'
result+='<A HREF="http://homedirections.com"> HOME DIRECTIONS</A>'
result+='</center>6</BODY></HTML>'
```

ConfirmClose()

All this function does is to confirm whether the browser window should be closed. Once you press **OK** at the prompt, the window will be closed. The code looks like this:

```
//Exit Window
function ConfirmClose() {
   if (confirm("Do you really wish to go back ?")) {
      window.close()}
   }
```

Putting the Script Together

Listing 7.8 shows the complete code for the homepage builder.

Listing 7.8 The Homepage Builder Script

```
<html>
<Head>
<SCRIPT LANGUAGE="JavaScript">
<!-
//
//    Homepage Creation Script
//    (C) Copyright 1996 by Kevin Gorsline(gorsline@ix.netcom.com)
//    For more examples go to the Home Directions Web site at
```

```
//                    http://homedirections.com
//
//     You may freely use this script.
//     If you do, please leave this section in place and drop me a note.
//
//   The function drawPage is called to create the new homepage

function drawPage() {
    document.open ("text/html");
    var result=doText();
    document.write (result)
    document.close();
}
//
// The function doText is called from drawPage and is used to format the new //homepage
//
function doText(){
/*
//         Obtain the selectedIndex properties from the list box options for
//Background, text, visited links, active links, and link colors.
//
//   NOTE: Backgrnd, textclr, links, vlinks, and alinks are form item names in the
//form called hp (homepage) you can substitute hp with <form name of your form>
*/
          bgSelIndex = document.hp.Backgrnd.selectedIndex;
          txSelIndex = document.hp.textclr.selectedIndex;
          lnSelIndex = document.hp.links.selectedIndex;
          vlSelIndex = document.hp.vlinks.selectedIndex;
          alSelIndex = document.hp.alinks.selectedIndex;
//
//         This section actually "builds/formats" the new homepage
//
            var result='<HTML><HEAD><TITLE>'
//
//             pgename = the name of the user's homepage in the form (hp)
//                            used in the title and the top line of the page
//
    result+=document.hp.pgename.value
    result+='</TITLE></HEAD>'
    result+='<BODY BGCOLOR= '
//
//     This sets up the BGCOLOR color of the homepage
//
    result+=document.hp.Backgrnd.options[bgSelIndex].text
            result+='  TEXT='
//
```

```
//      This sets up the TEXT color of the homepage
//
                 result+=document.hp.textclr.options[txSelIndex].text
//
//      This sets up the LINK color of the homepage
//
                 result+='  LINK='+document.hp.links.options[lnSelIndex].text
//
//      This sets up the ALINK color of the homepage
//
                 result+='  ALINK='+document.hp.alinks.options[alSelIndex].text
//
//      This sets up the VLINK color of the homepage
//
                 result+='VLINK='+document.hp.vlinks.options[vlSelIndex].text+'>'
//

result+='<CENTER><H1>'+document.hp.pgename.value+'</H1></CENTER>'
                 result+='<HR>'
//
//      This sets up the Text of the homepage
//
     result+=document.hp.textline.value
                 result+='<BLOCKQUOTE><br>'
                 result+='Here are some sites of interest that I found:<BLOCK
     QUOTE>'
//
//      this sets up the hypertext links and description of the LINKS submitted
//      for the homepage
//
     result+='<A HREF="http://'+document.hp.hypertext1.value+'">'
                 result+=document.hp.hyperdescr1.value+'</a><br>'
                 result+='<A HREF="http://'+document.hp.hypertext2.value+'">'
                 result+=document.hp.hyperdescr2.value+'</a><br>'
                 result+='<A HREF="http://'+document.hp.hypertext3.value+'">'
                 result+=document.hp.hyperdescr3.value+'</a><br>'
                 result+='<A HREF="http://'+document.hp.hypertext4.value+'">'
                 result+=document.hp.hyperdescr4.value+'</a><br>'
                 result+='<A HREF="http://'+document.hp.hypertext5.value+'">'
                 result+=document.hp.hyperdescr5.value+'</a><br>'
                    result+='</BLOCKQUOTE></BLOCKQUOTE><CENTER>'
//
//      this sets up the mailto of the user/creator of the homepage
//
                 result+='<HR>Send me mail at: <A HREF="mailto:'
                 result+=document.hp.email.value+'">'
```

```
         '+document.hp.uname.value+'</a>'
         result+='<br><A HREF="http://homedirections.com/homecre.html">Back'
         result+=' to Creator Page</a>'
                    result+='<br>Created by &copy'
                    result+='<A HREF="http://homedirections.com"> HOME DIREC
    TIONS</A>'
                    result+='</center>6</BODY></HTML>'
         return (result);
}
//
//Exit Window

function ConfirmClose() {

    if (confirm("Do you really wish to go back ?")) {

        window.close()}

    }

</SCRIPT>

<TITLE>Home Directions-Homepage Request Form</TITLE>
</HEAD>
<BODY BgColor=midnightblue TEXT="#F0F0F0" LINK="#FFFF00" VLINK="#22AA22"
ALINK="#0077FF">
<center><FONT SIZE=5><b>Create a Page</FONT></b><p>
</font>Fill in all fields, then submit the form and "VOILA" a brand new homepage of
your own.</center>

<FORM  name="hp" METHOD=POST>
<b>Your complete name:</b> <INPUT
name="uname" SIZE=50 onFocus="window.status='Enter your full name, First Name then Last
Name'; return true"><br>

<b>Your e-mail address:</b> <INPUT
name="email" SIZE=50 onFocus="window.status='Enter your e-mail address, i.e.,
    yourname@isp.com'; return true"><br>

<b>Your homepage name:</b> <INPUT
    name="pgename" SIZE=50 onFocus="window.status='This will appear in the title
    and the first line of your page, i.e., Kevin's First Page'; return true"
    onBlur="window.status=' '; return true"><p>

<CENTER><FONT COLOR="red">C</font><FONT COLOR="yellow">O</font><FONT
COLOR="pink">L</FONT><FONT COLOR="aquamarime">O</FONT><FONT
COLOR="purple">R</FONT><FONT
COLOR="green">S</font><p></CENTER>

<b>Select Your Page Background Color:</b> <SELECT name="Backgrnd" >
<OPTION>aliceblue <OPTION>antiquewhite <OPTION>aqua <OPTION>aquamarine
```

```
<OPTION>azure <OPTION>beige <OPTION>bisque <OPTION>black </select><br>

<b>Select Your Page Text Color:  </b> <SELECT name="textclr" >

<OPTION>aliceblue <OPTION>antiquewhite <OPTION>aqua <OPTION>aquamarine
<OPTION>azure <OPTION>beige <OPTION>bisque <OPTION>black

<OPTION>yellow    <OPTION>yellowgreen </select><br>

<b>Select the color of your "hot" links:</b>
<SELECT name="links" >
<OPTION>aliceblue <OPTION>antiquewhite <OPTION>aqua <OPTION>aquamarine
<OPTION>azure <OPTION>beige <OPTION>bisque <OPTION>black
<OPTION>yellow    <OPTION>yellowgreen
</select><br>

<b>Select the color of your active links:</b> <SELECT name="alinks" >
<OPTION>aliceblue <OPTION>antiquewhite <OPTION>aqua <OPTION>aquamarine
</select><br>

<b>Select the color of your visited links:</b> <SELECT name="vlinks" >
<OPTION>aliceblue <OPTION>antiquewhite <OPTION>aqua <OPTION>aquamarine
<OPTION>azure <OPTION>beige <OPTION>bisque <OPTION>black
 </select><p>

<b>Hypertext Links <i>NOTE: Enter the site's address only, i.e., home.netscape.com. DO
NOT
    INCLUDE http://. We'll provide that for you:</i><p>
Site Address (url.xyz.html)<IMG Site Name (Yahoo!)</b><br><center>
<INPUT name="hypertext1" SIZE=30><INPUT name="hyperdescr1" SIZE=30><br>
<INPUT name="hypertext2" SIZE=30><INPUT name="hyperdescr2" SIZE=30><br>
<INPUT name="hypertext3" SIZE=30><INPUT name="hyperdescr3" SIZE=30><br>
<INPUT name="hypertext4" SIZE=30><INPUT name="hyperdescr4" SIZE=30><br>
<INPUT name="hypertext5" SIZE=30><INPUT name="hyperdescr5" SIZE=30><p>
<p><b>Enter the twenty-five lines of text as they should appear on your
    page:<XMP>Include <p> to start a new paragraph, include <br> to start a new
    line</XMP></b>
<TEXTAREA name="textline" ROWS=25 COLS=70></TEXTAREA><br>
<p><INPUT TYPE ="submit" Value=" Create Your Page " onClick=drawPage()>
<INPUT TYPE ="reset" Value=" Clear the Form "><br>
<INPUT TYPE ="button" Value=" Back to Home Directions " onClick=ConfirmClose()>
</PRE></FORM></center>
</BODY>
</HTML>
```

After the user finishes all the input, you could easily verify the name, e-mail address, homepage name, and site address fields. You can call a verification function from the **Submit** button via the `onClick` event handler. For example: `onClick='verify_input(this.form)'`

When you call this function, it verifies the data and then calls our `drawPage()` function. If the entry is incorrect, it will alert the user. Here is what the function looks like:

```
function verify_input (form) {
var error=false;
if (form.Title.value=="") {
alert('Please fill in the Title');
error=true;}
if (form.URL.value=="http://" && error==false) {
alert('Please fill in the URL address');
error=true; }
if (form.Keywords.value=="" && error==false) {
alert('Please fill in some Keywords');
error=true; }
if (form.Org.value=="" && error==false) {
alert('Please fill in your Organization');
error=true;}
if (form.City.value=="" && error==false) {
alert('Please fill in your City');
error=true; }
if (form.State.value=="" && error==false) {
alert('Please fill in your State');
error=true; }
if (form.Contact.value=="" && error==false) {
alert('Please fill in your Name');
error=true; }
if (form.Email.value=="" && error==false) {
alert('Please fill in the e-mail address');
error=true; }
if (form.Description.value=="" && error==false) {
alert('Please fill in the description');
error=true; }
if (!error){
drawPage();
}
```

CHAPTER EIGHT

CUSTOM COMPUTER COST ESTIMATOR

In first part of the book, you learned how to work with forms. This chapter deals with forms in greater depth. You will learn how to do calculations on the fly as you create an on-line computer cost estimator. This program presents a number of choices that users can select to design a custom computer; then the application calculates the cost of the computer. The difference between a typical CGI-based form and a JavaScript-based form such as our cost calculator is that JavaScript operates on the client side. Form submission is much faster, because you don't have to wait for the server to return the submitted request. Users can change their minds as much as they want and receive the new price information instantly.

This chapter covers:

- Creating the front end for the custom computer cost estimator
- Creating the back end for the custom computer cost estimator
- Putting the script together

Creating the Front End

The first step is to create the front end: the form. Let's look at how to create HTML forms and elements.

To format the form attractively, we will take advantage of tables. We create the form inside a table and make sure that the form is properly centered. To create the table, we use the following keywords:

```
<TABLE>....</TABLE>
```

Next we define the form:

```
<FORM method=post>
```

Notice that a form method was used. As you know, you can use either POST or GET in this case.

In the form, our first job is to create the selection options. To create the first selection option, we use the following code:

```
<SELECT NAME="processor">
<OPTION Selected>      Select
<OPTION>       68LCO45 DD [$540]
<OPTION>       68LCO45 EE  [$340]
<OPTION>       68LCO45 FF   [$680]
<OPTION>       68LCO45 GG  [$421]
</SELECT>
```

Notice that we used the NAME attribute to name the selection. This attribute is important, because when we call this form from our JavaScript function, JavaScript will need to know which selection option we are calling. The <OPTION> tag lets you create the options (which appear in the text written after each <OPTION> tag). All the selection options are created in the same way. The only difference is that some forms might have five options, and others might have only two options. When we compile this HTML page, you will notice that all the selection options are displayed and the first option in each list is highlighted.

We will also create two buttons. One button updates the user's choices and puts the calculated price in a text box. To create this button, we use the following code:

```
<INPUT TYPE="BUTTON" NAME="price" Value="Update Price"
    onClick="compute(this.form)">
```

Notice that for this button to work, we used the event handler `onClick`. As described in Chapter 2, `onClick` executes JavaScript code when the user clicks on the button. In the preceding code, `onClick` calls the JavaScript function `compute()`. The `this.form` parameter makes sure that the data is exported to the function from the current form.

Next, we create a button called **Print Preview**. This button creates a window that displays a list of the user's choices for the custom computer as well as the price for each chosen component. The new window also lets a user print this information. We create the button by using the following code:

```
<INPUT TYPE="BUTTON" NAME="Print_data" Value="Print Preview"
    onClick="print(this.form)">
```

WARNING

If users do not click the **Update Price** button before they click **Print Preview**, the Print Preview window will not give them the list of selections. For example, if users make all their selections and then click **Print Preview**, their selections will not appear in the new window. Every time they change their selections, they must close the Print Preview window (if it is opened), click **Update Price**, and then click **Print Preview**.

Again, we have used the `onClick` event handler. When this button is pressed, the function `print()` is called.

Now we create the text box that will show the updated price. To define the text box, we use the following code:

```
<INPUT TYPE="text" NAME="T_Price" Value="">
```

Notice that we left the value blank (`Value=""`). As you might guess, we want to leave the text box blank until the **Update Price** button is pressed.

The front end of the custom computer cost estimator is shown in Figure 8.1.

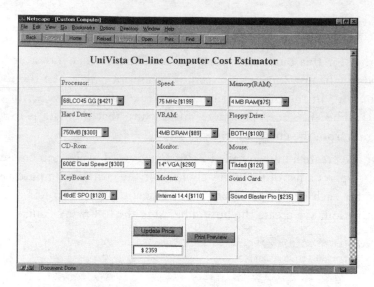

Figure 8.1 The on-line cost estimator program.

Creating the Back End

Now let's go step by step to create the back end of the program. First, we define the variables shown in Listing 8.1.

Listing 8.1 Variables for Custom Computer Estimator Scripts

```
var called=false;      //to make sure the function compute() is called
var T_Price=0;     //the default for total price is always $ 0
var pr_flag;       //processor flag for keeping track of the choices
var pr_print="";

var sp_flag;       //flag for Speed
var sp_print;

var ram_flag;      //flag for RAM
var ram_print;

var hdrive_flag;       //flag for Hard Drive
var hdrive_print;

var vram_flag;      //flag for VRAM
var vram_print;
```

```
var fdrive_flag;      //flag for Floppy Drive
var fdrive_print;

var cd_flag;       //flag for CD-ROM
var cd_print;

var mn_flag;       //flag for Monitor
var mn_print;

var mos_flag;       //flag for Mouse
var mos_print;

var kb_flag;       //flag for Keyboard
var kb_print;

var modem_flag;      //flag for Modem
var modem_print;

var software_flag; //flag for software
var software_print;

var card_flag;        //flag for Sound Card
var card_print;
```

As you can see from the comments, most of the variables are used to keep track of the selection options. The variable T_Price is used to total the price of all the selected components. The Boolean variable called is used to make sure the compute() function is called.

compute() Function

This is the most important function in this program. It keeps track of all the options chosen by the user and does the final calculation. Listing 8.2 shows the code for the function.

Listing 8.2 The compute() Function

```
function compute(form){
called=true;

//——-Processor——
if (form.processor[0].selected){
    pr_flag=0;
    pr_print= "None [$0]";
}

else if (form.processor[1].selected){
```

```
        pr_flag =540;
        pr_print="68LCO45 DD [$540]";
}

else if (form.processor[2].selected){
        pr_flag =340;
        pr_print="68LCO45 EE [$340]";
}

else if (form.processor[3].selected){
        pr_flag =680;
        pr_print="68LCO45 FF [$680]";
}

else if (form.processor[4].selected){
        pr_flag =421;
        pr_print="68LCO45 GG [$421]";
}

//-----Speed------
if (form.speed[0].selected){
        sp_flag=0;
        sp_print="None [$0]";
}

else if (form.speed[1].selected){
        sp_flag=110;
        sp_print="60 MHz [$110]";
}

else if (form.speed[2].selected){
        sp_flag=145;
        sp_print="66/33 MHz [$145]";
}

else if (form.speed[3].selected){
        sp_flag=199;
        sp_print="75 MHz [$199]";
}

else if (form.speed[4].selected){
        sp_flag=235;
        sp_print="100 MHz  [$235]";
}

//-----RAM------
if (form.ram[0].selected){
        ram_flag=0;
        ram_print="None [$0]";
}
```

```
else if (form.ram[1].selected){
    ram_flag=75;
    ram_print="4 MB RAM [$75]";
}

else if (form.ram[2].selected){
    ram_flag=120;
    ram_print="8 MB RAM [$120]";
}

else if (form.ram[3].selected){
    ram_flag=200;
    ram_print="16 MB RAM [$200]";
}

else if (form.ram[4].selected){
    ram_flag=350;
    ram_print="32 MB RAM [$350]";
}

//-----Hard Drive-----
if (form.hdrive[0].selected){
    hdrive_flag=0;
    hdrive_print="None [$0]";
}

else if (form.hdrive[1].selected){
    hdrive_flag=100;
    hdrive_print="250MB [$100]";
}

else if (form.hdrive[2].selected){
    hdrive_flag=200;
    hdrive_print="500MB [$200]";
}

else if (form.hdrive[3].selected){
    hdrive_flag=300;
    hdrive_print="750MB [$300]";
}

else if (form.hdrive[4].selected){
    hdrive_flag=399;
    hdrive_print="1.0GB [$399]";
}

//-----VRAM-----
if (form.vram[0].selected){
    vram_flag=0;
    vram_print="None [$0]";
```

```
        }
else if (form.vram[1].selected){
    vram_flag=50;
    vram_print="1MB DRAM [$50]";
    }
else if (form.vram[2].selected){
    vram_flag=89;
    vram_print="4MB DRAM  [$89]";
    }

else if (form.vram[3].selected){
    vram_flag=125;
    vram_print="8MB DRAM [$125]";
    }

else if (form.vram[4].selected){
    vram_flag=200;
    vram_print="16MB DRAM [$200]";
    }

//——-Floppy——-
if (form.fdrive[0].selected){
    fdrive_flag=0;
    fdrive_print="None [$0]";
    }

else if (form.fdrive[1].selected){
    fdrive_flag=75;
    fdrive_print=" 1.4 inch. [$75]";
    }

else if (form.fdrive[2].selected){
    fdrive_flag=50;
    fdrive_print="5.25 inch. [$50]";
    }

else if (form.fdrive[3].selected){
    fdrive_flag=100;
    fdrive_print="BOTH [$100]";
    }

//——-CD ROM——-

if (form.cd[0].selected){
    cd_flag=0;
    cd_print="None [$0]";
    }

else if (form.cd[1].selected){
```

```
        cd_flag=300;
        cd_print="600E Dual Speed [$300]";
        }

else if (form.cd[2].selected){
        cd_flag=450;
        cd_print="800E Quadruple-Speed  [$450]";
        }

//————Monitor————-
if (form.monitor[0].selected){
        mn_flag=0;
        mn_print="None [$0]";
        }

else if (form.monitor[1].selected){
        mn_flag=210;
        mn_print="12 inch VGA [ $210]";
        }

else if (form.monitor[2].selected){
        mn_flag=300;
        mn_print="12 inch Super VGA [$300]";
        }

else if (form.monitor[3].selected){
        mn_flag=290;
        mn_print="14 inch VGA [$290]";
        }

else if (form.monitor[4].selected){
        mn_flag=370;
        mn_print="14 inch Super VGA [$370]";
        }

else if (form.monitor[5].selected){
        mn_flag=350;
        mn_print="17 inch VGA [$350]";
        }

else if (form.monitor[6].selected){
        mn_flag=475;
        mn_print="17 inch Super VGA [$475]";
        }

//————-Mouse——
if (form.mouse[0].selected){
        mos_flag=0;
        mos_print="None [$0]";
}
```

```
else if (form.mouse[1].selected){
    mos_flag=35;
    mos_print=" Vesa6 [$35]";
}

else if (form.mouse[2].selected){
    mos_flag=120;
    mos_print=" Titda9 [$120]";
}

//———keyboard———-
if (form.keyboard[0].selected){
    kb_flag=0;
    kb_print= "None [$0]";
}

else if (form.keyboard[1].selected){
    kb_flag=75;
    kb_print="473E SPO [$75]";
}

else if (form.keyboard[2].selected){
    kb_flag=120;
    kb_print="48dE SPO [$120]";
}

else if (form.keyboard[3].selected){
    kb_flag=150;
    kb_print="874K SPO [$150]";
}

else if (form.keyboard[4].selected){
    kb_flag=175;
    kb_print="888i SPO [$175]";
    }

//———Modem———-
if (form.modem[0].selected){
    modem_flag=0;
    modem_print=" None [$0]";
}

else if (form.modem[1].selected){
    modem_flag=100;
    modem_print=" External 14.4 [$100]";
}

else if (form.modem[2].selected){
    modem_flag=110;
    modem_print=" Internal 14.4 [$110]";
```

```
    }
else if (form.modem[3].selected){
    modem_flag=150;
    modem_print=" External 28.8 [$150]";
}

else if (form.modem[4].selected){
    modem_flag=160;
    modem_print=" Internal 28.8 [$160]";
    }

//————Sound Card————
 if (form.card[0].selected){
    card_flag=0;
    card_print="None [$0]";
}

else if (form.card[1].selected){
    card_flag=300;
    card_print=" Adlib [$300]";
}

else if (form.card[2].selected){
    card_flag=258;
    card_print=" Sound Blaster [$258]";
}

else if (form.card[3].selected){
    card_flag=235;
    card_print=" Sound Blaster Pro   [$235]";
}

else if (form.card[4].selected){
    card_flag=320;
    card_print=" MIDI Mapper    [$320]";
}

//————calculation of price
T_Price=pr_flag+sp_flag+ram_flag+hdrive_flag+vram_flag+ fdrive_flag
+cd_flag+mn_flag+mos_flag+ kb_flag+modem_flag+card_flag;

//—-display of price————
form.T_Price.value="      $ "+ T_Price;
}
```

You might be saying to yourself that the code repeats itself with different objects. You are absolutely right! We used the same code pattern to handle each of the component selections.

  If you look at the first line of this function, you will notice that we assigned true to called. We made this variable a Boolean because the user might press

Print Preview before **Update Price**. As you have seen, this function keeps track of all the options. If users pressed **Print Preview** before they pressed **Update Price**, the information about all the choices would not be seen in the Print Preview window.

Next, you will notice an `if` statement. This statement is used to create the array of choices for the first component. Notice that in JavaScript, the first element of an array is defined as the 0th element. So the array for the first selection option looks like this:

```
Array[0]=Select
Array[1]= 68LOCO45 DD [$540]
Array[2]= 68LCO45 EE   [$340]
Array[3]= 68LCO45 FF    [$680]
Array[4]= 68LCO45 GG   [$421]
```

Notice carefully that we call our first option from `processor` inside the `if` statement. Remember that we did not name the form anything in HTML. So all we need to do is to call the array element of the object, and we get the object (in our case, a form).

In the `if` statement, if the user chooses the first option from `processor`, we assign `pr_flag=0` and `pr_print="None [$0]"`. The reason we assign `pr_flag=0`, and in other selection options as well, is that `Select` has a value of 0. Naturally, if the user presses the **Price** button before choosing any of the options from any of the selection options, the price will be zero. When that happens, if the user presses the button **Print Preview**, all the components will have `None [$0]` next to them.

As you can see, we use `else if` statements in `processor` to assign the appropriate price for each option to `pr_flag` ($540, $40, $680, and $421). We also assign the appropriate component choice for each selection in `pr_print` for the Print Preview window.

The next selection option is speed. As before, we use `if` and `else if` statements to find out which item was selected from this object.

After we are finished with all the selection options, we need to add all the flags. For this purpose we use the variable `T_Price` for the simple addition.

```
T_Price=pr_flag+sp_flag+ram_flag+hdrive_flag+vram_flag+fdrive_flag+cd_fla
    g+ mn_flag+  mos_flag+ kb_flag+modem_flag+card_flag;
```

Finally, we display the value of `T_Price` in our text box. To do that, we replace the blank property of the text box, `value`, with `T_Price`:

```
form.T_Price.value="    $ "+ T_Price;
```

print() Function

This function creates a window that lists all the choices made by the user as well as the computed price. Listing 8.3 shows the `print()` function.

Listing 8.3 The print() Function

```
function print(form){
if(!called){
     compute(form);
}

text = ("<HEAD><TITLE>'UniVista On-line Computer Cost
Estimator'</TITLE></HEAD>");
text = (text +"<BODY BGCOLOR =  '#FFFFFF' ><CENTER><B><FONT SIZE = 4>
<FONT COLOR=BLUE>UniVista On-line Computer Cost Estimator<BR>
</FONT></FONT></B></CENTER>");

text=(text+"<hr>");

text=(text+"<TABLE BORDER =0><TR VALIGN=Top><TD VALIGN=Top>");
text=(text+"<B>Processor:<BR>Speed: <BR>Monitor: <BR>Hard Drive:
    <BR>Floppy Drive: <BR>Memory:");
text=(text+" <BR>VRAM: <BR>CD-ROM: <BR>Sound Card: <BR>Modem:
    <BR>Keyboard: <BR>Mouse: ");
text=(text+"</B></TD><TD>")

text=(text+"<B>"+ pr_print+"<BR>"+sp_print+"<BR>"+ mn_print+"<BR>"+
    hdrive_print+"<BR>");
text=(text+ fdrive_print+"<BR>"+ram_print+"<BR>"+ vram_print+"<BR>"+
    cd_print+"<BR>");
text=(text+card_print+"<BR>"+ modem_print+"<BR>"+kb_print +"<BR>"
    +mos_print );
text=(text+"<TD></TR></TABLE><hr>");
text=(text+"<B><FONT COLOR=RED>Total Cost:</FONT>"+"      
    $"+T_Price);
text=(text+"<BR><BR><BR><BR><BR><FONT SIZE=-1><FONT COLOR=GREEN>To print,
    choose FILE and PRINT.</FONT></FONT>");
text=(text+"</body></html>");

msgWindow=window.open("","displayWindow","toolbar=no,width=375,height=480
```

```
    ,directories=no,status=yes,scrollbars=yes,resize=no,menubar=yes");
msgWindow.document.write(text);

}
```

In this function, we first make sure that the compute() function is called. Next, we declare a variable, text, that carries all the information necessary to create a new page. For example, we define the BGCOLOR of the document, as we would do to make a new HTML page (Figure 8.2).

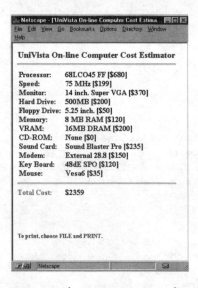

Figure 8.2 The Print Preview window.

After our page is made, we use the window object to create a new window. Notice the properties that are used in our new window:

```
toolbar=no
width=375
height=480
directories=no
status=yes
scrollbars=yes
resize=no
menubar=yes
```

We showed you how to make new windows in Chapter 6, so we won't repeat the explanation in this chapter. The final step is to use the document property write to display the text.

Putting the Code Together

Listing 8.4 shows the script for the custom computer cost estimator.

Listing 8.4 The Custom Computer Cost Estimator

```
<HTML>
<TITLE>Custom Computer</TITLE>
<HEAD>
<SCRIPT LANGUAGE="JAVASCRIPT">

var called=false;      //to make sure the function compute() is called
var T_Price=0;
var pr_flag;       //processor flag for keeping track of the choices
var pr_print="";

var sp_flag;       //flag for speed
var sp_print;

var ram_flag;       //flag for RAM
var ram_print;

var hdrive_flag;       //flag for Hard Drive
var hdrive_print;

var vram_flag;       //flag for VRAM
var vram_print;

var fdrive_flag;       //flag for Floppy Drive
var fdrive_print;

var cd_flag;       //flag for CD-ROM
var cd_print;

var mn_flag;       //flag for Monitor
var mn_print;

var mos_flag;       //flag for Mouse
var mos_print;

var kb_flag;       //flag for Keyboard
var kb_print;
```

```
var modem_flag;        //flag for Modem
var modem_print;

var software_flag; //flag for software
var software_print;

var card_flag;          //flag for sound card
var card_print;

function compute(form){
called=true;

if (form.processor[0].selected){
    pr_print= "None [$0]";
    pr_flag=0;
}

 if (form.processor[1].selected){
    pr_flag =540;
    pr_print="68LCO45 DD [$540]";
}

else if (form.processor[2].selected){
    pr_flag =340;
   pr_print="68LCO45 EE [$340]";
}

else if (form.processor[3].selected){
    pr_flag =680;
    pr_print="68LCO45 FF [$680]";
}

else if (form.processor[4].selected){
    pr_flag =421;
    pr_print="68LCO45 GG [$421]";
}

//——-Speed———
if (form.speed[0].selected){
    sp_flag=0;
    sp_print="None [$0]";
}

if (form.speed[1].selected){
    sp_flag=110;
   sp_print="60 MHz [$110]";
}

if (form.speed[2].selected){
    sp_flag=145;
sp_print="66/33 MHz [$145]";
```

```
}

if (form.speed[3].selected){
    sp_flag=199;
    sp_print="75 MHz [$199]";
}

if (form.speed[4].selected){
    sp_flag=235;
    sp_print="100 MHz  [$235]";
}

//-----RAM------
if (form.ram[0].selected){
    ram_flag=0;
    ram_print="None [$0]";
}

if (form.ram[1].selected){
    ram_flag=75;
    ram_print="4 MB RAM [$75]";
}

if (form.ram[2].selected){
    ram_flag=120;
    ram_print="8 MB RAM [$120]";
}

if (form.ram[3].selected){
    ram_flag=200;
    ram_print="16 MB RAM [$200]";
}

if (form.ram[4].selected){
    ram_flag=350;
    ram_print="32 MB RAM [$350]";
}

//-----Hard Drive------
if (form.hdrive[0].selected){
    hdrive_flag=0;
    hdrive_print="None [$0]";
}

if (form.hdrive[1].selected){
    hdrive_flag=100;
    hdrive_print="250MB [$100]";
}

if (form.hdrive[2].selected){
```

```
        hdrive_flag=200;
        hdrive_print="500MB [$200]";
}

if (form.hdrive[3].selected){
        hdrive_flag=300;
        hdrive_print="750MB [$300]";
}

if (form.hdrive[4].selected){
        hdrive_flag=399;
        hdrive_print="1.0GB [$399]";
}

//——-VRAM——-

if (form.vram[0].selected){
        vram_flag=0;
        vram_print="None [$0]";
        }

if (form.vram[1].selected){
        vram_flag=50;
        vram_print="1MB DRAM [$50]";
        }

if (form.vram[2].selected){
        vram_flag=89;
        vram_print="4MB DRAM  [$89]";
        }

if (form.vram[3].selected){
        vram_flag=125;
        vram_print="8MB DRAM [$125]";
        }

if (form.vram[4].selected){
        vram_flag=200;
        vram_print="16MB DRAM [$200]";
        }

//——-Floppy——-
if (form.fdrive[0].selected){
        fdrive_flag=0;
        fdrive_print="None [$0]";
        }

if (form.fdrive[1].selected){
        fdrive_flag=75;
        fdrive_print=" 1.4 inch [$75]";
```

```
        }

if (form.fdrive[2].selected){
    fdrive_flag=50;
    fdrive_print="5.25 inch [$50]";
    }

if (form.fdrive[3].selected){
    fdrive_flag=100;
    fdrive_print="BOTH [$100]";
    }

//——-CD-ROM——-

if (form.cd[0].selected){
    cd_flag=0;
    cd_print="None [$0]";
    }
if (form.cd[1].selected){
    cd_flag=300;
    cd_print="600E Dual Speed [$300]";
    }

if (form.cd[2].selected){
    cd_flag=450;
    cd_print="800E Quadruple-Speed [$450]";
    }

//——Monitor——-
if (form.monitor[0].selected){
    mn_flag=0;
    mn_print="None [$0]";
    }

if (form.monitor[1].selected){
    mn_flag=210;
    mn_print="12 inch VGA [ $210]";
    }

if (form.monitor[2].selected){
    mn_flag=300;
    mn_print="12 inch Super VGA [$300]";
    }

if (form.monitor[3].selected){
    mn_flag=290;
    mn_print="14 inch VGA [$290]";
    }

if (form.monitor[4].selected){
```

```
      mn_flag=370;
      mn_print="14 inch Super VGA [$370]";
      }

if (form.monitor[5].selected){
    mn_flag=350;
    mn_print="17 inch VGA [$350]";
      }

if (form.monitor[6].selected){
    mn_flag=475;
    mn_print="17 inch Super VGA [$475]";
      }

//———-Mouse——
if (form.mouse[0].selected){
    mos_flag=0;
    mos_print="None [$0]";
}

if (form.mouse[1].selected){
    mos_flag=35;
    mos_print=" Vesa6 [$35]";
}

if (form.mouse[2].selected){
    mos_flag=120;
    mos_print=" Titda9 [$120]";
}

//———Keyboard———-
if (form.keyboard[0].selected){
    kb_flag=0;
    kb_print= "None [$0]";
}

if (form.keyboard[1].selected){
    kb_flag=75;
    kb_print="473E SPO [$75]";
}

if (form.keyboard[2].selected){
    kb_flag=120;
    kb_print="48dE SPO [$120]";
}

if (form.keyboard[3].selected){
    kb_flag=150;
    kb_print="874K SPO [$150]";
```

```
       }

if (form.keyboard[4].selected){
     kb_flag=175;
     kb_print="888i SPO [$175]";
     }

//——Modem———-

if (form.modem[0].selected){
     modem_flag=0;
     modem_print=" None [$0]";
}

if (form.modem[1].selected){
     modem_flag=100;
     modem_print=" External 14.4 [$100]";
}

if (form.modem[2].selected){
     modem_flag=110;
     modem_print=" Internal 14.4 [$110]";
}

if (form.modem[3].selected){
     modem_flag=150;
     modem_print=" External 28.8 [$150]";
}

if (form.modem[4].selected){
     modem_flag=160;
     modem_print=" Internal 28.8 [$160]";
     }

//——Sound Card———-

if (form.card[0].selected){
     card_flag=0;
     card_print="None [$0]";
}

if (form.card[1].selected){
     card_flag=300;
     card_print=" Adlib [$300]";
}

if (form.card[2].selected){
     card_flag=258;
     card_print=" Sound Blaster [$258]";
}
```

```
if (form.card[3].selected){
    card_flag=235;
    card_print=" Sound Blaster Pro  [$235]";
}

if (form.card[4].selected){
    card_flag=320;
    card_print=" MIDI Mapper    [$320]";
}

T_Price=pr_flag+sp_flag+ram_flag+hdrive_flag+vram_flag+ fdrive_flag
+cd_flag+mn_flag+mos_flag+ kb_flag+modem_flag+card_flag;

form.T_Price.value="    $ "+ T_Price;

}
function print(form){
if(!called){
    compute(form);
}

text = ("<HEAD><TITLE>'UniVista On-line Computer Cost
    Estimator'</TITLE></HEAD>");
text = (text +"<BODY BGCOLOR =  '#FFFFFF' ><CENTER><B><FONT SIZE =
    4><FONT COLOR=BLUE>UniVista On-line Computer Cost
    Estimator</FONT></FONT></B>");
text= (text +"</CENTER>");
text=(text+"<hr>");

text=(text+"<TABLE BORDER =0><TR VALIGN=Top><TD VALIGN=Top>");
text=(text+"<B>Processor:<BR>Speed: <BR>Monitor: <BR>Hard Drive:
    <BR>Floppy Drive: <BR>Memory:");
text=(text+" <BR>VRAM: <BR>CD-ROM: <BR>Sound Card: <BR>Modem:
    <BR>Keyboard: <BR>Mouse: ");
text=(text+"</B></TD><TD>")

text=(text+"<B>"+ pr_print+"<BR>"+sp_print+"<BR>"+ mn_print+"<BR>"+
    hdrive_print+"<BR>");
text=(text+ fdrive_print+"<BR>"+ram_print+"<BR>"+ vram_print+"<BR>"+
    cd_print+"<BR>");
text=(text+card_print+"<BR>"+ modem_print+"<BR>"+kb_print +"<BR>"
    +mos_print );
text=(text+"<TD></TR></TABLE><hr>");
text=(text+"<B><FONT COLOR=RED>Total Cost:</FONT>"+"      
    $"+T_Price);
text=(text+"<BR><BR><BR><BR><BR><FONT SIZE=-1><FONT COLOR=GREEN>To print,
    choose FILE and PRINT.</FONT></FONT>");
text=(text+"</body></html>");
```

```
msgWindow=window.open("","displayWindow","toolbar=no,width=375,height=480
     ,directories=no,status=yes,scrollbars=yes,resize=no,menubar=yes")
                msgWindow.document.write(text)
                msgWindow.document.close()
}

</SCRIPT>
</HEAD>
<BODY BGCOLOR="#fffbf0" TEXT="#1f1f1f">

<H2><font color=Blue> <Center>UniVista On-line Computer Cost Estimator
<FORM method=post>
<TABLE BORDER CELLPADDING="2" border=0><CAPTION>
</CAPTION><TR><TD>Processor:
<P>
<SELECT NAME="processor">
<OPTION Selected>        Select
<OPTION>         68LCO45 DD [$540]
<OPTION>         68LCO45 EE   [$340]
<OPTION>         68LCO45 FF      [$680]
<OPTION>         68LCO45 GG    [$421]
</SELECT>
</TD><TD>Speed:
<P>
<SELECT NAME="speed">
<OPTION Selected>        Select
<OPTION>         60 MHz  [$110]
<OPTION>         66/33 MHz  [$145]
<OPTION>         75 MHz        [$199]
<OPTION>         100 MHz       [$235]
</SELECT>
</TD><TD>Memory(RAM):

<P>
<SELECT NAME="ram">
<OPTION>         Select
<OPTION>         4 MB RAM[$75]
<OPTION>         8 MB RAM [$120]
<OPTION>         16 MB RAM [$200]
<OPTION>         32 MB RAM [$350]
</SELECT>
</TD></TR><TR><TD>Hard Drive:
<P>
<SELECT NAME="hdrive">
<OPTION>         Select
<OPTION>         250MB [$100]
<OPTION>         500MB  [$200]
```

```
<OPTION>         750MB   [$300]
<OPTION>         1.0GB    [$399]
</SELECT>
</TD><TD>VRAM:
<P>
<SELECT NAME="vram">
<OPTION>         Select
<OPTION>         1MB DRAM   [$50]
<OPTION>         4MB DRAM    [$89]
<OPTION>         8MB DRAM    [$125]
<OPTION>         16MB DRAM    [$200]
</SELECT>
</TD><TD>Floppy Drive:
<P>
<SELECT NAME="fdrive">
<OPTION>         Select
<OPTION>         1.4MB [$75]
<OPTION>         5.25MB [$50]
<OPTION>         BOTH    [$100]
</SELECT>
</TD></TR><TR><TD>CD-ROM:
<P>
<SELECT NAME="cd">
<OPTION>          Select
<OPTION>          600E Dual Speed [$300]
<OPTION>          800E Quadruple-Speed  [$450]
</SELECT>
</TD><TD>Monitor:

<P>
<SELECT NAME="monitor">
<OPTION Selected>        Select
<OPTION>         12" VGA   [ $210]
<OPTION>         12" Super VGA   [$300]
<OPTION>         14" VGA   [$290]
<OPTION>         14" Super VGA [$370]
<OPTION>         17" VGA   [$350]
<OPTION>         17" Super VGA   [$475]
</SELECT>
</TD><TD>Mouse:
<P>
<SELECT NAME="mouse">
<OPTION Selected>        Select
<OPTION>         Vesa6   [$35]
<OPTION>          Titda9    [$120]
</SELECT>
```

```
</TD></TR><TR><TD>Keyboard:
<P>
<SELECT NAME="keyboard">
<OPTION Selected>        Select
<OPTION>            473E SPO    [$75]
<OPTION>            48dE SPO    [$120]
<OPTION>            874K SPO    [$150]
<OPTION>            888i SPO        [$175]
</SELECT>
</TD><TD>Modem:
<P>
<SELECT NAME="modem">
<OPTION Selected>        Select
<OPTION>            External 14.4 [$100]
<OPTION>            Internal 14.4    [$110]
<OPTION>            External 28.8    [$150]
<OPTION>            Internal 28.8        [$160]
</SELECT>
</TD><TD>Sound Card:
<P>
<SELECT NAME="card">
<OPTION>            Select
<OPTION>            Adlib    [$300]
<OPTION>            Sound Blaster        [$258]
<OPTION>            Sound Blaster Pro   [$235]
<OPTION>            MIDI Mapper    [$320]
</SELECT>
</TD></TR></TABLE><P>
<TABLE BORDER CELLPADDING="2"><TR><TD><center><BR>
<INPUT TYPE="BUTTON" NAME="Price" Value="Update Price"
onClick="compute(this.form)"></center>
<BR>
<INPUT TYPE="text" SIZE=15 NAME="T_Price" value=""><br>

</TD><TD><INPUT TYPE="BUTTON" NAME="Print_data" Value="Print Preview"
onClick="print(this.form)"></center>
</TD></TR></TABLE><P>
</FORM><P>
</FORM></BODY></HTML>
```

CHAPTER NINE

AN AREA CODE LOOKUP DATABASE

This chapter will show you how to create a client-side database using JavaScript. You can store all your data in one HTML page and access the data via an HTML form. The sample application, an area code lookup database, accepts as input an area code (integer) or city name (string) and searches for a match. One useful feature of this script is that the database responds immediately to each letter input by users, accelerating the query. This script does not employ a server, so it doesn't require you to know how to connect with a database or use database concepts such as ODBC. This script is a time-saver for those who build it and for those who use it.

This chapter covers:

- Building the front end for the area code lookup database
- Building the back end
- Putting the script together

Building the Front End

For the front end, we create two files: one that displays the search (a blank HTML page) and one that handles the query. We combine both files using a frame.

In our query file, **search.htm**, a text box takes the input and displays a list of options that lets you choose which search (by area code or by city name) to perform. We also create two buttons: one to reset the form and perform a new search, and a submit button that calls the search function for the query (Figure 9.1).

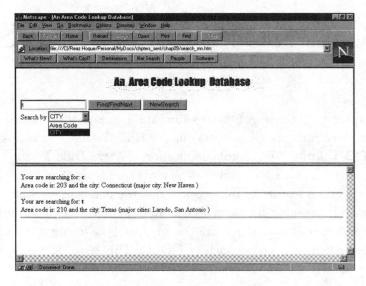

Figure 9.1 Area code lookup database in action.

Building the Back End

If you look at the JavaScript code in the **search.htm** page, you will notice that most of the syntax is for the data. So although this script may seem long, in reality it is quite simple and straightforward.

First, notice the function createArray(). As the name suggests, this function is used to define an array. You don't have to use this function if you are using Netscape 3.0+, which has an array object. All you have to do is use the keyword new to define a new array.

The createArray() function takes one parameter: how many data items the array should define, or the array length. It then loops through the length and returns the array. The function is shown in Listing 9.1.

Listing 9.1 Creating an Array

```
function createArray(length)
{
        this.length = length;
        for( var i = 1; i<= length; i++)   this[i] = null;
        return this;
}
```

Next, we define a bunch of variables:

```
var n_data = 169;       // Number of data items in the database
var Separator = "|"     // Separator for the Data fields
var Fields = 2;          // Number of Data Fields
var input_str="";            // the input field
var s_data= new createArray(n_data); //creating the array element for the data
```

Next, we list the data for each array element. Remember that the items are separated by "|" and are inside double quotes:

```
s_data[1]= "201|New Jersey (only at: Hackensack, Jersey City and  Newark )|";
s_data[2]= "202|District of Columbia (D.C. )(all areas )|";
s_data[3]= "203|Connecticut (only at: New Haven )|";
s_data[4]= "204|Manitoba (all areas )|";
    .
    .
    .
s_data[166]= "941|Florida (only at: Ft. Myers, Naples and  Sarasota )|";
s_data[167]= "954|Florida (only at: Fort Lauderdale )|";
s_data[168]= "970|Colorado (only at: Aspen, Fort Collins and  Grand Junction )|";
s_data[169]= "972|Texas (only at: Dallas )|";
```

Then define another variable, LastMatch, that stores the last matched data index. Now that we have created the array and stored the data, let us concentrate on the essential functions of the script.

FindNext()

This function takes two parameters: String, which is the input string, and number, which is the field that we will search in (either the city or the area code). Inside the function, we have two loops: one that loops through the whole list in a row and another that loops through each data item in a column.

Notice that we have declared a variable called CompareWith. This variable takes only the values from the field chosen. For example, if the user chooses to search for a city only, CompareWith will hold only the values of the city names. We also have two other variables, named bl and sl. These variables are used to take the length of the compared string and the input string. If the length of the two strings is not the same, then we compare up to the string length that is input by the user. Finally, we try to find a string match. If the match is not found, the function returns a zero; otherwise, the function returns a 1.

The function appears in Listing 9.2.

Listing 9.2 The FindNext Function

```
function FindNext(String, number)
{
    var CompareWith = "";
    for(var i = LastMatch + 1; i <=s_data.length; i++)
    {
        var FirstChar=0;
        var LastChar=-1;

        for(var j = 1; j <=number; j++) {
            FirstChar = LastChar + 1;
            LastChar = s_data[i].indexOf(Separator, FirstChar);

        }

        CompareWith = s_data[i].substring(FirstChar,LastChar);
        var bl = parseInt(CompareWith.length);
        var sl = parseInt(String.length);
        if(bl > sl) CompareWith = CompareWith.substring(0,sl );
if (CompareWith.toLowerCase() == String.toLowerCase())  {
    LastMatch = i; return i}
    }

    LastMatch = 0; return 0;
}
```

ResetSearch()

This function resets the form as well as clears the input string and puts the cursor for the data search on the top of the array. The function is shown in Listing 9.3.

Listing 9.3 The ResetSearch Function

```
function ResetSearch()//reset to start a new search
{
    LastMatch = 0;
    document.SearchForm.elements[0].value = "";
    input_str="";

}
```

valid()

This function ensures that the user input is valid. If the input is invalid, the function returns `false`; otherwise, the function returns `true`.

We have five variables. `input_len` takes the length of the entered string, `search_by_area` holds the value for the first selection (area code), `search_by_city` holds the value for the second selection (city), and `temp` and `temp2` hold the value of the text that will be displayed for invalid input.

First, we check whether the input length is 0 (there is no input). If the length is zero, we alert the user that the input is not valid and return `false`.

If there is input and the search is by area code, we make sure that the user inputs a string that contains characters between 0 and 9. We use a loop to check the input string. If we find that the string does not follow our criteria, we alert the user that the input is not valid and return `false`.

Finally, if the input length is not 0 and the search is by city, we make sure that the user inputs a string that contains characters between *a* and *z*. Again, we use a loop to check the input string. If we find that the string does not follow our criteria, we alert the user that the input is not valid and return `false`.

The `valid()` function is shown in Listing 9.4.

Listing 9.4 The valid Function

```
function valid(form){

    var input_len=input_str.length;
    var search_by_area =document.SearchForm.elements[3].options[0].selected;
    var search_by_city=document.SearchForm.elements[3].options[1].selected;

    var temp="When you choose to search\n"
            + "by area code, you have to\n"
            + "input a valid integer value.";

    var temp2="When you choose to search\n"
            + "by city, you cannot\n"
            + "input an invalid string value.";

    if (input_len==0){
        alert("Please input something, at least!");
        return false;
    }
    else if ((input_len!=0) && (search_by_area)){
            for (var i = 0; i < input_len; i++) {
                var ch = input_str.substring(i, i + 1);
                if ((ch < "0" )||( ch > "9" )) {
                        alert(temp);
                        return false;
                    }
                }
            }
    else if ((input_len!=0) && (search_by_city)){
            for (var j = 0; j < input_len; j++) {
                var ch2 = input_str.substring(j, j + 1);
                if (((ch2 < "a") ||  (ch2 > "z")) && ((ch2 < "A") ||  (ch2 >
                    "Z"))){
                    alert(temp2);
                        return false;
                    }
                }
            }

    return true;
}
```

TypeNext()

This function either outputs the search result or alerts the user that the search item was not found.

This function defines seven variables: SearchString holds the input string, index holds the value of the search option, and j holds the result (0 or 1) of calling the function FindNext(). FirstChar holds the position of the first character, LastChar holds the position of the last character, temptext holds the text that will be printed on the document for the search result, and temp holds the value of the search result.

First, we see whether j is 0 or whether the function FindNext() returns a 0. If that is the case, we alert the user that the search was not successful. If that is not the case in our second frame (**blank.htm**) we print the search string that is being searched for and then print the search result. Notice that we have used two important methods here: indexOf and substring. If you do not remember what these methods do, please check out Chapter 4 for more details.

The TypeNext function is shown in Listing 9.5.

Listing 9.5 The TypeNext Function

```
function TypeNext(field)
{

 if (valid(field.value)){
    var SearchString = document.SearchForm.Text.value;//takes the input from the
    form
    var index =document.SearchForm.elements[3].options.selectedIndex + 1;
    //find out the search option the user selected! Remember that the first
    array element is 0

    var j = FindNext(SearchString, index);//call the function FindNext and hold
    the value in j

    if (j == 0)//if the string not found
    {
        alert("Search string is not found OR \n" +
            "end of list is reached\n" +
            "Press 'NewSearch'  to start searching with a new string.");
        return;
    }

    var FirstChar=0;
```

```
        var LastChar=-1;//we want a zeroth position for the first time
        var temptext=" ";

        parent.bottom.document.write("You are searching for: <b>' " + SearchString
    +" '</b><br>");

        for(var i = 1; i <=Fields; i++)
        {
            FirstChar = LastChar + 1;
            LastChar = s_data[j].indexOf(Separator, FirstChar);//new position for
    //last character
            var temp=s_data[j].substring(FirstChar,LastChar);
            if(i==1) temptext = "<b><font color=blue>Area code: </font></b>";
            if(i==2) temptext = "<font color=blue><b>City: </font></b>";
            parent.bottom.document.bgColor="ffffff"; //preserve background color
            parent.bottom.document.write(temptext+"<font
    color=0889f>"+temp+"</font><br>");
        }
        parent.bottom.document.write("<br><hr>");

    }
}
```

Putting the Script Together

Listing 9.6 shows the complete listing for the area code lookup database.

Listing 9.6 The Area Code Lookup Database

```
<html>
<HEAD>
<TITLE> An Area Code Lookup Database </TITLE>
<SCRIPT LANGUAGE = "JavaScript">

function createArray(length)
{
        this.length = length;
        for( var i = 1; i<= length; i++)   this[i] = null;
        return this;
}

var n_data = 169;          // Number of data items in the database

var Separator = "|"        // Separator for the Data fields

var Fields = 2;            // Number of Data Fields
```

```
var input_str="";              // the input field

var s_data= new createArray(n_data);

    s_data[1]= "201|New Jersey (only at: Hackensack, Jersey City and  Newark
)|";

    s_data[2]= "202|District of Columbia (D.C. )(all areas )|";

    s_data[3]= "203|Connecticut (only at: New Haven )|";

    s_data[4]= "204|Manitoba (all areas )|";

    s_data[5]= "205|Alabama (only at: Birmingham and  Huntsville )|";

    s_data[6]= "206|Washington (only at: Seattle and  Tacoma )|";

    s_data[7]= "207|Maine (all areas )|";

    s_data[8]= "208|Idaho (all areas )|";

    s_data[9]= "209|California (only at: Fresno and  Modesto )|";

    s_data[10]= "210|Texas (only at: Laredo and  San Antonio )|";

    s_data[11]= "212|New York (only at: New York City )|";

    s_data[12]= "213|California (only at: Los Angeles )|";

    s_data[13]= "214|Texas (only at: Dallas and  Tyler )|";

    s_data[14]= "215|Pennsylvania (only at: Philadelphia)|";

    s_data[15]= "216|Ohio (only at: Akron, Canton, Cleveland and  Youngstown)|";

    s_data[16]= "217|Illinois (only at: Champaign|Urbana and  Springfield )|";

    s_data[17]= "218|Minnesota (only at: Duluth )|";

    s_data[18]= "219|Indiana (only at: Gary, Hammond and  South Bend )|";

    s_data[19]= "250|British Columbia|";

    s_data[20]= "281|Texas (only at: Houston )|";

    s_data[21]= "301|Maryland (only at: Hagerstown and  Rockville )|";

    s_data[22]= "302|Delaware (all areas )|";

    s_data[23]= "303|Colorado (only at: Boulder and  Denver )|";

    s_data[24]= "304|West Virginia (all areas )|";

    s_data[25]= "305|Florida (only at: Key West and  Miami )|";

    s_data[26]= "306|Saskatchewan (all areas )|";

    s_data[27]= "307|Wyoming (all areas )|";
```

```
s_data[28]= "308|Nebraska (only at: Grand Island, North Platte and
Scottsbluff )|";

s_data[29]= "309|Illinois (only at: Peoria and  Rock Island )|";

s_data[30]= "310|California (only at: Long Beach )|";

s_data[31]= "312|Illinois (only at: Chicago )|";

s_data[32]= "313|Michigan (only at: Ann Arbor and  Detroit )|";

s_data[33]= "314|Missouri (only at: Columbia, Jefferson and  St. Louis )|";

s_data[34]= "315|New York (only at: Syracuse and  Utica )|";

s_data[35]= "316|Kansas (only at: Dodge City, Hutchinson and  Wichita )|";

s_data[36]= "317|Indiana (only at: Indianapolis and  Kokomo )|";

s_data[37]= "318|Louisiana (only at: Lake Charles and  Shreveport )|";

s_data[38]= "319|Iowa (only at: Cedar Rapids, Davenport and  Dubuque )|";

s_data[39]= "320|Minnesota|";

s_data[40]= "330|Ohio|";

s_data[41]= "334|Alabama (only at: Montgomery and  Mobile )|";

s_data[42]= "352|Florida (only at: Gainesville )|";

s_data[43]= "360|Washington (only at: Bellingham, Olympia and  Vancouver
)|";

s_data[44]= "401|Rhode Island (all areas )|";

s_data[45]= "402|Nebraska (only at: Lincoln and  Omaha )|";

s_data[46]= "403|Alberta (all areas )|";

s_data[47]= "404|Georgia (only at: Atlanta )|";

s_data[48]= "405|Oklahoma (only at: Enid and  Oklahoma City )|";

s_data[49]= "406|Montana (all areas )|";

s_data[50]= "407|Florida (only at: Boca Raton, Orlando and  West Palm Beach
)|";

s_data[51]= "408|California (only at: Monterey and  San Jose )|";

s_data[52]= "409|Texas (only at: Beaumont and  Galveston )|";

s_data[53]= "410|Maryland (only at: Annapolis and  Baltimore )|";

s_data[54]= "412|Pennsylvania (only at: Pittsburgh )|";

s_data[55]= "413|Massachusetts (only at: Pittsfield and  Springfield )|";
```

```
s_data[56]= "414|Wisconsin (only at: Green Bay, Milwaukee and  Racine )|";

s_data[57]= "415|California (only at: San Francisco )|";

s_data[58]= "416|Ontario (only at: Toronto )|";

s_data[59]= "417|Missouri (only at: Joplin and  Springfield )|";

s_data[60]= "418|Quebec (only at: Quebec )|";

s_data[61]= "419|Ohio (only at: Toledo )|";

s_data[62]= "423|Tennessee (only at: Chattanooga and  Knoxville )|";

s_data[63]= "441|Bermuda (all areas )|";

s_data[64]= "501|Arkansas (all areas )|";

s_data[65]= "502|Kentucky (only at: Bowling Green, Louisville and  Paducah
)|";

s_data[66]= "503|Oregon (only at: Portland and  Salem )|";

s_data[67]= "504|Louisiana (only at: Baton Rouge and  New Orleans )|";

s_data[68]= "505|New Mexico (all areas )|";

s_data[69]= "506|New Brunswick (all areas )|";

s_data[70]= "507|Minnesota (only at: Rochester )|";

s_data[71]= "508|Massachusetts (only at: Lowell, New Bedford and  Worcester
)|";

s_data[72]= "509|Washington (only at: Spokane, Walla Walla and  Yakima )|";

s_data[73]= "510|California (only at: Oakland and  Berkeley )|";

s_data[74]= "512|Texas (only at: Austin and  Corpus Christi )|";

s_data[75]= "513|Ohio (only at: Cincinnati and  Dayton )|";

s_data[76]= "514|Quebec (only at: Montreal )|";

s_data[77]= "515|Iowa (only at: Des Moines )|";

s_data[78]= "516|New York (only at: Hempstead and  Long Island )|";

s_data[79]= "517|Michigan (only at: Bay City, Jackson and  Lansing )|";

s_data[80]= "518|New York (only at: Albany, Schenectady and  Troy )|";

s_data[81]= "519|Ontario (only at: Windsor )|";

s_data[82]= "520|Arizona (only at: Flagstaff, Tucson and  Yuma )|";

s_data[83]= "540|Virginia (only at: Roanoke )|";
```

```
s_data[84]= "541|Oregon (Southern and Eastern Oregon )|";

s_data[85]= "562|California (Southern California )|";

s_data[86]= "573|Missouri|";

s_data[87]= "601|Mississippi (all areas )|";

s_data[88]= "602|Arizona (only at: Phoenix )|";

s_data[89]= "603|New Hampshire (all areas )|";

s_data[90]= "604|British Columbia (all areas )|";

s_data[91]= "605|South Dakota (all areas )|";

s_data[92]= "606|Kentucky (only at: Ashland, Lexington and  Winchester )|";

s_data[93]= "607|New York (only at: Binghamton, Elmira and  Ithaca )|";

s_data[94]= "608|Wisconsin (only at: La Crosse and  Madison )|";

s_data[95]= "609|New Jersey (only at: Atlantic City, Camden and  Trenton
)|";

s_data[96]= "610|Pennsylvania (only at: Philadelphia suburbs and  Allentown
)|";

s_data[97]= "612|Minnesota (only at: Minneapolis, St. Paul and  Saint Cloud
)|";

s_data[98]= "613|Ontario (only at: Kingston and  Ottawa )|";

s_data[99]= "614|Ohio (only at: Columbus and  Steubenville )|";

s_data[100]= "615|Tennessee (only at: Nashville )|";

s_data[101]= "616|Michigan (only at: Battle Creek, Grand Rapids and
Kalamazoo )|";

s_data[102]= "617|Massachusetts (only at: Boston, Cambridge and  Winchester
)|";

s_data[103]= "618|Illinois (only at: Alton, Cairo and  East St. Louis )|";

s_data[104]= "619|California (only at: Barstow, Palm Springs and  San Diego
)|";

s_data[105]= "630|Illinois (only at: Chicago - cellular )|";

s_data[106]= "701|North Dakota (all areas )|";

s_data[107]= "702|Nevada (all areas )|";

s_data[108]= "703|Virginia (only at: Alexandria and  Arlington )|";

s_data[109]= "704|North Carolina (only at: Asheville and  Charlotte )|";
```

```
s_data[110]= "705|Ontario (only at: Sault Ste. Marie )|";

s_data[111]= "706|Georgia (only at: Augusta, Columbus and  Rome )|";

s_data[112]= "707|California (only at: Eureka and  Santa Rosa )|";

s_data[113]= "708|Illinois (only at: Chicago suburbs, Evanston and  Waukegan
)|";

s_data[114]= "709|Newfoundland (only at: Labrador City and  St. John's )|";

s_data[115]= "712|Iowa (only at: Council Bluffs and  Sioux City )|";

s_data[116]= "713|Texas (only at: Houston )|";

s_data[117]= "714|California (only at: Anaheim )|";

s_data[118]= "715|Wisconsin (only at: Eau Claire and  Wausau )|";

s_data[119]= "716|New York (only at: Buffalo, Niagara Falls and  Rochester
)|";

s_data[120]= "717|Pennsylvania (only at: Harrisburg, Scranton and  Wilkes-
Barre )|";

s_data[121]= "718|New York (only at: Bronx, Brooklyn, Queens and  Staten
Island )|";

s_data[122]= "719|Colorado (only at: Colorado Springs and  Pueblo )|";

s_data[123]= "770|Georgia (only at: Atlanta suburbs )|";

s_data[124]= "800|Toll-Free (free for caller )|";

s_data[125]= "801|Utah (all areas )|";

s_data[126]= "802|Vermont (all areas )|";

s_data[127]= "803|South Carolina (only at: Charleston, Columbia and
Florence )|";

s_data[128]= "804|Virginia (only at: Newport News, Norfolk and  Richmond
)|";

s_data[129]= "805|California (only at: Bakersfield and  Santa Barbara )|";

s_data[130]= "806|Texas (only at: Amarillo and  Lubbock )|";

s_data[131]= "807|Ontario (only at: Fort William )|";

s_data[132]= "808|Hawaii (all areas )|";

s_data[133]= "809|Anguilla, Antigua (Barbuda ), Bahamas, Barbados, British
Virgin Islands," +

                "Cayman Islands, Dominica, Dominican Republic, Jamaica,
Montserrat," +
```

```
          "Nevis, Puerto Rico, St. Kitts, St. Lucia, St. Vincent, The
Democratic" +

          "Republic Of Trinidad And Tobago, Virgin Islands|";

 s_data[134]= "810|Michigan (only at: Flint and  Northern Detroit suburbs
)|";

 s_data[135]= "812|Indiana (only at: Evansville )|";

 s_data[136]= "813|Florida (only at: St. Petersburg and  Tampa )|";

 s_data[137]= "814|Pennsylvania (only at: Altoona and  Erie )|";

 s_data[138]= "815|Illinois (only at: Joliet, La Salle and  Rockford )|";

 s_data[139]= "816|Missouri (only at: Independence, Kansas City and  St.
Joseph )|";

 s_data[140]= "817|Texas (only at: Fort Worth and  Waco )|";

 s_data[141]= "818|California (only at: Pasadena )|";

 s_data[142]= "819|Quebec (only at: Noranda )|";

 s_data[143]= "847|Illinois (only at: Chicago suburbs )|";

 s_data[144]= "860|Connecticut (only at: Hartford )|";

 s_data[145]= "864|South Carolina (only at: Greenville )|";

 s_data[146]= "888|Toll-Free (free for caller )|";

 s_data[147]= "900|Call paid by the caller|";

 s_data[148]= "901|Tennessee (only at: Memphis )|";

 s_data[149]= "902|Nova Scotia (all areas )|";

 s_data[150]= "903|Texas (only at: Texarkana and  Tyler )|";

 s_data[151]= "904|Florida (only at: Jacksonville, Pensacola and  Tallahassee
)|";

 s_data[152]= "905|Ontario (only at: Mississauga )|";

 s_data[153]= "906|Michigan (only at: Marquette and  Sault Ste. Marie )|";

 s_data[154]= "907|Alaska (all areas )|";

 s_data[155]= "908|New Jersey (only at: Elizabeth and  New Brunswick )|";

 s_data[156]= "909|California (only at: Riverside and  San Bernardino )|";

 s_data[157]= "910|North Carolina (only at: Greensboro and  Winston-Salem
)|";
```

```
    s_data[158]= "912|Georgia (only at: Albany, Macon and  Savannah )|";

    s_data[159]= "913|Kansas (only at: Lawrence, Salina and  Topeka )|";

    s_data[160]= "914|New York (only at: Peekskill, White Plains and  Yonkers
)|";

    s_data[161]= "915|Texas (only at: Abilene and  El Paso )|";

    s_data[162]= "916|California (only at: Sacramento )|";

    s_data[163]= "917|New York (only at: New York City - cellular )|";

    s_data[164]= "918|Oklahoma (only at: Tulsa )|";

    s_data[165]= "919|North Carolina (only at: Fayetteville and  Raleigh )|";

    s_data[166]= "941|Florida (only at: Ft. Myers, Naples and  Sarasota )|";

    s_data[167]= "954|Florida (only at: Fort Lauderdale )|";

    s_data[168]= "970|Colorado (only at: Aspen, Fort Collins and  Grand Junction
)|";

    s_data[169]= "972|Texas (only at: Dallas )|";
var LastMatch = 0; // Store Last Matched Data Index

function FindNext(String, number)
{
    var CompareWith = "";
    for(var i = LastMatch + 1; i <=s_data.length; i++)
    {
        var FirstChar=0;
        var LastChar=-1;

        for(var j = 1; j <=number; j++) {
            FirstChar = LastChar + 1;
            LastChar = s_data[i].indexOf(Separator, FirstChar);

        }

        CompareWith = s_data[i].substring(FirstChar,LastChar);
        var bl = parseInt(CompareWith.length);
        var sl = parseInt(String.length);
        if(bl > sl) CompareWith = CompareWith.substring(0,sl );
if (CompareWith.toLowerCase() == String.toLowerCase())  {
LastMatch = i; return i}
    }

    LastMatch = 0; return 0;
}

function ResetSearch()//reset to start a new search
```

```
{
    LastMatch = 0;
    document.SearchForm.elements[0].value = "";
    input_str="";

}
function valid(form){

    var input_len=input_str.length;
    var search_by_area =document.SearchForm.elements[3].options[0].selected;
    var search_by_city=document.SearchForm.elements[3].options[1].selected;

    var temp="When you choose to search\n"
            + "by area code, you have to\n"
            + "input a valid integer value.";

    var temp2="When you choose to search\n"
            + "by city, you cannot\n"
            + "input an invalid string value.";

    if (input_len==0){
        alert("Please input something, at least!");
        return false;
    }
    else if ((input_len!=0) && (search_by_area)){
            for (var i = 0; i < input_len; i++) {
                var ch = input_str.substring(i, i + 1);
                 if ((ch < "0" )||( ch > "9" )) {
                        alert(temp);
                         return false;
                    }
                 }
            }
    else if ((input_len!=0) && (search_by_city)){
            for (var j = 0; j < input_len; j++) {
                var ch2 = input_str.substring(j, j + 1);
                 if (((ch2 < "a") ||  (ch2 > "z")) && ((ch2 < "A") ||  (ch2 >
                    "Z"))){
                    alert(temp2);
                        return false;
                    }
                 }
                }

        return true;
    }
function TypeNext(field)
{
```

```
if (valid(field.value)){
     var SearchString = document.SearchForm.Text.value;//takes the input from the
    //form
     var index =document.SearchForm.elements[3].options.selectedIndex + 1;
     //find out the search option the user selected! Remember that the first
    //array element is 0

     var j = FindNext(SearchString, index);//call the function FindNext and hold
    //the value in j

    if (j == 0)//if the string not found
    {
        alert("Search string is not found OR \n" +
            "end of list is reached\n" +
            "Press 'NewSearch'  to start searching with a new string.");
        return;
    }

    var FirstChar=0;
    var LastChar=-1;//we want a zeroth position for the first time
    var temptext=" ";

    parent.bottom.document.write("You are searching for: <b>' " + SearchString
    +" '</b><br>");

    for(var i = 1; i <=Fields; i++)
    {
        FirstChar = LastChar + 1;
        LastChar = s_data[j].indexOf(Separator, FirstChar);//new position for
    last character
        var temp=s_data[j].substring(FirstChar,LastChar);
        if(i==1) temptext = "<b><font color=blue>Area code: </font></b>";
        if(i==2) temptext = "<font color=blue><b>City: </font></b>";
        parent.bottom.document.bgColor="ffffff"; //preserve background color
        parent.bottom.document.write(temptext+"<font
    color=0889f>"+temp+"</font><br>");
    }
    parent.bottom.document.write("<br><hr>");

    }
}

// ->

</SCRIPT>

</HEAD>

<BODY bgcolor=ffffff >

<CENTER>
```

```
<img src="phone.jpg"><br>
</CENTER>

<P>
<FORM NAME="SearchForm"  >

<INPUT NAME="Text" TYPE="TEXT">

<INPUT NAME="FindNext" TYPE="SUBMIT" VALUE="Find/FindNext" onClick='
    input_str=document.SearchForm.Text.value; TypeNext(this);return false; '>

<INPUT NAME="NewSearch" TYPE="Reset" VALUE="NewSearch" onClick ="ResetSearch();"><BR>

Search by <SELECT  VALUE="s_choice" SIZE=1 onChange='LastMatch = 0;'>

<OPTION>Area Code
<OPTION>CITY

</SELECT><BR>
</FORM>

</BODY>
</html>
```

CHAPTER TEN

A JavaScript Calendar: Using Cookies

In this chapter, we will create an appointment calendar. This JavaScript program presents a page where users store their appointments, recall and view them on a later date. This kind of script requires that you maintain state, thereby preserving your ability to retrieve the stored data correctly. You could use a database for this purpose, but an easier solution is to use a *cookie*, which stores the information in a browser. Whenever a user uses the browser, the user can retrieve the value of the cookie. The term *cookie* originates in the UNIX programming concept. It is also known as a *token*.

Before JavaScript, cookies were used only by server-side scripts written in languages such as Perl, but now you can use cookies on the client side. In brief, a cookie lets you store information in a file and read that information when needed. For the client side, the cookie information is stored in a plain text file called **cookies.txt**.

This chapter covers:

- Cookie basics
- JavaScript cookie functions
- Creating an appointment calendar

Cookie Basics

When a user of a cokkie based application requests a page, any data the user associates with that page is stored in **cookies.txt**. Suppose, for example, that you have a page where users can customize the look and feel of the page. When the user leaves the page and returns, the cookie makes sure the user's preferences are applied to that page.

To create a cookie, you use the `Set-Cookie` header in a CGI as part of an HTTP response. The `Set-Cookie` will let you set one required field, called `name`, and four optional fields: `expires`, `path`, `domain`, and `secure`. The syntax of `Set-Cookie` is as follows:

```
Set-Cookie: NAME=VALUE; expires=Date; path=PATH; domain=DOMAIN_NAME; secure
```

In JavaScript you use the syntax `document.cookie`, as we will see in the next sections in more detail. For example:

```
document.cookie = `cookieName=ReazHoque1996; expires=Sun, 31-March-2000 12:00:00 GMT;
path="/"; domain=".rhoque.com"; secure';
```

Now let's examine each of these fields.

NAME=VALUE

NAME is a required field that defines a specific name for the cookie. For example, `myCookie1` is a valid cookie name. NAME is a string with no semicolons, commas, or spaces.

The value of the cookie is nothing but a sequence of character strings. For example, `Sunday1994` is a valid value of a cookie.

expires=Date

If you want to, you can store your cookie in **cookies.txt** for as long as five years. The `expires` attribute is optional; if you don't specify the expiration date of the cookie, it is no longer stored or given out once the user closes the Netscape browser. The format for the date string must be in Greenwich mean time (GMT) strings:

```
wdy, DD-Mon-YY HH:MM:SS GMT
```

The easiest way to delete a cookie is set the date to any date before the present.

domain=DOMAIN_NAME

This string sets up the domain part of the URL, such as rhoque.com. If you were to specify the domain rhoque.com, by default it would become the basic domain for the site's location. So if you had a page such as jsbook.rhoque.com, any cookie set in it would be valid for the rhoque.com domain.

Note that the top-level domain names—COM, EDU, NET, ORG, GOV, MIL, and INT—must contain two periods (i.e., ".rhoque.com"), whereas other low-level domains, such as CA, must have three periods.

path=PATH

The `path` attribute specifies the subset of the URLs in a domain (for example, rhoque.com/book). If no path is set, Navigator automatically puts "/" for the current directory. After the domain is matched, the path name of the URL is compared with the `path` attribute. Only if there is a match is the cookie considered valid. Any page in the path, such as /jsbook or /jsbook/mypage.html, would be a valid match with the path /book.

Note that it is possible to create a duplicate copy of a cookie using a separate path and domain.

secure

When the secure attribute is specified, the cookie is sent via a secure channel. To do that, you must mark the cookie secure; otherwise, the cookie is sent over unsecured channels and its data will be accessible to any document. The secure flag is used as a Boolean value (True or False).

NOTE A client can store only 300 cookies, 4 KB per cookie and 20 cookies per server or domain. For more information on cookies, check out http://home.netscape.com/newsref/std/cookie_spec.html.

JavaScript Cookie Functions

In this section we will explain how you can create a cookie-setting function in which you can store a page visitor's name. We will also show you how to retrieve the value of the cookie so that every time the same person visits the page the cookie will show the person's name and the date of his or her first visit to that page.

The first thing you need is to have a page where a segment of JavaScript code checks whether the cookie value exists. If the cookie was not set for that particular browser, the page redirects the visitor to a page where he or she can set the cookie. When the cookie function finds a value from the visitor's browser, the page displays a greeting. The process is illustrated in Figure 10.1.

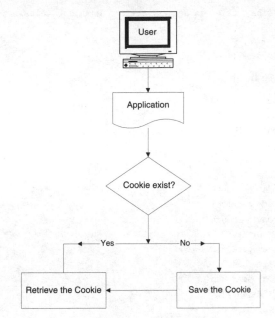

Figure 10.1 The cookie storage and retrieval process.

Listing 10.1 shows the page that sets the cookie.

Listing 10.1 The Set Cookie Page

```
<HTML>
<TITLE>Set the Cookie</TITLE>
<HEAD>
<SCRIPT LANGUAGE="JavaScript">

function addCookie(name, value)
{
        var expiredate= new Date("March 31, 1997, 12:30:00");

        document.cookie = name + "=" + escape (value) +
                "; expires=" + expiredate.toGMTString() +";"
}

function check(form){

        if (form.inputname.value==""){
                alert("Please input something \nand then press the 'Set the
                    Cookie' \nbutton!");
                return false;
        }
```

```
        else alert("The cookie was set to: " +form.inputname.value);
        return true;
  }
function find_date(mydate){

        var today=new Date();

        if (today.getMonth()==0)
                mydate="Jan";
        else if (today.getMonth()==1)
                mydate="Feb";
        else if (today.getMonth()==2)
                mydate="March";
        else if (today.getMonth()==3)
                mydate="April";
        else if (today.getMonth()==4)
                mydate="May" ;
        else if (today.getMonth()==5)
                mydate="June";
        else if (today.getMonth()==6)
                mydate="July";
        else if (today.getMonth()==7)
                mydate="Aug";
        else if (today.getMonth()==8)
                mydate="Sep";
        else if (today.getMonth()==9)
                mydate="Oct";
        else if (today.getMonth()==10)
                mydate="Nov";
        else if (today.getMonth()==11)
                mydate="Dec";

        mydate+= " " +today.getDate() + ", 19" +  today.getYear();
        return (mydate);

}

</SCRIPT>
</HEAD>
<BODY BGCOLOR=FFFFFF>
<form>
<font face="areal">
<font size="+2">Cookie Setting:</font><br>
<b>Please enter your name and click on "Set the Cookie".</b><p>
Name:
<input type="text" name="inputname" value="">
<input type="button" name="setcookie" value="Set the Cookie"
    onClick='

        if (check(this.form)) {
                var initialdate=find_date(this);
```

```
                var mydata=form.inputname.value + "<br>Your first visit was: "
                    +initialdate;
                addCookie("cookiereaz",mydata);
                window.location="getcookie.htm"
                }'>
</form>
</BODY>
</HTML>
```

First, we create a button and a text box. When the user enters a name in the text box and clicks on the button, the check() verifies the input. After that, we set the value of the text box in a variable called mydata. The variable mydata2 holds the returned value from the find_date() function. This function returns the current date of the user's visit in the format Month(as a string)-Date-Year. We then call the function addCookie() with the specific cookie name, cookiereaz. The value of this cookie is the user's name, the string "Your first visit was:," and the current date (Figure 10.2).

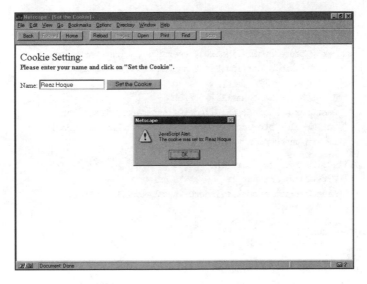

Figure 10.2 The output from the cookie-setting file.

Next, in addCookie() we create a new date instance with the date value March 31, 1997, 12:30:00. The cookie will be stored until 1997. Then we take document.cookie and set values for its name, value, and expires. Notice that we set the expiration date to GMT.

Now let's take a look at how we retrieve the value of the cookie. Listing 10.2 shows you how.

Listing 10.2 The Cookie-Retrieving Function

```
<HTML>
<TITLE>See the Cookie</TITLE>
<HEAD><body bgcolor=white>
<font face="areal">
<font size="+2"><center><b>Cookie Retrieving</a></a><hr noshade width=40%></font><br>
<SCRIPT LANGUAGE="JavaScript" >

function getcookie(name)
{
     var separator1="=";
     var separator2=";";
     var FirstChar=0;
     var LastChar=-1;

     var storedcookie=document.cookie + ";";

     while (FirstChar<storedcookie.length){

          FirstChar = LastChar+1;
          LastChar = storedcookie.indexOf(separator1, FirstChar);
          if (storedcookie.substring(FirstChar,LastChar)== name)
          {
               FirstChar = LastChar+1;
               LastChar = storedcookie.indexOf(separator2, FirstChar);
               var myvalue=storedcookie.substring(FirstChar,LastChar);
               return unescape(myvalue);

          }//if fails then go start the second cookie
               FirstChar=LastChar+1;
               LastChar=storedcookie.indexOf(separator2,FirstChar);

     }
     return "notfound";
}

if(getcookie("cookiereaz")!="notfound"){
     document.write("<h2>Welcome Back :" +getcookie("cookiereaz")+ "!</h2>");
     }
else if(getcookie("cookiereaz")=="notfound"){
     window.location="setcookie.htm";
     }

</SCRIPT>
</BODY>
</HTML>
```

We will pass the name of the cookie in the function `getcookie()`. If the name is matched, the value of the cookie is returned. Be aware that you need to add a semicolon (";") at the end of the cookie to separate it from other cookies. Although we separated each cookie with a ";" when setting the cookie, if you print **document.cookie** you will notice that all the cookie names and their values are displayed together without the semicolons.

So the first thing we need to do is to have two variables for two different separations: "=" and ";". The "=" is used between the name and the value when setting the cookie. We then define two other variables: `FirstChar` and `LastChar`. These variables hold positions of the first and last characters of the cookie. For this, we set the value of `FirstChar` equal to 0 and `LastChar` equal to the position (as an integer) before the "=" sign. Then we have a `while` loop that loops until `FirstChar` is less than the cookie length. Next, an `if` statement compares the requested cookie name with the saved cookie name. Once we have found the matching cookie, we position our `FirstChar` equal to the first character after the "=" sign; `LastChar` becomes the position before the second separator, which is ";". Finally, we use the `substring` method to get the cookie value and return it (Figure 10.3).

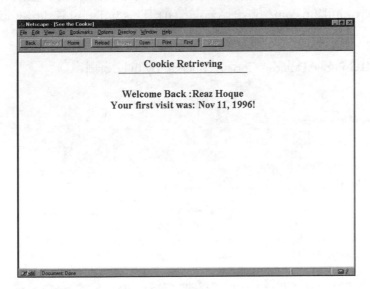

Figure 10.3 The output of the cookie-retrieving file.

If for some reason the cookie name does not match, we first set LastChar before the position of ";". Next, we set the FirstChar. Now if the LastChar is before ";" then the FirstChar must be two positions after the LastChar. That is why we add 2 with LastChar for the FirstChar. If the FirstChar is now at the beginning of the cookie name, we will need to set the LastChar up to the "=" sign. We do that using the following statement:

```
LastChar=(storedcookie.indexOf(separator1, FirstChar);
```

After the loop, if the specific cookie name is not found, we return notfound. Our next few statements after the function are quite simple. We call the function for the specific cookie name. If the cookie was set before, we simply print it. Otherwise, we take the user to the **setcookie.htm** page to set the cookie.

To show you how the two cookies were saved in **cookies.txt**, I copied the following lines from the file:

```
FALSE    /C|/Reaz Hoque/Personal/MyDocs/cookie    FALSE    859811400    cookiereaz
Reaz%2Hoque%3Cbr%3EYour%20first%20visit%20was%3A%20Nov%209%2C%201996
```

To store and retrieve client-side cookies with JavaScript, you can also use the public domain cookie function written by Bill Dortch from hIdaho Design (http://www.hidaho.com/cookies/cookie.txt). This function is shown in Listing 10.3.

Listing 10.3 Public Domain Cookie Function by Bill Dortch

```
<html>
<head>
<title>Cookie Functions</title>
</head>
<body>
<script language="javascript">
<!- begin script
//
//   Cookie Functions — "Night of the Living Cookie" Version (25-Jul-96)
//
//   Written by:  Bill Dortch, hIdaho Design <bdortch@hidaho.com>
//   The following functions are released to the public domain.
//
//   This version takes a more aggressive approach to deleting
//   cookies.  Previous versions set the expiration date to one
//   millisecond prior to the current time; however, this method
```

```
//  did not work in Netscape 2.02 (though it does in earlier and
//  later versions), resulting in "zombie" cookies that would not
//  die.  DeleteCookie now sets the expiration date to the earliest
//  usable date (one second into 1970), and sets the cookie's value
//  to null for good measure.
//
//  Also, this version adds optional path and domain parameters to
//  the DeleteCookie function.  If you specify a path and/or domain
//  when creating (setting) a cookie**, you must specify the same
//  path/domain when deleting it, or deletion will not occur.
//
//  The FixCookieDate function must now be called explicitly to
//  correct for the 2.x Mac date bug.  This function should be
//  called *once* after a Date object is created and before it
//  is passed (as an expiration date) to SetCookie.  Because the
//  Mac date bug affects all dates, not just those passed to
//  SetCookie, you might want to make it a habit to call
//  FixCookieDate any time you create a new Date object:
//
//     var theDate = new Date();
//     FixCookieDate (theDate);
//
//  Calling FixCookieDate has no effect on platforms other than
//  the Mac, so there is no need to determine the user's platform
//  prior to calling it.
//
//  This version also incorporates several minor coding improvements.
//
//  **Note that it is possible to set multiple cookies with the same
//  name but different (nested) paths.  For example:
//
//     SetCookie ("color","red",null,"/outer");
//     SetCookie ("color","blue",null,"/outer/inner");
//
//  However, GetCookie cannot distinguish between these and will return
//  the first cookie that matches a given name.  It is therefore
//  recommended that you *not* use the same name for cookies with
//  different paths.  (Bear in mind that there is *always* a path
//  associated with a cookie; if you don't explicitly specify one,
//  the path of the setting document is used.)
//
//  Revision History:
//
//     "Toss Your Cookies" Version (22-Mar-96)
//       - Added FixCookieDate() function to correct for Mac date bug
//
```

```
//     "Second Helping" Version (21-Jan-96)
//       - Added path, domain and secure parameters to SetCookie
//       - Replaced home-rolled encode/decode functions with Netscape's
//         new (then) escape and unescape functions
//
//     "Free Cookies" Version (December 95)
//
//
//   For information on the significance of cookie parameters, and
//   and on cookies in general, please refer to the official cookie
//   spec, at:
//
//       http://www.netscape.com/newsref/std/cookie_spec.html
//
//*******************************************************************
//
// "Internal" function to return the decoded value of a cookie
//
function getCookieVal (offset) {
  var endstr = document.cookie.indexOf (";", offset);
  if (endstr == -1)
    endstr = document.cookie.length;
  return unescape(document.cookie.substring(offset, endstr));
}
//
//   Function to correct for 2.x Mac date bug.  Call this function to
//   fix a date object prior to passing it to SetCookie.
//   IMPORTANT:  This function should only be called *once* for
//   any given date object!  See example at the end of this document.
//
function FixCookieDate (date) {
  var base = new Date(0);
  var skew = base.getTime(); // dawn of (Unix) time - should be 0
  if (skew > 0)  // Except on the Mac - ahead of its time
    date.setTime (date.getTime() - skew);
}
//
//   Function to return the value of the cookie specified by "name".
//     name - String object containing the cookie name.
//     returns - String object containing the cookie value, or null if
//       the cookie does not exist.
//
function GetCookie (name) {
  var arg = name + "=";
  var alen = arg.length;
  var clen = document.cookie.length;
```

```
    var i = 0;
    while (i < clen) {
      var j = i + alen;
      if (document.cookie.substring(i, j) == arg)
        return getCookieVal (j);
      i = document.cookie.indexOf(" ", i) + 1;
      if (i == 0) break;
    }
    return null;
  }
  //
  // Function to create or update a cookie.
  //    name - String object containing the cookie name.
  //    value - String object containing the cookie value.  May contain
  //       any valid string characters.
  //    [expires] - Date object containing the expiration date of the cookie.  If
  //       omitted or null, expires the cookie at the end of the current session.
  //    [path] - String object indicating the path for which the cookie is valid.
  //       If omitted or null, uses the path of the calling document.
  //    [domain] - String object indicating the domain for which the cookie is
  //       valid.  If omitted or null, uses the domain of the calling document.
  //    [secure] - Boolean (true/false) value indicating whether cookie transmission
  //       requires a secure channel (HTTPS).
  //
  // The first two parameters are required.  The others, if supplied, must
  // be passed in the order listed above.  To omit an unused optional field,
  // use null as a placeholder.  For example, to call SetCookie using name,
  // value and path, you would code:
  //
  //     SetCookie ("myCookieName", "myCookieValue", null, "/");
  //
  // Note that trailing omitted parameters do not require a placeholder.
  //
  // To set a secure cookie for path "/myPath", that expires after the
  // current session, you might code:
  //
  //     SetCookie (myCookieVar, cookieValueVar, null, "/myPath", null, true);
  //
  function SetCookie (name,value,expires,path,domain,secure) {
    document.cookie = name + "=" + escape (value) +
      ((expires) ? "; expires=" + expires.toGMTString() : "") +
      ((path) ? "; path=" + path : "") +
      ((domain) ? "; domain=" + domain : "") +
      ((secure) ? "; secure" : "");
  }
```

```
//  Function to delete a cookie. (Sets expiration date to start of epoch)
//  name -  String object containing the cookie name
//  path -  String object containing the path of the cookie to delete.  This MUST
//          be the same as the path used to create the cookie, or null/omitted if
//          no path was specified when creating the cookie.
//  domain - String object containing the domain of the cookie to delete.  This MUST
//          be the same as the domain used to create the cookie, or null/omitted if
//          no domain was specified when creating the cookie.
//
function DeleteCookie (name,path,domain) {
  if (GetCookie(name)) {
    document.cookie = name + "=" +
      ((path) ? "; path=" + path : "") +
      ((domain) ? "; domain=" + domain : "") +
      "; expires=Thu, 01-Jan-70 00:00:01 GMT";
  }
}

//
//  Examples
//
var expdate = new Date ();
FixCookieDate (expdate); // Correct for Mac date bug - call only once for given Date
object!
expdate.setTime (expdate.getTime() + (24 * 60 * 60 * 1000)); // 24 hrs from now
SetCookie ("ccpath", "http://www.hidaho.com/colorcenter/", expdate);
SetCookie ("ccname", "hIdaho Design ColorCenter", expdate);
SetCookie ("tempvar", "This is a temporary cookie.");
SetCookie ("ubiquitous", "This cookie will work anywhere in thisdomain",null,"/");
SetCookie ("paranoid", "This cookie requires secure
    communications",expdate,"/",null,true);
SetCookie ("goner", "This cookie must die!");
document.write (document.cookie + "<br>");
DeleteCookie ("goner");
document.write (document.cookie + "<br>");
document.write ("ccpath = " + GetCookie("ccpath") + "<br>");
document.write ("ccname = " + GetCookie("ccname") + "<br>");
document.write ("tempvar = " + GetCookie("tempvar") + "<br>");
// end script -->
</script>
</body>
</html>
```

Creating an Appointment Calendar

Now let's create the main application. The appointment calendar we'll build will rely on our knowledge of cookies. The example application will display different dates, including the month and year, in an HTML page and users will specify appointments. The appointments will be saved in the user's browser so that every time the page is opened, users will see the appointments (Figure 10.4). This example is by Darryl Stoflet (http://www.calweb.com/~dstoflet/ j_xmples.htm).

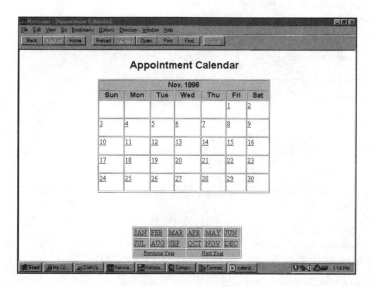

Figure 10.4 Appointment calendar in action.

Creating the Front End

The back end requires only three files: **calendar.htm**, **ctrls4.htm**, and **appt_set.htm**. The **calendar.htm** file creates two frames. The top frame holds the calendar, and the bottom frame displays the other months and years, which in turn contain links to the **ctrls4.htm** file. The calendar on the top frame is created using the functions shown in Listing 10.4.

Listing 10.4 PopCalendar() and calendar()

```
function PopCalendar (m) {
    if(m < 12){
        monthPage = m
    }else{
        monthPage = mo
        year -= m - 13
    }
    var hdg = "<HTML><HEAD><TITLE>Appt.Calender</TITLE></HEAD>";

    var bod = "<BODY  bgcolor=white  LINK=#004080  VLINK=#004080  ><CENTER>";
    var theTitle = "<FONT FACE='Modern'>"
    var xxx = parent.frames[0];
    xxx.document.open();
    xxx.document.clear();

    xxx.document.write(hdg);

    xxx.document.write(bod);
    xxx.document.write(theTitle);

    calendar(xxx);
}
function calendar(w) {

  var match1 = false

  monthNames = new Array("Jan","Feb","Mar","Apr","May","Jun","Jul","Aug",
      "Sep","Oct","Nov","Dec");

  var mD = "31,28,31,30,31,30,31,31,30,31,30,31";
  var monthDays = mD.split(",");  //split() method takes a string and creates an
      array of strings

  var thisDay = today.getDate();
  var mkBtn1 = "<FONT SIZE=1><A HREF = \"javascript:parent.ShowAppt("

  var mkBtn2 = "<A HREF = \"javascript:parent.openSetAppt("
  var mkBtn3 = ")\">"
  var mkBtn4 = "</A>"

  var end = "</CENTER></BODY></HTML>";

  if (((year % 4 == 0) && (year % 100 != 0)) || (year % 400 == 0))

    monthDays[1] = 29;

  var nDays = monthDays[monthPage];
  var firstDay = today;
  firstDay.setDate(1);
  firstDay.setMonth(monthPage);
```

```
firstDay.setYear(year);
var apptsThisMonth = 0;
var startDay = firstDay.getDay();

var FontString = "<STRONG><FONT COLOR=#004080 FACE=\"helvetica\"
    SIZE=1>  ";

var EndFont = "  </FONT></STRONG>";

var THeadFormat = "<TH  BGCOLOR=wheat >";

tmpMonth = monthNames[monthPage];

var TDFont = "<TD BGCOLOR=#ffffff ><FONT COLOR=#ffffff SIZE=1>";

w.document.write("<FORM><TABLE BORDER=1 CELLPADDING=1 CELLSPACING=1>");

w.document.write("<TH  BGCOLOR=wheat  COLSPAN=7>");

w.document.write(FontString + tmpMonth + ". " + year + EndFont + "<TR>");

w.document.write(THeadFormat + FontString + "   Sun   " + EndFont);

w.document.write(THeadFormat + FontString + "   Mon   " + EndFont);

w.document.write(THeadFormat + FontString + "   Tue    " + EndFont);

w.document.write(THeadFormat + FontString + "   Wed    " + EndFont);

w.document.write(THeadFormat + FontString + "   Thu    " + EndFont);

w.document.write(THeadFormat + FontString + "   Fri      " + EndFont);

w.document.write(THeadFormat + FontString + "   Sat     " + EndFont);

w.document.write("<TR>");

column = 0;

for (c=0; c<startDay; c++){

   w.document.write(TDFont);

   w.document.write("</FONT> </TD>");

   column++;

}

for (var i=1; i<=nDays; i++){

    w.document.write(TDFont);
    w.document.write(mkBtn2 +i + mkBtn3 + i + mkBtn4);
                for(var n = 0; n < splitapptDate.length; n++){
                    if(splitapptDate[n][1] == i & splitapptDate[n][0] ==
                        monthPage & splitapptDate[n][2] == year){
                            w.document.write("<br>" + mkBtn1 + i + "," + n +
```

```
mkBtn3  +   splitapptData[n][0] + mkBtn4 + "</FONT>");
                            }
                    }

    w.document.write("<br><br></FONT></TD>");

    column++;

    if (column == 7){

       w.document.write("<TR>"); // start a new row

       column = 0;

    }

  }

  w.document.write("</TABLE>");
  w.document.write("<BR>");

  w.document.write("</FORM>");

  w.document.write(end);
  w.document.close();

}
```

As you can see, `PopCalendar()` initiates the calendar draw. The parameter `m` is used to pass the month value, which is stored in the variable `monthPage`. We check to see whether `monthPage` is less than 12. If it is, we set the value of `monthPage` to 0 (for January), and the variable `year` is advanced to 1. Note that we have a variable `xxx`, which calls the top frame. To write anything to the top frame, note that we follow this instruction:

`xxx.document.write()`

Our next function, `calendar()`, is called from the `PopCalendar()` function. In addition to doing most of the calendar drawing, this function uses the `date` function mentioned in Chapter 5 to convert the months from integers to month names. Notice that we are using an array for the month names, and the `split()` method is used in the `monthDays` variable to create an array of strings for the total days in the month. Also note that for all the dates, we create a link to the `openSetApp()` function for setting up appointments. If there is a saved appointment, we link it to the function `ShowAppt()` to display it.

In the `calendar()` function we also have to worry about whether the year is a leap year. If it is, we assign the value 29 to the second month of the year. Let's see that segment of code again:

```
if (((year % 4 == 0) && (year % 100 != 0)) || (year % 400 == 0))
    monthDays[1] = 29;
```

Finally, we use the `document.write()` method to first draw the calendar heading with the month name and each day of the week and then to draw all the appointment dates in the current month.

The **ctrls4.htm** file displays hyperlinks to the 12 months and also links to the next and previous years. The `PopCalendar()` function actually is called from this file by the `<BODY>` tag using the `onLoad` event handler. The hyperlinks refer to the `PopCalendar()` function for each month, the previous year, and next year.

The **appt_set.htm** file is used as a pop-up window. When the user clicks on a date to set an appointment, this window opens with a simple HTML form. The form has three text inputs: the name, time, and description of the appointment. It also has a **Set Appointment** button that submits the information typed by the user.

Creating the Back End

For the back end, we will concentrate on the **calendar.htm** file, because most of the code is generated from this file. First, we define the variables shown in Listing 10.5.

Listing 10.5 Variables for the Calendar Script

```
var monthPage = 0;//sets the proper month
var tmpMonth;
var monthNames;
var month = 0;
var today = new Date();
var year = today.getYear() + 1900;
var mo = today.getMonth();
var tempMo;
var tempYear;
var theDay;
var apptsNum = GetCookie("appt"); // how many appointments are set

var apptDate = new Array();
//holds the appointment date information (month, day, year)

var apptData = new Array();
```

```
//holds the appointment information (name, time, description)

var splitapptDate = new Array();
//splits the above arrays to hold the appointment's individual data (e.g., day)

var splitapptData = new Array();
//splits the above arrays to hold the appointment's individual
//data (e.g., name)
var match1 = false;

var match2 = false;

var some = false;

var d = 0;

var mc;

var mcw_exists = false;
```

Next we use Bill Dortch's cookie functions to save the appointment information in the cookie.

NOTE
In the deleteCookie() function, the expiration date of the appointment is the date of the appointment. This means that entries older than the current time are deleted.

The following code segment runs as the **calendar.htm** file gets loaded:

```
if(apptsNum != null & apptsNum != 0){
        for(var i = 0; i < apptsNum; i++){
                apptDate[i] = GetCookie("apptDt" + i);  //get prior set appointment //
                                                                dates
                apptData[i] = GetCookie("apptDa" + i);  //get prior set appointment //
                                                                data
                var  tempString1 = "" + apptDate[i] + "";
                var tempString2 = "" + apptData[i] + "";
                splitapptDate[i] = tempString1.split(",");  //split dates array //(day,
                                                            month, year)
                splitapptData[i] = tempString2.split(",");  //split data array //(name,
                                                            time, notes)

        }

    }
```

The preceding code checks to see whether an appointment was set. If the variable apptsNum is not null or 0, then we loop apptsNum a number of times to retrieve the values of all the cookies that are stored with appointment data. This data is stored in the `apptDate` and `apptData` arrays, which are split to get the individual data (month, day, year, description, and so on). The variables `splitapptDate` and `splitapptData` are used for these new arrays. Note that these two variables hold `[n][x]` indexing, where `[n]` represents each `splitapptDate` and `splitapptData` index of the arrays and `[x]` represents either the month, day, or year (for `splitapptDate`) or the name, time, or description (for `splitapptData`). For example, in `splitapptDate[1][1]`, the first `[1]` would mean that it is the second `splitapptDate` array element, and the second `[1]` would refer to the day stored within the element.

Our next function, `openSetAppt()`, is called when the someone wants to make an appointment. This function opens the pop-up window and displays the **appt_set.htm** file. The function looks like this:

```
function openSetAppt(x){

        theDay = x;

        sa = window.open("appt_set.htm","appt","0,0,0,0,0,0,0,
            WIDTH=300,HEIGHT=340");

    }
```

Figure 10.5 shows the **calendar.htm** file in action.

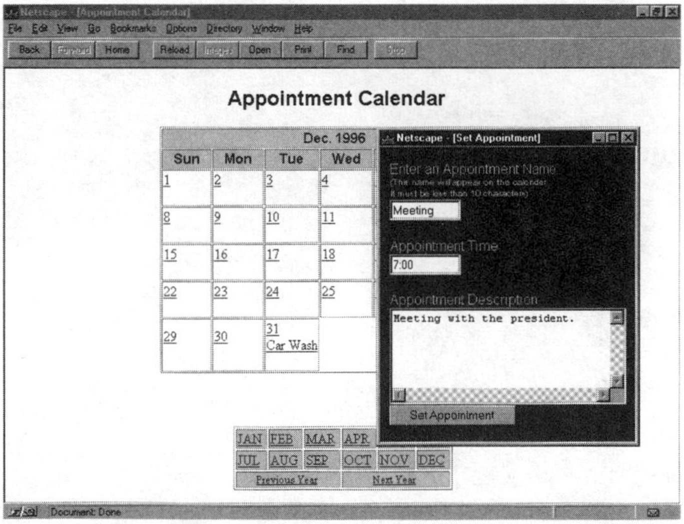

Figure 10.5 Creating an appointment.

The next two functions (Listing 10.6) convert the weekdays from integers to Sunday, Monday, and so on and the month names from 0–11 integers to January–December strings.

Listing 10.6 full() and mCon()

```
function full(sd){
                if(sd == 0)

                        sd = "Sunday, "

                else if(sd == 1)

                        sd = "Monday, "

                else if(sd == 2)

                        sd  = "Tuesday, "

                else if(sd == 3)

                        sd  = "Wednesday, "

                else if(sd == 4)

                        sd  = "Thursday, "

                else if(sd == 5)

                        sd  = "Friday, "

                else if(sd == 6)

                        sd  = "Saturday, "

                return sd;
    }

function mCon(theMonth){
    if(theMonth == 0)

    mnth = "-Jan-"

  else if(theMonth ==1)

    mnth = "-Feb-"

  else if(theMonth ==2)

    mnth = "-Mar-"

  else if(theMonth ==3)

    mnth = "-Apr-"

  else if(theMonth ==4)
```

```
        mnth = "-May-"
    else if(theMonth ==5)
        mnth = "-Jun-"
    else if(theMonth ==6)
        mnth = "-Jul-"
    else if(theMonth ==7)
        mnth = "-Aug-"
    else if(theMonth ==8)
        mnth = "-Sep-"
    else if(theMonth ==9)
        mnth = "-Oct-"
    else if(theMonth ==10)
        mnth = "-Nov-"
    else if(theMonth ==11)
        mnth = "-Dec-"
    return mnth;
}
```

Our next function, saveAppt(), is called when you fill out the form from the
appt_set.htm file. This function, shown in Listing 10.7, calls our cookie function and saves the appointment information. Note that the functions full()
and mCon() are called from this function. Once the function saves the information, the **appt_set.htm** file is closed and the calendar page is reloaded with the
current appointment information.

Listing 10.7 saveAppt()

```
function saveAppt(form, form_data){
        apptDates = monthPage + "," + theDay + "," + year
        exDate = new Date(year,monthPage,theDay,23,59,59);
        wkDayEx = exDate.getDay();
        wkDayFull = full(wkDayEx);
        monthFull = mCon(monthPage)
        mDayFull = exDate.getDate() + ""
        if(mDayFull.length < 2)
                mDayFull = "0" + mDayFull;
```

```
exFull = wkDayFull + mDayFull + monthFull + "96" + " 23:59:59 GMT"

apptsNum++

var xpires = today;

xpires.setTime(xpires.getTime() + (30*24*60*60*1000));

parent.SetCookie("appt", apptsNum, exFull);

var a = "apptDt" + (apptsNum - 1) + "";

var b = "apptDa" + (apptsNum - 1) + "";

parent.SetCookie(a, apptDates,xpires);

parent.SetCookie(b, form_data,xpires);

alert("Appointment has been saved!");

sa.close();

location.reload()

}
```

To show the saved appointments, we use a function called ShowAppt(). This function (Listing 10.8) retrieves the cookie information and then writes it in a pop-up window if a hyperlink to the appointment is clicked.

Listing 10.8 ShowAppt()

```
function ShowAppt(){

    theD = new Date();

    if(parent.apptsNum == null){

        alert("\n\nYou haven\'t set any appointments yet!\n\n");

    }else{

            var dtData = new Array();

            var dtDate = new Array();

            var theData = new Array();

            var theDate = new Array();

            for(var i = 1; i <= parent.apptsNum; i++){

                    var a = "apptDt" + (i - 1) + "";

                    var b = "apptDa" + (i - 1) + "";
```

```
                    dtData[i] = GetCookie(b);

                    dtDate[i] = GetCookie(a);

                    theData[i] = dtData[i].split(",");

                    theDate[i] = dtDate[i].split(",");

        }

var show = window.open("","","toolbar=no,location=no,directories=no,
    status=no,menubar=no,scrollbars=yes,resizable=no,WIDTH=300,
    HEIGHT=300");

var saw = show.document;

saw.open()

saw.write("<HTML><HEAD><TITLE>Saved Appts.</TITLE></TITLE>");

saw.write("<BODY BGCOLOR= wheat   TEXT=#004080>");

saw.write("<FONT FACE='Modern' SIZE=6>Your Saved Appts.<hr width=80%
    align = right><br></FONT>");

saw.write("<FONT FACE='Modern' SIZE=3>");

for(var a = 1; a <= parent.apptsNum; a++){

    var md = parseInt(theDate[a][0]);

    var td = parent.monthNames[md]

    saw.write("<hr><b> Month: </b>" + td);

    saw.write("<b> Day: </b>" + theDate[a][1]);

     saw.write("<b> Year: </b>" +  theDate[a][2] + "<br><br>");

        for(var p = 0; p< parent.splitapptData[parent.d].length-1;
            p++){

            if(theData[a][p] == null){

                break;

            }else{

                    saw.write("<b> Field " + (p+1) + ": </b>" +
                        theData[a][p] +  "<br>");

            }

        }

    }
```

```
        saw.write("</FONT></BODY></HTML>");

        saw.close();

    }

  }
```

Putting the Script Together

Listings 10.9, 10.10, and 10.11 show the scripts needed for this example.

Listing 10.9 Calendar.htm

```
<HTML>
<HEAD>

<TITLE> Appointment Calendar </TITLE>

<SCRIPT LANGUAGE="JavaScript">

<!— to hide script contents from old browsers
    //    This script is copyrighted by Darryl Stoflet

var monthPage = 0;
var tmpMonth;
var monthNames;
var month = 0;
var today = new Date();

var year = today.getYear() + 1900;
var mo = today.getMonth();
var tempMo;
var tempYear;
var theDay;
var apptsNum = GetCookie("appt");
var apptDate = new Array();
var apptData = new Array();
var splitapptDate = new Array();
var splitapptData = new Array();
var match1 = false;
var match2 = false;
var some = false;
var d = 0;
var mc;
var mcw_exists = false;

function getCookieVal (offset) {
  var endstr = document.cookie.indexOf (";", offset);
  if (endstr == -1)
```

```
      endstr = document.cookie.length;
   return unescape(document.cookie.substring(offset, endstr));
}

function GetCookie (name) {
  var arg = name + "=";
  var alen = arg.length;
  var clen = document.cookie.length;
  var i = 0;
  while (i < clen) {
    var j = i + alen;
    if (document.cookie.substring(i, j) == arg)
      return getCookieVal (j);
    i = document.cookie.indexOf(" ", i) + 1;
    if (i == 0) {

       break;
    }
  }
  return null;
}

function SetCookie (name, value) {
  var argv = SetCookie.arguments;
  var argc = SetCookie.arguments.length;
  var expires = (argc > 2) ? argv[2] : null;
  var path = (argc > 3) ? argv[3] : null;
  var domain = (argc > 4) ? argv[4] : null;
  var secure = (argc > 5) ? argv[5] : false;
  document.cookie = name + "=" + escape (value) +
    ((expires == null) ? "" : ("; expires=" + expires)) +
    ((path == null) ? "" : ("; path=" + path)) +
    ((domain == null) ? "" : ("; domain=" + domain)) +
    ((secure == true) ? "; secure" : "");
 //debugging info to check if cookies have been set
 //alert(name + " set to " + value);
}

    function deleteCookie(name){
      var exp = new Date();
      exp.setTime(exp.getTime()-1);
      var cval = GetCookie(name);
      document.cookie = name + "=" + cval + "; expires=" + exp.toGMTString();
    }

        if(apptsNum != null & apptsNum != 0){
          for(var i = 0; i < apptsNum; i++){
              apptDate[i] = GetCookie("apptDt" + i);  //get prior set appointment
                                            //dates
```

```
                apptData[i] = GetCookie("apptDa" + i);  //get prior set appointment
                                                        //data
            var  tempString1 = "" + apptDate[i] + "";
            var tempString2 = "" + apptData[i] + "";
            splitapptDate[i] = tempString1.split(",");  //split dates array
                (day, month, year)
            splitapptData[i] = tempString2.split(",");  //split data array
                (name, time, notes)
        }
    }

    function openSetAppt(x){
        theDay = x;
        sa = window.open("appt_set.htm","appt","0,0,0,0,0,0,0,WIDTH=300,HEIGHT=340");
    }

function full(sd){
                    if(sd == 0)
                            sd = "Sunday, "
                    else if(sd == 1)
                            sd  = "Monday, "
                    else if(sd == 2)
                            sd  = "Tuesday, "
                    else if(sd == 3)
                            sd  = "Wednesday, "
                    else if(sd == 4)
                            sd  = "Thursday, "
                    else if(sd == 5)
                            sd  = "Friday, "
                    else if(sd == 6)
                            sd  = "Saturday, "
                return sd;
    }

    function mCon(theMonth){
        if(theMonth == 0)
        mnth = "-Jan-"
      else if(theMonth ==1)
        mnth = "-Feb-"
      else if(theMonth ==2)
        mnth = "-Mar-"
      else if(theMonth ==3)
        mnth = "-Apr-"
      else if(theMonth ==4)
        mnth = "-May-"
      else if(theMonth ==5)
        mnth = "-Jun-"
      else if(theMonth ==6)
```

```
        mnth = "-Jul-"
    else if(theMonth ==7)
        mnth = "-Aug-"
    else if(theMonth ==8)
        mnth = "-Sep-"
    else if(theMonth ==9)
        mnth = "-Oct-"
    else if(theMonth ==10)
        mnth = "-Nov-"
    else if(theMonth ==11)
        mnth = "-Dec-"
  return mnth;
}

  function saveAppt(form, form_data){

      apptDates = monthPage + "," + theDay + "," + year
      exDate = new Date(year,monthPage,theDay,23,59,59);
      wkDayEx = exDate.getDay();
      wkDayFull = full(wkDayEx);
      monthFull = mCon(monthPage)
      mDayFull = exDate.getDate() + ""
      if(mDayFull.length < 2)
          mDayFull = "0" + mDayFull;
      exFull = wkDayFull + mDayFull + monthFull + "96" + " 23:59:59 GMT"

      apptsNum++
      var xpires = today;
      xpires.setTime(xpires.getTime() + (30*24*60*60*1000));
      parent.SetCookie("appt", apptsNum, exFull);
      var a = "apptDt" + (apptsNum - 1) + "";
      var b = "apptDa" + (apptsNum - 1) + "";
      parent.SetCookie(a, apptDates,xpires);
      parent.SetCookie(b, form_data,xpires);
      alert("Appointment has been saved!");
      sa.close();
      location.reload()
}
function ShowAppt(){
    theD = new Date();
    if(parent.apptsNum == null){
       alert("\n\nYou haven\'t set any appointments yet!\n\n");
    }else{
            var dtData = new Array();
            var dtDate = new Array();
            var theData = new Array();
            var theDate = new Array();
            for(var i = 1; i <= parent.apptsNum; i++){
```

```
                         var a = "apptDt" + (i - 1) + "";
                         var b = "apptDa" + (i - 1) + "";
                         dtData[i] = GetCookie(b);
                         dtDate[i] = GetCookie(a);
                         theData[i] = dtData[i].split(",");
                         theDate[i] = dtDate[i].split(",");
                 }

        var show = window.open("","","toolbar=no,location=no,directories=no,
            status=no,menubar=no,scrollbars=yes,resizable=no,WIDTH=300,
            HEIGHT=300");
        var saw = show.document;
        saw.open()
        saw.write("<HTML><HEAD><TITLE>Saved Appts.</TITLE></TITLE>");
        saw.write("<BODY BGCOLOR= wheat   TEXT=#004080>");
        saw.write("<FONT FACE='Modern' SIZE=6>Your Saved Appts.<hr width=80%
            align = right><br></FONT>");
        saw.write("<FONT FACE='Modern' SIZE=3>");
        for(var a = 1; a <= parent.apptsNum; a++){
            var md = parseInt(theDate[a][0]);
            var td = parent.monthNames[md]
            saw.write("<hr><b> Month: </b>" + td);
            saw.write("<b> Day: </b>" + theDate[a][1]);
             saw.write("<b> Year: </b>" +  theDate[a][2] + "<br><br>");
                for(var p = 0; p< parent.splitapptData[parent.d].length-1;
                    p++){
                       if(theData[a][p] == null){
                          break;
                       }else{
                              saw.write("<b> Field " + (p+1) + ": </b>" +
                                  theData[a][p] +  "<br>");
                       }
                }
        }
        saw.write("</FONT></BODY></HTML>");
        saw.close();
    }
}

    function PopCalendar (m) {
    if(m < 12){
        monthPage = m
    }else{
        monthPage = mo
        year -=  m - 13
    }
    var hdg = "<HTML><HEAD><TITLE>Appt.Calender</TITLE></HEAD>";
```

```
    var bod = "<BODY  bgcolor=white  LINK=#004080  VLINK=#004080  ><CENTER>";
    var theTitle = "<FONT FACE='Modern'>"
    var xxx = parent.frames[0];
    xxx.document.open();
    xxx.document.clear();

    xxx.document.write(hdg);

    xxx.document.write(bod);
    xxx.document.write(theTitle);

    calendar(xxx);
}

function calendar(w) {
  var match1 = false

    monthNames = new Array("Jan","Feb","Mar","Apr","May","Jun","Jul","Aug","Sep",
        "Oct","Nov","Dec");

    var mD = "31,28,31,30,31,30,31,31,30,31,30,31";
    var monthDays = mD.split(",");

    var thisDay = today.getDate();
    var mkBtn1 = "<FONT SIZE=1><A HREF = \"javascript:parent.ShowAppt("

    var mkBtn2 = "<A HREF = \"javascript:parent.openSetAppt("
    var mkBtn3 = ")\">"
    var mkBtn4 = "</A>"

    var end = "</CENTER></BODY></HTML>";

    if (((year % 4 == 0) && (year % 100 != 0)) || (year % 400 == 0))

        monthDays[1] = 29;

    var nDays = monthDays[monthPage];

    var firstDay = today;

    firstDay.setDate(1);
    firstDay.setMonth(monthPage);
    firstDay.setYear(year);
    var apptsThisMonth = 0;
    var startDay = firstDay.getDay();

    var FontString = "<STRONG><FONT COLOR=#004080 FACE=\"helvetica\"
        SIZE=1>  ";

    var EndFont = "  </FONT></STRONG>";

    var THeadFormat = "<TH  BGCOLOR=wheat >";

    tmpMonth = monthNames[monthPage];
```

```
var TDFont = "<TD BGCOLOR=#ffffff ><FONT COLOR=#ffffff SIZE=1>";

w.document.write("<FORM><TABLE BORDER=1 CELLPADDING=1 CELLSPACING=1>");

w.document.write("<TH  BGCOLOR=wheat  COLSPAN=7>");

w.document.write(FontString + tmpMonth + ". " + year + EndFont + "<TR>");

w.document.write(THeadFormat + FontString + "    Sun    " + EndFont);

w.document.write(THeadFormat + FontString + "    Mon    " + EndFont);

w.document.write(THeadFormat + FontString + "    Tue    " + EndFont);

w.document.write(THeadFormat + FontString + "    Wed    " + EndFont);

w.document.write(THeadFormat + FontString + "    Thu    " + EndFont);

w.document.write(THeadFormat + FontString + "    Fri     " + EndFont);

w.document.write(THeadFormat + FontString + "    Sat    " + EndFont);

w.document.write("<TR>");

column = 0;

for (c=0; c<startDay; c++){

    w.document.write(TDFont);

    w.document.write("</FONT> </TD>");

    column++;

}

for (var i=1; i<=nDays; i++){

    w.document.write(TDFont);
    w.document.write(mkBtn2 +i + mkBtn3 + i + mkBtn4);
            for(var n = 0; n < splitapptDate.length; n++){
                if(splitapptDate[n][1] == i & splitapptDate[n][0] ==
                    monthPage & splitapptDate[n][2] == year){
                        w.document.write("<br>" + mkBtn1 + i + "," + n + mkBtn3 +
                        splitapptData[n][0] + mkBtn4 + "</FONT>");
                    }
            }

    w.document.write("<br><br></FONT></TD>");

    column++;

    if (column == 7){

        w.document.write("<TR>"); // start a new row

        column = 0;

    }
```

```
    }

    w.document.write("</TABLE>");
    w.document.write("<BR>");

    w.document.write("</FORM>");

    w.document.write(end);
    w.document.close();

}

//  ->

</SCRIPT>

</HEAD>
    <FRAMESET ROWS="195,*"  FRAMEBORDER=no BORDER=0>
        <FRAME SRC="about:blank" MARGINWIDTH=0 MARGINHEIGHT=0>
        <FRAME SRC= "ctrls4.htm" MARGINWIDTH=0 MARGINHEIGHT=0 SCROLLING=NO >
    </FRAMESET>
</HTML>
```

Listing 10.10 ctrls.htm

```
<HTML>
<BODY BGCOLOR=#ffffff  LINK=#004080  VLINK=#ffffff  onLoad =
setTimeout("parent.PopCalendar(parent.mo)",200)>
<CENTER>
<TABLE BORDER=1 BGCOLOR=white >
<FONT SIZE=2 COLOR="0F000F">
<TR>
<TD  BGCOLOR=wheat>
<FONT SIZE=1 COLOR="#004080"><A HREF="javascript:parent.PopCalendar(0)">JAN</A>
</A>
</TD>
<TD  BGCOLOR=wheat>
<FONT SIZE=1 COLOR="#004080"><A HREF="javascript:parent.PopCalendar(1)">FEB</A>
</A>
</TD>
<TD BGCOLOR=wheat >
<FONT SIZE=1 COLOR="#004080"><A HREF="javascript:parent.PopCalendar(2)">MAR</A>
</A>
</TD>
<TD BGCOLOR=wheat >
<FONT SIZE=1 COLOR="#004080"<A HREF="javascript:parent.PopCalendar(3)">APR</A>
</A>
</TD>
<TD BGCOLOR=wheat >
<FONT SIZE=1 COLOR="#004080"><A HREF="javascript:parent.PopCalendar(4)">MAY</A>
```

```
</A>
</TD>
<TD  BGCOLOR=wheat >
<FONT SIZE=1 COLOR="#004080"><A HREF="javascript:parent.PopCalendar(5)">JUN</A>
</A>
</TD>
</TR>
<TR>
<TD BGCOLOR=wheat >
<FONT SIZE=1 COLOR="#004080"><A HREF="javascript:parent.PopCalendar(6)">JUL</A>
</A>
</TD>
<TD  BGCOLOR=wheat>
<FONT SIZE=1 COLOR="#004080"><A HREF="javascript:parent.PopCalendar(7)">AUG</A>
</A>
</TD>
<TD  BGCOLOR=wheat >
<FONT SIZE=1 COLOR="#004080"><A HREF="javascript:parent.PopCalendar(8)">SEP</A>
</A>
</TD>

<TD BGCOLOR=wheat >
<FONT SIZE=1 COLOR="#004080"><A HREF="javascript:parent.PopCalendar(9)">OCT</A>
</A>
</TD>
<TD  BGCOLOR=wheat >
<FONT SIZE=1 COLOR="#004080"><A HREF="javascript:parent.PopCalendar(10)">NOV</A>
</A>
</TD>
<TD BGCOLOR=wheat >
<FONT SIZE=1 COLOR="#004080"><A HREF="javascript:parent.parent.PopCalendar
    (11)">DEC</A>
</A>
</TD>
</TR>
<TR>
<TD  BGCOLOR=wheat  COLSPAN=3 ALIGN=CENTER>
<FONT SIZE=2 COLOR=0F000F>
<A HREF="javascript:parent.PopCalendar(14)">Previous Year</A>
</TD>
<TD BGCOLOR=wheat  COLSPAN=3 ALIGN=CENTER>
<FONT SIZE=2 COLOR=0F000F>
<A HREF="javascript:parent.PopCalendar(12)">Next Year</A>

</TD>
</TR>
</TABLE>
```

```
</FONT>
</CENTER>
</BODY>
</HTML>
```

Listing 10.11 appt_set.htm

```
<HTML>
<HEAD>
<TITLE>
      Set Appointment
</TITLE>
<SCRIPT LANGUAGE = "JavaScript">

<!–

    function accumulate(form){
         for(var i = 0; i < form.elements.length -1; i++){
              elem[i] = form.elements[i].value
         }
         theAppt = elem.join(",");
         opener.saveAppt(this.form,theAppt);
    }
//–>

</SCRIPT>
</HEAD>
<BODY BGCOLOR=#004080 TEXT=wheat>
<FORM NAME="a">
<FONT SIZE=3 FACE="Arial">
Enter an Appointment Name:<br>
</FONT>
<FONT SIZE=1 FACE="Arial">
(This name will appear on the calendar.
<br> It must be less than 10 characters.)<br>
</FONT>
<INPUT TYPE="text" SIZE=10><br><br>
<FONT SIZE=3 FACE="Arial">
Appointment Time:<br>
<INPUT TYPE="text" SIZE=10><br><br>
Appointment Description:
<TEXTAREA ROWS=5 COLS=32>
</TEXTAREA><br>
<INPUT TYPE="button" VALUE = "Set Appointment" onClick = "accumulate(this.form)">
</FORM>
<SCRIPT LANGUAGE="JavaScript">
```

```
<!—
var elem = new Array(document.a.elements.length)
//—>

</SCRIPT>
</BODY>
</HTML>
```

CHAPTER ELEVEN

A SHOPPING CART APPLICATION

A shopping cart application is based on the same concept as grocery shopping. Users choose a product, put it in their cart, and then check out. This is one of the easiest ways to buy products from the Internet, and JavaScript is probably the easiest tool you can use to create your own shopping cart application.

Our shopping cart application, called Jigowat, is taken from fabric8.com (http://www.fabric8.com/jigowat/index.html). This site uses frames, JavaScript, and VRML for a professional shopping cart application for selling rings. For the back-end code, we use the functionality of the JavaScript external file source and object-oriented programming concepts.

This chapter covers:

- Creating the front end for the shopping cart
- Creating the back end
- Putting the script together

Creating the Front End

At the fabric8.com site you will notice that there are four different frames on the page (Figure 11.1). The two left-hand frames are used for navigation, and the right-hand frame displays information about the rings. The frame in the upper-left corner holds a VRML graphic image that indicates where the user is in the site. The image is updated automatically when users click on the various navigation links. When the user checks out, for example, this frame displays a hand with a dollar bill. The middle-left frame is used for detailed navigation. For example, when a user chooses a ring style, this frame is automatically updated with links to descriptions of different styles. The bottom-left frame holds links to the main, sizing, ordering, and styles pages.

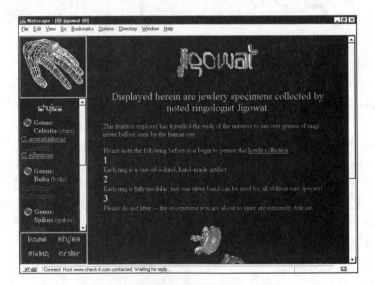

Figure 11.1 The Jigowat shopping cart site.

To let users choose styles and place orders, the application uses HTML forms, which should be easy for you to understand by now. Once the shipping information is complete, a CGI script is used to send the information to the respective division.

Creating the Back End

For the back end, an external file stores all the functions and variables. As mentioned in Chapter 1, having an external file lets you use the same code over and over and makes your code more object-oriented. Listing 11.1 shows you the script specified in the main page.

Listing 11.1 The index.html Page of the Shopping Cart Application

```
<html>
<head>
<title>@ jigowat @</title>
<script language="JavaScript" src="jigowat.js">
<!–
//  all code is copyright (c) 1996 fabric8.com
// –>
</script>
</head>
<frameset cols="160,*" border=1 bordercolor="#999999">
    <frameset rows="145,*,75"  border=1 bordercolor="#999999">
        <frame src="hand01.html" name="module1" marginwidth=0 marginheight=0
        scrolling=no noresize>
        <frame src="module2.html" name="module2" marginwidth=0 marginheight=0
        scrolling=auto noresize>
        <frame src="navigate.html" name="navigate" marginwidth=0 marginheight=0
        scrolling=no noresize>
    </frameset>
    <frame src="home.html" name="stage" marginwidth=0 marginheight=0 noresize>
</frameset>
<noframes>
<body>
The <b>jigowat Online Catalog</b> uses Frames, Javascript 1.1 , and VRML. You'll find
the software at http://www.netscape.com
</body>
</noframes>
</html>
```

If you look at the **jigowat.js** file, you will notice that some of the functions (such as rotating random HTML files) are not applicable for this chapter. We will discuss here only the essential functions associated with the shopping cart. Many of these functions are called from the orders and sizing page. Here is how functions are called from other pages:

```
parent.functionNAME()
```

Here, `functionName` is the name of the function. Figure 11.2 shows the structure of functions in Jigowat.

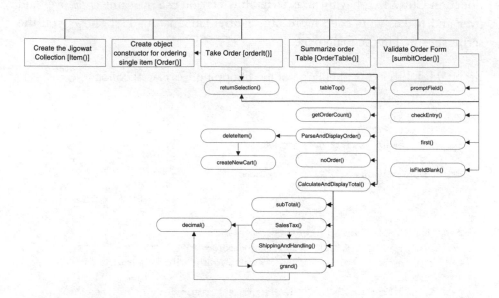

Figure 11.2 Jigowat function structure.

First, we create an object constructor called `Item`. Here we define four variables: `name`, `price`, `file`, and `variation`. This object also stores information about how many of the items have been ordered. Once it is created, we define an array (called `jigowat`) of `Item` objects and initialize them. The script is shown in Listing 11.2.

Listing 11.2 The Item Constructor and the Item Array

```
function Item(name, price, file, variation) {
    this.name = name;
    this.price = price;
    this.file = file;
    this.variation = variation;
    return this;
}

// Jigowat Collection *****
// Create an array of Item objects and initialize them
```

```
var jigowat = new Array();

jigowat[1] = new Item("Celestia acutatadiscus",85,"ring13.html",false);
jigowat[2] = new Item("Celestia cubelus",68,"ring14.html",true);
jigowat[3] = new Item("Celestia ellipticus",68,"ring15.html",true);
jigowat[4] = new Item("Bolta ellipticus",68,"ring20.html",false);
jigowat[5] = new Item("Bolta triangulus",77,"ring21.html",false);
jigowat[6] = new Item("Spikus oliviae",85,"ring30.html",true);
jigowat[7] = new Item("Spikus antonius",85,"ring31.html",true);
jigowat[8] = new Item("Spikus domusbrilliantis",68,"ring32.html",true);
jigowat[9] = new Item("Spikus ellipticus",68,"ring35.html",true);
jigowat[10] = new Item("Spikus domububblicious",68,"ring37.html",true);
jigowat[11] = new Item("Bubblum domus",68,"ring40.html",true);
jigowat[12] = new Item("Bubblum domustripae",77,"ring41.html",false);
jigowat[13] = new Item("Embezellea conus",68,"ring63.html",true);
jigowat[14] = new Item("Embezellea ellipticusbrilliantis",68,"ring65.html",true);
```

Our next function generates random HTML pages when the user clicks on styles. You can use this code to create random URLs for your page. The `random` function uses today's date to generate a random number from 1 to the number of items in the array:

```
function getRandomStyle() {
    var today = new Date();
      var seed = today.getTime();
      seed = (seed * 29  + 1) % (jigowat.length - 1);
      parent.stage.location = jigowat[seed + 1].file;
}
```

Next, we create a function that opens a pop-up window (using the `window.open()` method) when the user clicks on the material link from the selection page. This window shows the different materials that users can choose for their ring (Figure 11.3). The function looks like this:

```
function materials(type) {
    var selectionWindow;
    if(type == "Metals")
                selectionWindow = window.open("http://www.fabric8.com/jigowat/
                    ma-met.html", "Metals", "scrollbars,WIDTH=150,HEIGHT=285");
    if(type == "Gem01")
                selectionWindow = window.open("http://www.fabric8.com/jigowat/
                    ma-gem01.html", "Gem01","scrollbars,WIDTH=150,HEIGHT=285");
    if(type == "Gem02")
                selectionWindow = window.open("http://www.fabric8.com/jigowat/
                    ma-gem02.html", "Gem02", "scrollbars,WIDTH=150,HEIGHT=285");
}
```

Figure 11.3 The pop-up window for choosing metals.

Now we create another object called `Order`. This object has the `item`, `quantity`, `size`, `band`, and `material` properties. The object contains the information about a single item ordered. Then we create another array that stores all the orders. The script looks like this:

```
function Order(item, quantity, size, band, material) {
    this.item = item;
    this.quantity = quantity;
    this.size = size;
    this.band = band;
    this.material = material;
    return this;
}
var cart = new Array;
```

Next, we create a function to handle the customer order. This function is invoked when the **order-it** button is clicked in the styles page. The function makes sure that a size was entered and a ring band was selected. It also confirms whether a gem or metal was chosen for rings with variations. Once the order is validated, the user is asked if he or she really wants to place the order. Once the order is confirmed, the function adds a `new` element to the cart array and alerts the user with the team and its subtotal. Listing 11.3 shows the function.

Listing 11.3 The orderIt() Function

```
function orderIt(form) {
    var incomplete = false;
    var orderIndex;
    var multiple = 1;

    // iterate through jigowat array to determine which item was ordered
    for(orderIndex = 1; orderIndex < jigowat.length; orderIndex++)
        if(jigowat[orderIndex].name == form.name) break;

    // confirm that a size was entered
        if(!incomplete && form.size.options[form.size.selectedIndex].value ==
            "") {
        alert("\nPlease select a size.\nIf you need assistance, select \"your
            ring size\".");
          incomplete = true;
    }

    // confirm a ring band was selected
    if(!incomplete && returnSelection(form.band)==null) {
        alert("\nPlease select a ring band.");
          incomplete = true;
    }

    // confirm a gem or metal was chosen for rings with variations
    if(!incomplete && jigowat[orderIndex].variation) {
        if(returnSelection(form.gem) == null) {
            alert("\nPlease select a Gem or Metal.");
              incomplete = true;
        }
     }

    if(!incomplete) {

        // get values from the form passed to this function
        var quantity = form.quantity.value;
        var size=form.size.options[form.size.selectedIndex].value;
        var band= returnSelection(form.band);
        var material = (jigowat[orderIndex].variation) ?
            returnSelection(form.gem) : "N/A";

        // add a new element to the cart array
        cart[cart.length] = new Order(jigowat[orderIndex], quantity, size,
            band, material);

        // calculate subtotals
        var subtotal = quantity * jigowat[orderIndex].price;
        if(band != "None") subtotal += quantity * 25;
```

```
        // create alert box to confirm order
        alert("\nThe " + jigowat[orderIndex].name +
        " has been added to your SPECIMEN JAR.\n\nQuantity:\t\t" +
        quantity + "\nSize:\t\t" + size + "\nBand:\t\t" + band+"\nGem/Metal:\t"
            + material +
        "\nPrice:\t\t" + "$" + subtotal + ".00" + "\n\nTo submit your order,
            select " +      "\"Pay For-It\".");
    }
}
```

Figure 11.4 shows the Jigowat order form.

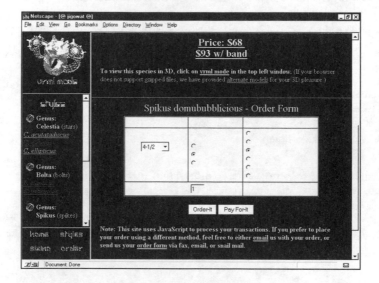

Figure 11.4 The styles page (submitting an order).

The orderTable function is used to create a table to display the customer order information on the order page. This function calls a function called table-top(). If there is no order, the function calls noOrder(). Otherwise, parseAndDisplayOrder() and calculateAndDisplayTotal() are called.

```
function orderTable(win) {
    tableTop(win);

    orderCount = getOrderCount();
    if(orderCount == 0) {
        noOrder(win);
    } else {
```

```
            parseAndDisplayOrder(win);
            calculateAndDisplayTotal(win, orderCount);
        }
    }
```

The `tableTop()` function creates the syntax for a table in the HTML page:

```
function tableTop(win) {
    win.document.write("<p><a name='specimens'><font size=+2><b>Specimen
        Jar</b></font></a><p>");
    win.document.write("<center><table cellpadding=5 border=1 width=95%>");
    win.document.write("<tr><th>Remove<br>Item</th><th>Style</th><th>Band</th><th>Pri
    ce</th>");
}
```

In the next function, `getOrderCount()`, we find out how many items were ordered. The order count helps us calculate shipping and handling charges as well as render the table:

```
function getOrderCount() {
    var orderCount=0;
    for (var i = 0; i < cart.length; i++) if(cart[i].quantity > 0) orderCount +=
        cart[i].quantity;
    return orderCount;
}
```

We then create another function, `noOrder()`, which displays information if no orders were made but the button **Pay For-it** was clicked (Figure 11.5). Here is how the function is set up:

```
function noOrder(win) {
    win.document.write("<tr><td colspan=4 align=center>" +
    "Our systems indicate that you have not ordered anything.<br>To order, click
        on any " +
    "<a href='genus.html' target='module2'>style</a>, select the " +
    "item and size you want, and click \"Order-It\".</td></tr>");
    win.document.write("</table></center></td>");
}
```

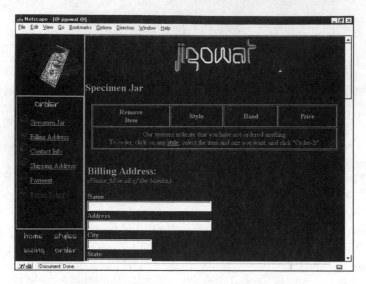

Figure 11.5 An incomplete order.

In `parseAndDisplayOrder()`, we display the order that was placed from the styles page. We loop through the `cart` array length and display the order information in the appropriate table cells. Notice that we create some hidden fields for submitting the final order to a CGI script. We also have a button named **remove** to remove any item from the cart. The function is shown in Listing 11.4.

Listing 11.4 The parseAndDisplayOrder() Function

```
function parseAndDisplayOrder(win) {
    var DELIMITER = "|";
    var counter = 0;
    for( var i=0; i < cart.length; i++) {
        if(cart[i].quantity > 0) {
            counter++;
            var extendedPrice = cart[i].quantity * cart[i].item.price;
            if(cart[i].band != "None") extendedPrice += cart[i].quantity * 25;
            win.document.write("<tr align=center><td><input type='button'
                name= '" + i +
            "' value='remove' onclick='parent.deleteItem(" + i + ")'></td>");
            win.document.write("<td>" + cart[i].quantity + "<br>" +
                cart[i].material +
            "<br>" + cart[i].item.name + "</td><td>" + cart[i].size + "<p>" +
                cart[i].band +
```

```
        "</td><td align=right>$" + extendedPrice + ".00" + "</td>");
        win.document.write("<input type='hidden' name='" + counter + "'
            value='" +
        cart[i].item.name + DELIMITER  + cart[i].quantity + DELIMITER +
        cart[i].size + DELIMITER + cart[i].band + DELIMITER +
            cart[i].material +"'>");
    }
}
for(var j = 0; j < ringSize.length; j++) {
    if(ringSize[j] != null) {
        win.document.write("<input type='hidden' name = 'sizer" + j + "'
            value = '" + ringSize[j].mm +
        DELIMITER + ringSize[j].converted + "'>");
    }
}
}
```

Figure 11.6 shows a completed order.

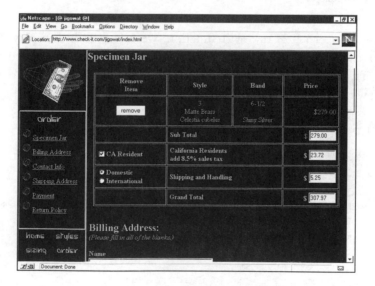

Figure 11.6 A completed order table.

When the user clicks the **remove** button, the following function is executed to delete the array element from the cart array:

```
function deleteItem(i) {
    if(confirm("Are you sure you want to delete this " + cart[i].item.name +
```

```
"?")) {
        cart[i] = null;
        createNewCart();
        parent.stage.location="payforit.html";
    }
}
```

The `createNewCart` function re-creates the `cart` array by removing all the null values:

```
function createNewCart() {
    var newCart = new Array();
    for(var i = 0, j = 0; i < cart.length; i++) {
        if(cart[i] != null) {
            newCart[j] = cart[i];
            j++;
        }
    }
    cart = newCart;
}
```

In the `calculateAndDisplayTotal` function, we calculate and display the total price for the order. Notice that we create some form elements to call the `salesTax()`, `subTotal()`, and `shippingAndHandling()` functions. Listing 11.5 shows how the function is set up.

Listing 11.5 The calculateAndDisplayTotal() Function

```
function calculateAndDisplayTotal(win, orderCount) {
    win.document.write("<tr><th><br></th><th colspan=2 align=left>Sub
        Total</th>" +
        "<td align=right><nobr>$ <input name='sub' value='" + parent.subTotal() +
        ".00' size=7 onfocus='this.blur()'></nobr></td>");
    win.document.write("<tr><th align=left><input " +
        "onclick='parent.salesTax(this.form.sub.value, this.form, " +
            orderCount + ")' " +
        "type='checkbox' name='california'>CA Resident</th>" +
        "<th colspan=2 align=left>California Residents<br>add 8.5% sales
            tax</th>" +
        "<th align=right><nobr>$ <input name='tax' value='0.00' size=7 onfo
            cus='this.blur()'></nobr></th>");
    win.document.write("<tr><th align=left><input type='radio' name='domestic'" +
        "onclick='parent.shippingAndHandling(this.form, " + orderCount + ",
            true)'>Domestic<br>" +
        "<input type='radio' name='domestic'" +
```

```
          "onclick='parent.shippingAndHandling(this.form, " + orderCount + ",
              false)'>International</th>" +
          "<th colspan=2 align=left>Shipping and Handling</th>" +
          "<th align=right><nobr>$ <input name='shipping' value='select' size=7
              onfocus='this.blur()'></nobr></th>");
     win.document.write("<tr><td><br></td><th colspan=2 align=left>Grand
        Total</th>" +
          "<th align=right><nobr>$ <input name='grand' value='' size=7
              onfocus='this.blur()'></nobr></th>");
     win.document.write("</table></center></td>");

}
```

The subTotal() function takes the item quantity and multiplies it by the price.
If a ring band was selected, we add $25 for each item.

```
function subTotal() {
    var subtotal=0;
    for(var i=0; i < cart.length; i++) {
        if(cart[i].quantity > 0) {
            extended=cart[i].quantity * cart[i].item.price;
            if(cart[i].band != "None") extended += (25 * cart[i].quantity);
            subtotal += extended;
        }
    }
    return subtotal;
}
```

The salesTax() function calculates the 8.5% California sales tax. If the order
is placed from outside California, we calculate $0.0 tax for the sale. Notice that
we use the click() method to click the radio button automatically if it is a
California order.

```
function salesTax(subtotal, form, orderCount) {
    if(form.california.checked) {
        subtotal *= 100;
        var salestax = Math.round(subtotal * .085);
        salestax = decimal(salestax);
        form.tax.value=salestax;
        form.domestic[0].click();
        shippingAndHandling(form, orderCount, true);
    } else      form.tax.value="0.00";
    grand(form);
}
```

In the `shippingAndHandling()` function, we check to see whether the order is domestic or international and then calculate the shipping and handling.

```
function shippingAndHandling(form, orderCount, domestic) {
    var shipping;
    if(domestic) {
        if(orderCount >= 1 && orderCount <=5) shipping="5.25";
        if(orderCount >5) shipping="8.50";
    } else {
        if(orderCount >=1 && orderCount <=5) shipping="15.25";
        if(orderCount >5) shipping="24.75";
    }
    form.shipping.value=shipping;
    grand(form);
}
```

The next function totals the sales tax, shipping and handling, and price for the ordered item and displays the value in the form element named `grand`. Notice that we call `decimal()` to convert the dollar value into decimal format.

```
function grand(form) {
    if(form.shipping.value != "select") {
        total = form.sub.value*100;
        total = total + (form.tax.value*100);
        total = total + (form.shipping.value*100);
        form.grand.value = decimal(total);
    }
}
```

As the name suggests, the `decimal()` function takes an integer and puts a decimal point before the last two digits of the number.

```
function decimal(number) {
    var addDecimal = "";
    var num = "" + number;
    addDecimal += num.substring(0, num.length - 2);
    addDecimal += ".";
    addDecimal += num.substring(num.length - 2, num.length);
    return addDecimal;
}
```

In the `returnSelection` function, we return the selection made from the radio options in both the order page and the styles page. This function is called from various functions in the page, such as the function to validate the customer order form.

```
function returnSelection(theRadio) {
    var selection=null;
    for(var i=0; i<theRadio.length; i++) {
        if(theRadio[i].checked) {
            selection=theRadio[i].value;
            return selection;
        }
    }
            return selection;
}
```

The rest of the code in the file validates the user input (please check Chapter 9 for details on input validation) and takes care of VRML loading. Some of these VRML loading functions are used to avoid JavaScript security violations. In some platforms, security alert dialog boxes would come up after we return to HTML mode from VRML mode. (This is because a ring page has an `onload()` that loads the other frame.) We set a flag so that nothing is reloaded in other windows, preventing the alert. Although we will not explain the functions, you can see the code in the completed listing in the next section.

Putting the Script Together

Listing 11.6 shows the full script of the shopping cart application.

Listing 11.6 The Complete Script for the Shopping Cart Application

```
//  All code is Copyright (C) 1996 fabric8.com
//  Please don't just copy our code, improve it!
//  Send suggestions to olivia ongpin ooo@fabric8.com

// Item Object Constructor *****
// Define field of Item object to contain information about an item's  name,
// price, html file, and whether
// it has variations (for gems, metals, etc.).
// The Item object also stores information about how many of the items have been
// ordered and is initialized to 0.

function Item(name, price, file, variation) {
    this.name = name;
    this.price = price;
    this.file = file;
    this.variation = variation;
    return this;
```

```
}

// Jigowat Collection *****
// Create an array of Item objects and initialize them

var jigowat = new Array();

jigowat[1] = new Item("Celestia acutatadiscus",85,"ring13.html",false);
jigowat[2] = new Item("Celestia cubelus",68,"ring14.html",true);
jigowat[3] = new Item("Celestia ellipticus",68,"ring15.html",true);
jigowat[4] = new Item("Bolta ellipticus",68,"ring20.html",false);
jigowat[5] = new Item("Bolta triangulus",77,"ring21.html",false);
jigowat[6] = new Item("Spikus oliviae",85,"ring30.html",true);
jigowat[7] = new Item("Spikus antonius",85,"ring31.html",true);
jigowat[8] = new Item("Spikus domusbrilliantis",68,"ring32.html",true);
jigowat[9] = new Item("Spikus ellipticus",68,"ring35.html",true);
jigowat[10] = new Item("Spikus domububblicious",68,"ring37.html",true);
jigowat[11] = new Item("Bubblum domus",68,"ring40.html",true);
jigowat[12] = new Item("Bubblum domustripae",77,"ring41.html",false);
jigowat[13] = new Item("Embezellea conus",68,"ring63.html",true);
jigowat[14] = new Item("Embezellea ellipticusbrilliantis",68,"ring65.html",true);

// View Ring Styles Randomly *****
// allow customer to view the styles randomly
// use today's date to generate a "random" number from 1 to the number of items
// in the jigowat collection
// use the random number to access file field of jigowat array

function getRandomStyle() {
    var today = new Date();
      var seed = today.getTime();
      seed = (seed * 29  + 1) % (jigowat.length - 1);
      parent.stage.location = jigowat[seed + 1].file;
}

//  Material Selection Window *****
// Open a floating window to allow customer to peruse jigowat's gem and material
// selection.
// Contents of window are located in separate html files

function materials(type) {
    var selectionWindow;
    if(type == "Metals")
                selectionWindow = window.open("http://www.fabric8.com/jigowat/
                    ma-met.html", "Metals", "scrollbars,WIDTH=150,HEIGHT=285");
                    if(type == "Gem01")
                selectionWindow = window.open("http://www.fabric8.com/jigowat/
                    ma-gem01.html", "Gem01", "scrollbars,WIDTH=150,
                    HEIGHT=285");
```

```
        if(type == "Gem02")
                selectionWindow = window.open("http://www.fabric8.com/jigowat/
                    ma-gem02.html", "Gem02", "scrollbars,WIDTH=150,
                    HEIGHT=285");
}

// Order Processing
// scripts for check-out

// Order object constructor
// this object contains the information about a single item ordered

 function Order(item, quantity, size, band, material) {
        this.item = item;
        this.quantity = quantity;
        this.size = size;
        this.band = band;
        this.material = material;
        return this;
}

// Cart array
// stores (no pun intended) all of the orders into one array

var cart = new Array;

//Order-it
// called when customer selects the "order-it" button

function orderIt(form) {
        var incomplete = false;
        var orderIndex;
        var multiple = 1;

        // iterate through jigowat array to determine which item was ordered
        for(orderIndex = 1; orderIndex < jigowat.length; orderIndex++)
            if(jigowat[orderIndex].name == form.name) break;

        // confirm that a size was entered
            if(!incomplete && form.size.options[form.size.selectedIndex].value ==
                "") {
            alert("\nPlease select a size.\nIf you need assistance, select \"your
                ring size\".");
              incomplete = true;
        }

        // confirm a ring band was selected
        if(!incomplete && returnSelection(form.band)==null) {
            alert("\nPlease select a ring band.");
              incomplete = true;
```

```
        }

        // confirm a gem or metal was chosen for rings with variations
        if(!incomplete && jigowat[orderIndex].variation) {
            if(returnSelection(form.gem) == null) {
                alert("\nPlease select a Gem or Metal.");
                incomplete = true;
            }
        }

        if(!incomplete) {

            // get values from the form passed to this function
            var quantity = form.quantity.value;
            var size=form.size.options[form.size.selectedIndex].value;
            var band= returnSelection(form.band);
            var material = (jigowat[orderIndex].variation) ?
                returnSelection(form.gem) : "N/A";

            // add a new element to the cart array
            cart[cart.length] = new Order(jigowat[orderIndex], quantity, size,
                band, material);

            // calculate subtotals
            var subtotal = quantity * jigowat[orderIndex].price;
            if(band != "None") subtotal += quantity * 25;

            // create alert box to confirm order
            alert("\nThe " + jigowat[orderIndex].name +
            " has been added to your SPECIMEN JAR.\n\nQuantity:\t\t" +
            quantity + "\nSize:\t\t" + size + "\nBand:\t\t" + band+"\nGem/Metal:\t"
                + material +
            "\nPrice:\t\t" + "$" + subtotal + ".00" + "\n\nTo submit your order,
                select " +     "\"Pay For-It\".");
        }
    }
}

// Order Summary Table
// creates a table that summarizes the customer's order

function orderTable(win) {
    tableTop(win);

    orderCount = getOrderCount();
    if(orderCount == 0) {
        noOrder(win);
    } else {
        parseAndDisplayOrder(win);
        calculateAndDisplayTotal(win, orderCount);
    }
```

```
}      // Table Top
// render top of order table

function tableTop(win) {
    win.document.write("<p><a name='specimens'><font size=+2><b>Specimen
        Jar</b></font></a><p>");
    win.document.write("<center><table cellpadding=5 border=1 width=95%>");
    win.document.write("<tr><th>Remove<br>Item</th><th>Style</th><th>Band</th><th>
    Price</th>");
}

// getOrderCount
// function to determine the number of items in this order
// used for rendering table and for calculating shipping and handling charges

function getOrderCount() {
    var orderCount=0;
    for (var i = 0; i < cart.length; i++) if(cart[i].quantity > 0) orderCount +=
        cart[i].quantity;
    return orderCount;
}

// No Order
// render table when no order has been submitted
// contains a link to the getRandomStyle function

function noOrder(win) {
    win.document.write("<tr><td colspan=4 align=center>" +
    "Our systems indicate that you have not ordered anything.<br>To order, click
        on any " +
    "<a href='genus.html' target='module2'>style</a>, select the " +
    "item and size you want, and click \"Order-It\".</td></tr>");
    win.document.write("</table></center></td>");
}

// Parse and Display Order
// obtains order information from field in the jigowat array and displays them in //
appropriate table cells
// writes order information to hidden fields for submittal to cgi script

function parseAndDisplayOrder(win) {
    var DELIMITER = "|";
    var counter = 0;
    for( var i=0; i < cart.length; i++) {
        if(cart[i].quantity > 0) {
            counter++;
            var extendedPrice = cart[i].quantity * cart[i].item.price;
            if(cart[i].band != "None") extendedPrice += cart[i].quantity * 25;
            win.document.write("<tr align=center><td><input type='button'
```

```
        name= `" + i +
                "` value='remove' onclick='parent.deleteItem(" + i + ")'></td>");
                win.document.write("<td>" + cart[i].quantity + "<br>" +
                    cart[i].material +
                "<br>" + cart[i].item.name + "</td><td>" + cart[i].size + "<p>" +
                    cart[i].band +
                "</td><td align=right>$" + extendedPrice + ".00" + "</td>");
                win.document.write("<input type='hidden' name='" + counter + "`
                    value='" +
                cart[i].item.name + DELIMITER  + cart[i].quantity + DELIMITER +
                cart[i].size + DELIMITER + cart[i].band + DELIMITER +
                    cart[i].material +"'>");
        }
    }
    for(var j = 0; j < ringSize.length; j++) {
        if(ringSize[j] != null) {
            win.document.write("<input type='hidden' name = 'sizer" + j + "`
                value = `" + ringSize[j].mm +
            DELIMITER + ringSize[j].converted + "'>");
        }
    }
}

// Delete item

function deleteItem(i) {
    if(confirm("Are you sure you want to delete this " + cart[i].item.name +
        "?")) {
        cart[i] = null;
        createNewCart();
        parent.stage.location="payforit.html";
    }
}

//Create new cart
// This function recreates the cart array by removing null values

function createNewCart() {
    var newCart = new Array();
    for(var i = 0, j = 0; i < cart.length; i++) {
        if(cart[i] != null) {
            newCart[j] = cart[i];
            j++;
        }
    }
    cart = newCart;
}
```

```
// Calculate and Display Total
// calculates purchase subtotal and calls functions to add applicable taxes and //
shipping costs

function calculateAndDisplayTotal(win, orderCount) {

    win.document.write("<tr><th><br></th><th colspan=2 align=left>Sub
        Total</th>" +
        "<td align=right><nobr>$ <input name='sub' value='" + parent.subTotal() +
        ".00' size=7 onfocus='this.blur()'></nobr></td>");
    win.document.write("<tr><th align=left><input " +
        "onclick='parent.salesTax(this.form.sub.value, this.form, " +
            orderCount + ")' " +
        "type='checkbox' name='california'>CA Resident</th>" +
        "<th colspan=2 align=left>California Residents<br>add 8.5% sales
            tax</th>" +
        "<th align=right><nobr>$ <input name='tax' value='0.00' size=7 onfo
            cus='this.blur()'></nobr></th>");
    win.document.write("<tr><th align=left><input type='radio' name='domestic'" +
        "onclick='parent.shippingAndHandling(this.form, " + orderCount + ",
            true)'>Domestic<br>" +
        "<input type='radio' name='domestic'" +
        "onclick='parent.shippingAndHandling(this.form, " + orderCount + ",
            false)'>International</th>" +
        "<th colspan=2 align=left>Shipping and Handling</th>" +
        "<th align=right><nobr>$ <input name='shipping' value='select' size=7
            onfocus='this.blur()'></nobr></th>");
    win.document.write("<tr><td><br></td><th colspan=2 align=left>Grand
        Total</th>" +
        "<th align=right><nobr>$ <input name='grand' value='' size=7
            onfocus='this.blur()'></nobr></th>");
    win.document.write("</table></center></td>");

}

function subTotal() {
    var subtotal=0;
    for(var i=0; i < cart.length; i++) {
        if(cart[i].quantity > 0) {
            extended=cart[i].quantity * cart[i].item.price;
            if(cart[i].band != "None") extended += (25 * cart[i].quantity);
            subtotal += extended;
        }
    }
    return subtotal;
}

function salesTax(subtotal, form, orderCount) {
```

```
        if(form.california.checked) {
            subtotal *= 100;
            var salestax = Math.round(subtotal * .085);
            salestax = decimal(salestax);
            form.tax.value=salestax;
            form.domestic[0].click();
            shippingAndHandling(form, orderCount, true);
        } else       form.tax.value="0.00";
        grand(form);
}

function shippingAndHandling(form, orderCount, domestic) {
    var shipping;
    if(domestic) {
        if(orderCount >= 1 && orderCount <=5) shipping="5.25";
        if(orderCount >5) shipping="8.50";
    } else {
        if(orderCount >=1 && orderCount <=5) shipping="15.25";
        if(orderCount >5) shipping="24.75";
    }
    form.shipping.value=shipping;
    grand(form);
}

function grand(form) {
    if(form.shipping.value != "select") {
        total = form.sub.value*100;
        total = total + (form.tax.value*100);
        total = total + (form.shipping.value*100);
        form.grand.value = decimal(total);
    }
}

function decimal(number) {
    var addDecimal = "";
    var num = "" + number;
    addDecimal += num.substring(0, num.length - 2);
    addDecimal += "."
    addDecimal += num.substring(num.length - 2, num.length);
    return addDecimal;
}

// Return selection from radio button

function returnSelection(theRadio) {
    var selection=null;
    for(var i=0; i<theRadio.length; i++) {
        if(theRadio[i].checked) {
```

```
                selection=theRadio[i].value;
                return selection;
        }
    }
                return selection;
}

// Form Validation
// these functions confirm the order has been completed before submitting
// the information to the server

var firstName;

function submitOrder(form) {
    if(form.sub == null) {
        alert("\nYou haven\'t ordered anything, silly.");
        return false;
    } else if(form.shipping.value == "select") {
        alert("\nPlease select a shipping option in the specimen jar.");
        return false;
    }
    if(ringSize.length == 0) {
        if(confirm("\nYou have not submitted your Jigowat finger measurements.
            For the best fit, we highly " +
        " recommend that you go to the SIZING area.")) return false;

    }
    if(isFieldBlank(form.fullname)) {
        var entry = null;
        var i = 0;
        while(++i <= 3) {
            if((entry = prompt("Please provide your name.", "Enter your
                name")) == null)
                    return false;
            if(checkEntry(entry)) break;
        }
        firstName = first(entry);
        form.fullname.value = entry;
    } else firstName = first(form.fullname.value);
            if(isFieldBlank(form.address)) promptField(form.address, "Address");
            if(isFieldBlank(form.city)) promptField(form.city, "City");
            if(isFieldBlank(form.state)) promptField(form.state, "State");
            if(isFieldBlank(form.country)) promptField(form.country, "Country");
            if(isFieldBlank(form.zip)) promptField(form.zip, "Zip Code");
            if(isFieldBlank(form.email)) promptField(form.email, "email address");
            if(isFieldBlank(form.phone)) promptField(form.phone, "phone number");
            if(isFieldBlank(form.phone_eve)) promptField(form.phone_eve,
```

```
        "evening phone number");
    if(!form.same.checked) {
            if(isFieldBlank(form.name_ship)) promptField(form.name_ship,
                "shipping name");
            if(isFieldBlank(form.address_ship))
                promptField(form.address_ship, "shipping address");
            if(isFieldBlank(form.city_ship)) promptField(form.city_ship,
                "shipping city");
            if(isFieldBlank(form.state_ship)) promptField(form.state_ship,
                "shipping state");
            if(isFieldBlank(form.country_ship))
                promptField(form.country_ship, "shipping country");
            if(isFieldBlank(form.zip_ship)) promptField(form.zip_ship,
                "shipping zip code");
    }
    if(returnSelection(form.payment) == null) {
        alert("Please select a payment method");
        return false;
    }
    else return true;
}

function checkEntry(entry) {
    entry = first(entry);
    if(entry == "Enter")
        return false;
    else return true;
}

function isFieldBlank(theField) {
            if(theField.value.length == 0)
        return true;
    else return false;
}

function first(entry) {
    var space = entry.indexOf(" ");
    return (space > 0) ? entry.substring(0, space) : entry;
}

function promptField(field, fieldName) {
    i = 0;
    while(++i <= 3) {
        if((entry = prompt(firstName + ", please provide your " + fieldName +
            ".", "Enter your " + fieldName)) == null)
            return false;
            if(checkEntry(entry)) break;
```

```
            }
        field.value = entry;
        return true;
    }

// Ring Sizer
// Function to store ring sizes submitted to the sizer

var ringSize = new Array();

function sizer(mm, converted) {
        ringSize[ringSize.length] = new Size(mm, converted);
    }

function Size(mm, converted) {
        this.mm = mm;
        this.converted = converted;
        return this;
    }

// load vrml **
// functions added to avoid javascript security violations

var vrmlCall = false;

function getVRML(vrmlFile) {
        with(parent.module1.location.href) vrmlCurrent = substring (lastIndexOf
            ("/") + 1);
        if(vrmlCurrent != vrmlFile) (vrmlCall) ? vrmlCall = false :
            parent.module1.location = vrmlFile;
    }

function vrmlLoad() {
        vrmlCall = true;
    }

function vrmlClear() {
        vrmlCall = false;
    }

var stageCall = false;

function loadStage(stageFile) {
        if(stageCall) {
            with(parent.stage.location.href) stageCurrent = substring (lastIndexOf
                ("/") + 1);
            if(stageCurrent != stageFile) parent.stage.location = stageFile;
        } else stageCall = true;
    }
```

CHAPTER TWELVE

JAVASCRIPT PAINTER

This chapter explains JavaScript's image object in detail, using a paint program to illustrate the concepts. To use the JavaScript Painter application, users select a color from among four palettes, adding the color to their own palette. Then they can use the color to paint on a canvas by clicking on the mouse or by dragging. This example is similar to Microsoft Paint program except that users cannot cut, copy, paste, undo, or save the drawing.

There are two ways to choose a color to add to your palette. One way is to choose color values from any of the three color palettes (red, green, and blue). Once you've chosen the desired combination, you can customize the color by increasing or decreasing the intensity of any of the colors. The other method is to choose from an RGB palette, in which case you can choose the final color with one mouse click. You can look at the chosen color in the preview box; the specified values for red, green, and blue are also displayed as decimals in three text boxes. When you click **ADD TO PALETTE**, the color is added to your palette (Figure 12.1). This example was created by David Ray at www.dream.com and is located at http://www.dream.com/JS-Painter. The JavaScript Paint program also demonstrates how to work with CGI, which calls colored images from the server.

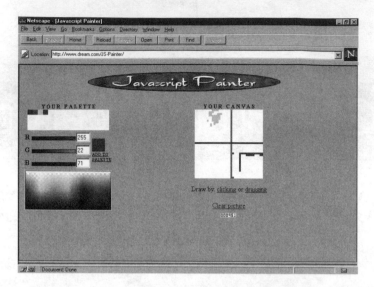

Figure 12.1 JavaScript Painter in action.

NOTE   To understand this example, you should know that we use image replacement functionality in JavaScript and invoke the same CGI over and over to do the replacements. Note that there is a set of image files on the server, and the JavaScript code refers to these filenames (we will see how these files are referenced). The CGI is used to display these images on the HTML page.

This chapter covers:

- Creating the front end for the JavaScript Painter
- Creating the back end for the JavaScript Painter
- Putting the script together

Creating the Front End

The example page is set up with two frames. The bottom frame is empty and the other frame contains the actual script. The **index.html** page puts the frames together:

```
var emptyFrame = '<html></html>';
var htmlOut = '<frameset rows="*,0">'
+ '  <frame name="main" src="main.html">'
+ '  <frame name="echo" src="javascript:parent.emptyFrame">'
+ '</frameset>';
document.write(htmlOut);
```

The **main.html** page first creates three hidden fields: drag (to find out whether the user wants to use drag or click to draw on the canvas), color (indicates the current drawing color), and palette (used to store the current selected palette). The default values for these fields are (in order) 0, ffffff, and 1. Next, we paint a grid of four rows by 16 columns containing the user's preferred palette. This grid contains **.gif** files that are returned by a CGI.

```
for (i=0;i<4;i++) {
 for (j=0;j<16;j++) {
   picnum = '' + ((4 * (i)) + j);
   document.write('<a href="javascript:setColor(+ picnum
     + '><img src="http://www.idiom.com/user-cgi/daver/giflet?' + colors[picnum] +
         '" border=0 height=12 width=12></a>');
 }
 document.write('<br>');
}
```

The formula that is set up for the picnum variable does not work properly. You should use this formula instead: 16*I+j.

WARNING

Now we display the palettes from which users select a color. Note that we place text boxes next to the red, blue, and green palettes to display the values for each color selection. Users can, however, use these boxes to input their own decimal values. For that reason, we use an input validation function to ensure correct input. Also note that for our **ADD TO PALETTE** link we call the function setPalette(). For the preview box, we use the same CGI. This color box is manipulated by the functions getR(), getG(), getB(), and getRGB().

The functions getR(), getG(), getB(), and getRGB() are located in the **index.html** page, so the keyword parent is used to call these functions from our **main.html** file.

NOTE

Initially, the preview box shows a white image, but once a color is selected, the CGI takes the URL of the **.gif** image that corresponds to the CGI argument and displays that color. The image file **palette1.gif** displays the RGB palette. Listing 12.1 shows the code.

Listing 12.1 The Front-End Code for Setting Up the Palettes

```
var htmlOut = '</td></tr><tr><td><b>R</b></td>'
+ '<td><a href="javascript:parent.echoR()//" target="echo"><img src="rpick.gif"
    height=9 width=103 border=0 ISMAP></a>'
+ '<input type="text" size=3 name="r" value="255" onBlur="checkVal(')"></td>'
+ '<td rowspan=3><img src="http://www.idiom.com/user-cgi/daver/giflet?FFFFFF"
    height=30 width=30><br>'
+ '<a href="javascript:setPalette()"><font size=1>ADD TO<br>PALETTE</a></td>'
+ '</tr><tr>'
+ '<td><b>G</b></td>'
+ '<td><a href="javascript:parent.echoG()//" target="echo"><img src="gpick.gif"
    height=9 width=103 border=0 ISMAP></a>'
+ '<input type="text" size=3 name="g" value="255" onBlur="checkVal(')"></td>'
+ '</tr><tr>'
+ '<td><b>B</b></td>'
+ '<td><a href="javascript:parent.echoB()//" target="echo"><img src="bpick.gif"
height=9 width=103 border=0 ISMAP></a>'
+ '<input type="text" size=3 name="b" value="255" onBlur="checkVal(∞')"></td>'
+ '</tr><tr>'
+ '<td colspan=3 align=center><a href="javascript:parent.echoRGB()//"
    target="echo"><img src="palette1.gif" height=93 width=204 border=0
    ISMAP></a>'
+ '</td>'
+ '</tr></table>';
document.write(htmlOut);
htmlOut=null;
```

For the canvas, we make a grid of 40 white images in a row by 40 white images in a column. If a user chooses to draw in the drag mode and puts the mouse over any of the images, the function dragColor() is invoked with the current row and column. Next, the clicked image is changed to the selected color from the palette. Otherwise, if the mode is "by clicking," then the function clickColor() is called with the current row and column, and the same process of image replacement occurs.

```
document.write('<center><table border=0><tr><td align=center>'
 + '<font size=2><b>Y O U R   C A N V A S</b></font><br>');
```

```
var picnum = '';
for (i=1;i<=40;i++) {
   for (j=1;j<=40;j++) {
      picnum = '' + ((40 * (i-1)) + j - 1);
      document.write('<a href="javascript:clickColor(' + picnum +
            ')" onMouseover="dragColor(' + picnum + ')"><img
               src="http://www.idiom.com/user-cgi/daver/giflet?FFFFFF" height=4
               width=4 border=0></a>');
   }
   document.write('<br>');
}
```

The page has three hyperlinks. Two of them call the function `setClick()` and the other one calls the `clearPict()` function.

```
htmlOut='<p>Draw by: '
+ '<a href="javascript:setClick(')">clicking</a> or '
+ '<a href="javascript:setClick(')">dragging</a><p>'
+ '<a href="javascript:clearPict()">Clear picture</a>'
+ '</td></tr></table></center>';
document.write(htmlOut);
htmlOut=null;
```

Creating the Back End

For the back end, we first create an array and store the value `ffffff` in 64 of its elements:

```
var colors = new StringArray(64);
for (i=0;i<64;i++) { colors[i]="FFFFFF"; }
```

Next, we define the following variable:

```
var hexchars="0123456789ABCDEF"; //holds the hex characters
```

Later, we will create 13 functions in total. I will list them here and walk you through the functionality of each one. Note that many of these functions are used to perform the same process for different colors. For example, the functions `getR()`, `getG()` and `getB()` are invoked from different palettes to manipulate a specific palette selection.

Function clickColor()

Here, we get the complete URL of the current image and pass it to the variable urlstring. Note that in the HTML page, we display 69 images in addition to the canvas. We index the images starting from 70. Then we extract all but the last six characters of the URL and add the value of the current color. For example, if the current value is 121212, the new image URL becomes color121212. Finally, we assign the newly created image URL to the current image.

```
function clickColor(i) {
 var urlstring = document.images[(70+i)].src;
 document.images[(70+i)].src = (urlstring.substring(0,urlstring.length-6)
    + document.miscdata.color.value);
}
```

 The color names are called like this by the CGI: http://www.idiom.com/user-cgi/daver/giflet?FFFFFF.

NOTE

Function dragColor()

This function basically does the same as the clickColor() function, but only when the dragging mode is selected:

```
function dragColor(i) {
 if (document.miscdata.drag.value == "1") {
  var urlstring = document.images[(70+i)].src;
  document.images[(70+i)].src = (urlstring.substring(0,urlstring.length-6)
    + document.miscdata.color.value);
 }
}
```

Function setClick()

This function sets a flag to indicate that the user wishes to draw by dragging:

```
function setClick(i) {
  document.miscdata.drag.value=i;
}
```

Function setColor()

Here, the function displays the decimal value for the red, green, and blue color selections in the text boxes `r`, `g`, and `b`.

```
function setColor(i) {
  i++;
  document.miscdata.color.value=colors[i];
  document.images[66].src="http://www.idiom.com/user-cgi/daver/giflet?" +
      colors[i];
  document.rgb.r.value=unhex(colors[i].substring(0,2));
  document.rgb.g.value=unhex(colors[i].substring(2,4));
  document.rgb.b.value=unhex(colors[i].substring(4,6));
}
```

Function unhex()

This function is used to convert two-digit text numbers to decimals.

```
function unhex(i) {
  return(16*(hexchars.indexOf(i.substring(0,1)))) + (hexchars.indexOf(i.sub
      string(1,2))));
}
```

Function clearPict()

The `clearPict()` function draws all the 1600 pictures in white using a loop from 0 to 1599.

```
function clearPict() {
  for (i=0;i<=1599;i++) {
    var urlstring = document.images[(70+i)].src;
    document.images[(70+i)].src = (urlstring.substring(0,urlstring.length-6) +
        'FFFFFF');
  }
}
```

Function getR()

This function is a little complex. In the red palette you use this function to choose from lighter to darker red. Now we're using this palette as image map, which returns an x and a y value. For example, when you point your mouse to this image, you can select a value something like 48,4. We must parse the coordinates to get the x value, which will give us the decimal value for red. Because the image is a linear decline, we do not worry about the y coordinate and thus we multiply x by 2.5. We then convert that value to hex for red and convert the current green and blue decimal values to hex. Thus, we get the two-digit hex values for all three colors: red, green, and blue. Next, we concatenate these values to a value that the CGI understands (Listing 12.2).

Listing 12.2 Function getR()

```
function getR(coords) {
    var comma = coords.indexOf(",");
    var x = parseInt(coords.substring(1,comma));
    var r = Math.floor(2.5 * x);
    document.rgb.r.value='' + r;
    var tmp = Math.floor(r/16);
    var RGB = hexchars.substring(tmp,tmp+1)
        + hexchars.substring(Math.floor(r - (tmp * 16)),Math.floor(r - (tmp *
16))+1);
    var g = parseInt(document.rgb.g.value);
    tmp = Math.floor(g/16);
    RGB += hexchars.substring(tmp,tmp+1)
        + hexchars.substring(Math.floor(g - (tmp * 16)),Math.floor(g - (tmp *
            16))+1);
    var b = parseInt(document.rgb.b.value);
    tmp = Math.floor(b/16);
    RGB += hexchars.substring(tmp,tmp+1)
        + hexchars.substring(Math.floor(b - (tmp * 16)),Math.floor(b - (tmp *
            16))+1);
    document.images[66].src="http://www.idiom.com/user-cgi/daver/giflet?" + RGB;
    document.miscdata.color.value=RGB;
}
```

NOTE   The getR() function is called only when the mouse is clicked on the red palette. So we left the blue and green values unchanged.

Function getG()

This function is the same as the getR() function except here we find the hex value for green by multiplying its x coordinate by 2.5. Listing 12.3 shows the code.

Listing 12.3 Function getG()

```
function getG(coords) {
    var comma = coords.indexOf(",");
    var x = parseInt(coords.substring(1,comma));
    var g = Math.floor(2.5 * x);
    document.rgb.g.value='' + g;
    var r = parseInt(document.rgb.r.value);
    var tmp = Math.floor(r/16);
    var RGB = hexchars.substring(tmp,tmp+1)
        + hexchars.substring(Math.floor(r - (tmp * 16)),Math.floor(r - (tmp *
            16))+1);
    tmp = Math.floor(g/16);
    RGB += hexchars.substring(tmp,tmp+1)
        + hexchars.substring(Math.floor(g - (tmp * 16)),Math.floor(g - (tmp *
            16))+1);
    var b = parseInt(document.rgb.b.value);
    tmp = Math.floor(b/16);
    RGB += hexchars.substring(tmp,tmp+1)
        + hexchars.substring(Math.floor(b - (tmp * 16)),Math.floor(b - (tmp *
            16))+1);
    document.images[66].src="http://www.idiom.com/user-cgi/daver/giflet?" + RGB;
    document.miscdata.color.value=RGB;
}
```

Function getB()

This function is same as the getR() and getB() functions except here we find the hex value for blue by multiplying its x coordinate by 2.5 (Listing 12.4).

Listing 12.4 Function getB()

```
function getB(coords) {
    var comma = coords.indexOf(",");
    var x = parseInt(coords.substring(1,comma));
    var b = Math.floor(2.5 * x);
    document.rgb.b.value='' + b;
    var r = parseInt(document.rgb.r.value);
    var tmp = Math.floor(r/16);
    var RGB = hexchars.substring(tmp,tmp+1)
        + hexchars.substring(Math.floor(r - (tmp * 16)),Math.floor(r - (tmp *
            16))+1);
    var g = parseInt(document.rgb.g.value);
    tmp = Math.floor(g/16);
    RGB += hexchars.substring(tmp,tmp+1)
```

```
       + hexchars.substring(Math.floor(g - (tmp * 16)),Math.floor(g - (tmp *
          16))+1);
   tmp = Math.floor(b/16);
   RGB += hexchars.substring(tmp,tmp+1)
       + hexchars.substring(Math.floor(b - (tmp * 16)),Math.floor(b - (tmp *
          16))+1);
   document.images[66].src="http://www.idiom.com/user-cgi/daver/giflet?" + RGB;
   document.miscdata.color.value=RGB;
}
```

Function getRGB()

This function is the same as the preceding three functions, but this time we
must worry about the y value because it is not a linear decline. We also must
compute all three colors' hex values at the same time. For the calculations, we
use the same math formulas from the preceding functions. Note that we must
make some decisions based on the x and y values. For example, if x is between
33 and 166 we put 255 for red/blue/green. If the value of x is between 34 and
66, the value is calculated as -255*x/33+510. If the value of x is between 67 and
132, the value for red/green/blue is calculated as 255*x/33-1020. Otherwise,
the value for red/blue/green is 0. Finally, we concatenate these values to a value
that the CGI understands, as we did in the previous three functions (Listing
12.5).

Listing 12.5 Function getRGB()

```
function getRGB(coords) {
   var comma = coords.indexOf(",");
   var x = parseInt(coords.substring(1,comma));
   var y = parseInt(coords.substring(comma+1,coords.length));

   if (x<=33 || x>=166) { var r=255; }
   else if (x<=66) { var r=Math.floor(-255*x/33)+510; }
   else if (x>=132) { var r=Math.floor(255*x/33)-1020; }
   else { var r = 0; }
   if (y<=45) { r=r+Math.floor( (255-r)*(-y+45)/45 ); }
   else { r=r-Math.floor( r*(y-45)/45 ); }
   document.rgb.r.value='' + r;
   var tmp = Math.floor(r/16);
   var RGB = hexchars.substring(tmp,tmp+1)
       + hexchars.substring(Math.floor(r - (tmp * 16)),Math.floor(r - (tmp *
          16))+1);

   if (x>=33 && x<=100) { var g=255; }
```

```
    else if (x<=33) { var g=Math.floor(255*x/33); }
    else if (x>=100 && x<=133) { var g=Math.floor(-255*x/33)+1020; }
    else { var g = 0; }
    if (y<=45) { g=g+Math.floor( (255-g)*(-y+45)/45 ); }
    else { g=g-Math.floor( g*(y-45)/45 ); }
    document.rgb.g.value='' + g;
    tmp = Math.floor(g/16);
    RGB += hexchars.substring(tmp,tmp+1)
        + hexchars.substring(Math.floor(g - (tmp * 16)),Math.floor(g - (tmp *
            16))+1);

    if (x>=100 && x<=166) { var b=255; }
    else if (x>=66 && x<=99) { var b=Math.floor(255*x/33)-510; }
    else if (x>=167) { var b=Math.floor(-255*x/33)+1530; }
    else { var b = 0; }
    if (y<=45) { b=b+Math.floor( (255-b)*(-y+45)/45 ); }
    else { b=b-Math.floor( b*(y-45)/45 ); }
    document.rgb.b.value='' + b;
    tmp = Math.floor(b/16);
    RGB += hexchars.substring(tmp,tmp+1)
        + hexchars.substring(Math.floor(b - (tmp * 16)),Math.floor(b - (tmp *
            16))+1);
    document.images[66].src="http://www.idiom.com/user-cgi/daver/giflet?" + RGB;
    document.miscdata.color.value=RGB;
}
```

Function setPalette()

As the name implies, this function sets up the top palette when you click on the
link **ADD TO PALETTE**. The function also checks to see whether you are
trying to put more than 64 colors on the palette. If you do, it alerts you that
you have exceeded your limit and cannot add any more new colors.

```
function setPalette() {
    document.images[(parseInt(document.miscdata.palette.value))].src=
        "http://www.idiom.com/user-cgi/daver/giflet?" +
            document.miscdata.color.value;

colors[(parseInt(document.miscdata.palette.value))]=document.miscdata.color.value;
    document.miscdata.palette.value = '' +
        (parseInt(document.miscdata.palette.value) + 1);
    if (parseInt(document.miscdata.palette.value) > 64) {
        document.miscdata.palette.value="64";
        alert('You have reached the limit of 64 colors on your Palette.'
            + 'You may change colors on the palette but you cannot add new ones.');
    }
}
```

Function checkVal()

As mentioned before, this function is called when a user inputs a value in one of the text boxes next to the red, blue, and green palettes. The function validates the input and, if the user inputs an appropriate decimal number, checkVal() finds the hex value for the input. Next, it concatenates that value with the preexisting other two values and creates a value that will be understood by the CGI. If the user inputs a number that is not between 0 and 255, the function alerts the user and displays the decimal value that was previously stored in that text box. Note that for the calculation of the RGB value, we use the same code as that used in getR(), getG() and getB(). The code appears in Listing 12.6.

Listing 12.6 Function checkVal()

```
function checkVal(i) {
   if (i == 'r') {
      if ((parseInt(document.rgb.r.value) < 256) &&
         (checkChars(document.rgb.r.value))) {
         var r = parseInt(document.rgb.r.value)
         var tmp = Math.floor(r/16);
         var RGB = hexchars.substring(tmp,tmp+1)
            + hexchars.substring(Math.floor(r - (tmp * 16)),Math.floor(r - (tmp *
               16))+1);
         var g = parseInt(document.rgb.g.value);
         tmp = Math.floor(g/16);
         RGB += hexchars.substring(tmp,tmp+1)
            + hexchars.substring(Math.floor(g - (tmp * 16)),Math.floor(g - (tmp *
               16))+1);
         var b = parseInt(document.rgb.b.value);
         tmp = Math.floor(b/16);
         RGB += hexchars.substring(tmp,tmp+1)
            + hexchars.substring(Math.floor(b - (tmp * 16)),Math.floor(b - (tmp *
               16))+1);
         document.images[66].src="http://www.idiom.com/user-cgi/daver/giflet?" +
            RGB;
         document.miscdata.color.value=RGB;
      }
      else {
         alert ('Value for d must be between 0 and 255.');
         document.rgb.r.value=unhex(document.miscdata.color.value.sub
            string(0,2));
      }
```

```
}
if (i == 'g') {
    if ((parseInt(document.rgb.g.value) < 256) &&
        (checkChars(document.rgb.g.value))) {
        var r = parseInt(document.rgb.r.value);
        var tmp = Math.floor(r/16);
        var RGB = hexchars.substring(tmp,tmp+1)
            + hexchars.substring(Math.floor(r - (tmp * 16)),Math.floor(r - (tmp *
                16))+1);
        var g = parseInt(document.rgb.g.value);
        tmp = Math.floor(g/16);
        RGB += hexchars.substring(tmp,tmp+1)
            + hexchars.substring(Math.floor(g - (tmp * 16)),Math.floor(g - (tmp *
                16))+1);
        var b = parseInt(document.rgb.b.value);
        tmp = Math.floor(b/16);
        RGB += hexchars.substring(tmp,tmp+1)
            + hexchars.substring(Math.floor(b - (tmp * 16)),Math.floor(b - (tmp *
                16))+1);
        document.images[66].src="http://www.idiom.com/user-cgi/daver/giflet?" +
            RGB;
        document.miscdata.color.value=RGB;
    }
    else {
        alert ('Value for eenust be between 0 and 255.');
        document.rgb.g.value=unhex(document.miscdata.color.value.sub
            string(2,4));
    }
}
if (i == 'b') {
    if ((parseInt(document.rgb.b.value) < 256) &&
        (checkChars(document.rgb.b.value))) {
        var r = parseInt(document.rgb.r.value);
        var tmp = Math.floor(r/16);
        var RGB = hexchars.substring(tmp,tmp+1)
            + hexchars.substring(Math.floor(r - (tmp * 16)),Math.floor(r - (tmp *
                16))+1);
        var g = parseInt(document.rgb.g.value);
        tmp = Math.floor(g/16);
        RGB += hexchars.substring(tmp,tmp+1)
            + hexchars.substring(Math.floor(g - (tmp * 16)),Math.floor(g - (tmp *
                16))+1);
        var b = parseInt(document.rgb.b.value);
        tmp = Math.floor(b/16);
        RGB += hexchars.substring(tmp,tmp+1)
            + hexchars.substring(Math.floor(b - (tmp * 16)),Math.floor(b - (tmp *
```

```
16))+1);
        document.images[66].src="http://www.idiom.com/user-cgi/daver/giflet?" +
            RGB;
        document.miscdata.color.value=RGB;
    }
    else {
        alert ('Value for ∞ueust be between 0 and 255.');
        document.rgb.b.value=unhex(document.miscdata.color.value.sub
            string(4,6));
    }
  }
}
```

checkChars()

This function, called from the `checkVal()` function, looks for a character between 0 and 9. If the character is not found, the function returns `false`; otherwise, it returns `true`.

```
function checkChars(i) {
    var nums="0123456789";
    var bad=0;
    if (i == "") { bad=1; }
    for(j=0;j<i.length;j++) {
        if (nums.indexOf(i.substring(j,j+1)) == -1) { bad=1; }
    }
    if (bad==0) { return true; }
    else { return false; }
}
```

Putting the Script Together

Listings 12.7 and 12.8 show the full script for this example.

Listing 12.7 The index.html Page

```
<HTML>
<HEAD>

<TITLE>JavaScript Painter</TITLE>

</HEAD>

<script Language="JavaScript">
```

```
<!—
function echoR() {
    return '<body onload="parent.main.getR(location.search)"></body>';
}

function echoG() {
    return '<body onload="parent.main.getG(location.search)"></body>';
}

function echoB() {
    return '<body onload="parent.main.getB(location.search)"></body>';
}

function echoRGB() {
    return '<body onload="parent.main.getRGB(location.search)"></body>';
}

var emptyFrame = '<html></html>';
var htmlOut = '<frameset rows="*,0">'
+ '   <frame name="main" src="main.html">'
+ '   <frame name="echo" src="javascript:parent.emptyFrame">'
+ '</frameset>';
document.write(htmlOut);
// —>
</script>

</HTML>
```

Listing 12.8 The main.html Page

```
<HTML>
<!— Copyright 1995, 1996 by David Ray, Dream Designs. All rights reserved. —>
<!— No portion of this document may be reproduced without prior written permis-
sion from author. —>

<HEAD>

<TITLE>JavaScript Painter Lite</TITLE>

<script language="JavaScript">
<!—
var colors = new StringArray(64);
for (i=0;i<64;i++) { colors[i]="FFFFFF"; }

function clickColor(i) {
 var urlstring = document.images[(70+i)].src;
 document.images[(70+i)].src = (urlstring.substring(0,urlstring.length-6)
    + document.miscdata.color.value);
}
```

```
function dragColor(i) {
 if (document.miscdata.drag.value == "1") {
  var urlstring = document.images[(70+i)].src;
  document.images[(70+i)].src = (urlstring.substring(0,urlstring.length-6)
    + document.miscdata.color.value);
 }
}

function setClick(i) {
  document.miscdata.drag.value=i;
}

function setColor(i) {
  i++;
  document.miscdata.color.value=colors[i];
  document.images[66].src="http://www.idiom.com/user-cgi/daver/giflet?" +
      colors[i];
  document.rgb.r.value=unhex(colors[i].substring(0,2));
  document.rgb.g.value=unhex(colors[i].substring(2,4));
  document.rgb.b.value=unhex(colors[i].substring(4,6));
}

var hexchars="0123456789ABCDEF";

function unhex(i) {
   return(16*(hexchars.indexOf(i.substring(0,1)))) + (hexchars.indexOf
      (i.substring(1,2)));
}

function clearPict() {
  for (i=0;i<=1599;i++) {
    var urlstring = document.images[(70+i)].src;
    document.images[(70+i)].src = (urlstring.substring(0,urlstring.length-6) +
      'FFFFFF');
  }
}

function getR(coords) {
   var comma = coords.indexOf(",");
   var x = parseInt(coords.substring(1,comma));
   var r = Math.floor(2.5 * x);
   document.rgb.r.value='' + r;
   var tmp = Math.floor(r/16);
   var RGB = hexchars.substring(tmp,tmp+1)
      + hexchars.substring(Math.floor(r - (tmp * 16)),Math.floor(r - (tmp *
          16))+1);
   var g = parseInt(document.rgb.g.value);
   tmp = Math.floor(g/16);
```

```
       RGB += hexchars.substring(tmp,tmp+1)
          + hexchars.substring(Math.floor(g - (tmp * 16)),Math.floor(g - (tmp *
             16))+1);
       var b = parseInt(document.rgb.b.value);
       tmp = Math.floor(b/16);
       RGB += hexchars.substring(tmp,tmp+1)
          + hexchars.substring(Math.floor(b - (tmp * 16)),Math.floor(b - (tmp *
             16))+1);
       document.images[66].src="http://www.idiom.com/user-cgi/daver/giflet?" + RGB;
       document.miscdata.color.value=RGB;
}

function getG(coords) {
    var comma = coords.indexOf(",");
    var x = parseInt(coords.substring(1,comma));
    var g = Math.floor(2.5 * x);
    document.rgb.g.value='' + g;
    var r = parseInt(document.rgb.r.value);
    var tmp = Math.floor(r/16);
    var RGB = hexchars.substring(tmp,tmp+1)
       + hexchars.substring(Math.floor(r - (tmp * 16)),Math.floor(r - (tmp *
          16))+1);
    tmp = Math.floor(g/16);
    RGB += hexchars.substring(tmp,tmp+1)
       + hexchars.substring(Math.floor(g - (tmp * 16)),Math.floor(g - (tmp *
          16))+1);
    var b = parseInt(document.rgb.b.value);
    tmp = Math.floor(b/16);
    RGB += hexchars.substring(tmp,tmp+1)
       + hexchars.substring(Math.floor(b - (tmp * 16)),Math.floor(b - (tmp *
          16))+1);
    document.images[66].src="http://www.idiom.com/user-cgi/daver/giflet?" + RGB;
    document.miscdata.color.value=RGB;
}

function getB(coords) {
    var comma = coords.indexOf(",");
    var x = parseInt(coords.substring(1,comma));
    var b = Math.floor(2.5 * x);
    document.rgb.b.value='' + b;
    var r = parseInt(document.rgb.r.value);
    var tmp = Math.floor(r/16);
    var RGB = hexchars.substring(tmp,tmp+1)
       + hexchars.substring(Math.floor(r - (tmp * 16)),Math.floor(r - (tmp *
          16))+1);
    var g = parseInt(document.rgb.g.value);
    tmp = Math.floor(g/16);
```

```
    RGB += hexchars.substring(tmp,tmp+1)
       + hexchars.substring(Math.floor(g - (tmp * 16)),Math.floor(g - (tmp *
          16))+1);
    tmp = Math.floor(b/16);
    RGB += hexchars.substring(tmp,tmp+1)
       + hexchars.substring(Math.floor(b - (tmp * 16)),Math.floor(b - (tmp *
          16))+1);
    document.images[66].src="http://www.idiom.com/user-cgi/daver/giflet?" + RGB;
    document.miscdata.color.value=RGB;
}

function getRGB(coords) {
    var comma = coords.indexOf(",");
    var x = parseInt(coords.substring(1,comma));
    var y = parseInt(coords.substring(comma+1,coords.length));

    if (x<=33 || x>=166) { var r=255; }
    else if (x<=66) { var r=Math.floor(-255*x/33)+510; }
    else if (x>=132) { var r=Math.floor(255*x/33)-1020; }
    else { var r = 0; }
    if (y<=45) { r=r+Math.floor( (255-r)*(-y+45)/45 ); }
    else { r=r-Math.floor( r*(y-45)/45 ); }
    document.rgb.r.value='' + r;
    var tmp = Math.floor(r/16);
    var RGB = hexchars.substring(tmp,tmp+1)
       + hexchars.substring(Math.floor(r - (tmp * 16)),Math.floor(r - (tmp *
          16))+1);

    if (x>=33 && x<=100) { var g=255; }
    else if (x<=33) { var g=Math.floor(255*x/33); }
    else if (x>=100 && x<=133) { var g=Math.floor(-255*x/33)+1020; }
    else { var g = 0; }
    if (y<=45) { g=g+Math.floor( (255-g)*(-y+45)/45 ); }
    else { g=g-Math.floor( g*(y-45)/45 ); }
    document.rgb.g.value='' + g;
    tmp = Math.floor(g/16);
    RGB += hexchars.substring(tmp,tmp+1)
       + hexchars.substring(Math.floor(g - (tmp * 16)),Math.floor(g - (tmp *
          16))+1);

    if (x>=100 && x<=166) { var b=255; }
    else if (x>=66 && x<=99) { var b=Math.floor(255*x/33)-510; }
    else if (x>=167) { var b=Math.floor(-255*x/33)+1530; }
    else { var b = 0; }
    if (y<=45) { b=b+Math.floor( (255-b)*(-y+45)/45 ); }
    else { b=b-Math.floor( b*(y-45)/45 ); }
    document.rgb.b.value='' + b;
    tmp = Math.floor(b/16);
```

```
      RGB += hexchars.substring(tmp,tmp+1)
         + hexchars.substring(Math.floor(b - (tmp * 16)),Math.floor(b - (tmp *
            16))+1);
      document.images[66].src="http://www.idiom.com/user-cgi/daver/giflet?" + RGB;
      document.miscdata.color.value=RGB;
}

function setPalette() {
   document.images[(parseInt(document.miscdata.palette.value))].src=
      "http://www.idiom.com/user-cgi/daver/giflet?" +
         document.miscdata.color.value;

colors[(parseInt(document.miscdata.palette.value))]=document.miscdata.color.value;
   document.miscdata.palette.value = '' +
      (parseInt(document.miscdata.palette.value) + 1);
   if (parseInt(document.miscdata.palette.value) > 64) {
      document.miscdata.palette.value="64";
      alert('You have reached the limit of 64 colors on your Palette.'
         + 'You may change colors on the palette but you cannot add new ones.');
   }
}

function checkVal(i) {
   if (i == 'r') {
      if ((parseInt(document.rgb.r.value) < 256) &&
         (checkChars(document.rgb.r.value))) {
         var r = parseInt(document.rgb.r.value);
         var tmp = Math.floor(r/16);
         var RGB = hexchars.substring(tmp,tmp+1)
            + hexchars.substring(Math.floor(r - (tmp * 16)),Math.floor(r - (tmp *
               16))+1);
         var g = parseInt(document.rgb.g.value);
         tmp = Math.floor(g/16);
         RGB += hexchars.substring(tmp,tmp+1)
            + hexchars.substring(Math.floor(g - (tmp * 16)),Math.floor(g - (tmp *
               16))+1);
         var b = parseInt(document.rgb.b.value);
         tmp = Math.floor(b/16);
         RGB += hexchars.substring(tmp,tmp+1)
            + hexchars.substring(Math.floor(b - (tmp * 16)),Math.floor(b - (tmp *
               16))+1);
         document.images[66].src="http://www.idiom.com/user-cgi/daver/giflet?" +
            RGB;
         document.miscdata.color.value=RGB;
      }
      else {
         alert ('Value for d must be between 0 and 255.');
```

```
            document.rgb.r.value=unhex(document.miscdata.color.value.
                substring(0,2));
        }
    }
    if (i == 'g') {
        if ((parseInt(document.rgb.g.value) < 256) &&
            (checkChars(document.rgb.g.value))) {
            var r = parseInt(document.rgb.r.value);
            var tmp = Math.floor(r/16);
            var RGB = hexchars.substring(tmp,tmp+1)
                + hexchars.substring(Math.floor(r - (tmp * 16)),Math.floor(r - (tmp *
                    16))+1);
            var g = parseInt(document.rgb.g.value);
            tmp = Math.floor(g/16);
            RGB += hexchars.substring(tmp,tmp+1)
                + hexchars.substring(Math.floor(g - (tmp * 16)),Math.floor(g - (tmp *
                    16))+1);
            var b = parseInt(document.rgb.b.value);
            tmp = Math.floor(b/16);
            RGB += hexchars.substring(tmp,tmp+1)
                + hexchars.substring(Math.floor(b - (tmp * 16)),Math.floor(b - (tmp *
                    16))+1);
            document.images[66].src="http://www.idiom.com/user-cgi/daver/giflet?" +
                RGB;
            document.miscdata.color.value=RGB;
        }
        else {
            alert ('Value for eenust be between 0 and 255.');
            document.rgb.g.value=unhex(document.miscdata.color.value.
                substring(2,4));
        }
    }
    if (i == 'b') {
        if ((parseInt(document.rgb.b.value) < 256) &&
            (checkChars(document.rgb.b.value))) {
            var r = parseInt(document.rgb.r.value);
            var tmp = Math.floor(r/16);
            var RGB = hexchars.substring(tmp,tmp+1)
                + hexchars.substring(Math.floor(r - (tmp * 16)),Math.floor(r - (tmp *
                    16))+1);
            var g = parseInt(document.rgb.g.value);
            tmp = Math.floor(g/16);
            RGB += hexchars.substring(tmp,tmp+1)
                + hexchars.substring(Math.floor(g - (tmp * 16)),Math.floor(g - (tmp *
                    16))+1);
            var b = parseInt(document.rgb.b.value);
```

```
        tmp = Math.floor(b/16);
        RGB += hexchars.substring(tmp,tmp+1)
            + hexchars.substring(Math.floor(b - (tmp * 16)),Math.floor(b - (tmp *
                16))+1);
        document.images[66].src="http://www.idiom.com/user-cgi/daver/giflet?" +
            RGB;
        document.miscdata.color.value=RGB;
      }
      else {
        alert ('Value for ∞ueust be between 0 and 255.');
        document.rgb.b.value=unhex(document.miscdata.color.value.sub
            string(4,6));
      }
   }
}

function checkChars(i) {
   var nums="0123456789";
   var bad=0;
   if (i == "") { bad=1; }
   for(j=0;j<i.length;j++) {
      if (nums.indexOf(i.substring(j,j+1)) == -1) { bad=1; }
   }
   if (bad==0) { return true; }
   else { return false; }
}

function setHistory () {
   GetChips();
   var theHist = Chips[9];
   if (theHist == '') { theHist = ","; }
   if (theHist.indexOf(",8,") == -1) { theHist += "8," }
   SetChip(9,theHist);
}

// ->
</script>
</HEAD>
<body>
<center>
<img src="../Media/Painter.gif" width=460 height=50 border=0
   alt="Javascript Painter">
<p>
<form name="miscdata">
<input type="hidden" name="drag" value="0">
<input type="hidden" name="color" value="FFFFFF">
<input type="hidden" name="palette" value="1">
```

```
</form>

<script language="JavaScript">
<!—

document.write('<form name="rgb"><table border=0 align=left><tr><td colspan=3 a
    lign=center>'
 + '<font size=2><b>Y O U R   P A L E T T E</b></font><br>');

for (i=0;i<4;i++) {
 for (j=0;j<16;j++) {
   picnum = '' + ((4 * (i)) + j);
   document.write('<a href="javascript:setColor(+ picnum
     + '><img src="http://www.idiom.com/user-cgi/daver/giflet?' + colors[picnum] +
        '" border=0 height=12 width=12></a>');
 }
 document.write('<br>');
}

var htmlOut = '</td></tr><tr><td><b>R</b></td>'
+ '<td><a href="javascript:parent.echoR()//" target="echo"><img src="rpick.gif"
    height=9 width=103 border=0 ISMAP></a>'
+ '<input type="text" size=3 name="r" value="255" onBlur="checkVal(')"></td>'
+ '<td rowspan=3><img src="http://www.idiom.com/user-cgi/daver/giflet?FFFFFF"
    height=30 width=30><br>'
+ '<a href="javascript:setPalette()"><font size=1>ADD TO<br>PALETTE</a></td>'
+ '</tr><tr>'
+ '<td><b>G</b></td>'
+ '<td><a href="javascript:parent.echoG()//" target="echo"><img src="gpick.gif"
    height=9 width=103 border=0 ISMAP></a>'
+ '<input type="text" size=3 name="g" value="255" onBlur="checkVal(')"></td>'
+ '</tr><tr>'
+ '<td><b>B</b></td>'
+ '<td><a href="javascript:parent.echoB()//" target="echo"><img src="bpick.gif"
    height=9 width=103 border=0 ISMAP></a>'
+ '<input type="text" size=3 name="b" value="255" onBlur="checkVal(∞')"></td>'
+ '</tr><tr>'
+ '<td colspan=3 align=center><a href="javascript:parent.echoRGB()//"
    target="echo"><img src="palette1.gif" height=93 width=204 border=0
    ISMAP></a>'
+ '</td>'
+ '</tr></table>';

document.write(htmlOut);
htmlOut=null;

document.write('<center><table border=0><tr><td align=center>'
 + '<font size=2><b>Y O U R   C A N V A S</b></font><br>');
```

```
var picnum = '';
for (i=1;i<=40;i++) {
   for (j=1;j<=40;j++) {
      picnum = '' + ((40 * (i-1)) + j - 1);
      document.write('<a href="javascript:clickColor(' + picnum +
            ')" onMouseover="dragColor(' + picnum + ')"><img
                src="http://www.idiom.com/user-cgi/daver/giflet?FFFFFF" height=4
                width=4 border=0></a>');
   }
   document.write('<br>');
}

htmlOut='<p>Draw by: '
+ '<a href="javascript:setClick(')">clicking</a> or '
+ '<a href="javascript:setClick(')">dragging</a><p>'
+ '<a href="javascript:clearPict()">Clear picture</a>'
+ '</td></tr></table></center>';
document.write(htmlOut);
htmlOut=null;
// -->
</script>
</BODY>
</HTML>
```

PART THREE

USING LIVECONNECT

Chapter 13 by Piroz Mohseni

Chapter 14 and 15 by Louis Schumacher

CHAPTER THIRTEEN

LIVECONNECT

Now that we have talked about plain JavaScript, it's time to move forward with the knowledge gained in the first two parts of the book. In the next few chapters, we will focus on how you can use JavaScript with other tools such as plug-ins and Java. Don't be nervous if you don't know Java. Chapter 14 will give you enough information about Java that you can easily get a head start working with the LiveConnect concept.

This chapter introduces a relatively new, powerful tool called LiveConnect. As its name implies, LiveConnect is a mechanism for connecting two or more entities. The specification provides a robust and standardized method for this interface, which adds flexibility and usefulness to your Web applications.

This chapter covers:

- Understanding the LiveConnect concept
- Plug-in detection using JavaScript
- Calling Java methods from a JavaScript
- Calling JavaScript methods from Java applets
- Calling plug-in methods from Java applets
- Calling Java methods from plug-ins

Understanding the LiveConnect Concept

As part of a paradigm shift to client-side computing, Netscape has introduced three distinct solutions. First came the plug-in technology, which enabled an independent module to load and run within the browser process. This technology was a major stepping-stone, because it enabled a browser to show more than HTML pages with pictures. Many companies based their core technology on the plug-in API.

The next two technologies were developed alongside each other, although there was no relationship between them originally. Netscape introduced LiveScript as a scripting language within HTML. The name was changed to JavaScript soon after the introduction of Java. JavaScript brought life to Web pages not by invoking a separate module but by interpreting JavaScript commands embedded within HTML code. Alongside the development of JavaScript was the Java language. Soon after its emergence, it found a home on the Web as an embedded object in HTML pages known simply as an *applet*.

Each of these technologies was an important milestones in the development of the Web, and each technology found its own niche for the types of applications it supported. Before long, the need to link these components became evident. The answer, of course, was LiveConnect. This technology establishes a standard method by which the components (plug-ins, JavaScript, and Java applets) communicate and are used collectively to build an application. This concept is shown in Figure 13.1. Programmers are no longer limited to choosing one technology and trying to implement an entire application using it. Instead, they can build each part of an application from the piece most suited to the need.

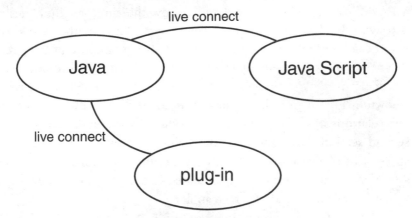

Figure 13.1 LiveConnect allows three core technologies (plug-ins, JavaScript, and Java applets) to communicate.

To understand the LiveConnect concept, we'll concentrate on the similarities among the three technologies. LiveConnect takes advantage of these similarities to establish a communication mechanism. For one thing, all three technologies are based on objects. Therefore, it would make sense for one technology (say, JavaScript) to call methods and access properties of an object in another technology (say, a Java applet). The object-oriented nature of these technologies hides the implementation details and allows the communication to take place at a higher abstraction level. You already know that JavaScript treats elements of a Web page as separate objects. In Chapter 14, you will learn how Java programs are built from a collection of objects. If you study the documentation for Netscape Plug-ins, you will find that it, too, is based on an object-oriented paradigm.

In addition to their object-oriented nature, all three technologies can be viewed as application builders. A complete application can be written as a plug-in or a Java applet. Despite their collective nature, these technologies are also considered separate components; an application can have a component written in Java and another component written in JavaScript. LiveConnect allows these components to merge and create an application. You can think of LiveConnect as the glue. The concept of components becomes more powerful as greater numbers of generic and of highly specific applications are built. You can build more-complex applications by simply putting the right pieces next to each other and connecting them via LiveConnect.

In the following sections, we describe how the three technologies mentioned previously are connected by LiveConnect. Along with the discussion, we present examples of this integration. You'll also get a sense of the strengths and weaknesses of each technology as you try to choose which component best fits a particular part of your application. This chapter is based on the relationships shown in Figure 13.1. In the first section, we discuss the most natural of the four relationships: how a JavaScript code calls methods written in Java. The second section shows the opposite relationship, which is the ability of a Java applet to call methods written in JavaScript. The third part focuses on how a Java applet calls methods implemented in the plug-in. Finally, we show how a plug-in calls Java methods in an applet.

Plug-in Detection Using JavaScript

One of the first issues that come up as you begin using LiveConnect is lack of knowledge about the object you are trying to access. Suppose your JavaScript needs to call a method in a Java applet. How do you know what the method's name is and what parameters it needs? To give you a taste of some of the detective work you must do, we use JavaScript to detect the existence of a particular plug-in. The following discussion assumes that you are familiar with MIME types. Multipurpose Internet mail extensions is the technique used by browsers to identify external source types and determine how they will be processed by the browser. The Netscape Navigator **Options|General Preferences|Helpers** item lists numerous MIME types that your browser may be asked to handle. The list will most likely have several dozen entries covering everything from plain ASCII text to QuickTime movies. MIME types follow a simple type/subtype naming convention. For example, "text/plain" denotes plain ASCII text, and "video/quicktime" denotes a QuickTime player. Note that the **Help|About Plug-ins** panel lists all the plug-ins installed on your Navigator browser and includes a simple explanation of their purpose.

The following JavaScript code fragment checks to see whether the MacroMedia Shockwave plug-in is available:

```
function probePlugIn(mimeType) {
    var havePlugIn = false
```

```
    var tiny = window.open("", "teensy", "width=1,height=1")
    if (tiny != null) {
        if (tiny.document.open(mimeType) != null)
            havePlugIn = true
            tiny.close()
    }
    return havePlugIn
}

var haveShockWavePlugIn = probePlugIn("application/x-director")
if (haveShockWavePlugIn)
    document.writeln("<EMBED SRC="Movie.dir" HEIGHT=100 WIDTH=100>")
else
    document.writeln("You don't have Shockwave installed!")
```

You could use the `probePlugIn` function to check for the availability of any plug-in required by your Web page as long as you know the MIME type. But there is a much better method available with Navigator 3.0.

JavaScript has a global `navigator` object that contains properties for information not associated with any particular document. This object now has two more properties: a `mimeTypes` object and a `plugins` object.

The `mimeTypes` object is an array of all MIME types supported by the browser (either internally, via helper apps, or by plug-ins). Each array element is a `mimeType` object, which has properties for its type, description, and file extension. The `plugins` object is an array of all plug-ins currently installed on the client system. Each element of the array is a `plugin` object, which has properties for its name and description as well as a subarray of `mimeType` objects listing the types supported by that plug-in.

The following code fragment can be used in place of the previous one. It displays a Shockwave file if the Shockwave plug-in is available; otherwise, it will let users know they need Shockwave.

```
var haveShockWavePlugIn = navigator.plugins["Shockwave"];
if (haveShockWavePlugIn)
    document.writeln("<EMBED SRC="Movie.dir" HEIGHT=100 WIDTH=100>")
else
    document.writeln("You don't have Shockwave installed!")
```

The following JavaScript example displays all the plug-ins loaded in a browser:

```
<HTML>
<HEAD>
```

```
<TITLE>Plug-ins Supported by This Browser</TITLE>
</HEAD>
<BODY>
<SCRIPT>
var PlugInCount = navigator.plugins.length
var Index
var MIMEcount
document.write( "<B>There are ",PlugInCount," plug-ins supported by this
    browser.</B>
<BR><BR>")
for (Index = 0; Index < PlugInCount; Index++) {
    document.write("  Plug-in name '",navigator.plugins[Index].name, "'<BR>")
    document.write("  Plug-in file '",navigator.plugins[Index].filename,
        "'<BR>")
    document.write("  Plug-in description
        '",navigator.plugins[Index].description, "'<BR>")
    MIMEcount = navigator.plugins[Index].length
    plural = (MIMEcount > 1) ? "s" : ""
    document.write("  Plug-in supports ",MIMEcount," MIME
        type",plural,"<BR><BR>")
}
</SCRIPT>
</BODY>
</HTML>
```

Calling Java Methods from a JavaScript

The mechanism that lets JavaScript call methods in a Java applet is simple and straightforward. Basically, you need to enable both Java and JavaScript on your Netscape 3.0 or later browser (from **General Preference | Network Preference | Languages**). You can then directly call native Java methods from JavaScript. This technique is shown in Figure 13.2.

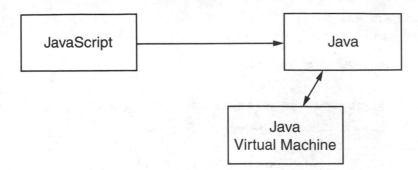

Figure 13.2 Calling Java methods from a JavaScript via LiveConnect.

Let's start with a simple example that doesn't even involve a Java applet. In Netscape, you can turn on the Java console and display messages the Java program would have displayed if it were running as a standalone program and not as an applet. To turn on the Java console, from the Options menu, select **Show Java Console**. Now create a simple HTML file containing the following:

```
<html>
<head>
<script Language="JavaScript">
function PrintHello() {
     java.lang.System.out.println("Hello World!");
}
</script>
</head>
<body>
Very simple LiveScript demo <p>

<form>
<input type="button" value="Click here" onClick="PrintHello()">
</form>

</body>
</html>
```

After creating the file, load it in Netscape and click the button. You will note that the message "Hello World" appears on the Java console, as shown in Figure 13.3. Congratulations! You have just called a native Java method from a JavaScript using LiveConnect. Note that your JavaScript has treated the Java method just like any other method. The big difference is that JavaScript does not have a method named `println`, but Java does. You must reference any Java method starting with its package name. The naming hierarchy is as follows:

```
[Packages.]packageName.className.methodName
```

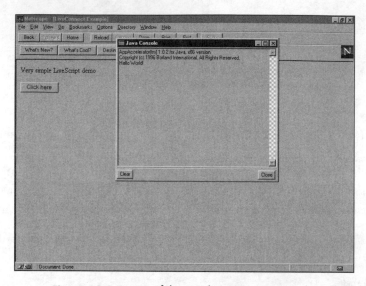

Figure 13.3 Output of the simple LiveScript example.

If the method is part of the `java`, `sun`, or `netscape` package, you do not need to explicitly use `Packages` as the first part of the naming hierarchy. Table 13.1 shows the default aliasing for `java`, `sun`, and `netscape`.

Table 13.1 Default Aliases for java, sun, and netscape Packages

Alias	Expansion
java	Packages.java
sun	Packages.sun
netscape	Packages.netscape

The `PrintHello()` function in our example could have accessed the `println()` method in either of the following ways. Both would be valid.

```
Packages.java.lang.System.out.println("Hello World!");
java.lang.System("Hello World!");
```

The preceding example is very simple but should give you a preview of what is possible with LiveConnect. Once again, LiveConnect allows you to invoke a method that is native to Java in a JavaScript function. Now we turn to a more useful example. Java applets have been adding life to Web pages for the past year. Java applets are limited in what they can do, so they can implement only a subset of the Java API. Nonetheless, they are a powerful source for Web applications. We won't discuss the specifics of how an applet works or how you should write one. Assuming you have an applet, we'll show you how your JavaScript can access methods implemented in your Java applet.

Based on the previous example, you might guess that you can directly call the Java method as you did with the `println()` method, and you are correct. The only restriction is that the method you are trying to call must be public. Let's look at an example to see how all this works.

Listing 13.1 shows the code for a Java applet that displays the postal rate (first class, presorted, and express mail) for weights less than 10 oz. For simplicity, we have hard-coded the rates into the code. A more practical application would perhaps use Java Database Connectivity to get the rates from a database.

Listing 13.1 po.java: The Java Source for the po Class

```java
import java.awt.*;
import java.io.*;
import java.applet.Applet;

public class po extends java.applet.Applet {

    public int appletHeight = 100;
    public int appletWidth = 100;

    public final static String FC = "First Class";
    public final static String PS = "Presorted";
    public final static String EXPRS = "Express";

    public String fc, ps, exprs;
    public OrderPanel orderPanel;

    public void init() {
        setLayout(new BorderLayout());

        orderPanel = new OrderPanel(this);
        add("Center", orderPanel);
```

```
        layout();
        resize(appletWidth, appletHeight);
        repaint();
}

public void start() {
        resize(appletWidth, appletHeight);
        layout();
        repaint();
}

public void set_rate(String aWeight) {
        int weight;
        weight = java.lang.Integer.parseInt(aWeight);

        clear();

        switch (weight) {
            case 1 :
                orderPanel.fcTextF.setText("0.32");
                orderPanel.psTextF.setText("0.295");
                orderPanel.exprsTextF.setText("10.50");
                break;

            case 2 :
                orderPanel.fcTextF.setText("0.55");
                orderPanel.psTextF.setText("0.525");
                orderPanel.exprsTextF.setText("10.50");
                break;

            case 3 :
                orderPanel.fcTextF.setText("0.78");
                orderPanel.psTextF.setText("0.709");
                orderPanel.exprsTextF.setText("11.95");
                break;

            case 4 :
                orderPanel.fcTextF.setText("1.01");
                orderPanel.psTextF.setText("0.939");
                orderPanel.exprsTextF.setText("13.05");
                break;

            case 5 :
                orderPanel.fcTextF.setText("1.24");
                orderPanel.psTextF.setText("1.169");
                orderPanel.exprsTextF.setText("14.15");
                break;

            case 6 :
                orderPanel.fcTextF.setText("1.47");
```

```
                    orderPanel.psTextF.setText("1.399");
                    orderPanel.exprsTextF.setText("15.30");
                    break;

            case 7 :
                    orderPanel.fcTextF.setText("1.70");
                    orderPanel.psTextF.setText("1.629");
                    orderPanel.exprsTextF.setText("16.40");
                    break;

            case 8 :
                    orderPanel.fcTextF.setText("1.93");
                    orderPanel.psTextF.setText("1.859");
                    orderPanel.exprsTextF.setText("17.55");
                    break;

            case 9 :
                    orderPanel.fcTextF.setText("2.16");
                    orderPanel.psTextF.setText("2.089");
                    orderPanel.exprsTextF.setText("18.70");
                    break;

            case 10 :
                    orderPanel.fcTextF.setText("2.39");
                    orderPanel.psTextF.setText("2.319");
                    orderPanel.exprsTextF.setText("19.75");
                    break;

            default :
                    orderPanel.fcTextF.setText("Rate unknown");
                    orderPanel.psTextF.setText("Rate unknown");
                    orderPanel.exprsTextF.setText("Rate unknown");
                    break;
        }
    }

    public void clear() {
        orderPanel.fcTextF.setText("");
        orderPanel.psTextF.setText("");
        orderPanel.exprsTextF.setText("");
    }
}

class OrderPanel extends java.awt.Panel {
    po applet;
    Label fcLabel;
    Label psLabel;
    Label exprsLabel;
    TextField fcTextF;
```

```
      TextField psTextF;
      TextField exprsTextF;
      String aWeight;

      public OrderPanel(po applet) {
          this.applet = applet;

          setLayout(new GridLayout(3,2));

          fcLabel = new Label(po.FC);
          psLabel = new Label(po.PS);
          exprsLabel = new Label(po.EXPRS);

          fcTextF = new TextField(20);
          psTextF = new TextField(20);
          exprsTextF = new TextField(20);

          fcTextF.setEditable (false);
          psTextF.setEditable (false);
          exprsTextF.setEditable (false);

          add(fcLabel);
          add(fcTextF);
          add(psLabel);
          add(psTextF);
          add(exprsLabel);
          add(exprsTextF);
      }

      public void update(Graphics g) {
          paint(g);
      }
  }
```

The applet draws a layout to hold three text boxes that are not editable. Each box is used to display one of the three rates. As far as our discussion is concerned, the focal point is the set_rate(String Weight) method of the class OrderPanel. This method accepts a string that is basically a digit from 1 to 10 representing the weight of the package in ounces. Notice that the Java applet does not provide the user with a place to enter the value. In other words, the Java applet cannot directly accept the weight value from the user. An HTML input box is used to accept the weight value, and LiveConnect is used to convey this value to the Java applet. This simple application is shown in Figure 13.4, and Listing 13.2 shows the code.

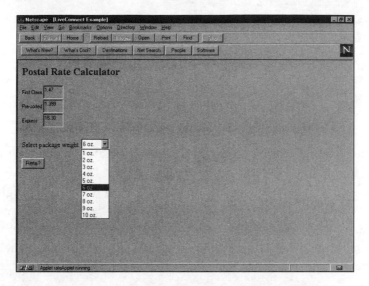

Figure 13.4 Simple postal rate application.

Listing 13.2 The HTML Code for the Page

```html
<html>
<head>
</head>

<body>
<h2> Postal Rate Calculator</h2>

<applet CODE="po.class" NAME="rateApplet" WIDTH=100 HEIGHT=100>
</applet>

<form name=rate>

Select package weight:
<select name = "weight">
<option selected value="1"> 1 oz.
<option select value="2"> 2 oz.
<option select value="3"> 3 oz.
<option select value="4"> 4 oz.
<option select value="5"> 5 oz.
<option select value="6"> 6 oz.
<option select value="7"> 7 oz.
<option select value="8"> 8 oz.
<option select value="9"> 9 oz.
<option select value="10"> 10 oz.
```

```
</select>
<p>

<input type="button" value="Rate?" name="getRate"
    onClick="document.rateApplet.set_rate(document.rate.weight.selectedIndex+1)">

</form>

</body>
</html>
```

To reference the Java applet in JavaScript, we associate a name with the Java applet by using the NAME attribute to the applet tag. In this case, we call the applet rateApplet. An ordinary text input box is used to accept a weight value. Then we directly invoke the set_rate method (which is part of the Java applet) and pass to it the value entered in the input box. The applet then goes to work, acting on the value passed to it by going through the switch statement and displaying the correct rates in the rate boxes.

The way the applet is referred to in the JavaScript needs some extra discussion. The applet is treated as another object on the Web page and therefore is part of the document object. So you can refer to it in several different ways, as with other JavaScript objects:

```
document.rateApplet
document.applets["rateApplet"]
document.applets[0]
```

The last reference assumes that the rateApplet is the first applet on the page.

The communication mechanism between JavaScripts and Java is not limited to Java methods. A JavaScript can access and change public variables. These variables usually are referred to as applet properties, and usually applets provide accessor methods for manipulating such variables. By changing these values, you can customize the applet or have it perform specific tasks. Finally, JavaScript can call methods that return values of type boolean, numeric, and string.

As you have seen, LiveConnect provides a natural way for integration of Java methods and properties into JavaScript code. One pressing issue is how you find out what methods and properties are available in the Java applet and how you know whether that method or variable is public. Currently, unless you have the source code or documentation for the applet, you can't automatically extract that information from the applet. As LiveConnect becomes more wide-spread, more applet authors will provide appropriate documentation about their applets and how their methods can be used from within JavaScript. It's also possible that future technologies might allow you to inspect the applet and receive information about its methods and properties via some standard API.

Calling JavaScript Methods from Java Applets

In this section we describe how a Java applet can call methods and change properties of JavaScript objects. This process, the opposite of the one discussed in the previous section, is shown in Figure 13.5. Objects in JavaScript represent almost all the elements of a Web page, such as frames, forms, and the HTML document itself. By allowing a Java applet to manipulate JavaScript methods and properties, we in turn give the applet the ability to modify the elements of the HTML page, and that is a powerful and useful tool.

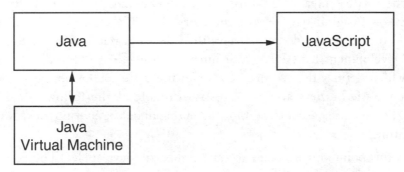

Figure 13.5 Calling JavaScript methods from Java via LiveConnect.

There are many applications in which Java-to-JavaScript communication is an invaluable feature. For example, an animation applet could change the background color of the host page for a more visually appealing display. In another case, an applet could use JDBC or another mechanism to retrieve information from a database and fill out an HTML form. The reverse could also be done.

Basically, any JavaScript method or property can be accessed by a Java applet. The question is whether you want that to happen. If you don't want the applet you just downloaded to make any changes to your HTML page what should you do? This is a serious issue. Most of the time, you don't know exactly what the applet will be doing until you download and execute it. The designers of LiveConnect address this issue by requiring a special attribute to the `<applet></applet>` tag. You must supply the MAYSCRIPT attribute if you want to give the applet access to JavaScript methods and properties. Here is an example:

```
<applet code="myapplet.class" width="300" height="200" name="myapplet" MAYSCRIPT>
```

The inclusion of the MAYSCRIPT attribute is the only thing you have to do on the JavaScript/HTML side of the communication. The rest of the work is on the Java applet side. Your Java code must import the Netscape `javascript` package using code similar to the following:

```
import netscape.javascript.*
```

The Netscape `javascript` package is part of a collection of packages contained in the file java_30. This file is usually located in the Navigator\Program\java\classes directory. This file contains a more secure version of the `java` and `sun` packages than the ones released in the Sun 1.0.2 Java Development Kit (JDK). Your interest is the `netscape.javascript` package, which defines the `JSObject` class and the `JSException` object. Complete reference of the netscape packages is available at the following address: http://home.netscape.com/eng/mozilla/3.0/handbook/javascript/packages/packages.html.

At this point you are ready to start coding the Java applet. The `getWindow` method in the class `netscape.javascript.JSObject` is used to get a window handle. Here is a typical usage:

```
public void setupApplet() {
    browser = JSObject.getWindow(this);
}
```

With the window handle in hand, you can then call `getMember()` to access a particular JavaScript object on the page. You must follow the usual hierarchy of JavaScript objects. For example, to gain access to the content of a text box, you must first make a call to `getMember()` for the text box itself, the form that the text box is in, and the document that contains the form. The following example captures the content of a text box `myBox` and assigns that value to a Java variable of type `string`:

```
browser = JSObject.getWindow(this);
JSObject mydoc = (JSObject) browser.getMember("document");
JSObject myform = (JSObject) mydoc.getMember("myform");
JSObject mytext = (JSObject) myform.getMember("myBox");
String mycontent = (String) mytext.getMember("value");
```

The hierarchy for the preceding example is shown in Figure 13.6.

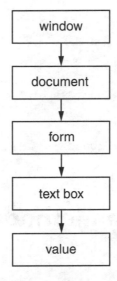

Figure 13.6 JavaScript hierarchy for the value of the text input box.

The ability to access JavaScript properties is useful but not sufficient for practical applications. Thankfully, LiveConnect does not limit you to properties. It also allows you to call JavaScript methods. With this combination, your Java applets can have full interaction with the Web page through JavaScript properties and methods. The `netscape.javascript.JSObject` provides two methods that are your main tool for calling JavaScript methods. They are `call` and `eval`. You need to get a handle for the window before using any of these methods. Here are the two most common syntax forms for `call` and `eval`:

```
JSObject.getWindow().call("methodName", arguments);
JSObject.getWindow()eval("expression");
```

Here, `methodName` is the name of the JavaScript method you want to call, `arguments` is an array of arguments that will be passed to the JavaScript method, and `expression` is a valid JavaScript expression that evaluates to a valid JavaScript method.

Suppose that before your applet begins its work, you want to ask the user for some information such as a password or identification number. You can have your applet display a prompt window and accept input from the user. We implement this functionality using both `call` and `eval` methods in the method `verify`:

```
public void init() {
    JSObject browser = JSObject.getWindow(this);
}

public boolean verify () {
    browser.call(" prompt(\"Enter ID number: \"; ");
}

public boolean verify() {
    browser eval(" prompt(\"Enter ID number:\"; ");
}
```

Calling Plug-In Methods from Java Applets

This section covers the last arrow in our original diagram. Sometimes you want your Java applet to call a method that belongs to the plug-in. For example, if the desired function cannot be implemented in Java, you may need the lower level of access provided by C and C++. Also, methods implemented in C or C++ execute faster than Java code. Such methods are usually referred to as *native* methods, perhaps because they are written for the native operating system. The communication mechanism discussed in this chapter is shown in Figure 13.7.

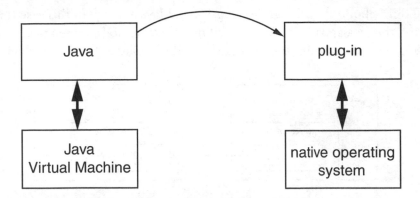

Figure 13.7 Calling plug-in methods from Java via LiveConnect.

The association of Java applets and plug-ins comes at three different levels. The first level is shown in Figure 13.8. In this configuration, the Java applet and the plug-in are two separate entities. Although the plug-in can call Java methods, the Java methods cannot call the plug-in.

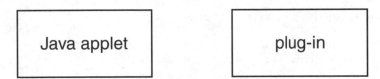

Figure 13.8 No association between the Java applet and the plug-in.

The second option defines a narrow connection between the two and is shown in Figure 13.9. The Java applet includes the class `Plugin` and therefore has an association with the `plugin`. This association is minimal, because the Java applet does not define any methods for the `plugin` class.

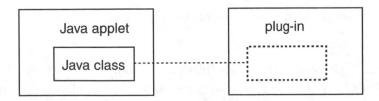

Figure 13.9 Minimal association between the Java applet and the plug-in.

The third choice fully integrates plug-ins and Java applets. In this case (Figure 13.10), the Java applet is capable of calling native methods written in C or C++. The Java applet contains the class Plugin and makes use of native methods.

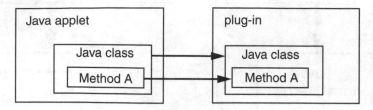

Figure 13.10 Full integration of the Java applet and the plug-in.

To take advantage of native plug-in methods requires minimal work on your Java code. Suppose there is a plug-in that acts as a chat service. We'll call this plug-in ChatPlugin. In your Java code, you first import the netscape.plugin.Plugin class:

```
import netscape.plugin.Plugin
```

You then define the subclass ChatPlugin:

```
class ChatPlugin extends Plugin {
    public native boolean setConnection (int handle);
}
```

This is the only reference made in your Java code. The actual implementation occurs as part of the C/C++ code. Before you compile your Java code, you use javah to create the necessary header files and also stubs to link the native method in Java to its implementation in C or C++. To get the header files, simply run javah as follows:

```
javah -jri ChatPlugin
```

To get the stubs, use the -stubs command-line option:

```
javah -jri -stubs ChatPlugin
```

You already know what the header files generated by javah contain. They have a number of macros that allow you to get or set the Java class properties. For a detailed description of the syntax and naming convention, please refer to the previous section.

The `-stubs` command-line option causes `javah` to create a **.c** file. This file contains an important routine that prepares the class for usage and registers the native methods so that Java applets can call them. This important routine has a name of the form `use_ClassName`, so we look for a function `use_ChatPlugin` in the generated C code. Here is the syntax for C:

```
extern java_lang_Class* use_ChatPlugin (JRIEnv* env);
```

And for C++:

```
java_lang_Class* ChatPlugin::_use(JRIEnv* env);
```

In the new specification, an `unuse` function is also defined. You should call it when you're finished with the class. Here is the C syntax and the C++ syntax:

```
extern void unuse_ChatPlugin (JRIEnv* env);
void ChatPlugin::_unuse(JRIEnv* env);
```

A word of caution: the `-stubs` option was never meant to be used with classes, such as system classes, that have private fields and methods. To interface with these fields and methods, use the `get` and `set` macros defined in the header file.

In the plug-in code, you will need to associate with a Java class in your code. The plug-in API uses the `NPP_GetJavaClass` function:

```
extern java_lang_Class* NPP_GetJavaClass (void);
```

Here is an example:

```
java_lang_Class* NPP_GetJavaClass() {
    return use_ChatPlugin (NPN_GetJavaEnv() );
}
```

Note how we use the `use` function generated in the stub file to make the association. If you don't want to make an association, simply return NULL. Also note our use of the `NPN_GetJavaEnv()` function to get a handle on the current execution environment. You need to call the `use` routine for all the classes in which you will have native method implementation. Also, you should get in the habit of using the `unuse` routine when you are finished with the plug-in. Here is an example:

```
NPError NPP_Shutdown() {
    JRIEnv* env = NPN_GetJavaEnv();
    unuse_ChatPlugin(env);
```

}

Go ahead and compile your plug-in code. Be sure the stub file is included so that the use and unuse functions are defined.

When you implement the native method, it must follow a specific naming guideline that includes the word native, followed by the class name, followed by the method name. Here is the syntax:

```
ResultType native_ClassName_methodName ( JRIEnv* env, ClassName *self, args...);
```

So for our Chat plug-in, the setConnection method would be implemented as follows:

```
int native_ChatPlugin_setConnection (JRIEnv* env, ChatPlugin* self, int handle) {

    /*
    actual code goes here
    */

}
```

One final note regarding garbage collection in Java: as you know, Java has a built-in garbage collection mechanism that frees objects when they are no longer in use. So what happens when you have a reference to a Java class in your C++ code and Java frees the object? Your program will probably crash. To prevent headaches, either avoid or cautiously use pointers to Java objects. Java runtime interface (JRI) has a native type, jref, that is used to point to (reference) Java objects. Pointers to variables of this type are dangerous. Also, be careful with pointers to stubs and types generated by javah. You need to be familiar with how garbage collection really works in Java if you are going to use these types of pointers effectively. Generally, the lifetime of Java pointers is the same as that of the stack frame in which they are being used. As a result, putting a variable of type jref in the heap or in a global variable will certainly cause problems as the stack frames change during the lifetime of such variables.

Calling Java Methods from Plug-Ins

We now shift gears a little bit and concentrate on how Java applets and plug-ins can communicate using LiveConnect technology. Plug-ins were the first attempt to add non-HTTP functionality to Web browsers. A plug-in is usually written in C or C++ and based on a strict plug-in standard developed by Netscape. Using MIME types, you can configure Netscape browsers to load a particular plug-in when they receive a particular type of document. A plug-in is inherently platform-dependent. Netscape makes available a Software Development Kit for the Windows, Macintosh, and UNIX operating systems. Examples of popular plug-ins are Shockwave, Real Audio, and PointPlus.

NOTE If you want to learn how to make plug-ins, check out the Netscape plug-in guide at http://home.netscape.com/eng/mozilla/3.0/handbook/plugins/pguide.htm. For a LiveConnect/plug-in SDK, try http://home.netscape.com/eng/mozilla/3.0/handbook/plugins/sdk.html.

Because Java applets and plug-ins share space on the Web page, a plug-in might need to call some Java methods to manipulate the applet. In this section, we outline the steps you must take to give your plug-in this functionality. The interaction is shown in Figure 13.11. This section in no way attempts to cover plug-in programming details. For that material, please refer to the Netscape Web site, where you'll find a number of examples and detailed explanation of the development of plug-ins.

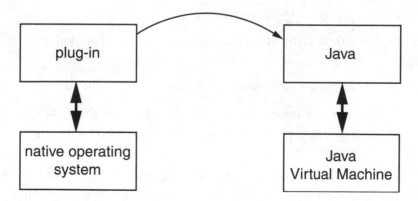

Figure 13.11 Calling Java methods from plug-ins via LiveConnect.

Let's assume you are using the Netscape SDK to develop a plug-in in C or C++. You should first decide which Java classes you will be calling from the plug-in. You need to run the new JRI `javah` on each class. `javah` generates C header files that describe the specified classes. For example, if you plan to call methods from `java.net.URL`, you should run the following:

```
javah -jri java.net.URL
```

Don't forget the `-jri` option. Also, remember to set the CLASSPATH environmental variable or use the `-classpath` option. If the preceding command executes successfully, you will get the file **java_net_URL.h** with a series of macros that enable you to call Java methods and manipulate Java properties. This is all you need to do on the Java side.

If you look at the **java_net_URL.h** file, you will soon see the convention used by `javah` to create the macros. For each class property, `javah` generates two macros: one to set that property and one to get the value of the property. The naming convention is as follows:

```
ResultType get_ClassName_fieldName (JRIEnv* env, ClassName* self);

void set_className_field_Name (JRIEnv * env, ClassName* self, ResultType value);
```

Here is an example that gets the value of the `pathSeparatorChar` from the `java.io.File` class:

```
jchar separator = get_java_io_File_pathSeparatorChar (env, myFile);
```

Similarly, you can use the `set` method to set the value for the `pathSeparatorChar`:

```
set_java_io_File_pathSeparatorChar (env, myFile, "/");
```

The `env` argument is a handle to the current execution environment and is needed by all `getter` and `setter` methods. We will discuss the `env` argument in more detail later in the chapter.

If you are implementing your plug-in using the C++ language, you don't have to be concerned with the preceding naming convention. You implement the necessary methods to change the properties of the class as C++ methods. The class defined in C++ has the same name as its counterpart in Java. Here is the general syntax:

```
class ClassName : ... {
    ResultType fieldName (JRIEnv* env)  { ... }
    void fieldName (JRIenv* env, ResultType value) { ... }
}
```

As you might suspect, the first method is the `getter` method, and the second one is the `setter` method. With the C++ implementation, setting the `pathSeparatorChar` property becomes a matter of ordinary C++ notation:

```
myFile->pathSeparatorChar (env, "/");
```

Similarly, to get the value of this property, you use something like the following:

```
jchar separator = myFile->pathSeparatorChar (env);
```

Your plug-in will certainly need to call Java methods in addition to `getter` and `setter` methods for Java properties. The manner in which Java methods are called is the same as the one shown previously. To get the minute of the current time, you can use the `getMinutes()` method in the `java.util.Date` class. Here is the syntax for the C language implementation:

```
int minutes = java.util.Date.getMinutes();
```

The syntax for C++ is as follows:

```
int minutes = mydate->getMinutes();
```

As you have seen, plug-ins written in C or C++ can call Java methods or access Java properties or both. By doing so, LiveConnect provides a standard mechanism for this one-way communication. You may be concerned about security. Recall that JavaScripts can call only Java methods or access only Java properties that are specifically declared as public. Also, recall that a Java applet can call JavaScript methods only when the MAYSCRIPT attribute is specified in the applet tag. How does this apply to plug-ins calling Java methods? The simple answer is that C and C++ interfaces to Java objects have unrestricted access privileges. Regardless of how a Java method or property is defined, it can be accessed by C and C++, although the LiveConnect specification discourages this practice. The reasoning is that although such a practice might work with some Java implementations (such as Sun JDK and Netscape), it might fail with other implementations.

Earlier we promised to discuss the execution environment handle, which is the env parameter. This parameter is part of all JRI operations created by javah. Aside from being a handle on the current execution environment, it is an encapsulation of the *current* Java thread of execution. Therefore, you should not use the env parameter for other threads. To get this handle, simply call the following, which is part of the plug-in API:

```
extern JRIEnv* NPN_GetJavaEnv (void);
```

We finish this section with a discussion of JRI types. Because C and C++ compilers exist for many different operating systems and because programs written in these languages don't enjoy the uniformity provided by a Java virtual machine, designers for LiveConnect rely on JRI types to achieve interplatform compatibility. Instead of using standard C or C++ types such as int or float, use the JRI types shown in Table 13.2.

Table 13.2 JRI Types

Java Type	C/C++ Type	Size (bytes)
boolean	jbool	1
byte	jbyte	1
char	jchar	2
short	jshort	2
int	jint	4
long	jlong	8
float	jfloat	4
double	jdouble	8

These JRI types are in the file **jri_md.h**, which is included in the main file, **jri.h**.

CHAPTER FOURTEEN

QUICK COURSE IN JAVA

In Chapter 13, we introduced LiveConnect, which facilitates communication among several types of Web tools. One thing LiveConnect lets you do is to call a Java program from a JavaScript. In many ways, Java is a "big brother" of JavaScript. This chapter expands on the Java syntax we described briefly in Chapter 13 and introduces JavaScript's more mature sibling.

Java has received an incredible amount of publicity in its relatively short lifetime. No other application development language in the history of computing has had such an impact in its first two years. The software development tools industry has been gearing up for a major thrust into the Java arena. Sun Microsystems, the originator of Java, has been touting it as the Swiss Army knife of software development environments. Is Java worthy of all the hype surrounding it? Only time will tell, but one thing is certain. For Web designers and application developers, Java is definitely a technology worth knowing a bit about.

The intent of this chapter is to give you a quick, thorough overview of Java. This chapter is not intended to take the place of an entire book devoted to teaching the Java language. The intent is to arm JavaScriptors with enough information to create modest Java programs and to become proficient enough in Java to use it via LiveConnect. Just as JavaScript can be seen as expanding the Web page design capabilities of HTML, Java can be viewed as expanding on JavaScript's limitations. Mastering Java is more challenging than mastering

JavaScript, but JavaScriptors can gain a great deal from only a modest amount of Java knowledge and experience.

This chapter will also give you an idea of the breadth of Sun's Java initiative and will describe how other companies are involved, especially development tool vendors. Java began life quietly as a language named Oak. Oak was designed for use in embedded consumer electronics applications. Java has quickly gone from a mere language to an Internet phenomenon.

JavaScript is a relatively simple language that's easy to learn and use. Thus it's an ideal candidate for those "moving up" the Web page development tool hierarchy. Many people with little software development experience can quickly master JavaScript. Java, on the other hand, fits somewhere between JavaScript on the low end and C++ on the high end. Java is a much more exacting and disciplined language. It might best be thought of as "C++ Light" (only half the fat of the cumbersome C++ syntax). Developers with C language experience should have no trouble learning Java.

Java programs come in two varieties: applications and applets. Java can be used to develop full-scale commercial applications, but to date only a few of them exist. More applications will appear as the language moves from the tools development stage to deployment among application writers and corporate MIS shops. But for now, Java applets, which began as small-scale programs used to add animation to Web pages, are much more common then Java applications. Because they are of more interest to JavaScriptors, this chapter will cover only Java applets.

This chapter will cover:

- The primary differences between Java and JavaScript
- The Java Development Kit: a free Java tool from Sun Microsystems
- Introduction to Java coding via a simple applet
- Java variable types and the operations that can be performed on them
- Java methods
- Java classes
- Arrays in Java
- Java statements
- A second, more complex applet
- Standard Java packages

- Java development tools
- The scope of Sun Microsystems' Java plans
- A few Java Web sites of note

Java and How It Differs from JavaScript

Sun Microsystems introduced Java in the spring of 1995. Sun's first white paper on Java defined it as a "simple, object-oriented, distributed, interpreted, robust, secure, architecture-neutral, portable, high-performance, multi-threaded, and dynamic language." Although this definition may seem like the best collection of buzzwords ever seen in a single sentence, it does say a lot about Java in a minimum of space. Let's look at how Java is different from JavaScript.

Java is an object-oriented language that expands on JavaScript's object-based approach. Java follows the traditional object-oriented language paradigm; everything is defined in the context of an object. Object-oriented languages describe interactions among objects. An object has two primary components: state and behavior. An object's state consists of all data elements and their values. An object's behavior is embodied in its functions, or *methods* as they are called in Java. JavaScript allows functions to stand alone; Java methods must belong to an object. Java, like C++, supports the concept of an object template or *class*. Java classes allow for inheritance; JavaScript objects do not.

Java is compiled and interpreted and sometimes is compiled twice! That may sound a bit strange, but it isn't quite as odd as it seems. Java was designed to be architecture-neutral, meaning that it is meant to run on many types of operating systems (Windows 95, Windows NT, UNIX variants, OS/2, and so on) using various brands of CPUs. Java code is created using a text editor and is compiled using a Java compiler; unlike JavaScript code, Java code is not tied directly to the HTML page. The compiled Java code is kept in a separate file that must be referenced in the HTML page in order for the applet to run. Java follows the more traditional software development loop of separate edit, compile, and debug phases.

The Java compiler creates a *binary bytecode* file from the Java source code file. The bytecode format is not tied to any particular type of existing microprocessor, such as the Intel X86 line. The bytecode format defines a *virtual machine* environment that is easier to execute than the original source code, but more abstract than a typical microprocessor's instruction set. The code generated for a given Java program will be the same no matter which machine it was compiled on. The machine-independent, compiled Java program is then interpreted on a given system using a platform-specific runtime environment. Thus, to enable Java programs to run on a new system, the Java runtime environment is ported to that system. No recompilation of existing Java programs is necessary. Downloading and execution of a Java program are orchestrated by your Web browser.

A quick historical note: The technique of creating portable software by compiling to an abstract bytecode format is not new. Thoroughbred BASIC used this technique to run on numerous operating environments for over 15 years. Others have also used this same principle.

The performance of an interpreted bytecode file will never match that of a program compiled down to a specific processor's instruction set. So some Java environments also include a *just in time* (JIT) secondary compiler to convert the bytecode to machine code as the Java program is being loaded by the browser. A JIT compiler is available for Windows 95.

The Java Development Kit

Although numerous Java development tools are coming to market, the original Java development tool is the Java Development Kit (JDK) from Sun Microsystems. The JDK included in the accompanying CD-ROM is for Windows 95. You can download the software for other platforms from http://java.sun.com/products/JDK. The JDK is currently available for Windows 95, Windows NT, Solaris (Sun's version of UNIX), Linux, other UNIX versions, and the Macintosh. The current release of the JDK is 1.0.2 and is approximately four megabytes in size (compressed). The next major release will be version 1.1, which is due to be released in the last quarter of

1996. Note that there are some differences among the JDKs available on the various platforms.

There are seven major components in the JDK:

- **appletviewer**, a tool that allows viewing (execution) of Java applets without using a browser.

- **java**, a Java interpreter for running standalone Java applications. Note that Java applet execution is performed by a browser or the appletviewer.

- **javac**, the Java compiler. This program converts the source code for a Java program to its bytecode equivalent.

- **javadoc**, an application that automatically generates HTML documentation from specially formatted comments found in Java source code and the code itself. Javadoc creates several HTML files. The files document the inheritance hierarchy of user-created objects, the methods used in these objects, and links to existing HTML documentation of the API objects and methods used.

- **javah**, which generates files that allow Java code to be mixed with C or C++ code. Note that Java applets are currently forbidden to use any language other than Java. However, Java applications can be mixed with code from other languages.

- **javap**, which disassembles compiled Java files and prints a representation of the Java bytecodes. This tool is a sort of "reverse" compiler. It gives you an idea of what the original source code of a Java program looked like.

- **jdb**, a Java debugger. This tool permits symbolic debugging of compiled Java programs.

Full reference page descriptions of each of these tools can be found at http://java.sun.com/products/JDK/tools.

JavaScriptors would need to use only one or two of the JDK tools when creating Java applets. The Java compiler and javac would definitely be used. The appletviewer utility may also be of use.

First Java Applet

Let's dive into a simple Java applet and see what it is made of. It consists of two parts: the source code for the Java applet and the HTML page that references it. Listing 14.1 shows the Java source code for our first applet.

Listing 14.1 DisplayParm.java

```
// DisplayParm.java - Simple Java applet - written by Louis Schumacher
//
// This applet displays a single parameter passed from an HTML page in
// both a window and on the Java console.

// External Java packages used by this applet
import java.applet.*;              // Java applet package
import java.lang.*;                // Java language package
import java.awt.*;                 // Java AWT (windows) package

// Declare applet class
public class DisplayParm extends java.applet.Applet {
    String inputparm = null;       // string to hold passed parameter

    // Called when applet is loaded
    public void init() {
        // get the string from PARAM tag in HTML page
        inputparm = getParameter("displaystring");
    }

    // Called when applet starts (called after the init method)
    public void start() {
        System.out.println(inputparm);  // display on system console
        repaint();                      // redraw string in window
    }

    // Override built-in paint() method
    public void paint(Graphics g) {
        g.setColor(Color.red);       // string will be red in the window
        g.drawString(inputparm, 20, 20);
    }
}
```

Listing 14.2 shows the HTML used to invoke the DisplayParm applet.

Listing 14.2 The DisplayParm Applet HTML

```
<HEAD>
<TITLE>Displaying a string using Java<TITLE>
```

```
</HEAD>
<BODY>
<P>
<HR>
<APPLET CODE="DisplayParm.class" WIDTH=250 HEIGHT=100 ALIGN="CENTER">
<PARAM NAME="displaystring" VALUE="Hello, World!">
You will only see this if your browser cannot handle Java
</APPLET>
<HR>
The source <A HREF="DisplayParm.java" </A>
</P>
</BODY>
</HTML>
```

The HTML APPLET Tag

Unlike JavaScript programs, Java applets are contained in separate files and must be referenced within an HTML page in order to execute. The HTML APPLET tag is used to invoke a Java applet.

The APPLET tag is used in a block that consists of four parts:

- The opening <APPLET> tag
- An optional set of parameters that can be passed to the applet
- Optional alternate text to display on Java-impaired browsers
- The closing </APPLET> tag

Note that the APPLET tag is not an HTML block attribute. APPLET tags should be enclosed within a block delimiter such as paragraph (<P>).

The CODE attribute is mandatory and tells the browser which Java bytecode file to load. By default, the browser searches for Java bytecode files relative to the document's BASE. The WIDTH and HEIGHT attributes describe the size of the window that the browser will create to run the applet in. The values for WIDTH and HEIGHT are in pixels.

The following are optional APPLET tag attributes:

- ALIGN specifies the location of the applet's window relative to adjacent text and graphics. Values for this attribute include ABSBOTTOM, ABSMIDDLE, BASELINE, BOTTOM, LEFT, MIDDLE, RIGHT, TEXTTOP, and TOP.

- CODEBASE -is used to give the browser another search path for Java files. If the path is an absolute path, then only that path is searched for the Java bytecode file. If the path is a relative one, it is added to the end of the document's BASE. This arrangement can be useful if you want to keep your HTML files in one directory and your Java bytecode files in another directory.

- HSPACE and VSPACE define the amount of border space, in pixels, to create as a border for the applet.

- NAME is used to give the applet a name. The name need not be related to any of the names used for the applet's classes. Applet names are used for applet-to-applet communication and to reference applet methods from a JavaScript.

The HTML PARAM Tag

The APPLET block may contain any number of PARAM tags. The PARAM tag is used to pass parameters, one per PARAM tag, from the Web page to the Java applet. The PARAM tag has two attributes: NAME and VALUE. The value of each of these attributes is a string. The Java method getParameter() is used to retrieve the value associated with a PARAM tag. The getParameter() method takes a single parameter, the string defined by the NAME attribute.

Applet One

A Java applet has two files associated with it (not counting references in Web pages). The Java source code is kept in a file with the **.java** extension, **DisplayParm.java** in our example. The compiled bytecode file has the same name but with a **.class** extension. Note that the Java compiler, javac, will enforce the rule of naming the file the same as the class defined in it for *public* classes.

The DisplayParm applet begins with a set of comment lines. *Regular* Java comments follow the same rules as C++. A single-line comment or comment from the current position to the end of the line is denoted using double slashes (*//*). A multiline comment begins with */** and ends with **/*.

Java also has another type of comment, *documentation* comments, which are multiline comments bounded by */*** and **/*. They are used to automatically generate hypertext Web pages from the Java source file. Documentation comments include a few special @ keyword tags. For example, @author denotes a paragraph about the author of the Java program, and @version would indicate the version and date information.

NOTE   Details about various Java language syntax and semantic topics can be found in the Java Language Specification at http://java.sun.com/doc/language_specification/index.html. This is a detailed and somewhat large reference book. (If you print all 22 chapters, it will produce a document three inches thick.) It's a good place to find a full description of a specific Java topic and can fill in many of the details not found in this chapter.

The applet then uses the import command to let the Java compiler know that classes and methods external to this source file will be referenced. The import command is analogous to the C #include command. The import command takes as a parameter the name of a Java package, a group of related classes. Package names start with a lowercase letter; class names start with a capital letter. This makes it easy to tell a package name from a class name. The packages used in DisplayParm will be described in detail later in this chapter.

The Java environment uses packages to deliver common routines and functions useful to all applets and applications. These system packages fill a role similar to that of the standard libraries of other graphically oriented third-generation language programming environments, such as the Microsoft Foundation Classes (MFC) found in Microsoft's Visual C++.

The next item in the applet is the class declaration. Java has a rich set of built-in classes. All applets start by *extending* the built-in Applet class. This means that our `DisplayParm` class inherits all the capabilities of the `Applet` class, which is part of the `java.applet` package. The `DisplayParm` class is declared `public`. The `public` designation gives all other classes access to this class.

The next line is where the one and only variable in the `DisplayParm` class is declared. The variable type `String` is actually a class and not a simple data type. All literals in Java are of type `String`—for example, `abc`. Java has eight built-in data types, which we will get to shortly. The variable `inputparm` is initialized to `null`.

The next item is the example applet is the `init()` method. Four standard methods are called during the lifetime of an applet; `init()` is one of them. The `init()` method is called when the applet is first loaded. Its purpose is pretty straightforward. Here, you perform any one-time startup chores in your applet. In our case, `init()` is where the `displaystring` parameter passed from the HTML document is retrieved.

The `start()` method is next. It is the second in the set of four standard applet methods called during the applet's lifetime. The `start()` method is called as soon the applet begins to run, so it would generally be called automatically by the Java runtime system right after the `init()` method.

In our example, two things are done in the `start()` method. The string passed to the applet is printed two ways. Java has the concept of a *system console*. Messages can be printed to the Java console using the `System.out.println()` method. Under the Options menu of the Netscape browser, viewing the Java console can be enabled or disabled. Console output can be used as a simple debugging tool to allow debug print statements to be separated from the applet window. The JDK appletviewer tool displays console output directly in the DOS window from which it is run.

The call to the `repaint()` method in the `start()` method causes the system to redraw the applet's window. Part of this redraw process is handled by the `paint()` method, which we have overridden in our applet. All the methods that have been coded in the DisplayParm applet already exist in the `Applet` class that we inherited from. Because we coded a version of our own, the system will call the version of these methods in our class and not the version in the built-in class.

The `paint()` method takes a single parameter, the graphics context of our applet. The current color is set to red. The passed-in string is printed again, this time in the applet's graphics window.

The other two standard methods called during an applet's lifetime are `stop()` and `destroy()`. The `stop()` method is called when an applet is stopped by the browser. The usual cause for stopping an applet is that another Web page is visited. The `destroy()` method is called when the browser is completely finished with an applet.

Compiling and Running Applet One

To use the Java javac compiler under Windows 95, you need to start an MS-DOS session (also known as a DOS box). Copy the **DisplayParm.java** and **DisplayParm.html** files from the accompanying CD-ROM to your hard drive. Enter the following command at the DOS prompt to compile DisplayParm:

```
javac DisplayParm.java
```

The file **DisplayParm.class** should be created. This is the bytecode version of the Java applet. The applet is now ready to execute. Let's try it first via the JDK appletviewer tool. Enter the following command at the DOS prompt:

```
appletviewer DisplayParm.html
```

A small graphics window should appear in your DOS window containing a red "Hello, World!" message. The same message should also appear as text in the DOS window (Figure 14.1).

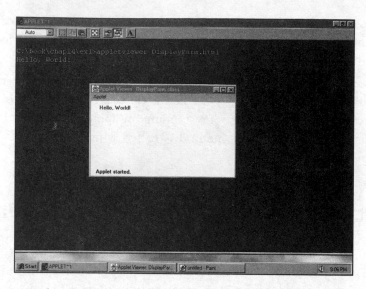

Figure 14.1 The results of running the DisplayParm applet using the appletviewer.

You can also try it from the browser. Remember to enable the Java console so that you can see the console output version of the message. Note that trying to run an applet in a browser by loading it from the local hard drive does not always work. After using the **File|Open** menu item to load the HTML file that references an applet, try clicking in the area that the applet should appear in if it doesn't start. I have had problems getting local Java applets to start in the Netscape Navigator (versions 2 and 3).

That completes the first example applet. It may have seemed like an extremely simple applet, but many important concepts have been covered. You now have an idea of how to use the two most useful JDK tools: the compiler and the appletviewer. It is certainly not a fancy development environment, but the price is right. You also now have a idea of Java's object orientation and use of packages, and you understand how Java applets live outside the HTML page.

The next section will take a deeper look into the components of the Java language syntax: data types, methods, variable scope, arrays, Java statements, and built-in Java packages.

Java Variable Types

Java is a strongly typed language. Every variable in Java must be declared as a particular data type. Strong typing helps detect errors at compile time.

Variable declaration is one of the areas in which Java and JavaScript are quite different. When declaring a variable in JavaScript, you do not have to think about what type of variable you need to create. You simply declare a variable using the var statement. In Java, you must think about the kind of information the new variable will hold (numeric, string, or reference). Then you must use the appropriate variable type keyword when declaring the variable in the applet. As you will see in a moment, Java has many variable types.

Java has two basic kinds of variables: primitive and reference. Java's primitive data types are similar to those of the C and C++ programming languages except that Java's primitive data types are rigidly defined to avoid confusion (and thus help to make Java programs portable). Reference type variables hold instances of a class, interface, or array. Java's primitive variable types are as follows:

- boolean
- byte
- char
- double
- float
- int
- long
- short

The boolean type represents a logical quantity with only two possible values: true or false. Java is more strict than other typed languages, such as C, in that you cannot use a numeric expression where a boolean expression is expected. The statement while(1) would not be allowed in Java; while(true) would have to be used instead. Boolean expressions determine the flow of control in the following types of statements: if, while, do, and for.

The integral numeric types are `byte`, `short`, `int`, and `long`. These variable types hold signed 8-, 16-, 32-, and 64-bit values, respectively. Unlike C, in Java the size of a `short`, `int`, or `long` does not vary according to the word size of the machine (16-bit Windows, 32-bit Windows or UNIX, or 64-bit UNIX). Java does not have any unsigned integral numeric types.

The floating-point types are `float` and `double`, representing the single-precision 32-bit and the double-precision 64-bit formats as defined by the IEEE (Institute of Electrical and Electronics Engineers) 754 specification. This is the floating-point specification that nearly all computers conform to.

The `char` type is a little bit different from the one you would find in most computer languages. The `char` type is 16 bits and is based on the Unicode standard. Unicode, unlike eight-bit ASCII, was designed to accommodate almost all written human languages. All string literals in Java are converted to Unicode. Any Unicode character can be represented using the \uxxxx form, where xxxx is a hexadecimal number. Java includes the `String` class for handling groups of Unicode characters. Note that strings and arrays of bytes are not the same length, as they would be in an ASCII-based language. In a practical sense, Java's internal use of Unicode instead of ASCII means that a conversion may have to be performed when string data is sent into or out of a Java program.

Java has a rich set of built-in operations that can be performed on its primitive data types. The following operators can be used with the integral types (`byte`, `short`, `int`, `long`, and `char`).

Comparison operators:

- The numerical comparison operators <, <=, >, and >=
- The numerical equality operators == and !=

Numeric operators:

- The unary plus and minus operators + and -
- The multiplicative operators *, /, and %
- The additive operators + and -
- The increment operator ++, both prefix and postfix

- The decrement operator ++, both prefix and postfix
- The signed and unsigned shift operators <<, >>, and >>>
- The bitwise complement operator ~
- The integer bitwise operators &, |, and ^
- The conditional operator ? :
- The cast operator, which can convert from an integral to a value of any specified numeric type
- The string concatenation operator +. When given a `String` operand and an integral operand, this operator converts the integral operand to a `String` representing its value in decimal form and produces a newly created `String` that is the concatenation of the two strings

Floating-point values can be operated on with the same operators as the integral types except for the following:

- The signed and unsigned shift operators <<, >>, and >>>
- The bitwise complement operator ~
- The integer bitwise operators &, |, and ^

Here are a few variable declaration examples:

```
boolean ready = FALSE;    // Can only be TRUE or FALSE
short   flags = 0x1234;   // Hexadecimal constants start with 0x
int     counter = 0;
String  message = "All Java statements end with a semi=colon";
```

Java Methods

A *method* declares executable code that can be called, passing a fixed set of parameters in a specific order. In other languages, a method might be called a *function* or a *procedure*. The actual work of the Java program takes place in its methods. Every operation, except variable initialization, that is performed on a data type happens in the context of a method.

All methods have the same four basic components:

- The return type (constructor methods don't have a return type)
- The method name
- The argument list
- The method body

The return type is given right before the method name. A special type of method, a *constructor*, is the only type that does not have a return type. If the method returns a value, it must declare what type of value is returned. If a value is not returned by the method, it must declare its return type as void. The Java compiler makes sure that all methods are called with an appropriate parameter list and that any returned value matches the type receiving it in the calling method.

The method name is the name by which the method is invoked. This works just like function and method names in JavaScript, with one exception. If the name of the method matches the name of the class exactly, it is known as a constructor method. We'll look at constructor methods a little later.

The argument list comes next. It can be blank if no arguments are to be passed to this method. The argument list declares the argument types as well as the argument names.

The body of the method comes next and contains the Java statements that do the actual work of the method. The method body is contained within braces ({}), as with JavaScript functions. Method bodies generally consist of local variable declarations, statements, possibly calls to other methods, and a return statement (if the return type isn't void).

For example, the following simple method returns the square of the int passed to it:

```
public int square_it( int input ) {
    int product;
    // return the square of the input
    product = input * input;
    return( product );
}
```

Methods are one of the fundamental building blocks of the most important Java language construct: the class.

Java Classes

A *class* is a data structure that groups an object's data and methods. A class is used as a template to create (*instantiate*) one or more copies of an object at run-time. Class development, and interaction among classes, is the focal point of programming in Java. Java classes are similar to JavaScript objects and to classes in C++.

Java has a rich set of predefined classes. These classes are incorporated into the packages that are standard in the Java development environment. We have already used some of them in the `import` statements in Listing 14.1.

All classes in Java are part of a structured hierarchy of classes. All Java classes are descendents of a single class: the `Object` class. Every Java class has exactly one parent, or *superclass*, that it is derived from. If a new class is created that does not explicitly state which class it is derived from, the `Object` class is its default superclass. This type of organization makes it easy to add more built-in functionality to all Java classes by adding methods to the `Object` class. In our first class in Listing 14.1, the class `DisplayParm` was declared as extending the `Applet` class.

Class declarations consist of three basic parts:

- The class declaration line
- Instance variable declarations
- Class methods

The class declaration line is used to declare the class name and also to denote any special attributes for the whole class. Traditionally, class names begin with an uppercase letter, and variables with a lowercase letter. This arrangement makes it easy to tell class names apart from variable names.

The class may be declared to be *public*, *abstract*, or *final*. Declaring a class public allows all other classes access to it; otherwise, the class can be accessed only by classes that are part of the same package. An abstract class is one that is not meant to be used as is; another class must derived from it first and "flesh out" the original class. The `final` keyword denotes a class that cannot be derived from. By far the class declaration modifier that you will use the most is the keyword `public`.

The next items in the class declaration are the instance variables. They are the data elements that are part of the whole class and exist as long as the instantiated object of that class exists. Each copy of the object has its own copy of the instance variables.

A twist on instance variables is the *class variable*, which is declared just like an instance variable except that the keyword `static` is added to the declaration. All copies of a specific class that exist at runtime share a single copy of a class variable.

Another useful modifier for instance variables is `final`. This is how you declare a constant in Java. A variable with the `final` keyword must be initialized when it is declared, and any attempt to assign a value to it later will cause a compile error.

Two other types of instance variable modifiers exist: *transient* and *volatile*. These types are not used as much and most likely wouldn't be used by an applet developer unless a multithreaded or database application was being developed. See http://java.sun.com/doc/langauge_specification/8.doc.html for details.

Next are the method declarations. They make up the bulk of most class definitions. We learned previously about methods, the workhorse of Java. We will now expand on that knowledge. Methods have eight modifier keywords that can be used in their declaration: `public`, `protected`, `private`, `abstract`, `static`, `final`, `synchronized`, and `native`. Some of these keywords can be used in combination in a single method declaration.

`Public`, `private`, and `protected` are the classic access control attributes seen in many object-oriented languages. `Public` means that anyone who has access to this class can call this method. `Private` denotes a method that can be used only by the class defining it. `Protected` is sort of an in-between level of access rights; only the original class and those derived from it can use the given method.

An abstract method would fit into the category of "advanced topics." It is a method that declares what parameters the method should be called with and what it will return, but it does not implement the method. Implementation is up to classes derived from this class.

A static method is a *class method*. Static methods are called without reference to a particular instance of an object. Static methods are analogous to static class variables. In contrast, all nonstatic methods (the usual case) are often referred to as *instance classes*.

A method can be declared final to prevent *subclasses* (derived classes) from overriding it.

A native method is a method implemented in some other language such as C. Applets cannot have native methods (applets must consist entirely of Java for security reasons).

A synchronized method acquires a lock before it executes. This type of method is used in multithreaded Java programs. This type of method will often be seen in applets that are declared with the `runnable` attribute.

A constructor method, if it exists, is called by Java when a new copy of a class is created. As in C++, any special object startup work is done in the constructor method. No special keyword is used to denote a constructor; the method simply has the same name as the class itself.

Method declaration can also optionally have a `throws` clause, which is how a method can state which runtime errors, or *exceptions*, may occur when the method is used. A full explanation of Java exceptions can be found at http://java.sun.com/doc/langauge_specification/11.doc.html. Listing 14.3 shows an example of a simple class declaration.

Listing 14.3 A Simple Class Declaration

```
public class Election {
    protected int voters = 0;                  // Count the voters
    protected int incorrect = 0;               // Incorrect votes
    protected static final int DEMOCRAT = 1;   // Political parties
    protected static final int REPUBLICAN = 2;
    protected static final int INDEPENDENT = 3;
    protected static final int UNKNOWN = 4;
    protected int results[] = { 0, 0, 0 };     // Votes by party

    // Count a vote - pass in the candidate name
    public void vote( String candidate ) {
        int party = UNKNOWN;
        voters++;
        if (candidate == "Clinton")
            party = DEMOCRAT;
        else if (candidate == "Dole")
            party = REPUBLICAN;
        else if (candidate == "Perot")
            party = INDEPENDENT;
        switch( party ) {
          case DEMOCRAT:
```

```
        results[DEMOCRAT]++;
         break;
      case REPUBLICAN:
        results[REPUBLICAN]++;
         break;
      case INDEPENDENT:
        results[INDEPENDENT]++;
         break;
      case UNKNOWN:
        incorrect++;
    }
  }
}
```

The previous listing creates a simple class that has a method to count votes. All the instance variables are protected, so only this class and others derived from it may access the variables directly. To be useful, another class could be derived from this class that would have methods to return vote counts and display them.

 Java does not have "header" files, such as those in C that are commonly used to define constants (#define statements in C). Instead, `static final` integers are used here for the same purpose.

NOTE

We'll mention one last item under the topic of Java classes: the special variables this and super. The keyword this refers to the current object, and super references its parent. These two keywords are often seen in object-oriented languages. The keyword this is used when you need to denote the current copy of an object when passing itself as a parameter or as a portable way to reference one of its own methods. super is often used to reference variables or methods in the direct ancestor of the current object.

Calling Java Methods from a JavaScript

When LiveConnect is enabled, JavaScript can reference Java methods in two ways. You can make direct calls to Java methods, or you can call methods in an applet attached to the document. An example of the former would be to call the `System.out.println` method to display a message on the Java console.

In JavaScript, Java packages and classes are properties of the `Packages` object. Java syntax is used to reference Java objects in JavaScript, with the name of the `Packages` object optionally prepended:

```
[Packages.]packageName.className.methodName( parameters....)
```

The name `Packages` is optional for `java`, `sun`, and `netscape` packages. These three package groups come standard with the Netscape Navigator browser. The name `Packages` is required when you're making references to methods in other packages.

Each applet in a document is reflected in JavaScript by `document.appletName`, where `appletName` is the value of the NAME attribute of the APPLET tag. The applet's methods can be called in three different ways. For example, the following HTML code launches an applet called MyApplet:

```
<APPLET CODE=MyApplet.class NAME=MyApplet WIDTH=70 HEIGHT=50>
</APPLET>
```

The applet can be referenced in JavaScript in either of the following ways:

```
document.MyApplet
document.applets["MyApplet"]
```

You can also reference this applet through the `applets` array. For example, if it is the first applet in the document it is referenced this way:

```
document.applets[0]
```

The `applets` array has a length property, `document.applets.length`, that indicates the number of applets in the document. A reference to a particular method within the applet could then be appended to any of the preceding three applet calling techniques.

Further information on accessing Java methods from JavaScript can be found at the following URL: http://home.netscape.com/eng/mozilla/3.0/handbook/javascript/moja.html#Enable_LiveConnect. Look for the section called "JavaScript to Java communication." If this URL is not found, search the Netscape site for the topic "LiveConnect communication."

Arrays

Arrays are actually classes in Java. Java and JavaScript differ significantly in how they handle arrays. Unlike JavaScript arrays, Java arrays cannot be extended. Java is extremely picky when it comes to array handling. Working with arrays is one of the classic ways to crash a C program. In contrast, Java doesn't let arrays get out of hand.

Java has five rules for array handling:

- Arrays can be created only via the `new` operator or by explicit initialization.

- Every array element must be of the same type.

- Every array has a fixed length, given by its `length` instance variable.

- Accessing memory before the beginning of an array (negative array index) is impossible.

- Accessing memory beyond the end of an array is impossible. (Indexes are checked at runtime against the upper bound of the array.)

You usually create an array in Java in one of two ways. The most common way involves the use of the `new` operator on the declaration line. The `new` operator is used to create the desired number of array elements. The second common way is via explicit initialization of all the array's elements. The following two statements declare an integer array of the same size. The second statement sets each element to the desired initial value:

```
int[] results = new int[3];
int results[] = { 0, 0, 0 };
```

Java arrays are zero-indexed (the first element in the array is element zero). In this respect, Java arrays are like C and JavaScript arrays.

Java arrays have an instance variable that can be referenced at runtime to find out the number of elements in an array. The `length` instance variable can be used to make sure an array reference is valid before it is used. In the following example, `index` is the element in the array that we wish to operate on:

```
if ( 0 <= index && index < results.length )
```

You could use a statement like this to make sure that the program does not generate an array bounds exception at runtime.

Indexing Java arrays is usually done using a variable of type `int`. Variable types `short`, `byte`, and `char` may also be used, but variables of type `long` may not. This implies that Java arrays are "limited" to a maximum of four billion elements (an `int` in Java is 32 bits long).

Java does not support multidimensional arrays. It does, however, allow arrays of arrays. A full discussion of the complex topic of Java arrays can be found at the following URL: http://java.sun.com/doc/langauge_specification/10.doc.html.

Java Statements

The syntax of Java statements is very similar to that of JavaScript statements. The most obvious difference between Java and JavaScript statements is that Java statements must end with a semicolon. Java statements would also look somewhat familiar to C and C++ programmers.

Java and JavaScript differ in some of the control structures available. Java has several control statements not found in JavaScript: the `switch` statement (as seen in Listing 14.3), the `do...while` statement, and `break` and `continue` statements that work with a label. Java does not have the `for...in` statement found in JavaScript. This section will be devoted to control statements not found in JavaScript.

The switch Statement

The `switch` statement in Java is very similar to the switch statement of C and C++. The `switch` statement transfers control to one of several statements depending on the value of an expression. The `switch` statement can often be used in place of a series of `if-then-else` statements. For example:

```
switch( day ) {
  case 1:
  case 7:
    weekend_day++;
```

```
        break;
    case 2:
    case 3:
    case 4:
    case 5:
    case 6:
        work_day++;
        break;
    default:
        System.out.println("Day of week must be between 1 and 7");
}
```

The switch statement takes a byte, char, short, or int expression (day in the example), evaluates the expression, and then jumps to a statement with a matching case label. The optional default label, if used, is where control jumps to if none of the case labels matches the value of the switch expression.

The break statement causes the flow of the program to continue with the next statement after the end of the switch statement. If the break statement is not used, execution of the block of statements for one group of case labels will fall into the statements for the block directly after it.

The do...while Statement

The do...while statement is very similar to the standard while statement. The only difference is that the test is at the end of the loop and not at the top. The effect is that the body of the loop is executed at least once. The following is the general format for the do...while statement:

```
do {
    while-loop-body;
} while( conditional ) ;
```

The body section of the loop is always executed once, because the conditional statement controlling the loop is not tested until the end of the control structure. This variety of while statement is not used nearly as often as the standard kind.

The break Statement

You have already seen one use of the break statement: controlling flow in a switch statement block. This was the first of two ways to use a break statement. It was an example of using an *unlabeled* break statement. An unlabeled break statement transfers control to the enclosing switch, while, do, or for statement.

Java does not have a goto statement; instead, it has a *labeled* break statement. The labeled break can be used to transfer control to an arbitrary place in a method. The labeled break simply transfers control to the statement *after* the statement identified with the same label. This technique can be useful to get out of a complex series of conditional statements or control structures.

The continue Statement

A continue statement with no label transfers control to the enclosing while, do, or for statement. The current iteration of the loop is terminated, and the loop over starts on the next iteration.

A continue statement may also take a label. This approach allows the continue statement to go directly to the next iteration of an outer loop in a nested loop control structure.

Try, catch, and throw Statements

These statements are the backbone of Java's exception handling functionality, which is beyond the scope of this "introduction to Java for JavaScriptors" chapter. In a nutshell, Java allows a block of statements to be executed while under the "protection" of error-handling statements. The error-handling statements are executed only if an error occurs.

The synchronized Statement

Java supports multithreaded applets and applications. In simple terms, this means that more than one part of an applet can be running at the same time or that multiple copies of a single part of an applet may run concurrently. This statement can also be useful in animation and other areas.

The synchronized statement is used to gain an exclusive lock on a block of code. The effect is that only one thread may execute the block at a given time. The ability to serialize access to certain resources is often needed in multi-threaded programming.

Second Java Applet

This section is devoted to the second demo applet. This applet, donated by Darryl Stoflet, prints a scrolling text string. The applet has several parameters that can be adjusted via HTML parameters to modify the color of the area around the string. The applet also demonstrates the use of some built-in object methods and of a second thread. Listing 14.4 shows the Java code, and Listing 14.5 shows the HTML.

Listing 14.4 An Applet that Continually Scrolls a Text Message

```
// Copyright 1996 by Darryl Stoflet.
import java.awt.Graphics;
import java.awt.Font;
import java.awt.Color;
import java.awt.FontMetrics;
import java.awt.Image;
import java.applet.Applet;
import java.util.StringTokenizer;

public class Scroller extends Applet implements Runnable {
  String input_text;
  String rgbDelimiter = ":,.";
  StringTokenizer st;
  Color fgColor, bgColor;
  int xpos;
  int width, height;
  int realHeight, realLength;
  Thread killme = null;
  Image im;
  Graphics osGraphics;
  int input_width, input_fontsize, input_height;
  Font f;

  public void init() {
    String s;
```

```
input_text = getParameter("text");
if(input_text == null) input_text = "applet by Darryl Stoflet";

input_width = Integer.parseInt(getParameter("width"));
if(input_width == 0) input_width = 400;

input_height = Integer.parseInt(getParameter("height"));
if(input_height == 0) input_height = 30;

input_fontsize = Integer.parseInt(getParameter("fontsize"));
if(input_fontsize == 0) input_fontsize = 16;

im = createImage(size().width,size().height);
osGraphics = im.getGraphics();
f = new Font("Times Roman",1,input_fontsize);

s = getParameter("fgColor");
if (s != null) st = new StringTokenizer(s, rgbDelimiter);
if (s == null)
  fgColor = Color.black;
else if (s.equalsIgnoreCase("red"))
  fgColor = Color.red;
else if (s.equalsIgnoreCase("blue"))
  fgColor = Color.blue;
else if (s.equalsIgnoreCase("green"))
  fgColor = Color.green;
else if (s.equalsIgnoreCase("yellow"))
  fgColor = Color.yellow;
else if (s.equalsIgnoreCase("white"))
  fgColor = Color.white;
else if (s.equalsIgnoreCase("orange"))
  fgColor = Color.orange;
else if (s.equalsIgnoreCase("cyan"))
  fgColor = Color.cyan;
else if (s.equalsIgnoreCase("magenta"))
  fgColor = Color.magenta;
else if (st.countTokens() == 3) {
  Integer r = new Integer(st.nextToken());
  Integer g = new Integer(st.nextToken());
  Integer b = new Integer(st.nextToken());
  fgColor = new Color(r.intValue(), g.intValue(), b.intValue());
}
else
  fgColor = Color.black;

s = getParameter("bgColor");
if (s != null) st = new StringTokenizer(s, rgbDelimiter);
if (s == null)
```

```
        bgColor = Color.lightGray;
     else if (s.equalsIgnoreCase("red"))
       bgColor = Color.red;
     else if (s.equalsIgnoreCase("blue"))
       bgColor = Color.blue;
     else if (s.equalsIgnoreCase("green"))
       bgColor = Color.green;
     else if (s.equalsIgnoreCase("yellow"))
       bgColor = Color.yellow;
     else if (s.equalsIgnoreCase("white"))
       bgColor = Color.white;
     else if (s.equalsIgnoreCase("orange"))
       bgColor = Color.orange;
     else if (s.equalsIgnoreCase("cyan"))
       bgColor = Color.cyan;
     else if (s.equalsIgnoreCase("magenta"))
       bgColor = Color.magenta;
     else if (s.equalsIgnoreCase("black"))
       bgColor = Color.black;
     else if (st.countTokens() == 3) {
       Integer r = new Integer(st.nextToken());
       Integer g = new Integer(st.nextToken());
       Integer b = new Integer(st.nextToken());
       bgColor = new Color(r.intValue(), g.intValue(), b.intValue());
     }
     else
       bgColor = Color.lightGray;

     System.out.println("Applet by Darryl Stoflet");
  }

  public void paint(Graphics g) {
     paintText(osGraphics);
     g.drawImage(im,0,0,null);
  }

  public void paintText(Graphics  g) {
     g.setColor(bgColor);
     g.fillRect(0,0,size().width,size().height);
     g.clipRect(0,0,size().width,size().height);
     g.setFont(f);
     g.setColor(fgColor);
     FontMetrics  fmetrics = g.getFontMetrics();
     realLength = fmetrics.stringWidth(input_text);
     realHeight = fmetrics.getHeight();
     g.drawString(input_text,input_width,(input_height + realHeight)/2);
  }
```

```java
  public void start() {
    if (killme == null){
      killme = new Thread(this);
      killme.start();
    }
  }

  public void setcoord() {
    input_width = input_width - 5;
    if (input_width < -realLength) {
      input_width = size().width;
    }
  }

  public void run() {
    while (killme != null) {
      try { Thread.sleep(60); } catch (InterruptedException e) { }
      setcoord();
      repaint();
    }
  }

  public void update(Graphics g) {
    paint(g);
  }

  public void stop() {
    if (killme != null) {
      killme.stop();
      killme = null;
    }
  }

}
```

Listing 14.5 Scroller.html

```html
<HTML>
<BODY  BGCOLOR=#ffffff>
<CENTER>
<FONT SIZE = 5><b><i>
Scrolling Text Applet
</FONT></b></i>
<FONT SIZE = 2>
<br>
 by Darryl Stoflet<br>
</FONT>
<IMG WIDTH = 300 SRC = "hruler04.jpg">
```

```
<br><br>

<APPLET NAME = "Scroller" CODE = "Scroller.class" HEIGHT = 20 WIDTH = 400>
<PARAM NAME = "text" VALUE = "Welcome to Darryl's Java Applets">
<PARAM NAME = "width" VALUE = "400">
<PARAM NAME = "height" VALUE = "20">
<PARAM NAME = "fontsize" VALUE = "12">
<PARAM NAME = "fgColor" VALUE = "black">
<PARAM NAME = "bgColor" VALUE = "white">
</APPLET>

<br><br>
<FORM>

This applet offers you parameters for text, text color, background color, height,
width, and font size. <br><br>

<A HREF = "Scroller.java">SOURCE</A>
<br><br>
</CENTER>
</BODY>
</HTML>
```

Example applet two is a major step up in complexity from the first example applet. Applet two begins by importing classes from the Advanced Windowing Toolkit (AWT) package. The first applet imported all the classes from the AWT package (`java.awt.*`), and this example shows that you can import only those classes that you need. The applet also uses the string-parsing class from the Java "utility" package. The applet class declaration looks similar to the one for the first applet example, except that the phrase `implements Runnable` denotes a multithreaded applet.

This applet has many instance variables. Many of them deal with the parameters that can be read from the HTML `PARAM` tags. Several of the variables are used to hold graphics constructs for the font and window display area. Two of the variables are used to control parsing of RGB (color) values from the `PARAM` tags. The `Thread` instance variable is used to create a separate thread to run the applet.

The `init()` method has a lot of work to do in this applet. Remember that `init()` is called as the applet is being loaded. Here is where all the startup work of the applet is performed. In this applet there are numerous parameters to be read. Note the use of the built-in `StringTokenizer` class to parse any RGB input values. The RGB values can use any one of three separator characters ":", "," or ".". The other item of interest in the `init()` method is the use of the `String` class's method to compare strings regardless of case, allowing user to specify "red" as "RED" and "Red," and so on. Even some of the most basic classes in Java have many useful methods.

The `paint()`, `paintText()`, and `update()` methods handle all the graphics issues for this applet, setting the size and color of the rectangle in which the text will be displayed. These two methods also handle the actual display of the text message.

The `start()` method is called by Java just after `init()`. Here, the applet creates a new execution thread. The creation of the new thread causes the `run()` method for the class to be called. So at the end of the `start()` method, we have two Java threads running: the original thread that comes when the Java runtime is started and the new thread we just created.

The `setcoord()` method controls the placement of the text message in the display.

The real action happens in the `run()` method. Here, our new thread loops forever, sleeping for a short time and then repainting the string at a new location to give it movement. The `sleep()` method is built into the `Thread` class. The `try/catch` statement is used to put the applet to sleep for 60 milliseconds while handling the single exception, `InterruptedException`.

The `stop()` method, called automatically when the browser goes to another page, kills the text display thread created in the `start()` method.

Now try running the applet from either your browser or the appletviewer (Figure 14.2). Experiment with changing the values sent to the applet via the PARAM tags. Use the file **Scroller2.html** instead of **Scroller.html** to see a different message and different colors. As I mentioned earlier, often it is difficult to get the browser to start a Java applet from a file on the hard disk. If you can't get the browser to start the applet, try using the appletviewer instead.

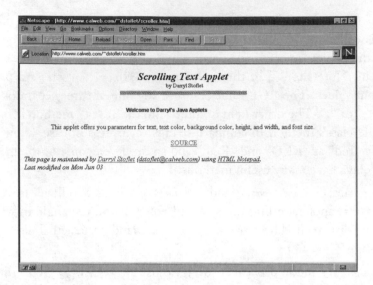

Figure 14.2 The results of running the Scroller applet using a browser.

The next section will be a brief discussion of the standard packages that come with the Java development environment.

Standard Java Packages

Java packages are groupings of related classes and their methods. Each of the example applets uses some of the packages that come with the Java development environment. There are six packages that are part of the base Java system delivered by Sun. These packages have classes that perform numerous useful and needed functions. This group of packages gives every Java developer a common baseline to work with. These packages are all part of the `java` package group.

Several of these packages are documented in the final chapters of the Java Language Specification: http://java.sun.com/doc/langauge_specification/index.html.

The java.lang Package

This the probably the most fundamental package in Java. It defines objects that mirror the primitive data types. It handles Strings and Threads. This package also contains the System class (used in our examples to print console output) and a math library.

The java.util Package

As its name implies, this package is a grab bag of utility functions. This package contains the string token processing class used in the second applet example as well as classes for dates, random number generation, vectors, stacks, and hash functions.

The java.io Package

This package contains classes that handle stream and file I/O. The numerous classes include support for buffered or unbuffered I/O as well as line-oriented text file I/O.

The java.net Package

This package contains the basic classes to support network communications, including sockets and URLs.

The java.awt Package

The AWT gives Java a set of common GUI components. Java programmers must construct their own buttons, text entry fields, and so on. This is the package that helps you do that. The items in this package can be grouped into three areas: display items (for example, a Checkbox), layouts (such as BorderLayout), and general graphics items (Color and Font). The list of display items includes: Button, Checkbox, CheckboxGroup (radio buttons), Choice (pop-up menu), Dialog, Frame, Image (GIF or JPEG), Label (static text), List (a listbox of items), Menu, Panel (a container), Point (a single pixel), Polygon, Rectangle, Scrollbar, TextArea (multiline edit area), and TextField (single-line edit).

The AWT has several layout styles, including BorderLayout, CardLayout, FlowLayout, and GridLayout. The default layout style is FlowLayout. Using these styles directly is an advanced topic. If you end up doing complex Java development, it's a good idea to use a tool that handles the layout with a GUI editor.

The java.applet Package

This package has just one class, the applet class. This is the class that all Java applets begin by extending (inheriting from). The applet class has several useful functions, including getParameter, which is used extensively to obtain applet startup values from the HTML page. The applet class contains the four methods called by the browser during the lifetime of an applet: init(), start(), stop(), and destroy(). This is a rather small, but important, Java package.

You can find further information on these packages in the "APIbook" documentation that can be downloaded from the Sun site mentioned earlier.

You have now been exposed to all the concepts needed to get started developing your own Java applets. This chapter will finish up by taking a few minutes to talk about a few other Java topics: third-party development tools, the breadth of Sun's Java push into the software development arena, and a final word on a few Java URLs of interest.

Java Development Environment

The JDK from Sun Microsystems was the initial development tool for Java programming, and it is still free. But as you will quickly find out, this tool is inadequate to do anything but play with Java.

Many other development products have been created as the software tools industry has geared up for the Java environment. Table 14.1 is a list of first- and second-generation tools available as of this writing. I urge you to investigate these and any other tools that are delivered by the development tools community.

Table 14.1 Java Development Tools

Product	Vendor	Platform
Cafe Mac, http://cafe.symantec.com	Symantec	Macintosh
Cafe Win	Symantec	Windows 95 and Windows NT
Code Warrior, http://www.metrowerks.com	Metrowerks	Macintosh
Roaster, http://www.roaster.com	Natural Intelligence	Macintosh
Visual J++, http://www.microsoft.com	Microsoft	Windows 95 and Windows NT
Java Workshop, http://www.sun.com	Sun Microsystems	Solaris (Sparc and X86), Windows 95, and Windows NT

Sun's "Java Everywhere" Push

Sun does not intend Java to be a language used to add only cute little animations to HTML pages. Sun has much higher hopes for Java. The depth of its plans can seen in several areas.

One of the best indicators of where Sun intends to take Java is its broad API push. The site http://www.javasoft.com/products/apiOverview.html has a complete overview of the extensive list of APIs proposed by Sun for Java. These APIs cover database connectivity, object management and interaction over a network, Internet servers, security, electronic commerce, network management, multimedia, workgroup applications, and software components. If even half of them succeed, Java will have a big impact on the computer industry.

Sun is also working with several chip manufacturers to build Java microprocessors. These chips will execute Java directly and enable the use of Java in inexpensive, network-based computers and consumer electronics.

The site http://www.sun.com/javacomputing has a white paper ("Java Computing Changes Everything") articulating Sun's strategy for Java and describing how it will change the world. This paper is perhaps the quickest way to get a handle on what Sun sees as the reasons Java will take over the world. This site also has a paper to explain Java to a CIO. Will Java take over the world? Who knows? But Sun certainly thinks it has a compelling list of reasons for it to happen.

Java is just starting to have an impact on corporate MIS shops. To date, I have read of only one major development project that has used Java (a major transportation company used Java in place of C++). The strategy paper mentions several other examples of large-scale Java application development.

A Few Java Sites of Note

Numerous Internet sites have information on Java and Java applets. To be sure, the mother lode of Java information flows from the Sun sites http://www.sun.com and http://www.javasoft.com. The shareware site http://www.jumbo.com has a Java section with links to many Java applets and other resources. This site has links to Java programs entered into the "Java Cup" contest: http://sunsite.utk.edu/winners_circle.

The author of the second Java applet example has several other examples and a group of interesting Java links at http://www.calweb.com/~dstoflet. For an extensive look at games written in Java and a few other Java links, try http://plug.pair.com/javagame.htm. Techweb has a site with an extensive amount of Java information and links: http://techweb.com/tools/java.

For a list of all the latest Java books, try http://www.javapages.com/java-pages/index.htm. The Online eZine of Java News and Opinion, by MagnaStar, Inc., is located at: http://www.javology.com/.

CHAPTER FIFTEEN

LIVECONNECT EXAMPLES

The previous two chapters have covered the main LiveConnect topics: the types of communication enabled by LiveConnect, and the Java language. Chapter 13 covered the four types of communication now available among JavaScripts, plug-ins, and Java applets. Chapter 14 was an introduction to Java, the important new technology that LiveConnect allows JavaScriptors to use.

The complexity of using the various LiveConnect communication types or Java programming may seem overwhelming. But don't let that scare you away from LiveConnect. Many sophisticated, professional-quality Web tools have been built with JavaScript in mind.

This chapter will take a look at several LiveConnect examples that you can control using JavaScript. The aim of this chapter is to give you an idea of the types of tools that LiveConnect can add to the JavaScriptor's bag of tricks.

This chapter is intended to be highly interactive. You are encouraged to try out the various examples mentioned here (they are available on the accompanying CD-ROM). This chapter will be a productive learning experience if you try out the examples as you read through them.

This chapter will cover:

- An example of a Java applet calling a plug-in

- Examples of a JavaScript calling a plug-in
- An example of a JavaScript calling a Java applet

Calling a Plug-in from Java

In the following example, a Java applet calls a plug-in, currently the most advanced use of LiveConnect. Action takes place that is not controlled directly from an HTML page once the applet is started. The initial step in using any Java applet is to launch it from an HTML page via an <APPLET> tag and pass any initial values via <PARAM> statements.

PointPlus by Net-Scene

PointPlus allows a Microsoft PowerPoint presentation to be displayed on a Web page (Figure 15.1). PointPlus comes in two flavors: a plug-in that you can download free and install in a Netscape browser, and a Java applet that can be downloaded dynamically as a Web page is accessed. Net-Scene, the makers of PointPlus, can be reached at http://www.net-scene.com.

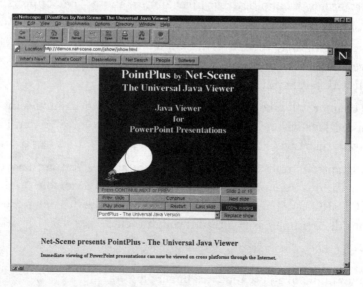

Figure 15.1 The PointPlus viewer for PowerPoint slide presentations (Java version).

The demo of the Java version of the PowerPoint slide player has several slide presentations that you can choose from. The buttons on the player reflect the methods that can be called from Java. The methods are documented later in this section. The demo of this product is quite nice. Note that the Java version of PointPlus also uses the plug-in.

Listing 15.1 is the HTML used to control the page and start the Java version of the slide player. Of particular interest is the applet declaration for SSapplet.class. The PARAM values reflect the choice of slide shows available in the viewer. Note that it may take a minute to download the player and slides when you're viewing this page (http://demos.net-scene.com/jshow/jshow.html). The HTML listing may be a bit long, but it gives you an idea of the features of this product. It also gives an indication of the level of effort and the quality reflected in many of the tools made available to JavaScriptors by LiveConnect.

Listing 15.1 HTML to Invoke the Java PowerPoint Slide Show Viewer

```
<HTML>
<HEAD>
<TITLE>PointPlus by Net-Scene - The Universal Java Viewer - Copyright 1996 by
    Net-Scene</TITLE>
</HEAD>
<BODY bgcolor="#FFFFFF" background="../image/bkg1_g.gif" text="#000000" link="#0000EE"
vlink="#551A8B" alink="#FF0000">
<center>
<table width=80%>
<tr>
<td>
<img src="../image/t-banner.gif" alt="Net-Scene - Welcome to PointPlus" border=0
    vspace=7>
</td>
<td align=center valign=center>
  <h1>The Universal Java Viewer</h1>
</td>
</tr>
</table>
<h3>Beta Version</h3>
<b>Best viewed with hi-color display</b><br>
<!font color=#0000FF>
<i>Please wait while the Java applet is loading...</i>
</center>
<p>
```

```
<center>
<APPLET CODE="SSapplet.class" codebase="classes" WIDTH=480 HEIGHT=460>
<PARAM NAME=SRC VALUE="javaview.jvs">
<PARAM NAME=DEBUG VALUE="false">
<PARAM NAME=TITLES VALUE="PointPlus - The Universal Java Version|ISO: Example for
    an on-line course|TQM: Example for an on-line course|First Aid: Sample presenta-
    tion">
<PARAM NAME=JVS VALUE="javaview.jvs|iso.jvs|tqm.jvs|abc.jvs">
</APPLET>
</center>
<pre>
</pre>
<blockquote>
<blockquote>
<h2>Net-Scene presents PointPlus - The Universal Java Viewer</h2>
<h4>Immediate viewing of PowerPoint presentations can now be achieved across
    platforms through the Internet.</h4>
<pre>
</pre>
<h3>The Viewer</h3>
You may be familiar with the PointPlus Plug-in Viewer, which enables users of Microsoft
PowerPoint to publish their presentations on the Web as compressed files. These presen-
tations are viewed on-line and immediately within the Web browser window.
<p>
Net-Scene has taken this technology one step further by developing a new Java viewer
for PowerPoint presentations that can run on all major platforms.
<p>
The new player does not require installation on the local computer but rather is trans-
ferred automatically via the Internet on entering the HTML page. The Java viewer uses
advanced compression algorithms to reduce the loading time.
<p>
The Java viewer uses streaming to load the slides and can therefore start displaying
the slides 2-3 seconds from the moment the Java applet appears.
<pre>
</pre>
<h3>Advantages</h3>
<ol>
<b><li>Cost-effective content publishing</b><br>
Many people in the organization can create Web content by using MS PowerPoint, without
requiring special expertise. Moreover, past investments are reused when you publish
existing presentations.
<p>
<b><li>Immediate display with minimal waiting time</b><br>
The PointPlus technology produces very compact files. Its streaming capability allows
for almost immediate display of the presentation.
<p>
```

```
<b><li>Viewing across platforms</b><br>
The Universal Java Viewer can display PointPlus presentations on all computer systems
that support Java, including Windows 95, Windows NT, Macintosh, and UNIX systems.
</ol>
<pre>
</pre>
<h3>Main features</h3>
<ul>
<li>Plays PowerPoint presentations on the Web.
<li>Uses streaming and thus allows almost immediate play.
<li>Runs under all major platforms (Windows 95, Windows NT, Macintosh, UNIX , OS/2).
<li>Runs within all browsers that support Java (Netscape 2.0 and later, Explorer
    3.0).
<li>Doesn't need to be installed.
<li>Small Java code allows quick loading.
<li>Automatic and quick converting of PowerPoint presentations into a Web com
    pressed format.
</ul>
<pre>
</pre>
<h3>Release Notes </h3>
The Java Viewer is still in the beta stage and may still be unstable in certain circum-
stances. Also note that different browsers suffer from different problems and bugs in
the Java environment.<br>
Therefore, we recommend:<br>
<ul>
<li>Enable the Just-In-Time (JIT) compiler in your browser to make the application
faster. (This is the default setting in Netscape Navigator 3.0. When using the MS
Internet Explorer, go to the View/Options/Advanced menu command).</li>
<li>To get the most from the presentation, we recommend using a high-color dis
    play.</li>
</ul>
<b>Note:</b> We will update the player version used in this page every few days as we
add more functionality to it. The version number is written on the logo slide, which is
displayed first.<br>
</blockquote>
</blockquote>
<pre>
</pre>
<center>
<A HREF="http://www.net-scene.com"><h3>Visit Net-Scene home page</h3></A>
</center>
```

The page http://www.net-scene.com/DevData.htm lists how to use the plug-in
version of PointPlus from either a JavaScript or a Java program. The directions

for calling the plug-in via Java are much more complex than those needed to call it via JavaScript. This makes sense, because, for the Java version, you must build a whole Java program of your own. The task isn't very difficult, though, because Net-Scene has an example version of the Java program that you can download. (Look for **PPMain.java** and **PPReceiver.java**, which are also listed later in this section.)

The following five Java classes are used when you're building a Java program to control the PointPlus plug-in:

- `PPPlugin.class` defines the PointPlus events that you can activate.

- `PPInterface.java` is a file known to the PointPlus plug-in as well as to your Java applet. It defines a Java interface for the class that receives events from PointPlus. Note that when you're using PointPlus, events will be sent to the plug-in from your program and will also be sent in the other direction.

- `PPReceiver.java` implements the `PPInterface` interface and is responsible for receiving events from the PointPlus plug-in and sending them to your applet.

- `PPSender.java` is used to send events to the plug-in.

- `PPApplet.java` is the interface that must be implemented by your applet. Your code goes here.

The following is a list of the some of the methods that can be called in the PointPlus plug-in via Java. The details of how to put together the Java program are covered in the previously mentioned URL. Note that `PPSender` is the Java class used to send events to the PointPlus plug-in from Java and that all calls to the plug-in must go through the `SendPointPlus` method:

- Go to the first slide:

    ```
    ppsender.SendPointPlus( PPsender.GO_FIRST_SLIDE, 0, null )
    ```

- Go to the last slide:

    ```
    ppsender.SendPointPlus( PPsender.GO_LAST_SLIDE, 0, null )
    ```

- Go backwards and forwards:

```
ppsender.SendPointPlus( PPsender.GO_BACKWARD, num, null )
ppsender.SendPointPlus( PPsender.GO_FORWARD, num, null )
```

- Pause the slide show:

```
ppsender.SendPointPlus( PPsender.PAUSE_SHOW, 0, null )
```

- Start the slide show:

```
ppsender.SendPointPlus( PPsender.PLAY_SHOW, 0, null )
```

- Get the number of slides already loaded by the plug-in:

```
ppsender.SendPointPlus( PPsender.GET_CUR_LOADED_NUM, 0, null )
```

- Get the index of the slide currently being show:

```
ppsender.SendPointPlus( PPsender.GET_CUR_SLIDE, 0, null )
```

When we get to the JavaScript version of the preceding methods, you will see that using the plug-in via JavaScript is much less work than using it via Java. As with all things in coding, the easy way may not be as flexible or give you as many features.

The following listings comprise the PointPlus Java applet example mentioned earlier. Notice that the PPMain class (Listing 15.2) "extends" the PPApplet class. The PPMain code can be used as a basis for writing your own Java applet to control the PointPlus plug-in.

Listing 15.2 The PPMain.java Class

```
/************************************************************************
 *                                                                    *
 * Copyright (c) 1996 Net-Scene Inc.  All Rights Reserved.            *
 * Permission to use, copy, modify, and distribute this software      *
 * and its documentation for NON-COMMERCIAL or COMMERCIAL purposes and *
 * without fee is hereby granted.                                     *
 *                                                                    *
 ************************************************************************
 *  File Name     : PPMain.java                                       *
```

```
 *  Project       : A simple example - getting connected to PointPlus *
 *  Written By    : Oded Cna'an    (OC)                               *
 *  Language      : Java                                              *
 ********************************************************************
 *    Creation   :  OC   16 Jun 96    1:14 pm                        *
 *    Last change:  OC   27 Jun 96   11:09 am                        *
 ********************************************************************/
import PPApplet;
import netscape.javascript.JSObject;
import netscape.javascript.JSException;
import java.util.*;
import java.awt.*;
import java.lang.*;
import java.applet.Applet;
//********************************************************************
//  Class name  : PPMain
//  Description : a simple example
//********************************************************************
public class PPMain extends Applet implements PPApplet {
private String title = null;
private Controls controls;

        //————————————————————
        //  Function name  : init
        //  Description     : get parameters from html
        //————————————————————
        public void init() {
            title = getParameter("title");
            title = (title == null) ? "Simple example - Connecting to PointPlus"
                : title;
            setLayout(new BorderLayout());
```

```
    }
    //—————————————————————————

    //  Function name  : start

    //  Description    : create the controls. passes the 'Controls' class a

    //  pointer to the document.

    //—————————————————————————

    public void start() {

        removeAll();

        add("Center",controls = new Controls(getDocument()));

    }   //end of function start

    //—————————————————————————

    //  Function name  : stop

    //  Description    : when reloading, the connection must be

    //                      created again

    //—————————————————————————

    public void stop() {

        controls.resetConnected();

    }   //end of function stop

    //—————————————————————————

    //  Function name  : getDocument

    //  Description    : returns a pointer to the document

    //—————————————————————————

    public JSObject getDocument() {

            return (JSObject)JSObject.getWindow(this).getMember("document");

    }   //end of function getDocument

}   //end of class PPMain

//********************************************************************

//  Class name  : Controls

//  Description : Create the interface and respond to events

//********************************************************************
```

```
class Controls extends Panel {

private JSObject         doc;

private boolean          connected;

private Button           startBt,stopBt;

private TextField        text,from,to;

private int              totSlides;

private int              state;

private final String     START     = "Start";

private final String     STOP      = "Stop";

private final int        RUNNING   = 1;

private final int        READY     = 2;

private PPSender ppSender;

private PPReceiver ppReceive;

        //————————————————————————

        // Function name  : Controls

        // Description    : Constructor

        //————————————————————————

        public Controls(JSObject doc) {

                this.doc = doc;      // save the document for future use

                connected = false;

                totSlides = 0;

                setLayout(new BorderLayout());

                setBackground(Color.white);

                // add text field

                add("North",text = new TextField(30));

                text.setEditable(false);

                text.setBackground(Color.blue);

                text.setForeground(Color.white);

                // add info areas

                Panel inf = new Panel();
```

```
inf.setLayout(new GridLayout(4,30));

inf.add(new Label("Messages sent to PointPlus : "));

inf.add(to = new TextField(30));

inf.add(new Label("Messages received from PointPlus : "));

inf.add(from = new TextField(30));

add("Center",inf);

to.setEditable(false);

to.setBackground(Color.blue);

to.setForeground(Color.white);

from.setEditable(false);

from.setBackground(Color.blue);

from.setForeground(Color.white);

// add some buttons

Panel p = new Panel();

p.setLayout(new GridLayout(2,30));

p.add(startBt = new Button(START));

p.add(stopBt = new Button(STOP));

add("South",p);

state = READY;

// connection is opened just once

// unless after reload

if ( !connected ) {

        ppReceive = new PPReceiver(this);

        // the string "css" is the name of the embedded
        // plug-in as defined in the HTML file

        PPPlugin css = (PPPlugin)doc.getMember("css");

        ppSender = new PPSender(ppReceive,PPSender.C_PP_SEND,
            css);

        connected = true;  // mark it as connected

}
```

```
        to.setText("Asking PointPlus to stop at the first slide");

        ppSender.SendPointPlus(ppSender.GO_FIRST_SLIDE,0," ");

        text.setText("Connection established. Press start to see the
            show.");

}

//——————————————————————

//  Function name  : action

//  Description     : event handler for buttons

//——————————————————————

public boolean action(Event evt, Object arg) {

            // help button

        if ( START.equals(arg) ) {

            onStart();

            return true;

        }

        else if ( STOP.equals(arg) ) {

            onStop();

            return true;

        }

        else

            return false;

} //end of function action

//——————————————————————

//  Function name  : onStart

//  Description     :

//——————————————————————

private void onStart() {

        state = RUNNING;

        to.setText("Asking PointPlus to play the show from the beginning");

        ppSender.SendPointPlus(ppSender.PLAY_FROM_SLIDE,1," ");
```

```
        totSlides = ppSender.SendPointPlus(ppSender.GET_TOT_SLIDE_NUM,0," ");

        from.setText("total number of slides is "+totSlides);

        text.setText("Starting show");
}  //end of function onStart
//————————————————————————
//  Function name  : onStop

//  Description    :
//————————————————————————-
private void onStop() {

        state = READY;

        to.setText("Asking PointPlus to stop the show");

        ppSender.SendPointPlus(ppSender.PAUSE_SHOW,0," ");

        text.setText("Show stopped");
}  //end of function onStop
//————————————————————————
//  Function name  : onSlideChangeMsg

//  Description    :
//————————————————————————
public void onSlideChangeMsg(int currSlide) {

    if ( state == RUNNING )

            from.setText("Current Slide is "+currSlide+"   out of
                "+totSlides+"  slides");
}  //end of function onSlideChangeMsg
//————————————————————————
//  Function name  : resetConnected

//  Description    :
//————————————————————————
public void resetConnected() {

    connected = false;
}  //end of function resetConnected
```

```
} //end of class Controls
```

The following routine (Listing 15.3) receives the events from PointPlus that
will be sent to your program.

Listing 15.3 The PPreceiver.java Class

```
/************************************************************************
 *                                                                      *
 * Copyright (c) 1996 Net-Scene Inc. All Rights Reserved.               *
 * Permission to use, copy, modify, and distribute this software        *
 * and its documentation for NON-COMMERCIAL or COMMERCIAL purposes and*
 * without fee is hereby granted.                                       *
 *                                                                      *
 ************************************************************************

 *  File Name      : PPReceiver.java
 *                            *
 *  Project        : Connection between PointPlus and Java
 *              *
 *  Written By     : Oded Cna'an     (OC)                                *
 *  Language       : Java                                                *
 ************************************************************************

 *     Creation   :  OC    3 Jun 96   11:45 am                          *
 *     Last change:  OC   16 Jun 96    3:16 pm                           *
 *                        *
 ***********************************************************************/
//************************************************************************

// Class name  : PPReceiver

// Description : this class is specific to a certain application. It
//   must implement the interface (known to PointPlus as well) and
//   may contain calls to specific classes of an application.

//************************************************************************

public class PPReceiver implements PPInterface {

private Controls    showCont;

private int currSlide;
```

```
//─────────────────────────

//  Function name   : PPReceiver

//  Description     : Constructor. Gets the class that it should call.

//─────────────────────────

public PPReceiver(Controls sc) {

        showCont = sc;

        currSlide = 0;

}

//─────────────────────────

//  Function name   : onSlideChange

//  Description     : called by PointPlus. Calls the
//                    ShowControls class.

//─────────────────────────

public void onSlideChange(int newSlide) {

        currSlide = newSlide;

        showCont.onSlideChangeMsg(newSlide);

}

//─────────────────────────

//  Function name : onCssLoaded

//  Description    : in this example it is not in use. Works the same as
//  the onSlideChange member.

//─────────────────────────

public void onCssLoaded(int success) {

}  //end of function onCssLoaded

//─────────────────────────

//  Function name   : onPPError

//  Description     : in this example it is not in use. Works
//                    the same as the onSlideChange member.

//─────────────────────────

public void onPPError(int errCode) {
```

```
        } //end of function onPPError

} //end of class PPReceiver
```

The final listing from the NetScene Java programming example is the sample HTML to invoke the Java applet (Listing 15.4).

Listing 15.4 HTML to Start the Example Java Applet

```
Written by : Oded Cna'an

<html>
<head>
   <title>PointPlus LiveConnect - Example</title>

</head>

<body>

<H1 ALIGN=center>A simple example of a Java application<br>
interacting with PointPlus</h1></center>
<center>
<table width=590 border=3 align=center>
<tr>
<td width=303 height=400>

<applet name=app  code=PPMain.class width=300 height=390
mayscript></applet>
</td>

<td width=280>
<embed name=css SRC=intro2.css WIDTH=280 HEIGHT=400 MOUSE=OFF
BGCOLOR=#AFAFAF CYCLE=NO ></td>
</tr>
</table>
</center>
<p>
</p>

</body>

</html>
```

Calling a Plug-in from JavaScript

The first example in this section builds on the previous example. It uses the same tool, PointPlus, but this time uses JavaScript to invoke the PointPlus plug-in. For most JavaScriptors, manipulating a plug-in in this fashion is preferable to having to write a Java program. LiveConnect allows four types of communication. For most people, JavaScript control of plug-ins and Java applets is the most useful.

The second example in this section uses Envoy, from Tumbleweed Software. Envoy can make it easy to publish formatted documents (non-HTML) on the Web. WebXpresso, by the DataViews Corporation, is the third example in this section. WebXpresso allows data to be fed dynamically to a graphic animation over the Web. The final two examples in this chapter are the FutureSplash product, from FutureWave Software, and Astound's WebMotion animation player.

A JavaScript Control Panel for PointPlus

Again we will take a look at the Net-Scene PointPlus product. The steps needed to use the plug-in via JavaScript are simpler and easier for the average person to handle. One of the reasons I'll show you both ways to use this tool is give you a look at the relative range of complexity covered by LiveConnect.

There are more than a dozen simple methods that can be called from JavaScript to manipulate a PowerPoint slide show. Here are eight of them.

- Go to the first slide:
  ```
  void goToFirstSlide( void )
  ```
- Go to the last slide:
  ```
  void goToLastSlide( void )
  ```
- Go backward and forward:
  ```
  void goBackward( int howMany )
  void goForward( int howMany )
  ```
- Pause the slide show:
  ```
  void pauseShow( void )
  ```
- Start the slide show:
  ```
  void playShow( void )
  ```
- Get the number of slides already loaded by the plug-in:
  ```
  int getCurrentLoadedNum( void )
  ```
- Get the index of the slide currently being shown:
  ```
  int getCurrentSlide( void )
  ```

The plug-in methods can be called using the following syntax:

```
document.css.FUNCTION()
```

FUNCTION is one of the plug-in methods, and css is the name in the PointPlus HTML EMBED tag.

You can see how easy it would be to display a PowerPoint slide show on one of your Web pages using this tool (Figure 15.2). A demo of the plug-in version of the Net-Scene product can be viewed at the following URL: http://www.net-scene.com/JSplayer/JSdemo.htm

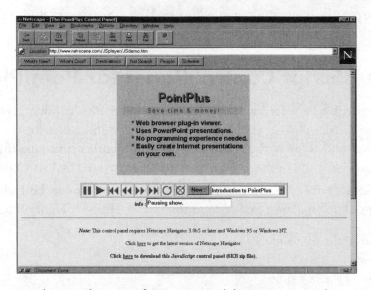

Figure 15.2 The PointPlus viewer for PowerPoint slide presentations (plug-in version).

Note the mention of the ZIP file that contains all the files needed to use the JavaScript control panel. The HTML contained in the ZIP file is included in Listing 15.5. Net-Scene makes it easy for JavaScriptors to use its product. The calls to the plug-in can be seen in the references to document.css. The name of the plug-in is css, as named in the <EMBED> tag.

Listing 15.5 HTML to Create the JavaScript Control Panel for the Plug-in Version of the PowerPoint Slide Show Viewer.

```
<html>
<head>
<title>The PointPlus Control Panel- Copyright 1996 by Net-Scene</title>
</head>
<BODY  background="../image/bkg1_b.gif" BGCOLOR="#FFFFFF" TEXT="000000" LINK="#000080"
VLINK="#000080" ALINK="#FFFFFF">
<center>
<embed name=css SRC="../intro.css" WIDTH=400 HEIGHT=300 mouse=off cycle=yes
bgcolor=#86AEBF>
</center>
<!hr size=1>
<!————————— Control Panel ——————————>
<form name=myform>
<center>
<table border=1 cellpadding=0 >
<td>
<a href="javascript: document.css.pauseShow()" OnMouseOver="top.window.status='Pause
show'; return true;" onClick='myform.info.value="Pausing show."'>
<img src="pause.gif" border=0></a>
</td>
<td>
<a href="javascript: document.css.playShow()" OnMouseOver="top.window.status='Play from
the current slide'; return true;" onClick='myform.info.value="Playing from the current
slide."'>
<img src="play.gif" border=0></a>
</td>
<td>
<a href="javascript: document.css.goToFirstSlide()" OnMouseOver="top.window.status='Go
to first slide'; return true;" onClick='myform.info.value="Returning to first slide."'>
<img src="go-first.gif" border=0></a>
</td>
<td>
<a href="javascript: document.css.goBackward(1)" OnMouseOver="top.window.status='Go to
previous slide'; return true;" onClick='myform.info.value="Returning to previous
slide."'>
<img src="backward.gif" border=0></a>
</td>
<td>
<a href="javascript: document.css.goForward(1)" OnMouseOver="top.window.status='Go to
next slide'; return true;"  onClick='myform.info.value="Advancing to next slide."'>
<img src="forward.gif" border=0></a>
</td>
<td>
<a href="javascript: document.css.goToLastSlide()" OnMouseOver="top.window.status='Go
to last slide'; return true;" onClick='myform.info.value="Advancing to last slide."'>
<img src="go-last.gif" border=0></a>
```

```html
</td>
<td>
<a href="javascript: document.css.setCyclicMode(1)"
OnMouseOver="top.window.status='Make the show cyclic'; return true;"
onClick='myform.info.value="Now in cyclic mode."'>
<img src="loop.gif" border=0></a>
</td>
<td>
<a href="javascript: document.css.setCyclicMode(0)"
OnMouseOver="top.window.status='Cancel cyclic mode'; return true;"
onClick='myform.info.value="Now in non-cyclic mode."'>
<img src="no-loop.gif" border=0></a>
</td>
<td>
<script>
<!--
function changeCss() {
    document.myform.info.value="Loading a new show."
    document.css.changeCss(document.myform.cssName.options
      [document.myform.cssName.selectedIndex].value);
}
// end script -->
</script>
<input type=button
    onclick="changeCss()"
    value="New :">
<!------ Control Panel Files ------>
<SELECT NAME="cssName">
<OPTION SELECTED VALUE="../intro.css">Introduction to PointPlus
<OPTION VALUE="../coke.css">Always CocaCola
<OPTION VALUE="../museum.css">At the museum
<OPTION VALUE="../intranet/intro.css">Intranet Applications Suite
<OPTION VALUE="../mexico.css">Mexican food
</SELECT>
</td>
</table>
<b>info :</b><input name=info type=text value="Net-Scene Player" size=30>
<br>
</center>
</form>
<!---------- End of Control Panel ----------->
<hr size=1>
<pre>
</pre>
<center>
<b><i>Note</i>:</b> This control panel requires Netscape Navigator 3.0b5 or later and
```

```
Windows 95 or Windows NT.
<p>
Click <a href="http://home.netscape.com/comprod/mirror/client_download.html">here</a>
to get the latest version of Netscape Navigator.
<p>
<b>Click <a href="ftp://net-scene.inter.net/pub/net-scene/controlp.zip">here</a> to
download this JavaScript control panel (6KB zip file).</b>
</center>
<pre>
</pre>
<center>
<a href="../down2.htm"><img src="../image/bullet1.gif"  alt="Download" border=0
hspace=5></a>
<a href="../demos2.htm"><img src="../image/bullet2.gif" alt="Demos" border=0></a>
<a href="../try_it.htm"><img src="../image/bullet8b.gif" alt="Try it !" border=0></a>
<a href="../buy_it.htm"><img src="../image/bullet9b.gif" alt="Buy it !" border=0></a>
<a href="../product2.htm"><img src="../image/bullet3.gif" alt="PointPlus" border=0
></a>
<a href="../devprog.html"><img src="../image/bullet11.gif" alt="Developer Program" bor-
der=0></a>
<br>
<a href="../about2.htm"><img src="../image/bullet4.gif" alt="About Us" border=0></a>
<a href="../tech/welcome.html"><img src="../image/bullet10.gif" alt="Tech Support" bor-
der=0></a>
<a href="../press2.htm"><img src="../image/bullet6.gif" alt="Press Releases" border=0
hspace=5></a>
<a href="../contact2.htm"><img src="../image/bullet5.gif" alt="Contact" border=0></a>
<a href="../intranet/welcome.html"><img src="../image/bullet12.gif" alt="Intranet
Applications Suite" border=0></a>
<pre>
</pre>
<a href="../welcome.html">
<img src="../image/bullet7.gif" alt="Net-Scene"  border=0></a>
</center>
<pre>
</pre>
<hr size=1>
<center>
<font size=-1>
<img src="../image/net-logo.gif" width=85 height=22 border=0 alt="Net-Scene"><br>
<a href="../contact2.htm">Questions or  Comments?</a> Please use our contact form<br>
For more information email: <a href="mailto:info@net-scene.com">info@net-
scene.com</a><br>
<pre>
</pre></font><font size=1>
Created  by:
```

```
<a href="http://www.inet.co.il" target=_top>iNet Marketing, Ltd.</a><br>
For comments about this Web site email: <a href="mailto:webmaster@inet.co.il">webmas-
ter@inet.co.il</a><br>
</font>
</center>
</body>
</html>
```

Envoy by Tumbleweed Software

Envoy (Figure 15.3) enables the electronic distribution of formatted documents. The basic idea behind Envoy is that any application can be used to create a document that can then be converted to the Envoy format for publishing on the Web. The Envoy viewer and plug-in are available free of charge from Tumbleweed Software at http://www.tumbleweed.com/viewer.htm. Try out the Envoy LiveConnect demo at http://www.tumbleweed.com/demo/lcmouse.htm

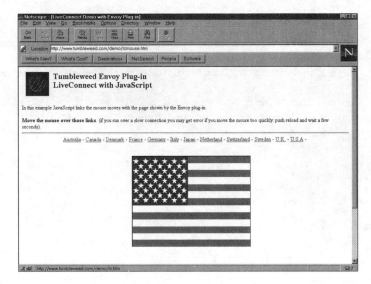

Figure 15.3 The Envoy LiveConnect example displaying flags of the world.

As you move the mouse over the various country names, you will see a color image of that country's flag.

You can view the JavaScript source to this demo by clicking on **View/Document Source** in a Netscape browser. The items listed under **Commands** give you an idea of what can be done with this tool. The code to display each flag as a page in an Envoy document is essentially just a single line:

```
document.myenvoydoc.setCurrentPage(current);
```

The main LiveConnect Envoy page is http://www.tumbleweed.com/demo/lc.htm

WebXpresso by DataViews Corporation

WebXpresso is a sophisticated tool that allows you to dynamically feed information to a graphic animation over the Web. You can embed dynamic WebXpresso drawings into any HTML document or use dynamic WebXpresso drawings in custom Java applets. Dynamic WebXpresso drawings can display information from any data source. You can make connections to databases and real-time data sources using any Web data connection. Alternatively, you can develop data connections via custom programs written as a Common Gateway Interface (CGI) script or as Java, C, or C++ applications.

Graphics are animated by feeding a stream of resources into the drawing after it has been loaded into the plug-in. This resource stream can originate from a client-side script or from the Web server.

The home page for WebXpresso is http://www.dvcorp.com/wx/index.html. Figure 15.4 shows one of the demos found at the WebXpresso site http://www.dvcorp.com/wx/lcautodemo/index.html. This is an interesting demo to play around with.

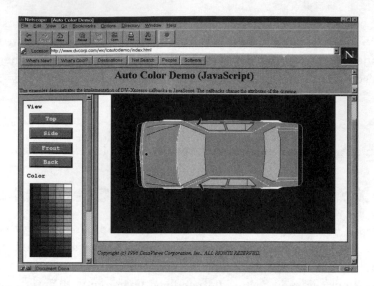

Figure 15.4 An interactive car painting program, an example of WebXpresso.

Listing 15.6 is the HTML used to control the car painting demo.

Listing 15.6 HTML and JavaScript to Control the Car Demo

```
<html>
<head>
<script>
function get_data(form) {
   var red = top.tocframe.display.document.auto.getGResourceX("back/body/FillColor");
   var green = top.tocframe.display.document.auto.getGResourceY("back/body/FillColor");
   var blue = top.tocframe.display.document.auto.getGResourceZ("back/body/FillColor");
   form.data0.value = red;
   form.data1.value = green;
   form.data2.value = blue;
}
function reg_call() {
   document.simple1.setSelectCallback("select_callback");
   document.simple1.setInputCallback("input_callback");
}
function settingsArray (name) {
   this.name = name;
}
function splitString (stringToSplit) {
   arrayOfStrings = stringToSplit.split("&")
```

```
        settings = new settingsArray("settings");
        for (var i=0; i < arrayOfStrings.length; i++) {
            nameVal = arrayOfStrings[i].split("=")
            settings[nameVal[0]] = nameVal[1]
        }
        if (settings["Origin"] == "top") {
          top.tocframe.display.document.auto.setDResource("top/Visibility", 1);
          top.tocframe.display.document.auto.setDResource("side/Visibility", 0);
          top.tocframe.display.document.auto.setDResource("front/Visibility", 0);
          top.tocframe.display.document.auto.setDResource("back/Visibility", 0);
          top.tocframe.display.document.auto.update();
        }
        if (settings["Origin"] == "side") {
          top.tocframe.display.document.auto.setDResource("top/Visibility", 0);
          top.tocframe.display.document.auto.setDResource("side/Visibility", 1);
          top.tocframe.display.document.auto.setDResource("front/Visibility", 0);
          top.tocframe.display.document.auto.setDResource("back/Visibility", 0);
          top.tocframe.display.document.auto.update();
        }
        if (settings["Origin"] == "front") {
          top.tocframe.display.document.auto.setDResource("top/Visibility", 0);
          top.tocframe.display.document.auto.setDResource("side/Visibility", 0);
          top.tocframe.display.document.auto.setDResource("front/Visibility", 1);
          top.tocframe.display.document.auto.setDResource("back/Visibility", 0);
          top.tocframe.display.document.auto.update();
        }
        if (settings["Origin"] == "back") {
          top.tocframe.display.document.auto.setDResource("top/Visibility", 0);
          top.tocframe.display.document.auto.setDResource("side/Visibility", 0);
          top.tocframe.display.document.auto.setDResource("front/Visibility", 0);
          top.tocframe.display.document.auto.setDResource("back/Visibility", 1);
          top.tocframe.display.document.auto.update();
        }
        if (settings["Origin"] == "color") {
top.tocframe.display.document.auto.setGResource("back/body/FillColor",
            parseFloat(settings["Value1"]),parseFloat(settings["Value2"]),
            parseFloat(settings["Value3"]));
          top.tocframe.display.document.auto.update();
        }
}
function select_callback(query) {
}
function input_callback(query) {
    splitString(query)
}
var myPlugin = navigator.plugins["WebXpresso"];
```

```
if (myPlugin) {
    document.writeln("<embed SRC=autoinput.xpg NAME=simple1 WIDTH=100%
        HEIGHT=100%>");
    document.writeln("<body onLoad = reg_call()>");
    document.writeln("<form NAME=demo>");
    document.writeln("<input name=data0 type=text size=5 >");
    document.writeln("<input name=data1 type=text size=5 >");
    document.writeln("<input name=data2 type=text size=5 >");
    document.writeln("<input type=button value=Get Data
        onclick='get_data(this.form)'>");
    document.writeln("</form>");
}
</script>
<I>
<p> Copyright (c) 1996 DataViews Corporation, Inc., ALL RIGHTS RESERVED. </p>
</I>
```

Following are the JavaScript methods you can use in WebXpresso HTML files to control the plug-in:

- Set a resource that takes a double value. resource is a string and value is a float.

  `setDResource( resource, value )`

- Set a resource that takes three double values, such as a geometrical point with x, y, and z values or an RGB value. resource is a string and value1, value2, and value3 are floats.

  `setGResource( resource, value1, value2, value3 )`

- Set a resource that takes a string value. resource is a string and value is a string.

  `setSResource( resource, value )`

- Set a callback to be called on a select event. callback is a string.

  `setSelectCallback( callback )`

- Set a callback to be called on an input event. callback is a string.

  `setInputCallback( callback )`

- Update the graph.

  `update()`

- Reset the graph to its original state. This method applies only under Windows.

  `reset()`

- Draw the graph. This method applies only under Windows.

```
        draw()
```
- Set up the widget drawing hierarchy.
```
        setup()
```
- Get the value of a resource that takes a double value. `resource` is a string. Returns a float value.
```
        getDResource( resource )
```
- Get the first value of a resource that takes three double values such as a geometrical point with x, y, and z values or an RGB value. `resource` is a string. Returns a float value.
```
        getGResourceX( resource )
```
- Get the second value of a resource that takes three double values such as a geometrical point with x, y, and z values or an RGB value. `resource` is a string. Returns a float value.
```
        getGResourceY( resource )
```
- Get the third value of a resource that takes three double values such as a geometrical point with x, y, and z values or an RGB value. `resource` is a string. Returns a float value.
```
        getGResourceZ( resource )
```
- Get the value of a resource that takes a string value. `resource` is a string. Returns a string value
```
        getSResource( resource )
```

To get a look at the complete documentation for the WebXpresso plug-in, check out http://www.dvcorp.com/wx/webxprdoc/index.html.

FutureSplash by FutureWave Software

FutureSplash is a LiveConnect-enabled animation plug-in that can be used to create highly interactive Web pages. FutureSplash can be used to play a movie or zoom in on areas of a map. FutureSplash buttons and frame actions can use JavaScript to control a FutureSplash movie, Java applet, or LiveConnect-enabled plug-in.

To view the FutureSplash demo (Figure 15.5) you will need to install the FutureSplash plug-in. The URL for the Windows 95/NT version can be found at http://www.futurewave.com/fssetup/downloadfsw95.htm.

After installing the plug-in, try taking the "tour of Hawaii" at http://www.futurewave.com/scripting/index.html.

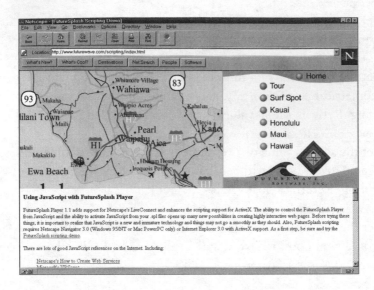

Figure 15.5 The FutureSplash demo: a tour of the state of Hawaii.

There are two basic actions you can perform with FutureSplash scripting. First, you can control the FutureSplash Player using a method such as `Play()`, `GotoFrame()`, or `CurrentFrame()`. The second type of action is to send a message from a FutureSplash button or frame action to JavaScript code in your Web page using `FSCommand`.

Following are the callable methods of the FutureSplash player.

- Start playing the animation:

    `Play()`

- Stop playing the animation:

    `StopPlay()`

- Find out whether the movie is currently playing:

    `IsPlaying()`

- Go to a specific frame of the movie:

    `GotoFrame( int frameNum )`

- Get the total number of frames in the movie:

```
TotalFrames()
```
- Go to the first frame:
```
Rewind()
```
- Zoom in on a rectangular area of the movie:
```
SetZoomRect( int left, int top, int right, int bottom )
```
- Zoom the view by a relative scale factor:
```
Zoom( int percent )
```
- Pan a zoomed-in movie:
```
Pan()
```
- Find out what percentage of the movie has been loaded by the browser so far:
```
PercentLoaded()
```

Calling a Java Applet from JavaScript

This section contains an example of a Java-based tool that can be called from JavaScript. The example is the WebMotion Java animation player by Astound.

WebMotion by Astound

WebMotion is a Java animation player that can be controlled via JavaScript. The player can be controlled using more than 20 methods, all callable from JavaScript. A LiveConnect example using WebMotion (Figure 15.6) can be viewed at http://www.astoundinc.com/webmotion/demo/liveconnect.html.

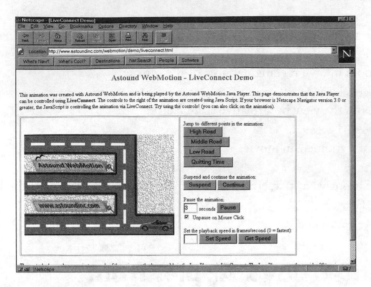

Figure 15.6 A demonstration of the WebMotion Java animation player.

If you view the document source of the page shown in Figure 15.6, you can see how simple it is to control the animation player from JavaScript. For example, here is the code to control pausing the player:

```
Suspend and continue the animation:<br>
<INPUT TYPE="button"
       VALUE="Suspend"
       onClick="document.animApp1.suspendAnim()">
<INPUT TYPE="button"
       VALUE="Continue"
       onClick="document.animApp1.playAnim()">
```

Following is a sampling of the WebMotion methods available to JavaScript. The full list of them can be seen at http://www.astoundinc.com/webmotion/demo/awmapi.html.

- Load an animation playback file:
  ```
  loadAnim ( String strDataPath, String strDataFile, boolean bStream )
  ```
- Start playing the animation file:
  ```
  playAnim()
  ```
- Pause the animation for a given amount of time:
  ```
  pauseAnim( int iSeconds, boolean bCancelOnClick )
  ```

- Go to a given frame in the animation:

    `gotoFrame( int iFrame )`
- Get the number of frames in the animation:

    `int getFrameCount()`
- Set the speed of the animation in frames per second:

    `setSpeed( int iFPS )`
- Tell the player to play the animation in a continuous loop:

    `setDoLoop( boolean bLoop )`

Conclusion

This chapter could go on for quite a while longer, listing one LiveConnect-enabled plug-in or Java applet after another. By this time you must have a sense of the breadth, quantity, and sophistication of the tools available on the Web that JavaScriptors can take advantage of.

I hope you have enjoyed our little journey into the world beyond the cozy confines of the HTML page and JavaScript. It may be more complicated than you are used to, but the potential for building lively, rich Web sites is enormous! As they say in the weight room, no pain, no gain. With LiveConnect, JavaScriptors can leverage someone else's pain for their own gain.

Part Four

Using LiveWire

Chapters 16-18 by Edward Sfreddo

CHAPTER SIXTEEN

USING LIVEWIRE

Now that we've covered some of the core JavaScript technologies, it's time to talk about server-side JavaScript. In this chapter, we'll introduce LiveWire, a tool that, among other things, communicates with an existing database, letting you put your product catalog on the World Wide Web. LiveWire also gives you a frame work for collaborating with other Web users so that you can, for example, create your own chat room.

Why is LiveWire such a popular tool? First, it uses JavaScript for its scripting language. It's also one of the easiest tools you can use to connect with a range of industry-standard databases, including Sybase, Informix, and others. After you've read this chapter and Chapter 17, which discusses Structured Query Language, you'll be ready to start creating your own applications.

This chapter covers:

- An overview of LiveWire
- The LiveWire development environment
- LiveWire and LiveWire Pro
- The LiveWire application architecture
- Developing a LiveWire application
- The LiveWire object framework

An Overview of LiveWire

LiveWire is a development environment that allows developers to create the next generation of interactive Web applications. LiveWire gives us the tools and techniques to develop Web sites that provide easy access to stores of data. For example, we can develop applications that search and display information from corporate databases. Or we can create applications that allow shopping or other types of electronic commerce. LiveWire also lends itself to the development of applications that provide interactivity and collaboration between multiple users at the same time. These applications may run over the Internet or over a corporate intranet. When combined with existing Netscape development technologies such as Java applets and inline plug-ins, LiveWire lets us add multimedia capability to interactive, data-centric applications, resulting in innovative, sophisticated Web sites.

LiveWire includes software tools to create and edit pages containing HTML and JavaScript, support the scripting language JavaScript on the Web server, build, debug, and install Web applications, and manage Web site pages and links.

LiveWire frees us from the limitations and complexities of CGI, the method employed by most interactive Web-based applications. The limitations of CGI result in a rather one-dimensional type of interactivity. The complexity of CGI stems from having to program in C or Perl to create external scripts. LiveWire gives us a scripting language, called server-side JavaScript, to create scripts that run on the Web server. This arrangement has the effect of extending the functionality of the server.

Server-side JavaScript shares its syntax and statements with client-side JavaScript, but server-side JavaScript can use objects that exist only on the server. Creative use of the methods and properties of these objects, and the use of the JavaScript server functions, is the key to unlocking the potential of server-side JavaScript.

System Requirements

LiveWire runs on the Windows NT and UNIX operating systems. To make full use of the LiveWire development environment, you first need to install and configure the Netscape FastTrack server or Netscape Enterprise server.

You can download LiveWire for a 60-day test drive for free. Check the Netscape Web site for details (www.netscape.com).

Because LiveWire is new and because Internet software is evolving quickly, you'll want to become familiar with the Netscape Web site to get the latest information on product availability. At the time of this writing, a release version of LiveWire was available only for Windows NT. Beta versions of LiveWire were available for UNIX and Macintosh. However, there is no MacOS version of a Netscape server, so you won't be able to run any applications without moving them to another platform.

The LiveWire Development Environment

LiveWire consists of a suite of tools that makes it easier to create Web pages, develop Web applications, and manage Web sites. Let's look at these tools in detail.

Netscape Navigator Gold

This is the same Navigator browser software we've all come to know and love, plus features that make it easy to create Web pages for LiveWire applications. You view the current document with the browser and edit the same document using the built-in HTML editor. You can see the results of your changes immediately in the browser. Navigator Gold creates HTML for you by using a point-and-click user interface.

Netscape Navigator Gold has a number of features:

- Edit mode saves a document to your local drive for editing.
- The HTML editor is WYSIWYG (what you see is what you get).
- You can create links using drag and drop
- The browser supports text editing for client-side and server-side JavaScript. Use **Properties | Character** to color-code and tag JavaScript.

- You can upload Web pages to your server using **File | Publish**.
- You can adjust links automatically for local editing or remote publishing.

You don't have to use Navigator Gold to develop LiveWire applications. You can use regular Navigator plus a text editor to accomplish the same job, but Navigator Gold makes some Web development tasks a little more pleasant.

Site Manager

Site Manager is a tool that provides a point-and-click interface for managing Web sites. It helps you detect and correct invalid links, a tedious task when done manually. Site Manager also contains gurus that can automatically create a framework for new Web sites. Another important feature is the LiveWire compiler, sometimes called Build WEB because of its location on the menu bar. You don't need Site Manager to use the compiler, because it has a command-line interface. In fact, the command line is preferable to most programmers. Nevertheless, the compiler is packaged with Site Manager.

Application Manager

Application Manager is a tool that is used to install, start, stop, modify, and debug your LiveWire applications. It's easy to use. You must use this tool to develop, operate, and maintain a LiveWire application.

LiveWire Server Extensions

LiveWire server extensions provides the following functionalities to a Netscape Web server:

- The ability to process server-side JavaScript.
- Support for activities conducted using Application Manager.
- The ability for server-side JavaScript to call functions in external libraries written in C or C++.

LiveWire and LiveWirePro

LiveWire Pro is identical to LiveWire except that it includes a version of Informix, a commercial relational database management system (RDBMS). The Windows NT version of LiveWire Pro also includes the Crystal Reports report generator. If you don't already have a database, you may want to buy this package. You'll have to install the database separately before you can use it. However, LiveWire gives you connectivity to most major databases through Microsoft's Open Database Connectivity (ODBC), and you may want to use an existing database or one that you are more comfortable with. The Crystal Reports report generator may come in handy if you need a quick method to extract and format data from your database. The installation and use of these two software products are beyond the scope of this chapter. I suggest that you browse Netscape's Web site or contact Netscape directly for more information.

LiveWire Application Architecture

A LiveWire application consists of files that reside on a Web server. The Web server must be a Netscape Enterprise server or Netscape FastTrack server, and it must have LiveWire installed on it. The application comprises source files and a Web file.

Source files are generally HTML pages and usually contain some embedded server-side JavaScript. Another type of source file has the file extension **.js** and contains only JavaScript functions. These functions may be referenced by the application at runtime.

The Web file is an executable file created by the application developer using the LiveWire compiler. The compiler takes the source files as input and creates the Web file as output. The Web file executes when you run the application.

The files that make up the LiveWire application reside in the application directory. This directory on the Web server is specified by the developer.

A LiveWire application has its own URL on the server. For example:

```
http://myserver.domain/myfirstapp
```

When a browser requests a URL beginning with `http://myserver.domain/myfirstapp`, the Web server will generate HTML using the specified URL.

When the URL of a LiveWire application is entered on a browser, the server receives the request just as it would for any other URL. However, the LiveWire-enabled server recognizes the URL as belonging to a LiveWire application. The server then gets the source file specified by the URL. The source file, or HTML page, is processed by the LiveWire server extension. Any embedded server-side JavaScript scripts on the page are processed. These scripts are generally used to modify the HTML page before it is sent to the browser. The page may be modified so that data from a file, a database, or a LiveWire object is embedded into the HTML. When the page has been processed from top to bottom, it is sent to the browser.

For example, suppose a page from a LiveWire application is requested that contains the following server-side script:

```
<SERVER>
write("You are using following browser:" + client.browser)
</SERVER>
```

The statements between the `<SERVER>` and `</SERVER>` tags are processed before the page is sent to the browser. In this case, LiveWire appends the value of `client.browser` (from the LiveWire object framework) to the text and writes it to the HTML page. When the browser receives the page, it doesn't care how the page was generated. It just formats the page and presents it to the user:

```
You are using the following browser: Netscape Navigator 2.0
```

This is dynamically generated HTML. It's yours for the taking.

After the user views the page, he or she may click on a link, requesting another page. This page is processed by the server and the cycle is repeated. The application is interactive, because server scripts can use information from the client, together with the current clicked link, to formulate an appropriate response in the form of the next dynamically generated page. A LiveWire application may generate HTML containing almost anything, including client-side JavaScript. In other words, LiveWire allows us to dynamically generate client-side functionality. In the world of the Internet, this is powerful stuff.

Figure 16.1 illustrates the sequence of events between a browser and a static Web site. The user types in a URL and presses **Enter**. A request for that URL is formulated by the browser and sent over the Internet to the desired server. The server receives the request, finds the requested page, and sends it back to the original browser. The browser receives the document and formats it on the screen for display.

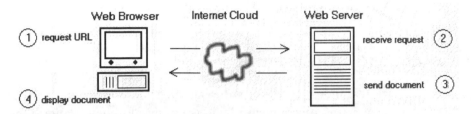

Figure 16.1 Browsing a Static Web site.

Figure 16.2 illustrates the sequence of events between a browser and a LiveWire application. The user types in the application URL and presses **Enter**. A request for that URL is formulated by the browser and sent over the Internet to the LiveWire-enabled server. The server receives the request and checks whether the URL belongs to a LiveWire application. If it does, the server parses the HTML page corresponding to the URL. It processes any server-side JavaScript on the page, getting data from the database server when necessary. Once the page has been generated, it is sent back to the browser. The browser receives the document and formats it on the screen for display.

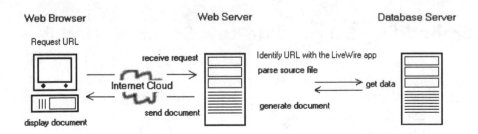

Figure 16.2 Browsing a LiveWire application.

Developing a LiveWire Application

The steps required to create a LiveWire application are as follows:

1. Create the source files.
2. Compile the LiveWire application.
3. Install the application using Application Manager.

Create the Source Files

Source files are text files that serve as the building blocks of your LiveWire application. They are used as input to build your LiveWire application using the LiveWire compiler. You can create source files by using Navigator Gold or your favorite text editor (or both).

Source files are of two types:

- HTML-only files, or HTML with embedded server-side JavaScript. These filenames usually end with **.htm** or **.html**. A special <SERVER> tag is used to delimit server-side JavaScript within the HTML.

- Files containing JavaScript functions only. These filenames end in **.js**. They may be referenced by server-side JavaScript in HTML files in the application. There are no special tags used in these files. The creation and use of these files is optional.

Embedding Server-Side JavaScript in HTML

Server-side JavaScript is embedded in HTML source files using the SERVER tag. You place your JavaScript statements between the <SERVER> and </SERVER> tags. The statements you write can generate HTML or may execute server-side JavaScript to do other things—use the object framework, access a database, or almost anything that JavaScript can do.

HTML is generated using the write() function or the backquote (`). You can use write() in almost every case. The only parameter required for the write() method is a string of HTML that you wish to send to the browser.

There can be many `write` statements in one HTML source file. In fact, your HTML source file may consist of nothing but `<HTML>` and `</HTML>` tags and a ton of `write` statements between SERVER tags. In this case, the entire HTML file is dynamically generated. So, from your server-side JavaScript, you can generate client-side JavaScript or anything else that is allowed in HTML. You need use backquotes only when you substitute the result of JavaScript expressions for HTML attribute names or values. This technique can get a little confusing because of the nesting of quotes and backquotes.

The following example creates an anchor tag with a hyperlink. In this scenario, the value of part of the hyperlink was read from a database table:

```
<A HREF = '"products/html/" + cursor.product_name + ".html"'> Adventure </A>
```

The backquotes enclose an entire JavaScript expression. They must be on the outside, because anything enclosed within double quotes is a string literal and is not processed by LiveWire. When LiveWire processes this HTML, it evaluates the expression within backquotes. It concatenates a string literal with an object property (`cursor.product_name`) and another string literal. Then it replaces the backquotes with double quotes and writes the anchor tag to the HTML as follows:

```
<A HREF = "products/html/adventure.html"> Adventure </A>
```

Compile the LiveWire Application

The source files are used as input to the LiveWire compiler. The compiler will create an executable file (**filename.Web**). You can use Site Manager for this step, or you can invoke the compiler at the command line of the operating system you are using. If you are using Site Manager, you must first bring the source files under site management by selecting the appropriate application directory and selecting **Site | Manage**. Then you choose the **Build | WEB** selection to compile the application.

The command-line interface is as follows:

```
lwcomp [-c|-v|?] [-o outputfile.Web] [mypage1.html . mypage2.html . mypageN.html]
    [jsfunctions1.js jsfunctions2.js ... jsfunctionsN.js]
```

Note the following:

- `lwcomp` invokes the compiler.
- Anything between brackets [ ] is optional.
- Choose –c or –v or ?, if you're choosing any one of them at all.
  - –c checks syntax only; it does not generate an executable application.
  - –v means verbose; give me all messages from the compiler.
  - ? gives you compiler usage help.
  - –o is required; it is the name of the executable application file
- At least one **.html** or **.js** source file is required by the compiler

The following example creates a **.web** file named **myfirstapp.web**, using three source files:

```
lwcomp -v -o myfirstapp.web mypage1.html mypage2.html jsfunctions1.js
```

In general, you must recompile your LiveWire application whenever you add or remove source files or make changes to any of your source files. To make the rebuilt application available to your browser, use Application Manager to restart the application.

Install the Application

To run a LiveWire application for the first time, you must install it using Application Manager (Figure 16.3). This one-time procedure registers the application with the Web server. To invoke Application Manager, enter the following URL in your browser:

```
http://myserver.domain/appmgr
```

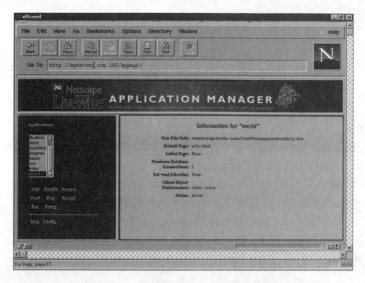

Figure 16.3 LiveWire Application Manager.

Application Manager displays a list of all LiveWire applications installed on the Web server. The sample applications that come with LiveWire are in this list. You can see information about an application when you select its name from the list. When you install your own application, you supply this information.

To install an application, click Add. Enter the following information:

- **Name**. Enter the name of your application. This name will become part of the URL (uniform resource locator) by which the application is run. For example, the name myfirstapp can be run from your browser by entering this URL:

  ```
  http://myserver.domain/myfirstapp
  ```

  Any requests beginning with this URL are satisfied from the Web file path. See the next item.

- **Web file path**. Enter the full file path of the **.web** file. This is the file that you created using the LiveWire compiler. The application source files typically reside here, too.

- **Default page**. This item is optional. If the browser requests the application URL and has already accessed the application, this page will be processed. For example, if the user clicks on a hyperlink containing this URL, the user will see the default page:

  ```
  http://myserver.domain/myfirstapp
  ```

- **Initial page**. This item is optional. If the browser requests the application URL and has not yet accessed the application, this page will be processed. The initial page is commonly used to do things that need to be done once at the start of a user's interaction with the application, such as connecting to a database. See Chapter 17 for details.

LiveWire Objects

The LiveWire server extensions give us objects that can be referenced by JavaScript on the client side or the server side. These objects provide the vehicle by which various types of communication become possible, including communication between pages of an application, user-to-user within an application, and application to application.

These objects have their own predefined methods. Some of the objects have predefined properties, but all of them allow JavaScript to create user-defined properties for custom use. LiveWire objects also differ by their longevity; each object is created and destroyed at different times. The sample LiveWire application in Chapter 18 illustrates how the LiveWire object framework can be used to create an interactive application in which different users exchange information.

Server Object

The server object outlives all other objects. It is created when the server is started and is destroyed when the server is shut down. All LiveWire applications on that server share the same server object. It can be used to pass information from one application to another. You can create your own property on the server object in a server-side script and read it from a script in another application.

The `server` object has default properties that contain information about it:

- `hostname` is the full name by which the server is known on the Internet, plus the port number (such as www.myserver.com:80).

- `host` is the full name, without the port number (www.myserver.com)

- `protocol` is the version of the HTTP protocol being used by the host (such as "HTTP/1.0").

- `port` is the port number (such as 80).

- `agent` is the type of Web server (such as "Netscape Enterprise server").

The server object has two methods: `lock()` and `unlock()`. These methods can be used when you want to update the value of a `server` object property. Locking the object protects the property value from being altered by other processes. When updating is done, you must unlock the object. The code might look this:

```
<HTML>
<SERVER>
server.lock()
server.access_count = server.access_count + 1
server.unlock()
</SERVER>
</HTML>
```

Project Object

The `project` object is a relatively long-lived LiveWire object. It is created when the application is started and is destroyed when the application is stopped. It does not have any predefined properties, but you can create your own properties in it simply by referring to one in a server-side script. `Project` object properties are shared between all clients that are currently accessing the application. This makes it a good place to store information that must be passed among clients. For example, let's assume you are developing a game which is played by several players at once. Each player can maneuver only when he or she holds the token. The token may be represented as a property of the `project` object containing the name of the player.

This example shows how to create your own property in the `project` object:

```
<HTML>
<SERVER>
project.player = "Nobody"
</SERVER>
</HTML>
```

The project object has two methods: `lock()` and `unlock()`. These methods are similar to those in the `server` object. They can be used when you want to protect the values of a `project` object's properties while you are updating them. If you don't unlock the object, LiveWire will unlock it for you after the client's request has been satisfied. Locking the object protects the property value from being altered by other processes.

Client Object

The `client` object contains data specific to one client. There can be many client objects coexisting simultaneously. A `client` object is created when a browser first accesses the server and can live across subsequent requests from the same client. This arrangement gives us a method for maintaining information about a client as it uses a particular application. Remember that the nature of the relationship between a client and a Web server on the Internet is stateless. The client asks for a page and the server sends it back. Neither the client nor the server remembers anything about the last page requested or served. The `client` object frees us from this limitation.

Let's say that you are developing an application that mimics a retail store. Visitors enter the store, browse the aisles, put items in a shopping cart, and check out. Browsing aisles while you fill your cart implies that you will navigate through several pages. In this case, you need a mechanism that lets you keep the contents of the shopping cart intact until you successfully check out of the store. Let me put it another way: the variables you declare in server-side JavaScript last only as long as it takes the Web server to satisfy a request for a page. After the page is sent to the browser, the variables are gone. The client object is a good place to store the values of these variables between requests.

The `client` object has no default properties; they are all user-defined. The first time you refer to a `client` object property, you create that `client` object. Before that time, it does not exist.

The following example shows how to create a `client` object:

```
<HTML>
<SERVER>
client.name = "Edward"
</SERVER>
</HTML>
```

The `client` object's life ends in one of two ways:

- By using the `destroy()` method of the client object:

  ```
  client.destroy()
  ```

- By expiration.

LiveWire allows us to maintain the `client` object on the server or on the client. When on the client, the `client` object is automatically destroyed when the browser is exited. When it is maintained on the server, the server cleans up old `client` objects by expiring them after a period of time. The default is 10 minutes, but you can change that by specifying an expiration period in seconds using the `expiration()` method:

```
client.expiration(seconds)
```

When the `client` object is destroyed, the values held by its properties are gone.

LiveWire gives us several ways to maintain the `client` object. When you install your application using Application Manager, you choose a single method that best suits your application. You can keep a client's information on the server or on the client.

One way to maintain the `client` object is to use a client Cookie. This technique uses the Netscape cookie protocol. It is an efficient technique, but not all browsers support it. It uses cookie files on the client to store client data. One major advantage of this technique is that it enables communication between client and server scripts. You can write client-side JavaScript and server-side JavaScript in the same application, and both scripts refer to the same `client` object properties. LiveWire adds an entry to the client cookie for each client property:

```
NETSCAPE_LIVEWIRE.property_name=property_value
```

We have already seen that `client` object properties can be created and referenced in server-side JavaScript. You can also write client-side JavaScript functions to create and update the client object properties. A code sample can be found in the LiveWire reference. However, this is an advanced topic and requires familiarity with the Netscape cookie specification, which can be found on the Netscape Web site at http://home.netscape.com/newsref/std/cookie_spec.html.

Another option for mastering the client object is client URL encoding. This technique's biggest advantage is that it works with all browsers. However, it will increase network traffic somewhat. Also, if your application generates any URLs dynamically, you must use the LiveWire function `writeURL()` in your server-side script. This function generates a URL that contains appended parameters that are necessary for maintaining the `client` object. For example, suppose your server-side script has code that uses the `write()` function to generate a hyperlink like this:

```
<A HREF='LinkTo'>
```

where `LinkTo` was a variable containing the name of a page on the server to link to. Then you'll have to code it like this instead:

```
<A HREF='writeURL(LinkTo)'>
```

These are server-side techniques for maintenance of the client object. Each uses a data structure on the server to store the `client` object properties between requests.

One server-side technique uses the client's IP address to match the client request to the corresponding `client` object. This technique works with all browsers and, unlike other methods, does not increase network traffic. However, it cannot be used in some applications. Because the client data is indexed by IP address, this technique relies on the assumption that each client's IP address will not change. Therefore, you cannot use this technique when your application may be accessed across proxy servers or by an Internet service provider that dynamically assigns IP addresses.

Yet another technique uses a server-generated name to identify the client object corresponding to each client. The first time a client accesses the application, the server generates a nickname for the client and stores the name in a server-side data structure. This name is returned to the client using the Netscape cookie protocol. The client identifies itself with the nickname on subsequent requests. Browsers that access an application using server cookies as the `client` object maintenance technique must support the Netscape cookie protocol.

Finally, the server URL encoding technique uses a server-generated name to identify the `client` object corresponding to each client, as with the server cookies approach. However, this technique does not use the Netscape cookie protocol to store and return this name in subsequent requests. Instead, it requires that you use the `writeURL()` function when dynamically generating URLs.

Request Object

The `request` object contains data associated with a client's request to the Web server. Each time you click on a hyperlink, for example, a `request` object is created on the server. This object's life can probably be measured in milliseconds. It lives as long as it takes for the server to satisfy the request. When the requested page is sent to the browser, the `request` object is destroyed automatically by LiveWire. The `request` object is typically used by server-side JavaScript to receive data sent by the client. Then the server-side script can process it appropriately. However, `request` object properties which are needed longer must be saved elsewhere. This can be in one of the other LiveWire objects (usually the `client` object) or a file or database. See "File Object" later in this chapter for more information on using a file, and Chapter 17 for more information on using databases. The `request` object has the following predefined properties:

- `agent` contains the name and version of the browser that made the request. This information can be used to write browser-specific code. For example, if Navigator supports an advanced HTML feature and other browsers do not, you can generate HTML in two different flavors, depending on the value of request.agent (for example, "Mozilla/2.0N" is the Netscape Navigator).

- ip is the IP address of the client. This value is always four numbers separated by periods (for example, "204.60.71.250"). This value can be used when you need to uniquely identify each client. However, although the IP address is generally unique on intranets, this may be true on the Internet only in special cases

- method. The HTTP method has the value GET, POST, or HEAD.

- protocol contains the HTTP protocol level used by the client (for example, "HTTP/1.0").

As in the other LiveWire objects, additional properties may be created by server-side scripts. However, this doesn't lend much value because the request object's life is short. The real value lies in creating properties that contain data values on the client and sending them to a server-side script for processing. You can do this in two ways. First, you can use form elements. When you submit an HTML form, each INPUT element becomes a request object property on the server. In the following example, the form creates a property that can be referred to as request.who. It will contain the value entered by the user, his or her name:

```
<FORM METHOD="post" ACTION = "index.html">
Please Enter Your Name
<INPUT TYPE = "text" NAME = "who">
<INPUT TYPE = "submit" VALUE = "Enter">
</FORM>
```

You can also create request object properties without using form elements. Request object properties can be encoded in the URL. The URL request is sent to the server, and request object properties are created there. You append the request object properties to the end of the URL. Each property takes the form of a name and value. Each name-value pair looks like this:

```
property_name=value
```

To use this method, append a question mark (?) to the end of the URL, followed by one or more name-value pairs. Each name-value pair must be separated by the AND symbol (&):

```
URL?property_name_1=value_1&property_name_2=value_2
```

The following example creates two `request` object properties on the server (`item_number`, `quantity`) that can be referenced from server-side scripts in **MyPage.html**:

```
MyPage.html?item_number=01453&quantity=1
```

File Object

The `file` object contains methods that allow applications to read and write files on the server. You can use files to store application information that can exist for any length of time. This technique is an alternative to using the LiveWire object framework or a database.

There are advantages to using a `file` object to store data. First, you have control over how long you want the file data to exist. Second a `file` object lends itself to storing repeating data, such as a list of user names. If your data access needs are modest, it may be easier to use the `file` object than a `database` object. And, unlike the `database` object, you don't have to wrestle with any database connectivity issues or install any third-party software in order to use it.

However, a file may not be appropriate for all applications. For example, if the data access requirements of your application include some of the following items, you may want to consider using a database to help you keep track of your data:

- Different types of data
- Selective update of data items
- Advanced searching
- Many users accessing the data simultaneously
- Large volume of data

When developing an application that allows files to be accessed, be aware that malicious users may try to disrupt the server. Take precautions so that users cannot create files on your server except what is written by your application.

WARNING

You create a `file` object using JavaScript. The following example creates a file whose name is placed in the variable `MyFileObject`. The file is created in the directory C:\LiveWire\MyApplication\MyFiles:

```
MyFileObject = new File("MyFiles")
```

The directory specified (MyFiles) must be under the directory in which the application's Web file exists (for example, C:\LiveWire\MyApplication\ MyApp.web) Use Application Manager to view this information about your application.

The basic operations you perform on a file are open, read, write, and close. After you create a `file` object, you must open it in order to use it. If the `open` method is successful, it returns the value `true`. This example opens the `file` object `MyFileObject` with a mode of `w`, or write:

```
return_code = MyFileObject.open("w")
```

The `open()` method takes `mode` as its only parameter. The value of this parameter dictates how the file can be accessed while it is open (Table 16.1). If you wish to change the mode, you must close the file and then open it again.

Table 16.1 File Access Modes for `open()`

Mode	Description
r	Open an existing file for reading. `Open()` returns `false` if the file does not exist. You cannot write to a file while it is opened in this mode.
w	Open a new file for writing. This mode first clears the contents of an existing file.
a	Open a file for writing at the end of the file. If the file doesn't exist, one is created.
r+	Open a file for reading and writing at the beginning of the file. `Open()` returns `false` if the file does not exist.
w+	Open a new file for reading and writing. This mode clears the contents of an existing file.
a+	Open a file for reading and writing at the end of the file. If the file doesn't exist, one is created.

Files are not designed to handle access by more than one user at a time. Consider this scenario.

User A reads the contents of a file and then user B reads the contents of the same file and updates the file. User A then updates the file from his or her old copy of the file. Now user B's updates are gone. This is not what is to be expected. To avoid this and other problems relating to simultaneous access, you must lock the file while a user is accessing it. You can do this by locking the `project` object or the `server` object. If the file will be accessed within one application, use the `lock()` method of the `project` object. If the file will be accessed by multiple applications, use the `lock()` method of the `server` object.

A `file` object has a pointer that contains the current position within the file. Reading and writing a file occur relative to the current position of the file. When you open a file, the current position is determined by the mode in which you opened it. You can change the current position by using the `setPosition()` method. This example sets the pointer to the 10th byte from the beginning of the file:

```
MyFileObject.setPosition(10,0)
```

The first parameter is the number of bytes relative to the position indicated by the second parameter. 0 = beginning of the file, 1 = current position, and 2 = end of the file.

If you opened your file for reading, you can use `readln()`, `read()`, or `readByte()` to get data out of the `file` object. If your file contains end-of-line characters (\n), `readln()` will return a string that contains the characters from the current position to the next end-of-line character:

```
line_var = MyFileObject.readln()
```

Alternatively, use `read()` to return a string that contains a specified number of bytes, starting with the current position:

```
string_var = MyFileObject.read()
```

To return the numeric value of the next byte, starting with the current position, use `readByte()`:

```
byte_var = MyFileObject.readByte()
```

If you opened your file for writing, you can use writeln(), write(), or writeByte() to write data to the file object. Writing to a file occurs relative to the current file position. All three methods return true if successful, or false if unsuccessful.

You can write remove strings ending with the end-of-line character using writeln:

```
return_code = MyFileObject.writeln()
```

Or you can use write() to write a string to the file without the end-of-line character:

```
return_code = MyFileObject.write()
```

To write a number representing a single byte to the file, use writeByte():

```
return_code = MyFileObject.readByte()
```

Here are other file object methods:

- eof returns true if the pointer is at the end of the file. While reading through a file, you should always use this method to avoid unnecessary reads. For example:

  ```
  while (!MyFile.eof() ) {
       line_var = MyFile.readln()
  }
  ```

- getPosition() returns a number that is the current position in the file, starting from 0.

- getLength() returns the number of bytes in the file, or –1 if an error occurs.

- exists() returns true if the file exists.

- error() returns a number that is the error status of the file. This value has different meanings depending on your operating system. Zero always means that no error has occurred.

- clearError() clears the value of the error status and the value of eof.

Here is an example using the `file` object that adds a string to the beginning of a file:

```
//create the file object
MyFile = new File("names.txt");

//lock the project so that the file cannot be accessed
//by more than one user at a time
project.lock()

//open the names file for reading
MyFile.open("r");

//read the contents of the file into old_contents
old_contents = MyFile.read(MyFile.getLength())

MyFile.close()

//open MyFile again, this time for writing
MyFile.open("w");

//add the new name to MyFile
MyFile.write(request.name + old_contents);

//close MyFile
MyFile.close();

//Unlock the project so that MyFile may be accessed
//by the next user
project.unlock();
```

Database Object

The `database` object contains methods and properties that allow applications to access databases. Database access gives LiveWire the potential to interact with countless existing stores of data. New databases are being created all the time. It is the industry standard way to organize and store data. Entire enterprises run their operations on databases. It gives rise to the possibility of applications that allow people to interact with all kinds of information. Chapter 17 discusses the `database` object in detail.

CHAPTER SEVENTEEN

USING DATABASES IN A LIVEWIRE APPLICATION

Building Web applications that can access repositories of data in a database management system (DBMS) is one of the major benefits of using LiveWire. Businesses of all sizes commonly use a DBMS to update, store, and retrieve data, and database-oriented Web applications are being implemented in growing numbers. Businesses can cut costs by giving their customers direct access to the information they need. Retailers want to create on-line catalogs to catch the coming wave of Internet commerce. Companies are building their own internal Web-based networks, or *intranets*, as a cost-effective method to distribute information within the company. And new databases containing multimedia features in the form of sound and video are pushing the envelope of hot sites. For all these reasons, it appears that LiveWire will play a part in the future of Web-based applications.

DBMSs are produced by many different vendors, and LiveWire supports a large number of them. Currently, this list includes Sybase, Informix, Oracle, and any other DBMS that is compliant with Microsoft's Object Database

Connectivity (ODBC) standard. However, this list is dependent on the operating system being used. As more combinations of DBMSs and operating systems are supported, this list is being updated, so check the LiveWire release notes at www.netscape.com.

This chapter is divided in two parts. For those who have never experienced Structured Query Language (SQL), we present an introduction to this industry standard for database access. Although it is by no means a comprehensive explanation of all SQL features, this section gives you enough information to write useful database applications without taking you on a long diversion. Experienced SQL developers may want to skim this section. The second part describes LiveWire database and cursor objects. You'll see how LiveWire incorporates the power of SQL so that you can create database-centric applications with server-side JavaScript.

This chapter will cover:

- What a DBMS is
- Introduction to SQL
- Using SQL and LiveWire together

What Is a DBMS?

A DBMS (Figure 17.1) is a collection of software programs that manage logically structured sets of data. It controls the organization, storage, and retrieval of data in a database. The DBMS accepts requests for data storage or retrieval from the application program and tells the operating system to perform the data transfer. Among the most important duties of the DBMS are to provide data security and to ensure the integrity of the data. Data security means that only authorized users have permission to read or update specific types of data. For example, one user may be permitted to view customer information, whereas another user may be allowed to update it. In any case, users must present their password before exercising any of their privileges. Data integrity is protected, because the DBMS ensures that data constraints, or rules, are not violated. For example, in a retail database, a sales order may not be placed unless the customer who is placing the order exists in the database.

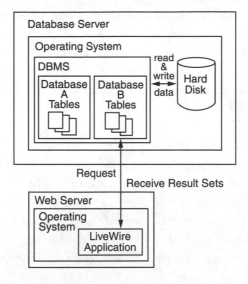

Figure 17.1 DBMS architecture.

Introduction to SQL

SQL (pronounced "see-quel") allows you to retrieve, add, update, and delete data. It also contains statements to create and administer databases. Mastering SQL may take considerable practice, but you can quickly learn the basics and use a database in a LiveWire application. However, be aware that there are variations in SQL from DBMS to DBMS, especially when it applies to advanced topics, so refer to your vendor's documentation for details. We will restrict this chapter's discussion of SQL to the features that allow us to retrieve and manipulate data.

To use a database in your application, you must have the following:

- A working knowledge of Structured Query Language (SQL). This includes SQL statements SELECT, INSERT, UPDATE, and DELETE.
- An understanding of the LiveWire database object and cursor object and their usage. These objects contain methods and properties that operate directly with your database.

• Familiarity with the logical structure of your of relational database. For example, a database used to contain customer orders for an on-line store may contain a customer table and an order table. If your application displays a customers and their orders, you'll have to know the names of the tables containing the data, as well as the relationships between them, in order to correctly retrieve the data.

A DBMS usually includes a program (Interactive SQL, or ISQL) for executing SQL on the database server. This is a good place to practice your SQL before incorporating it into any LiveWire applications. There are also third-party products that give you a graphical user interface in which to build your SQL statements. This approach may be easier than coding SQL using a text editor. These products provide a point-and-click method to select and assemble database object names and snippets of SQL into the final statement.

NOTE

ODBC is the industry-standard interface for providing database access. ODBC was created to satisfy the need to develop applications that are independent of any one DBMS vendor. In other words, an application should have the ability to access a database regardless of the database vendor. You should not need to do extensive reprogramming to move the database to a different DBMS.

Although SQL is an industry standard, each DBMS vendor has added extensions of its own. This means that an application coded to use a Sybase database, for example, may include statements that cannot be resolved by a Watcom database. ODBC resolves differences between versions of SQL provided by database vendors. ODBC provides a set of *drivers*, or programs that translate SQL into requests that are specific to the DBMS servicing the request. There are three levels of conformance between SQL syntax and the ODBC drivers that support them: minimum, core, and extended. Most commercial applications require at least core level conformance from their ODBC drivers. We will assume core level conformance for the purposes of this book. If you have a problem accessing your database using ODBC, check out your ODBC driver.

To use ODBC, you define a data source that includes the name of the DBMS vendor, the name of the database to be used, and other DBMS-specific information used to connect to the data source. The data source maps the data source name to the driver necessary to access the specific DBMS. To access your database, instead of referring to the DBMS and your database name, you refer to ODBC and the data source name.

ODBC gives LiveWire the ability to access many different DBMSs. If this is the only way to access the database of your choice, then you must use it. If your application uses a supported DBMS but needs to be portable among DBMSs, you should consider using ODBC. In other cases, the vendor-specific interface may be preferable, if one is available. Because you won't be adding a third-party ODBC driver to the mix, you may avoid long-term compatibility issues.

Database Tables

A relational database is a method of organizing related information so that queries and other data manipulation can be handled efficiently. The data in a relational database is organized into *tables*. A table may be thought of as a two-dimensional grid composed of *columns* and *rows*. Columns are the *attributes*, or data elements, of the table. *Instances* of data are held as horizontal rows. See Table 17.1.

Table 17.1 Customer Table

Customer ID	Last Name	First Name	Credit Limit	Customer Type	Customer Since
1	Burger	Nita	NULL	Edu	08/01/1996
2	Jones	Tao	12.50	Com	08/05/1996
3	Graw	Marty	200.00	Edu	07/30/1996
4	Nasium	Jim	0.00	Com	07/31/1996
5	Jackson	Martha	999.99	Gov	06/01/1996

In this example, the columns are Customer ID, Last Name, First Name, and so on. A row contains a value for each column. The first row in the table contains a customer ID of 1, a last name of Burger, and so on.

A table is designed so that it holds only one kind of data, without dependencies between its columns. You can see that the customer table contains attributes only of customers, such as name and address.

The logical structure of tables and databases should be designed according to so-called *rules of normalization*, taking into consideration issues such as DBMS performance. Commercial applications typically are designed by data modelers and database administrators. The techniques for designing databases are outside the scope of this book.

Tables are created by executing the CREATE TABLE statement. This SQL statement names the table and declares the columns that make up the table.

Create the customer table by executing the following SQL statement:

```
CREATE TABLE CUSTOMER
(Customer_ID      INTEGER     NOT NULL,
Last_Name         CHAR(30),
First_Name        CHAR(30),
Credit_Limit      NUMERIC(5,2),
Customer_Type     CHAR(3),
Customer_Since    DATE)
```

In the CREATE TABLE statement, a *data type* must be declared for each column. This technique offers some assurance that the data in the column can always be used by an application in a consistent manner. For example, displaying the credit limit of a customer will always result in a number and not an alphabetic string or a date. When a row of data is added (inserted) to a table, each data item being inserted must be compatible with the data type of the column it is targeted for. If it is not, the DBMS will return an error, and the data will not be inserted. For example, in our Customer table, the column Customer ID was declared as an integer, Last Name was defined as a string up to 30 characters long, and Customer Since was defined as a date.

Some DBMS vendors supply utility programs with graphical user interfaces that allow you to create tables without having to write any SQL. These utilities can be convenient, but you'll still need to name the table and columns and specify the data types.

To remove the table from the database, use this statement:

```
DROP TABLE CUSTOMER
```

You cannot change the data type or name of a column. You must DROP the table and CREATE it again. However, when you drop the table, you also delete all its data.

Retrieving Data from the Database

The SELECT statement is used to retrieve data from the database. This data is returned to the user or application in the form of rows, sometimes called the *result set*. You can execute a SELECT statement in any query tool provided by the DBMS vendor. Also, try using the sample application DBAdmin that is included in the LiveWire package.

The following statement is an example of a simple SELECT. The entire contents of the Customer table are retrieved. The "*" indicates that data should be selected from all columns. The ORDER BY is optional and specifies the columns by which the result set will be sorted (Table 17.2).

```
SELECT * FROM Customer ORDER BY Last_Name, First_Name
```

Table 17.2 A Sample Result Set

Customer ID	Last Name	First Name	Credit Limit	Customer Type	Customer Since
1	Burger	Nita	NULL	Edu	08/01/1996
3	Graw	Marty	200.00	Edu	07/30/1996
5	Jackson	Martha	999.99	Gov	06/01/1996
2	Jones	Tad	12.50	Com	08/05/1996
4	Nasium	Jim	0.00	Com	07/31/1996

Now let's limit the result set to only the columns that we want to see. This statement retrieves the last name, first name, and credit limit of all customers in the Customer table.

```
SELECT Last_Name, First_Name, Credit_Limit FROM Customer
```

Table 17.3 Result Set

Last Name	First Name	Credit Limit
Burger	Nita	NULL
Jones	Tad	12.50
Graw	Marty	200.00
Nasium	Jim	0.00
Jackson	Martha	999.99

Now let's narrow the result set further by retrieving only those rows that we are interested in. The following statement retrieves the first name, last name, and credit limit of customers whose credit limit is greater than $100. This example introduces the WHERE clause, which allows you to specify the criteria by which rows are retrieved from a table (Table 17.4).

```
SELECT Last_Name, First_Name, Credit_Limit FROM Customer WHERE Credit_Limit > 100.00
```

Table 17.4 Result Set

Last Name	First Name	Credit Limit
Graw	Marty	200.00
Jackson	Martha	999.99

A WHERE clause can employ a variety of *comparison operators* to narrow the result set (Table 17.5). WHERE clauses commonly take the form:

```
WHERE columnname <comparison operator> expression
```

Table 17.5 Comparison Operators

Operator	Description
=	Equal to
>	Greater than
<	Less than
>=	Greater than or equal to
<=	Less than or equal to
<>	Not equal to
!>	Not greater than
!<	Not less than
LIKE	String comparison using wildcards
ISNULL	Test if column value is equal to the NULL value
BETWEEN	Test if a value is within a range (for example, WHERE Credit_Limit BETWEEN 10.00 AND 50.00)
IN	Test if a value exists at least once in a list of values or result of subquery

A WHERE clause may contain many search criteria, and they are combined using AND and OR.

```
SELECT Last_Name, First_Name,
FROM Customer
WHERE Credit_Limit > 100.00
AND Customer_Since < "07/01/96"
```

The result of the preceding code is shown in Table 17.6.

Table 17.6 Result Set

Last Name	First Name
Jackson	Martha

Notice the use of parentheses in the following code to create a more complex Boolean expression. Rows in the Customer table that satisfy both search criteria within the parentheses are included in the result set. Also included are rows in the Customer table that satisfy the search criteria after the OR (Table 17.7).

```
SELECT Last_Name, First_Name, FROM Customer
WHERE (Credit_Limit > 100.00 AND Customer_Since < "07/01/96")
OR Credit_Limit = 0.00
```

Table 17.7 Result Set

Last Name	First Name
Nasium	Jim
Jackson	Martha

The following statement retrieves customers whose last names begin with the letter J. The % symbol is a wildcard indicating that a string of unknown characters may follow the letter J. Use the "_" symbol to indicate any single character. Table 17.8 shows the result set.

```
SELECT Last_Name, First_Name, FROM Customer WHERE Last_Name LIKE "J%"
```

Table 17.8 Result Set

Last Name	First Name
Jones	Tao
Jackson	Martha

The following statement retrieves customers whose Credit Limit has the value NULL, a special value used by databases to mean "undefined." It does not mean 0 or "" (an empty string). In this example, some customers may have a NULL credit limit simply because their credit has not yet been checked. Table 17.9 shows the result set.

```
SELECT Last_Name, First_Name
FROM Customer
WHERE Credit_Limit IS NULL
```

Table 17.9 Result Set

Last Name	First Name	Credit Limit
Burger	Nita	NULL

The BETWEEN operator compares a value to a range of values:

```
SELECT Last_Name, First_Name
FROM Customer
WHERE Credit_Limit BETWEEN 0.00 AND 20.00
```

Table 17.10 shows the result set.

Table 17.10 Result Set

Last Name	First Name	Credit Limit
Jones	Tao	12.50

The IN operator compares a value to a set of values. When you're comparing a column declared as CHARACTER to some value, that value must always be within quotes. Table 17.11 shows the result set.

```
SELECT Last_Name, First_Name
FROM Customer
WHERE Last_Name IN ("Burger", "Jackson")
```

Table 17.11 Result Set

Last Name	First Name
Burger	Nita
Jackson	Martha

You can substitute a *subquery* for the list of values in parentheses. A subquery is a select statement within another select statement. In the following case, it returns a result set of values. This is equivalent to listing the values as we did previously. In this example, we are looking for last names from the Customer table that also exist in the Employee table:

```
SELECT Last_Name
FROM Customer
WHERE Last_Name IN (SELECT Last_Name FROM Employee)
```

SQL includes *column functions* that can calculate a single value for a column in a result set (Table 17.12). Most DBMSs provide their own built-in functions to facilitate dealing with date formats, data conversion, and other special uses. Refer to your DBMS vendor's documentation for more information.

Table 17.12 Column Functions

Operator	Description
SUM	Returns the total value for that column in the result set (use on numeric columns only)
MIN	Returns the smallest value for that column in the result set
AVG	Returns the average value for that column in the result set (use on numeric columns only)
MAX	Returns the greatest value for that column in the result set
COUNT	Returns the number of rows in the result set

The following statement

```
SELECT MAX(Credit_Limit), MIN(Credit_Limit), COUNT(*)
FROM Customer
```

Table 17.13 shows the result set.

Table 17.13 Result Set

MAX(Credit Limit)	MIN(Credit Limit)	COUNT(*)
999.99	0.00	5

The GROUP BY clause is a powerful feature of the SELECT statement. When used in conjunction with column functions, it gives a summary of the data.

```
SELECT Customer_type, AVG(Credit_Limit)
FROM Customer
GROUP BY Customer_Type
```

Table 17.14 shows the result set.

Table 17.14 Result Set

Customer Type	AVG(Credit Limit)
Edu	200.00
Gov	999.99
Com	6.25

First, the SELECT is performed. Customer type and credit limit of all rows from the table are retrieved. Then the GROUP BY applies the AVG function once to each set of rows having the same customer type. Finally, we get a result set that contains only one row for each unique customer type.

The HAVING clause may be thought of as a WHERE clause for groups:

```
SELECT Customer_type, AVG(Credit_Limit)
FROM Customer
GROUP BY Customer_Type
HAVING COUNT(*) > 1
```

Table 17.15 shows the result set.

Table 17.15 Result Set

Customer Type	AVG(Credit Limit)
Edu	200.00
Com	6.25

The DISTINCT keyword eliminates duplicates from the result set.

```
SELECT COUNT(DISTINCT Customer_type)
FROM Customer
```

Table 17.16 shows the result set.

Table 17.16 Result Set

COUNT(DISTINCT Customer Type)
3

Table 17.17 lists all the SQL SELECT keywords.

Table 17.17 SQL SELECT Keywords

Keyword	Description
ALL	Tests if a value exists in every row returned from a subquery
DISTINCT	Eliminates rows containing duplicate values
NOT	Negates search criteria (for example, WHERE NOT Name = "Smith")
EXISTS	Tests if a subquery returns at least one row (WHERE EXISTS <subquery>)
ORDER BY	Sorts the result set by one or more columns
GROUP BY	Used with column functions (SUM, MIN, MAX, AVG, COUNT)
HAVING	Used with GROUP BY; filters groups in result set

Selecting Data from More than One Table (Join)

The tables in a relational database are usually tied together by *relationships*. The established database design methodology, *normalization*, produces designs with characteristics such as high data integrity, low data redundancy, a tendency toward smaller tables, and an expandable, logical design. In a normalized database, the data needed to satisfy a query is often located in more than one table. Retrieval of data in this case requires the use of a special type of SELECT statement called a *join*. A join usually occurs between tables, so that a column in one table refers to a column in another table. Joins are commonly used in commercial database applications.

Good database designs attempt to model real-world scenarios. For example, in the real world, an order cannot exist unless a customer exists to place it. This relationship should also be reflected in the logical database design.

Let's assume that our database contains customers and orders. (See Tables 17.18 and table 17.19.) In this example, the Customer table is a master list of all customers, and the Order table is a master list of all orders. If a table has a column for which there exists a master list, that column must appear in the master list; otherwise, the reference is invalid. Notice that the column named Customer ID appears in the Order table. It seems obvious that this column refers to the customer ID column in the Customer table, indicating that a relationship exists between the two tables. It is not the exact name of the column that indicates a relationship, although a good database design uses names that make it easy to see relationships. Rather, it is the meaning of the columns that is important in identifying a relationship.

Table 17.18 Customer Table

Customer ID	Last Name	First Name	Credit Limit
1	Burger	Nita	NULL
2	Jones	Tad	12.50
3	Graw	Marty	200.00
4	Nasium	Jim	0.00
5	Jackson	Martha	999.99

Table 17.19 Order Table

Order Number	Customer ID	Total Amount
1000	5	5.95
1001	4	155.00
1002	1	54.50
1003	2	18.96
1004	5	98.21

The tables in this simple relationship are often referred to as *parent* and *child* tables. The Customer table is the parent, because the customer must exist before the order is placed. The Order table is the child, because it contains a reference to the master list of customers.

There may be relationships defined between many tables in a database. To maintain data integrity, a DBMS must keep these relationships valid. There must not be any "missing" parent data references. The automatic enforcement of relationships is called *referential integrity*. A SQL developer must be aware of these relationships to avoid errors from invalid UPDATE and DELETE statements. (More on these SQL statements later in the chapter.) Also, knowledge of the relationships in your database will help you formulate your joins.

Now, back to the join. If you want to see a list of orders along with the customer's name, you must combine data from both tables. To get data from two tables, list both table names in the FROM clause. To make the SELECT meaningful, you must specify the relationship between the tables. This is done in the WHERE clause of the following example:

```
SELECT Order_number, Last_name
FROM ORDER, CUSTOMER
WHERE ORDER.Customer_Id = CUSTOMER.Customer_Id
```

Conceptually, a join is processed in two steps. First, DBMS takes each row from the Order table and pairs it with each row from the Customer table (Table 17.20). For clarity, we won't show each and every from both tables.

Table 17.20 Processing a Join, Step 1

Order Table		Customer Table	
Order Number	**Customer ID**	**Customer ID**	**Last Name**
1000	5	1	Burger
1000	5	2	Jones
1000	5	3	Graw
1000	5	4	Nasium
1000	5	5	Jackson
1001	4	1	Burger
1001	4	2	Jones
1001	4	3	Graw
1001	4	4	Nasium
1001	4	5	Jackson
1002	1	1	Burger

Table 17.20 Processing a Join, Step 1 (continued)

| Order Table | | Customer Table | |
Order Number	Customer ID	Customer ID	Last Name
1002	1	2	Jones
1002	1	3	Graw
1002	1	4	Nasium
1002	1	5	Jackson
1003	2	1	Burger
1003	2	2	Jones
1003	2	3	Graw
1003	2	4	Nasium
1003	2	5	Jackson
1004	5	1	Burger
1004	5	2	Jones
1004	5	3	Graw
1004	5	4	Nasium
1004	5	5	Jackson

Then, for each row in this intermediate result table, the value of Customer ID from the Order table is compared to the value of Customer ID from the Customer table. If the values are equal, the row is equal to the final result set (Table 17.21).

Table 17.21 Processing a Join, Step 2

Order Number	Last Name
1000	Jackson
1001	Nasium
1002	Burger
1003	Jones
1004	Jackson

The WHERE clause uses the relationship between tables to join them. In this case, we want the rows in which the two columns are equal (an *equijoin*). We could specify other comparison operators here (<>, >, and so on), but the equijoin is the most useful. Also, note that you must prefix the column name by the table that it is in. Otherwise, the DBMS does not know which column from which table you are referring to, and you will receive an error.

You can specify additional search criteria in a join. We'll modify the previous example and narrow the result set further:

```
SELECT Order_number, Last_name
FROM ORDER, CUSTOMER
WHERE ORDER.Customer_Id = CUSTOMER.Customer_Id
AND Credit_Limit > 100.00
```

Table 17.22 show the result set.

Table 17.22 Result Set

Order Number	Last Name
1000	Jackson
1004	Jackson

You can use the EXISTS clause with a join to find all occurrences that violate the integrity of a relationship. EXISTS returns true if its subquery returns at least one row. This query selects all order numbers for which a customer does not exist:

```
SELECT Order_Number
FROM ORDER
WHERE NOT EXISTS
    (SELECT *
    FROM Customer
    WHERE Customer.Customer_ID = Order.Customer_ID)
```

The DBMS processes this query by first selecting all order numbers from the Order table. Then, for each of these rows, it tries to select the row or rows in the Customer table that have the same Customer ID as that of the current order number.

Inserting Data into the Database

The INSERT statement is used to add rows to a table. The following example adds a row to the Customer table. You should list all of the table's columns, as well as a corresponding value for each, or the statement may fail.

```
INSERT INTO Customer
(Customer_ID,
Last_Name,
First_Name,
Credit_Limit,
Customer_Type,
Customer_Since)
VALUES
(6, "McCracken", "Jeff", 100.00, "Gion", "01-09-96")
```

You can also insert data based on data retrieved from another table. This technique comes in handy when you're creating some test data during development. In this example, we create a table called Customer_Temp:

```
CREATE TABLE Customer_Temp
(Name1     CHAR(30),
Name2      CHAR(30)
Type       CHAR(4) )


INSERT INTO Customer_Temp
SELECT First_name, Last_name, "TEMP"
FROM Customer
```

Updating the Database

The UPDATE statement is used to modify column values for existing rows in a table. The updated rows are those that meet the selection criteria specified by the WHERE clause. If no WHERE clause is specified, then all rows in the table are updated. This statement can update multiple rows at one time. The SET clause specifies the columns to be updated, and how they are to be updated.

This statement increases the Credit_Limit by 10 percent for every customer created before 01-01-96:

```
UPDATE Customer
SET Credit_Limit = Credit_Limit * 1.10
WHERE Customer_since < '01-01-96'
```

Deleting from the Database

The DELETE statement is used to remove rows of data from a table. The rows deleted are those that meet the selection criteria specified by the WHERE clause. If no WHERE clause is specified, all the rows in the table are deleted.

```
DELETE FROM Customer
WHERE Credit_Limit = 0.00
```

Using SQL and LiveWire Together

To access and manipulate the data in a database, you must first connect to the database. This is true whether you access the database via a LiveWire application or through the DBMS utility program. If you are connected to a network, the database will probably reside on a database server, a computer whose main purpose is to run DBMS software. If you are not connected to a network, your database will be on your hard drive. There may be many databases on a single server, but you will usually deal with a single database throughout a LiveWire application. For example, a customer service database may contain data that is related to customers and the status of their orders. Another database may contain articles, advertising materials, and photos used to produce on-line magazines.

Now let's connect to the database. LiveWire makes this easy with the connect() method. The connect() method requires some database connection information that we can't give you here. That information is unique to your database installation. If a database administrator is available, he or she should be able to supply this information:

```
database.connect("DBMSvendor", "servername", "userid", "password", "databasename")
```

For example, this statement connects to a Sybase database named "mydatabase" on the server "dbserver." I am connecting as user "me" with password "mypassword."

```
database.connect("SYBASE", "dbserver", "me", "mypassword", "mydatabase")
```

If you wanted to use ODBC to connect to a database defined as an ODBC data source, the connect statement might look like this:

```
database.connect("ODBC", "dbserver", "me", "mypassword", "mydatasource")
```

When you connect to a database, LiveWire creates a database object. The database object contains methods you need for working with your database.

To be sure that the connection has been established, use the `connected()` method. It returns the value `true` if the application has connected to the database:

```
if (!database.connected())
    {redirect ("connect_error.html"}        // statements that communicate connect //
                                            error to user
```

Use the `disconnect()` method when you want to cut the database connection. You must do this if you wish to connect to a different database. It is good programming practice to disconnect each time your work with the database is finished. Be aware that Web applications cannot maintain a continuous connection with the database. This stands in contrast to client-server and mainframe applications. In a Web application, after a page is requested by the browser, the application may connect to the database to satisfy the request. However, after the request is satisfied by the Web server, the connection is broken (Figure 17.2).

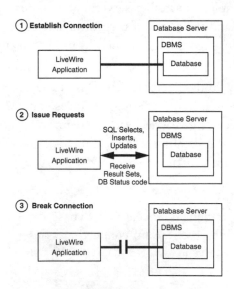

Figure 17.2 Using a Connection.

Techniques for Connecting

There are two techniques for connecting to a database in a LiveWire application. In the *standard* technique, the application establishes the connection in the initial page of the application. Subsequent pages use the same database connection, and other clients that access the application share the same connection. The video store sample application that comes with LiveWire uses this technique. It is suitable for applications that give public access to the database. Users do not have to identify themselves to the DBMS by entering a username and password to access the database.

In the *serial* technique, each client establishes his or her own connection using their own userid and password. A userid is associated with a set of permissions to use DBMS resources, such as databases and tables. In traditional database applications, a DBA (database administrator) creates userids and assign the appropriate permissions to them. A less restrictive approach commonly used on the Web is to let users add themselves to the database. This arrangement allows the application to gather user information for purposes such as marketing demographics or billing.

Retrieving Data

We've seen some examples of how SQL is used to retrieve data from a database. In a LiveWire application, you can use two techniques for displaying data retrieved using SQL. Each technique employs a different method of the database object.

Using SQLTable()

SQLTable() is a quick and easy way to display the result set from the SQL query on an HTML page. However, you cannot modify the way the data is formatted on the page. This is because the SQLTable() method gives you no control over how it creates an HTML table. Each column of the SQL result set becomes a column in the HTML table, and each row in the result set becomes a row in the HTML table. For example, this statement generates HTML that contains all the data in the Customer table:

```
database.SQLTable("select * from customer")
```

Note that the SQL statement must be within quotes. If you prefer, you can specify the name of a file containing the SQL select statement:

```
database.SQLTable(customer.sql)
```

Using a Cursor to Retrieve Data

Cursors provide a flexible approach for displaying data retrieved from a database. Using a cursor allows you to display data in any manner supported by HTML. This stands in contrast to the rigid format provided by `database.SQLTable()`.

A cursor is associated with the result set returned from a SQL SELECT statement. Using a cursor allows you to process the result set on a row-by-row basis. The row being processed is always the "current" row. When you are finished processing that row, you simply point to the next row.

You must create a cursor before you can use it. A cursor is created using this syntax:

```
CursorName = database.cursor ( "SQL SELECT statement", updatable )
```

Here, `CursorName` is a name you supply for the `cursor` object, and `updatable` is an optional true or false value. It indicates whether this cursor can be used for updating the database.

The following statement creates a cursor named `my_cursor`. The cursor contains rows from the customer table whose last name begins with the letter *J*.

```
my_cursor = database.cursor ( "SELECT First_Name, Last_Name from customer where
Last_Name like "J%")
```

This process is illustrated in Figure 17.3.

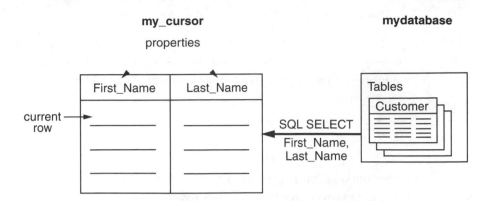

Figure 17.3 Creating a cursor.

A cursor is created with one property for each column in the cursor. In the current example, the cursor is created with the properties First_Name and Last_Name. You can display the First_Name of the current row with this statement:

```
write (my_cursor.First_Name)
```

You can also refer to the properties of the cursor object without having to know their names. This capability may come in handy when the SELECT statement is not known in advance. You can obtain column names and values from the current row of the result set by taking advantage of the fact that cursor object properties are held in an array, and array elements are referenced by the array index.

Use the array index value to refer to the value of a column for the current row in the result set. The following example displays the column name and column value of the first property, First_Name. The HTML output is identical to the previous example.

```
write (my_cursor[0] )
```

Note that the first property in the array is number zero, the second property is number 1, and so on.

Use the cursor.columnName() method to get the names of columns in the result set. Again, use the array index value to refer to the desired property name.

```
write (my_cursor.columnName(0) )
```

When you create a cursor, the first row is the current row. To refer to data in subsequent rows, you must point to the next row using the `next()` method of the cursor in a loop. In this example, we display each row in an HTML table:

```
while my_cursor.next()  {
    write ("<TR><TD>" + my_cursor.First_Name + "</TD>")
    write ("<TD>" + my_cursor.Last_Name + "</TD></TR>")
}
```

You can't jump around or go backward in a cursor; you can only go forward. Nor can you use `next()` to move from the last row to first row. `Next()` returns `false` if the current row is the last row in the cursor (Figure 17.4).

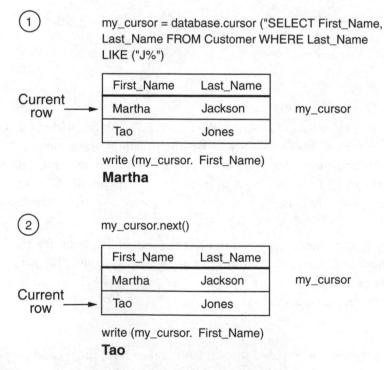

Figure 17.4 Navigating through a Cursor.

Another handy method of the `cursor` object is the `columns()` method. It returns the number of columns in the result set. It is commonly used to control a loop iterating through each column in a result set. This example outputs a row to an HTML table containing all the column names in a result set:

```
loop_counter = 0
column_count = my_cursor.columns()
write ("<TR>")

while loop_counter < column_count {
    write ("<TH>" + my_cursor.columnName(loop_counter) + "</TH>")
    loop_counter = loop_counter + 1
}
write ("</TR>")
```

Finally, when you are finished using a cursor, you should close it. Closing a cursor releases the memory used by the result set. When the cursor is closed, it is destroyed, but you can create it again if you need to.

```
my_cursor.close()
```

A cursor is automatically closed by LiveWire when the client request has been satisfied. In other words, you cannot keep the cursor open between pages.

Updating Data

LiveWire provides two techniques to update a database. You can use the method `database.execute()` to send a SQL statement directly to the DBMS. This statement can be an UPDATE, DELETE, or INSERT statement or any SQL statement that does not return a result set. The second technique uses a cursor to update, delete, or insert data using the current row. There are trade-offs between the two techniques. The execute method is more flexible, because you can submit SQL that is supported by the DBMS you are using. Remember that although SQL is a standard, DBMS vendors have their own extensions that you may want to take advantage of. On the other hand, using a cursor to update data produces an application that is more DBMS-independent.

Another difference between the two techniques lies in how each is processed. `Database.execute()` may update, delete, or insert many rows with a single statement. Using a cursor to update allows you to evaluate each row before you make any change to it. The nature of your application may help you decide which technique suits you better.

Using the Execute Method

Although the `database.execute()` method can be used to update a database, it may also be used to execute any SQL statement that does not return a result set. This includes statements that CREATE or DROP database tables, but does not include the SELECT statement. Some DBMS vendors provide stored procedures or triggers (or both) within which SQL statements are contained. These features are often used in commercial applications. The execute method is the prescribed way to invoke these and other extended features.

Using the execute method is also called *passthrough SQL*, because your SQL statement is passed directly to the server. This example updates the customer table:

```
database.execute ("UPDATE Customer SET Credit_Limit = Credit_Limit * 1.10")
```

Using a Cursor to Update the Database

We've seen how a cursor is used to retrieve data from a database. To use a cursor to update, delete, or insert data, you need to take extra steps. First, when you create the cursor, specify the `updatable` flag as `true`. For example:

```
my_cursor = database.cursor ( "SELECT First_Name, Last_Name from customer", True)
```

You can navigate through the cursor using the `cursor.next()` method. When you want to update the current row, assign new values to the columns to be updated. For example, we want to change a customer's name:

```
my_cursor.Last_Name = "Smith-Jones"
```

Then use the `cursor.updateRow()` method to update the table:

```
my_cursor.updateRow(Customer)
```

Inserting a row using a cursor is like using the current row as a template for a new row. You assign new values to the columns and then use `my_cursor.insertRow()`:

```
my_cursor.insertRow(Customer)
```

You may want to use this technique for inserting rows if you already have an open cursor and are processing rows. Otherwise, use the `database.execute` method if you just want to insert a row.

To delete the current row of the cursor, you don't need to assign any values. Just use `cursor.deleteRow()`.

```
My_cursor.deleteRow(Customer)
```

Managing Transactions

A database *transaction* consists of one or more SQL statements that must be executed as one unit of work. Statements are grouped in this way when you don't want to risk the possibility that the statements may be partially processed. Events such as system failure or SQL programming errors can cause incomplete processing.

Let's say you're at an ATM and you want to transfer $200 from your savings account to your checking account. Let's also assume that two things happen when you press **OK** to complete the transaction. First, $200 is subtracted from your balance in the savings accounts table. Then $200 is added to your checking account balance in the checking accounts table. There is a risk that if the computer goes down between the two steps, $200 will be "lost" from the savings account.

To ensure that this doesn't happen, SQL allows you to group both steps into one transaction. This arrangement gives you the assurance that either all statements in the group will be successfully processed, or will be processed. In our example, when you press **OK**, the ATM program will begin a database transaction. Then the program can update both tables. If all updates are successful, the changes are made permanent; the DBMS will *commit* the updates to the database, ending the transaction. If the system fails at any time between the beginning and the end of the transaction, the database may have been partially updated. When the DBMS is started again, it will automatically undo, or *roll back*, all changes made since the transaction began.

A rollback must sometimes be explicitly invoked from a program. To illustrate this, let's start the ATM scenario again. You press **OK**, begin the transaction and successfully execute the first update. This time, however, the DBMS fails to complete the second update because of a SQL error condition. The DBMS is still operating, so the ATM program must explicitly roll back the transaction.

For the most part, when implementing applications that do not update, insert, or delete data, you need not consider transaction management. However, if your application makes any changes to the database, you need to give it some thought. LiveWire implicitly begins a database transaction before each SQL statement and commits the transaction after each statement. This approach may be sufficient for your application. For example, consider a user activity that updates a customer's credit limit. This activity is performed within a single SQL update statement, and there are no other SQL statements related to it.

In summary, if the updating activity is composed of a single SQL statement that can be considered one unit of work, you need not explicitly begin, commit, and roll back transactions. However, if you have to process a unit of work that spans more than one SQL statement, you'll want to take explicit control over transactions. The amount of control over transaction management varies depending on the DBMS vendor. Check your vendor's documentation for details.

In LiveWire, explicit transaction management is handled with three methods of the database object: `beginTransaction()`, `commitTransaction()`, and `rollbackTransaction()`.

To begin a transaction, you must call the `beginTransaction()` method. Most DBMSs allow only a single transaction to exist at one time, so the transaction must end before you can begin another one. To make database changes permanent and end the transaction, use `commitTransaction()`. If you want to undo changes and end the transaction, call `rollbackTransaction()`.

Another way a transaction ends is when the Web page is exited. Keep this in mind when you are designing your Web application; you may not want to allow a unit of work to span Web pages. Keeping it within one page allows you to use the methods described. If you must design a unit of work that begins on one Web page and ends on another page, you cannot manage the transaction using these methods in a straightforward technique. Rather, if you commit changes on a Web page and then wish to undo them on a subsequent page, you'll have to keep track of those changes yourself and use the DELETE statement to roll back.

Handling Database Errors

Errors can occur while you're using a database in a LiveWire application, and a well-written application must be equipped to handle them. Errors happen for many reasons. For example, a statement might attempt to use a cursor object in an incorrect manner, such as referring to it when it doesn't exist. Or the DBMS may be unable to satisfy a SQL statement because the database server is down.

There are two ways to obtain information about database-related errors. First, many methods of the cursor and database objects return a status code as a result of their execution. These status codes are listed in Table 17.23. Second, there are four methods of the database object that return error codes and messages that have been issued by the DBMS.

Table 17.23 Database Status Codes

Status Code	Description
0	No error
1	Out of memory
2	Object never initialized
3	Data type conversion error
4	Database not registered
5	Error reported by database server
6	Message from database server
7	Error from DBMS vendor's library
8	Lost database connection
9	End of fetch (note: `fetch` and `next()` are synonymous)
10	Invalid use of object
11	Column does not exist
12	Invalid positioning within object
13	Unsupported feature
14	Null reference parameter
15	Database object not found
16	Required information is missing
17	Object cannot support multiple readers
18	Object cannot support deletions
19	Object cannot support insertions

Table 17.23 Database Status Codes (continued)

Status Code	Description
20,21	Object cannot support updates
22	Object cannot support indices
23	Object cannot be dropped
24	Incorrect connection supplied
25	Object cannot support privileges
26	Object cannot support cursors
27	Unable to open

The methods that return a LiveWire database status code are execute, insertRow, updateRow, deleteRow, beginTransaction, commitTransaction, and rollbackTransaction. It is a good idea to check the status code each time one of these methods is invoked. You can see the status codes when you run the application using the trace facility. Also, you can display a message in HTML when an error has interfered with a user's interaction with the application.

```
StatusCode = database.execute("DELETE FROM Customer WHERE Customer_Type = "xxx")
If (StatusCode <> 0) {
    write ("The customer could not be deleted due to a system error. <BR>")
    write ("Statement = database.execute("DELETE FROM Customer WHERE Customer_Type =
"xxx")
    write ("Database status code = " + StatusCode)
}
```

A nonzero LiveWire database status code is sometimes returned because the DBMS had a problem satisfying a request. For this reason, you must obtain error information from the DBMS by using the following database object methods:

- majorErrorCode() obtains the return code from the database server for the most recent database request.

- majorErrorMessage obtains the text corresponding to the major error code.

- minorErrorCode() obtains a secondary error code from the DBMS library.

- minorErrorMessage obtains the text corresponding to the minor error code.

The information you get from these methods varies according to the DBMS being used as well as the LiveWire database status code that occurred. Include these methods in your error-handling routine. It is up to you to interpret their results according to your DBMS error documentation.

LiveWire Database Object

Table 17.24 lists the LiveWire `database` object methods.

Table 17.24 Database Object Methods

Method	Description	Parameters	Returns
connect	Connect to a database	DB type, servername, username, password, Dbname	None
connected	Check for valid database connection	None	Return true if a valid database connection exists-
disconnect	Cut the database connection	None	None
beginTransaction	Begins a SQL transaction	None	Status code
commitTransaction	Commit the current transaction	None	Status code
rollbackTransaction	Cancel the current transaction	None	Status code
cursor	Create a cursor for a SQL SELECT statement	String containing SQL statement, boolean indicating updatable cursor	Cursor handle, used to refer to the cursor in subsequent operations
execute	Send any SQL to the server to be processed	String containing SQL statement	Status code
SQLTable	An easy way to produce an HTML page with SQL SELECT results	String containing SQL statement	None

Table 17.24 Database Object Methods (continued)

Method	Description	Parameters	Returns
majorErrorCode	Obtain the major error code returned by the DBMS	None	Returns the major error code returned by the DBMS
minorErrorCode	Obtain the minor error code returned by the DBMS	None	Returns the mino rerror code returned by the DBMS
majorErrorMessage	Obtain the text corresponding to the major error code returned by the DBMS	None	Returns the text corresponding to the major error code returned by the DBMS
minorErrorMessage	Obtain the text corresponding to the minor error code returned by the DBMS	None	Returns the text corresponding to the minor error code returned by the DBMS

LiveWire Cursor Object

Table 17.25 shows the cursor object methods.

Table 17.25 Cursor Object Methods

Method	Description	Parameters	Returns
columns	Obtains the number of columns in the cursor	None	Returns the number of columns in the cursor
columnName	Obtains the name of a column in the cursor	A number corresponding to the column name in the query. The first column is 0.	Returns the name of a column in the cursor

Table 17.25 Cursor Object Methods (continued)

Method	Description	Parameters	Returns
Close	Closes the cursor; discards the result set	None	None
deleteRow	Deletes the current row in the specified table	Name of table to delete from	Status code
insertRow	Inserts a row after the current row in the specified table	Name of table in which to insert	Status code
next	Makes the next row in the cursor the current row	None	Returns false if the current row is the last row in the cursor
updateRow	Updates the current row in the specified table	Name of table to update	Status code

CHAPTER EIGHTEEN

A SAMPLE LIVEWIRE APPLICATION: LIVEWIRE CHAT

In this chapter we will show you how to create live chat software using server-side JavaScript and LiveWire. LiveWire Chat was written by Darryl Stoflet (http://www.calweb.com/~dstoflet). It is a working application that provides an example of the kinds of interactive applications you can create using LiveWire. LiveWire Chat is a testimonial to the capabilities of LiveWire and gives an excellent illustration of the LiveWire object framework and how it is used. This chapter is based on Stoflet's documentation.

We will show you how easy it is to create places on the Internet where people can interact. To understand this application, you should be familiar with the general concept of how a LiveWire application works. See Chapter 16 for details.

This chapter covers:

- How LiveWire Chat works
- Source files used to build the application

How It Works

To illustrate how LiveWire Chat works, Figure 18.1 shows a visual representation of the source files and their relationships to each other. The main idea here is to convey an understanding of the runtime communication between source files.

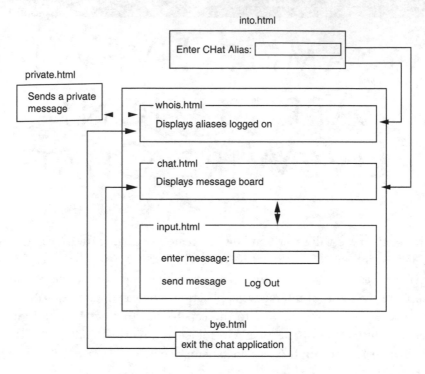

Figure 18.1 LiveWire Chat application architecture (created by Darryl Stoflet).

Source Files That Build the Application

LiveWire Chat is made up of eight source files. Let's look at each of them.

intro.html

When a browser requests the chat application, LiveWire responds with the **intro.html** page. This is the first page the user sees. It contains the following:

- A text box into which the user enters a chat alias
- A hidden form element
- A submit button

The name of the text box element in the HTML is who. Its value will be the chat alias entered by the user. The **intro.html** page also contains a hidden form element called enter. Its value is initially set to true. When the user clicks the submit button, the action attribute calls **index.html**, which processes the form contents.

Using the request and client Objects

When a browser requests a page from a LiveWire application, LiveWire creates an instance of the request object. The request object has predefined built-in properties. For example, IP is the IP address of the browser, and agent is the type of browser you are using. However, this chat application uses no built-in properties of the request object. Rather, it creates its own properties by using the names of the HTML form elements. When a user enters a chat alias into the text box called who and presses the submit button, a property identified as request.who is automatically created by LiveWire. Its value is set to the alias entered by the user. This request.who property is available to **index.html**, because **index.html** is POSTing itself to the server for processing by **index.html**, as in this line of code:

```
<FORM METHOD="post" ACTION = "index.html">
```

The request object is short-lived. It exists only for the duration of the page request. After the page has been requested and any server-side scripting has been performed, the request object is destroyed along with its properties and values. If you wish to have the values exist for a longer period of time, you must assign them to a property in the longer-lasting client object. By default, the client object keeps its property values for 10 minutes. An *instance* of the client object is created for every unique client that accesses a LiveWire application. This application uses the user's IP address to identify each client. This approach may be acceptable for a sample application. On the Internet, however, users accessing a Web site via a proxy server may not have unique IP addresses, so beware.

We want to retain the user's chat alias beyond a single page request, so **index.html** assigns the `request.who` value to `client.who`. Any time we want to reference this user's chat alias, we simply use `client.who`. Remember that many users may access the chat application at the same time. Each user will have his or her own `client` object, with its own values unique to that client.

We'll also copy `request.enter` to `client.enter` (this was set to `true` in the hidden form element of **intro.html**). We do this because we need a way to pass the value of `request.enter` from **index.html** to another page, **chat.html**. Remember that `request.enter` is destroyed immediately after **index.html** is retrieved. When `request.enter` is `true`, **chat.html** uses the chat alias to write "So-and-so has just entered." Figure 18.2 shows the LiveWire Chat entry page.

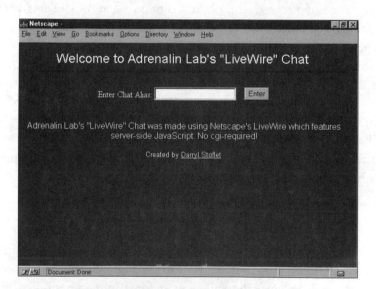

Figure 18.2 LiveWire Chat entry page.

Listing 18.1 shows **intro.html**.

Listing 18.1 intro.html

```
<!- After a user types in a chat alias and presses submit,
the form's data will be sent the server , which is running
LiveWire.  The LiveWire server extensions will take the chat
alias from the form element <INPUT TYPE = "text"
NAME = "who"> and put it into request.who.  Clicking the
submit button also retrieves the index.html page.  The
index.html page contains server-side JavaScript, which will
process the values stored in the request object.
!->
<HTML>
<BODY  bgcolor="#004080"  text="#ffffff"  link="#ffff80"  vlink="#ffff00"  >
<CENTER>
<FONT FACE="Arial" SIZE=5>
Welcome to Adrenalin Lab's "LiveWire" Chat
</FONT>
<hr>
<FORM METHOD="post" ACTION = "index.html">

<!-text box used to create request.who property, value set
to user's input. !->
Enter Chat Alias: <INPUT TYPE = "text" NAME = "who">

<!-hidden element used to create a request property called
"enter", value set to "true"!->
<INPUT TYPE= "hidden" NAME="enter" VALUE = "true">

<!-Clicking the submit button will post the form's data to
the server and retrieve the index.html page.!->
   <INPUT TYPE = "submit" VALUE = "Enter">
</FORM>
</FONT>
<br>
<FONT FACE="Arial" SIZE=3>
Adrenalin Lab's "LiveWire" Chat was made using Netscape's
LiveWire, which features server-side JavaScript.  No CGI required!<br><br>
</FONT>
<FONT FACE="Arial" SIZE=2>
Created by <A HREF="mailto:dstoflet@calweb.com">
Darryl Stoflet</A>
</CENTER>
</BODY>
</HTML>
```

index.html

Index.html creates a frameset consisting of three frames that make up the chat environment: **chat.html**, **input.html**, and **whois.html**. Refer to Figure 18.3 displays these pages during an actual chat session.

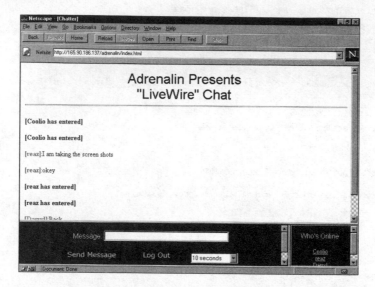

Figure 18.3 LiveWire Chat in action.

Listing 18.2 shows **index.html**.

Listing 18.2 index.html

```
<HTML>
<HEAD>
<TITLE>Chatter</TITLE>
<SCRIPT LANGUAGE = "JavaScript">
<!-
function showWhois(){
    parent.frames[2].location.href="whois.html";
    parent.frames[1].location.href = "input.html";
}
//-->
</SCRIPT>
</HEAD>
<SERVER>
```

```
    //request.enter and request.who passed from input.html.
    //Save values in longer-lived client object.
    client.enter = request.enter;
    client.who = request.who;

    //client.who was passed from intro.html.  Append it to
    //current list in the property object, which lives until
    //the application is stopped by an administrator.
    project.participants = "" + client.who + "|" +
        project.participants +     "";
</SERVER>

<!- Most of the message handling and displaying is handled
in the chat.html page !-->
<FRAMESET ROWS= "*, 100">
<FRAME SRC= "chat.html" NAME="content" >

<FRAMESET COLS = "80%,20%" onLoad ="showWhois()" >
  <FRAME SRC = "blank.html" NAME= "input">
  <FRAME SRC = "blank.html" NAME= "whois" SCROLLING=AUTO>
  </FRAMESET>
</FRAMESET>
</HTML>
```

input.html

Input.html is used to enter and send messages. It contains a form with the following elements:

- A text box in which the user enters a message
- Hidden form elements used to determine whether a user is sending a message or logging off
- A submit button requesting **chat.html** as the action

It is important to note that each form element has a `name` attribute. Each `name` attribute will become a `request` object property. **chat.html** will use the values passed by the form on **input.html**. Listing 18.3 shows **input.html**.

Listing 18.3 input.html

```
<HTML>
<!-On this page a user may send a message or log out.
!-->
```

```
<HEAD>
<SCRIPT LANGUAGE="JavaScript">
<!–
var  theRate = 20000;

//Following are a few client-side functions that mainly act as form input
//collectors and form submitters.
    function sendMsg(){
        document.forms[0].submit();
        document.forms[0].msg.value = "";
    }
    function logout(){
        document.forms[0].leave.value = "true";
        document.forms[0].submit();
    }
    function setRefresh(form){
        var w = form.refresh.selectedIndex
        theRate = form.refresh.options[w].value
    }
    function refresher(){
        parent.frames[0].history.go(0)
        setTimeout("refresher()",theRate);
    }

setTimeout("refresher()",theRate);

//–>
</SCRIPT>
</HEAD>
<BODY  bgcolor="#004080"  text="#ffffff" >
<FORM METHOD="post"    ACTION = "chat.html" TARGET="content">
<CENTER><FONT FACE="Arial">Message: </FONT>
<INPUT TYPE = "text" SIZE= 40 NAME="msg"><br><br>
<INPUT TYPE="hidden" NAME= "leave" VALUE = "">
<INPUT TYPE="hidden" NAME= "remove" VALUE = "">
<INPUT TYPE="hidden" NAME= "tour" VALUE = "">
<INPUT TYPE="hidden" NAME= "add" VALUE = "true">
<A HREF= "javascript:sendMsg()"><IMG BORDER=0 ALIGN=bottom WIDTH=140 HEIGHT=25
SRC="send_msg.gif"></A>
 
<A HREF= "javascript:logout()"><IMG BORDER=0 ALIGN=bottom WIDTH=140 HEIGHT=25 S
    RC="logout.gif"></A>
 
<FONT FACE="Arial"><SELECT NAME= "refresh" onChange = "setRefresh(this.form)">
<OPTION VALUE = "20000">Refresh Rate
<OPTION VALUE = "10000">10 seconds
<OPTION VALUE = "15000" >15 seconds
```

```
<OPTION VALUE = "20000" >20 seconds
<OPTION VALUE = "25000">25 seconds
<OPTION VALUE = "30000">30 seconds
</SELECT>
</CENTER>
</FORM>
</BODY>
</HTML>
```

Note that we have used the setTimeout() method to set the refresh rates. We pass the form element value to the function setRefresh() every time the user wants to change the refresh rate for the document.

chat.html

Chat.html displays all messages posted by chat users as well as messages generated from the entry and exit of users. It uses a file object created with the filename **jitters.txt**. This file is used to collect messages from all users of the chat application.

When a user accesses **chat.html**, the server-side script checks whether the client.enter property for that user equals true. If it does, the file is updated with the new user's chat alias. The file is opened for reading, and all the messages are read into a variable. Then a string consisting of the user's chat alias plus "has entered" is appended to the variable. The file is opened again and updated from the variable, and client.enter is reset to false. Finally, the file's contents are written to the page. This technique ensures that other chat users will see the new "has entered" message as well as the previous messages.

If client.enter does not equal true, the user may have sent a message from **input.html**. If so, the chat file is updated with the new message. In any case, after any update to the chat file, **chat.html** is regenerated using data from the chat file. The next request by any client for this page will contain the latest message.

Chat.html uses a hidden form element on **input.html** called add to detect when a user has submitted a message. **Input.html** contains a text box in which the user enters a message. When the user clicks the submit button, **chat.html** is the action requested. When **chat.html** is retrieved, the request.add property of the request object is created. Request.add is initially set to true by the `value` attribute of the hidden form element. **Chat.html** checks whether `request.add` = `true`. If it does, the chat file is updated with the new message.

Similarly, **chat.html** knows when a user has logged off from the chat application. **Input.html** has a logoff button. When a user clicks this button, a hidden form element called `logoff` is set to `true`. **Chat.html** checks whether `request.logoff` equals `true`. If it does, the chat file is updated with the appropriate message. Subsequently, the `redirect` function is used to send the **bye.html** page to the user.

Listing 18.4 shows **chat.html**.

Listing 18.4 chat.html

```
<HTML>
<HEAD>
<TITLE>Chat</TITLE>
</HEAD>
<BODY bgcolor="#ffffff"  text="#000000">
<CENTER>
<FONT FACE="Arial" SIZE= 6  COLOR ="#000000" >
Adrenalin Presents <br>
"LiveWire" Chat
<HR>
</FONT>
</CENTER>
<SERVER>
   //create a text file to store all the messages posted
   //to the chat.
   chatfile = new File("jitter.txt");
   //If the chatfile is large, let's clear it.
   if(chatfile.getLength() > 2000){
      //Lock the project so it cannot be accessed while we
      //alter the chatfile.
      project.lock()
      //open the chatfile for writing—clearing the file
      chatfile.open("w");
      //Unlock the project so the chatfile may be accessed
      project.unlock()
   }
   //If someone clicked the "logout" button,
   // send user to bye.html
   if(request.leave == "true"){
      client.expiration(30);
      redirect("bye.html");
```

```
}
//If the user came from intro.html
if(client.enter == "true"){
    // clear out the value of client.enter so this won't
    // be performed again.
    client.enter = "";
    project.lock()
    chatfile.open("r"); //open the chatfile for reading
    //read in the contents of the file into oldMsg
    oldMsg = chatfile.read(chatfile.getLength())
    chatfile.close()
    chatfile.open("w"); //open the chatfile for writing.
    //add the entering person's alias to the chatfile
    chatfile.write("<br><b>[" + client.who + " has entered]
        </b>" + "<br>" + oldMsg);
    chatfile.close(); //close the chatfile;
    //Unlock the project so the chatfile may be accessed
    project.unlock();
}
//If the user clicked Submit on the input.html page
if(request.add == "true"){
    project.lock()
    chatfile.open("r");  //open the chatfile for reading
    oldMsg = chatfile.read(chatfile.getLength())
    chatfile.close()
    chatfile.open("w");  //reopen the chatfile for writing
    //write user's name, message, plus existing chatfile
    chatfile.write("<br><b><FONT COLOR=#ff0000>
        [" + request.nom + "]</FONT></b>:" + request.msg
        + "<br>" + oldMsg);
    client.who = request.nom;
    chatfile.close();
    project.unlock()
}
//If we have updated the chatfile but not the page
if(chatfile.getLength() > 0 ){
    project.lock()
    chatfile.open("r");
    line = chatfile.read(chatfile.getLength());
    chatfile.close()
    project.unlock()
    flush();
    //Write the contents of the chatfile to the page
    //so the user may view all messages.
    write(line);
}
```

```
    client.enter ="false";
</SERVER>
</BODY>
</HTML>
```

whois.html

Whois.html displays all chat aliases that are currently on-line. When a user accesses **chat.html** for the first time, his or her chat alias is put into a property of the `project` object. A `project` object in the LiveWire object framework has the second longest life duration, second only to the `server` object. The `project` object is available to all users (clients) at any time from within any page that makes up the LiveWire application. In other words, it is shared by all users. The `project` object is created when the application is started and is destroyed when the application is stopped. (The `server` object is created or destroyed when the server is started or stopped.) `Project.participants` contains a list of all chat aliases, separated by the delimiting character "|".

    Whois.html scans the `project.participants` property, parses each alias, and creates an array to hold them. Each chat alias is written to the page. The chat aliases are written within an HTML anchor tag (A HREF) so that a user can click on an alias and send a private message to that person.

    Listing 18.5 shows **whois.html**.

Listing 18.5 whois.html

```
<HTML>
<!--
This page lists all user aliases currently in the chat.
!-->
<HEAD>
<SCRIPT LANGUAGE="JavaScript">
<!--
setTimeout("whois()",17000);

function whois(){
    location.href = "whois.html"
}
function directMsg(to){
    receiver = to;
    parent.frames[1].location.href = "private.html";
```

```
}

//-->
</SCRIPT>
</HEAD>
<BODY bgcolor="#004080" text="#ffffff" link="#ffffff" vlink="#ffffff" >
<CENTER>
<FONT SIZE=3 FACE= "Arial">
Who's Online
<hr align = center width=80%>
</FONT>
<FONT SIZE=2 FACE= "Arial">
<SERVER>
    //If the user clicked on a name for a private message
    if(request.priv == "true"){

        //Copy the request property values from the private.html
        //form to project properties so that they will be
        //available to other chat users
        project.privateMsg = request.priMsg;
        project.sound = request.sound;
        project.rec = request.to;
        project.from = client.who;
    }
    function makeArray(n){
      this.length = n;
      for(var i = 1; i <= n; i++)
          this[i] = "";
      return this;
    }
    pTotal = 0;
    pLen = project.participants.length
    for(var i = 1; i <= pLen; i++){
        if(project.participants.charAt(i) == "|"){
            pTotal++; //pTotal accumulates total participants
        }
    }
    delimLoc = new makeArray(pTotal + 1);
    userName = new makeArray(pTotal +1);
    iter = 1;

    for(var i = 1; i <= pLen; i++){
        if(project.participants.charAt(i) == "|"){
            delimLoc[iter] = i;
            iter++;
        }
    }
```

```
 oldLoc = 0;

//Load array of aliases using project.participants
for(var i = 1; i <=  pTotal; i++){
    userName[i] =
    project.participants.substring(oldLoc,delimLoc[i]);
    if(userName[i] == client.who){
        elemAt = i;
    }
    oldLoc = delimLoc[i] +1;
}

//Clear project.participants before we update it
project.participants = "";

//Create a link for every alias so that private messages
//can be sent.
for(var i = 1; i <= pTotal; i++){
    if(i != elemAt){
        project.participants +=  userName[i] + "|" ;
        write("<A HREF=\"javascript:directMsg(\'"
                + userName[i] + "\')\">" + userName[i]
                + "</A><br>");
    }else{
        project.participants +=  client.who + "|";
        write("<A HREF=\"javascript:directMsg(\'"
                + client.who + "\')\">" + client.who
                + "</A><br>");
    }
}
//If current user requesting whois.html has a private message pending
//to be sent to him, then open a window and display the message.
    if(project.rec == client.who){
        if(project.sound == "nuts"){
            soundMsg = "<EMBED SRC=\"nuts.au\" HIDDEN=TRUE>";
        }
        else if(project.sound == "ohjoy"){
            soundMsg = "<EMBED SRC=\"ohjoy.au\" HIDDEN=TRUE>";
        }
        else if(project.sound == "danger"){
            soundMsg = "<EMBED SRC=\"danger.au\" HIDDEN=TRUE>";
        }
        else if(project.sound == "null"){
            soundMsg = "No Sound Sent.";
        }
        write("<SCRIPT LANGUAGE = 'JavaScript'>")
        write("var priWin = window.open ('','privateMsg',
```

```
            '0,0,0,0,0,0,0,WIDTH=200,HEIGHT=200');");
        write("var w = priWin.document;w.open();
        w.write(\"<HTML><HEAD><TITLE>Private message
            </TITLE></HEAD>\");");
        write("w.write('<BODY BGCOLOR=\"white\"><CENTER>');");
        write("w.write('Private Message From: " + project.from
            + "<br><br>" + project.privateMsg + "<br>');");
        write("w.write('" + soundMsg + "<FORM>
            <INPUT TYPE=button
            VALUE=\"Close\"onclick=\"self.close()\"');");
        write("w.write('</FORM></BODY></HTML>');");
        write("w.close()");
        write("</SCRIPT>");
        //Clear project.rec so that the private message isn't
        //received again and another message can be sent.
        project.rec =""
    }
</SERVER>
</FONT>
</CENTER>
</BODY>
</HTML>
```

private.html

Private.html appears when a user clicks on a chat alias displayed in the **whois.html** page. **Private.html** allows the user to send a message or sound bite privately to a particular person. Once again, this capability is made possible by using form element names and values.

For example, when a user clicks on a radio button for a sound bite called "danger," a form element named `sound` is set to `danger`. When the user clicks the submit button (**Send Private Message**), **whois.html** is retrieved, displaying all chat aliases. **Whois.html** saves the sender, recipient, and message to the `project` object. Whenever any user requests **whois.html**, a check is made to see whether the requester's chat alias matches the name of the person who is to receive a message. If it matches, the message or sound bite is delivered to the requesting chat user. Figure 18.4 illustrates this process.

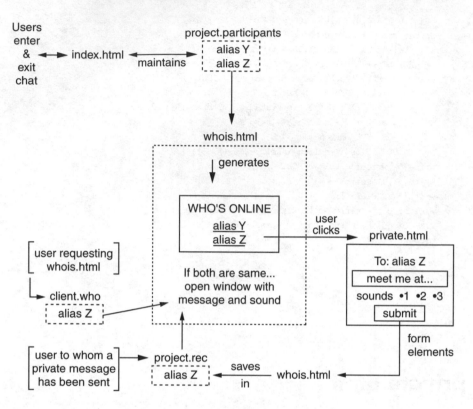

Figure 18.4 Sending a private message.

Listing 18.6 shows **private.html**.

Listing 18.6 private.html

```
<HTML>
<HEAD>
<TITLE>Private Message</TITLE>
<SCRIPT LANGUAGE="JavaScript">
   function retract(){
      parent.frames[1].location.href = "input.html";
   }
</SCRIPT>
</HEAD>
<BODY bgcolor="#ffffff">
<SCRIPT LANGUAGE='JavaScript'>
   document.write("<FORM METHOD = 'post'
```

```
        ACTION = 'whois.html' TARGET = 'whois'>");
    document.write("To: <b>" + parent.frames[2].receiver
        + "</b><br>");
</SCRIPT>
<INPUT TYPE="text" NAME="priMsg" SIZE=40 MAXLENGTH=100><br>
<b>Sound: </b><INPUT TYPE = "radio" NAME = "sound" VALUE= "nuts"><b>Nuts!</b>  
<INPUT TYPE="radio" NAME="sound" VALUE="ohjoy">
<b>Oh Joy</b>  
<INPUT TYPE="radio" NAME="sound" VALUE="danger">
<b>Danger!</b>  
 
<INPUT TYPE = "hidden" NAME="priv" VALUE = "true" >
<SCRIPT LANGUAGE="JavaScript">
    document.write("<INPUT TYPE = 'hidden' NAME='to'
        VALUE = \"" + parent.frames[2].receiver +  "\">");
</SCRIPT>
<INPUT TYPE="submit"VALUE="Submit">
<INPUT TYPE="button" VALUE="back to chat" onClick = "retract()">
</FORM>
</BODY>
</HTML>
```

bye.html

When a chat user clicks the logoff button, he or she is redirected to **bye.html**. The logoff button sets the value of a form element (logoff) to true. If request.logoff equals true, then **chat.html** calls the redirect function to send the user to **bye.html**. **Bye.html** then removes the exiting chat alias from project.participants. In this manner, the **whois.html** frame remains current. Listing 18.7 shows **bye.html**.

Listing 18.7 bye.html

```
<SERVER>
    //Update the chatfile that the user has logged off.
    //See similar code in chat.html
    chatfile = new File("jitter.txt");
    project.lock()
    chatfile.open("r");
    oldMsg = chatfile.read(chatfile.getLength())
    chatfile.close()
    chatfile.open("w");
    chatfile.write("<br><b>[" + client.who
```

```
          + "</FONT> has logged out.</b>]<br>" + oldMsg);
     chatfile.flush();
     chatfile.close();
     project.unlock()
     //Remove the alias from project.participants.
     //This keeps the Who's On-line frame current.
     //See similar code in whois.html
     function makeArray(n){
        this.length = n;
        for(var i = 1; i <= n; i++)
           this[i] = "";
        return this;
     }
     pTotal = 0;
     pLen = project.participants.length
     for(var i = 1; i <= pLen; i++){
        if(project.participants.charAt(i) == "|"){
           pTotal++;
        }
     }
     delimLoc = new makeArray(pTotal + 1);
     userName = new makeArray(pTotal +1);
     iter = 1;

     for(var i = 1; i <= pLen; i++){
        if(project.participants.charAt(i) == "|"){
           delimLoc[iter] = i;
           iter++;
        }
     }
      oldLoc = 0;
      for(var i = 1; i <=  pTotal; i++){
         userName[i] =
         project.participants.substring(oldLoc,delimLoc[i]);
         if(userName[i] == client.who){
            elemAt = i;
         }
         oldLoc = delimLoc[i] +1;
     }
     project.participants = "";
     for(var i = 1; i <= pTotal; i++){
        if(i == elemAt){
           project.participants +=  "";
        }else{
           project.participants +=  userName[i] + "|" ;
        }
     }
</SERVER>
```

```
<HTML>
<HEAD>
<SCRIPT LANGUAGE="JavaScript">
    //user is sent to bye2.html, where he or she can leave.
    parent.location.href = "bye2.html";
```

bye2.html

This page is sent to users after they have logged off. Listing 18.8 shows **bye2.html**.

Listing 18.8 bye2.html

```
<HTML>
<HEAD>
<TITLE>
Goodbye
</TITLE>
<BODY bgcolor="#004080" text="#ffffff" link="#ffff00" vlink="#ffff00">
<CENTER>
<FONT FACE="Arial" SIZE=4>
Thank you for visiting Adrenalin's "LiveWire" Chat
</FONT>
<br><br>
<BLOCKQUOTE>
<FONT FACE="Arial" SIZE=3>
Return to <A HREF="http://www.calweb.com/~dstoflet" TARGET="_parent">Adrenalin</A>
<br><br>OR
<br><br>
<A HREF="intro.html">I gotta go back</A>
</FONT>
</BLOCKQUOTE>
</FONT>
</CENTER>
</BODY>
</HTML>
```

PART FIVE

THE END?

CHAPTER NINETEEN

FINAL WORDS

I hope you've enjoyed this tour through the world of JavaScript. We've covered a great deal of territory—but it's good to keep in mind that the industry is changing rapidly. This book is only the first in your journey into the interactive age. We're not even close to seeing the end of that journey. The forthcoming Netscape and Microsoft browsers should bring major changes in JavaScript technology.

In this chapter we'll offer suggestions about how you can take advantage of your newly acquired knowledge. We'll discuss how to use your JavaScript expertise in working with other technologies, such as VRML and ActiveX. We'll also talk about some bugs you may encounter using JavaScript 1.1 on Netscape 3.0.

This chapter will cover:

- Using JavaScript with other technologies
- JavaScript bugs
- How do you keep up?

Using JavaScript with Other Technologies

In Chapter 12, we showed you how to use JavaScript with CGI, and the entire section on LiveConnect (Part 3) was about using JavaScript to communicate with plug-ins and Java applets. Here, we'll talk about two other technologies that can communicate with JavaScript. Using the JavaScript method `document.write()` you can write and manipulate a VRML model in a page. Using a LiveConnect-enabled browser such as Netscape 3.0+, you can manipulate ActiveX controls using JavaScript.

JavaScript with VRML

To illustrate how JavaScript can work with VRML, we have taken an example from Aereal Inc. The example, called Adrian's Grapher, is located at http://www.aereal.com/javascript/grapher.html. Adrian's Grapher presents three text boxes where users specify a number of intervals, the starting point of a graph, and the ending point of a graph. After users specify these coordinates, they can see what the VRML model will look like by pressing a button called **Create VRML**.

First, we create two frames. One frame holds plain HTML code, and the other holds the VRML model:

```
<HTML><HEAD>

<Frameset  cols="30%,70%">

 <Frame name="html" src="riemann.htm">

 <Frame name="vrmlFrame" src="http://www.aereal.com/home.wrl.gz" >

</Frameset>

</HEAD>

</HTML>
```

riemann.htm holds all the form elements with the button **Create VRML**. This button calls the function `doVRML()`, which displays the VRML in the other frame.

Listing 19.1 is the HTML file to show the JavaScript function displaying the VRML model.

Listing 19.1 riemann.html

```
<HTML>
<HEAD>
<TITLE>JavaScript test</TITLE>
<SCRIPT LANGUAGE="JavaScript">
<!— let's play "Hide the Script!"
/*
    Adrian's Grapher
    Copyright 1996 Adrian Scott
    http://www.aereal.com
    adrian@aereal.com
    scotta@rpi.edu
*/
function do_vrml() {
    var mime_type = "x-world/x-vrml";
//    var mime_type = "text/plain";

    vrml = parent.vrmlFrame;

    vrml.document.open( mime_type );

    vrmlheader(document.hello.x0.value, document.hello.x1.value);

//    vrml.document.writeln("Separator { AsciiText { string \"" +
        document.hello.funct.value + "\" } }");
    for(i=0;i<=document.hello.n.value;i++) {
        nextblock(i, document.hello.n.value, document.hello.x0.value, docu
            ment.hello.x1.value, vrml);
    }

    vrmlfooter();

    vrml.document.close();

}

// do the next Riemann block
function nextblock(i, n, x0, x1, vrml) {

    x = (x0/1) + i*(1/n)*(x1-x0);

    depth = Math.cos(x);  // function's derivative's value
    width = (1/n)*(x1-x0);
    height = Math.sin(x);  // function's value

    y = height/2;
    z = depth/2;

    depth = Math.abs(depth);
    height = Math.abs(height);
```

```
    vrml.document.writeln("Separator {");
    vrml.document.writeln(" Translation { translation " + x + " " + y + " " + z
        + " }");
    vrml.document.writeln(" Cube { height " + height + " depth " + depth + "
        width " + width + " }");
    vrml.document.writeln("}");
}

// VRML header
function vrmlheader(x0, x1) {
    cameramidpoint = ((x1 - x0)/2) + (x0/1);
    cameradistance = x1 - x0;
     vrml.document.writeln("#VRML V1.0 ascii");
     vrml.document.writeln("");
       vrml.document.writeln("Separator { DEF BackgroundColor Info { string \"1
           1 0\" }");
    vrml.document.writeln("DEF Cameras Switch { whichChild 0");
    vrml.document.writeln(" DEF Function PerspectiveCamera { position " + cam
        eramidpoint + " 0 " + cameradistance + " }");
    vrml.document.writeln(" DEF Derivative PerspectiveCamera { position " + cam
        eramidpoint + " " + cameradistance + " 0 ");
    vrml.document.writeln("                    orientation 1 0 0 -1.57 }");
    vrml.document.writeln("}");
    vrml.document.writeln(" Material { diffuseColor 0 .7 0 }");
}

// VRML footer
function vrmlfooter() {
    vrml.document.writeln("}");
}

// End of hide the script ->
</SCRIPT>
</HEAD>

<BODY>
<a href="http://www.aereal.com">Aereal Inc.</a> presents...<p>

<h1>Adrian's Grapher</h1>

<b>You can graph the <i>sin(x)</i>
function — and its derivative!</b>
The derivative (<i>cos(x)</i>) is the
depth of the cubes, so spin the graph
down 90 degrees to see the graph of the
derivative!<p>

<FORM name="hello">
```

```
<p>

The number of intervals, N, is
an integer greater than zero (e.g., 20).<br>

N: <input name="n" value="20"><p>

x0 is the starting point of the graph, a real
number (e.g., 0).<br>
x0: <input name="x0" value="0"><p>

x1 is the ending point of the graph, a real
number greater than x0 (e.g., 5).<br>

x1: <input name="x1" value="5"><p>
<INPUT TYPE="submit" value="Create VRML" onclick="do_vrml()">
</FORM>

<h6>Copyright 1996 by Adrian Scott.
<a href="mailto:adrian@aereal.com">adrian@aereal.com</a></h6>
</body>
</HTML>
```

Figure 19.1 shows the application in action.

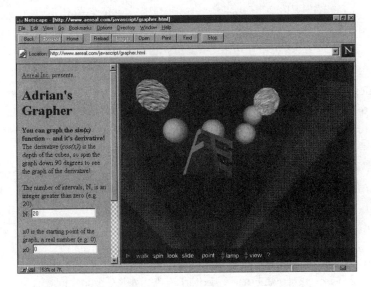

Figure 19.1 JavaScript working with VRML.

We have included this example along with a full VRML tutorial in the accompanying CD-ROM so that you can get more information on VRML. For VRML, Java, and JavaScript frequently asked questions, try http://www.aereal.com/faq/.

JavaScript with ActiveX

Using the LiveConnect framework on Netscape 3.0+, you can use JavaScript to call an ActiveX control. Because Netscape Navigator 3.0 does not support ActiveX at the time of this writing, you need a plug-in called ScriptActive, by Ncompasslabs Inc. To work with ActiveX, first you need to download the following software from the following sites:

- ScriptActive plug-in: http://www.ncompasslabs.com
- ActiveX control pad: http://www.microsoft.com

Once you install this software, you are ready to go. One note before we begin: you should probably look at the Ncompasslabs documentation to find out how its plug-in works. That documentation is located at http://www.ncompasslabs.com/documents/authoring.htm. For more information on ActiveX technology, try: http://www.microsoft.com/activex.

To demonstrate how JavaScript can work with ActiveX, I'll present a simple demo of an ActiveX button that is not captioned. I will show you how to caption the button from an HTML form. You can also change its background color.

First we use the ActiveX control pad and insert an ActiveX control called "Microsoft form 2.0 command button" in a dummy HTML page. We then specify its different properties just as we would in a Windows, Visual Basic, or Microsoft Access program. When we create the dummy HTML page that contains the object, it looks like the code shown in Listing 19.2.

Listing 19.2 Sample HTML Page Created in ActiveX Control Pad

```
<HTML>
<HEAD>
<TITLE>Dummy page</TITLE>
</HEAD>
<BODY>
```

```
<OBJECT ID="CommandButton1" WIDTH=148 HEIGHT=60
 CLASSID="CLSID:D7053240-CE69-11CD-A777-00DD01143C57">
    <PARAM NAME="ForeColor" VALUE="16777215">
    <PARAM NAME="BackColor" VALUE="16777215">
    <PARAM NAME="Caption" VALUE="JavaScript">
    <PARAM NAME="Size" VALUE="3916;1588">
    <PARAM NAME="FontEffects" VALUE="1073741825">
    <PARAM NAME="FontHeight" VALUE="480">
    <PARAM NAME="FontCharSet" VALUE="0">
    <PARAM NAME="FontPitchAndFamily" VALUE="2">
    <PARAM NAME="ParagraphAlign" VALUE="3">
    <PARAM NAME="FontWeight" VALUE="700">
</OBJECT>
</BODY>
</HTML>
```

The PARAM NAME= is the property name of the object that can be manipulated, as we will see later. After we save this file, we have two files: the name of this HTML page (**dummy.html**) and **CommandButton1.ODS**.

When you download the ScriptActive plug-in, you will find that it comes with an Ncompass HTML converter utility. Using this utility, we convert **dummy.html** to an **.OCX** file.

Figure 19.2 shows the demo program.

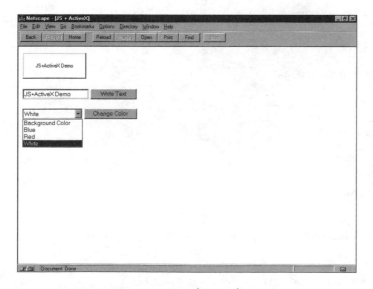

Figure 19.2 ActiveX working with JavaScript.

Next, we create another HTML page where we will call both the **.OCX** and the **.ODS** files. But before we do that, let's see the ActiveX methods you are allowed to call using the ScriptActive plug-in. From the Ncompasslabs documentation, you will see that only the following Java methods are publicly available to be invoked:

```
public Object GetProperty(String dispid)

public void SetProperty(String dispid, String property)
public void SetProperty(String dispid, Object property)

public Object Invoke(String dispid, Object params[])
public Object Invoke(String dispid)
public Object Invoke(String dispid, Object param1)
public Object Invoke(String dispid, Object param1, Object param2)
public Object Invoke(String dispid, Object param1, Object param2, Object param3)
public Object Invoke(String dispid, Object param1, Object param2, Object param3,
    Object param4)
```

Knowing that, we create the following HTML page and call only one Java method, `SetProperty()`. The file is shown in Listing 19.3.

Listing 19.3 HTML File to Call the ActiveX+JS Demo

```
<HTML>
<HEAD>
<TITLE>JS + ActiveX</TITLE>
</HEAD>
<BODY bgcolor=white>
<embed
    SRC="CommandButton1.ODS"
     NAME="buttonX"
    WIDTH=148
    HEIGHT=60
    CODEBASE="test_bug3.ocx"
    LIVECONNECT
>
<script>
function Change1(form){
temp=""
temp=form.input_name.value;
document.buttonX.SetProperty('caption', temp);
}
function change2(form){
if (form.bgcolor[1].selected){
```

```
        document.buttonX.SetProperty('BackColor',16744448);
        }
else if (form.bgcolor[2].selected){
        document.buttonX.SetProperty('BackColor',255);
        }
else document.buttonX.SetProperty('BackColor',16777215);
}
</script>
<form>
<input type=text value=" " name="input_name"><nobr>
<input    type=button onclick="Change1(this.form)" value="  Write Text   ">
<p>
<select name=bgcolor>
<option selected>Background Color
<option> Blue
<option> Red
<option> White
</select>
<input type=Button onclick="change2(this.form)"  value="Change Color">
</form>
</BODY>
</HTML>
```

Note that we use the `<embed>` tag to embed the object in the HTML Page. This object is given the name `buttonX`, and we call its `SetProperty()` methods to change its properties.

JavaScript Bugs

While writing this book, we found some bugs in Netscape Navigator 3.0. When Navigator 4.0 comes to the market, I am sure many of the bugs will be eliminated. If you would like to know about the current bugs in the Navigator version you are using, just click on **Help | Release note** from your browser. You will find all the known JavaScript bugs listed in the Netscape homepage.

The first bug we found is that the event handlers `onSelect` and `onBlur` do not work properly in some platforms. The solution to this problem is to have JavaScript write the form elements and event handlers using the `document.write()` method, such as

```
document.write("<form><input type=text onSelect='functionCall()'></form>");
```

The following is not really a bug, but when writing JavaScript code using `document.write()`, such as the following, you will get an error message: "Missing) after the argument list."

```
<html><head>
<script>
function myfunction(){
document.write("<html><body><script>alert('Help')</script></html></body>");
}
</script></head>
<body>
<form>
<input type=button value="click"onClick="myfunction()">
</form>
</body>
</html>
```

The solution to this problem is to put a "\" (escape sequence) before the `/script` tag like this:

```
document.write("<html><body><script>alert('Help')</script></html></body>");
```

The `lastModified` date for a page does not always display the correct date. Sometimes the `lastModified` date is 1970.

When you're writing a table, using `document.write()` can produce messy table formatting. For example:

```
<HTML>
<BODY BGCOLOR="#fffbf0" TEXT="#1f1f1f">
<SCRIPT>
document.write("<b><p align=right><font size=-1>"+ month);
document.write(myweekday+","+day+ " 19" + year + "</font></b>");
</SCRIPT>
</BODY></HTML>
```

The preceding code will give you the correct text output, but if you put the whole script inside a table, you get the output of the code itself as if you were using <XMP> tags around it.

Using the `onClick` event handler, you can hack anyone's e-mail in Netscape 3.0. All you need is a button that the user will need to click on. Here's an example:

```
<html>
```

```
<head>
<Script language="JavaScript">
function send_mail(form){
document.form1.elements[0].click();
alert("Email Sent!");
return;
}
</script>
</head>
<body bgcolor="white">
<FORM NAME="form1" METHOD="get" ACTION="mailto:youraddess@server.com"
ENCTYPE="text/plain">
<INPUT TYPE="hidden" name="emailaddress" VALUE="emailaddress">
<INPUT TYPE="submit" name="myhidden" value="Click Here" onClick="send_mail(this.form)"
>
</form>
</body>
</html>
```

Under some platforms, if you use text/plain in document.open(), such as document.open("text/plain"), it can cause the browser to crash.

If you create an HTML page using document.write() and if the page is loaded from a server, you will not be able to see the generated HTML in your print out, saved file, or source.

If you want to perform two different tasks using an onClick event handler, you might experience problems. To solve this problem, you should call a function from the event handler to perform the two different tasks. For example:

```
<HTML><title> Perform Two Tasks</title>
<HEAD>
<SCRIPT>
function do_two(){
alert("Entering page two!");
window.location="page2.htm";
}
</SCRIPT>
</HEAD>
<BODY>
<form>
<input type="button" value="Perform Two Tasks" onClick='do_two()'>
</form>
</FORM>
</BODY>
```

```
</HTML>
```

If you're creating dynamic pages using `document.write()` and don't define the HEIGHT and WIDTH of the image source, your browser can crash.

When `document.write()` is called from an event handler, the variable and the object can lose its functionality in the page.

Under some platforms, dividing an integer by another integer gives inconsistent answers. For example, if you divide 75 by 10, sometimes you get 7.5 and other times you get 7.50000000000000002.

Under some platforms, if you have a `document.write()` inside the `<body>` tag, you may not see any text after the `</script>` or your browser might crash. For example:

```
<html>
<body bgcolor="white">
A lot of text!
<script>
document.write("JavaScript Text");
</script>
More Text after this!
</body>
</html>
```

Say you have a text box that has an `onChange` event handler that calls an `alert()` method when the user changes the input in the text box. For example:

```
<HTML>
<BODY>
<FORM>
<INPUT TYPE="text" NAME="name" SIZE="19" value="" onChange="alert('You changed it!')">
</FORM>
</BODY>
</HTML>
```

After the page is loaded, if you put your cursor on the text box and then somewhere else in the page, you will find that the `alert()` method has been invoked (although you did not type anything). This happens only the first time that document is loaded. The solution is to add a text value in the `value=""` inside the input tag.

How Do I Keep Up?

Yes, that is a valid question! For this reason, we recommend that you try some of the following sites to make sure you can keep up with changes in the JavaScript language.

Author's Secure Site

As a buyer of this book, you get a bonus! My secure site is designed to point you in the right direction to get information about new JavaScript syntax changes, JavaScript news, and new examples. The site location is http://rhoque.com/secure. You need a valid user name and password to use this site, and the accompanying CD-ROM gives you more information about that.

Netscape Handbook

 This site is designed to give you information on the current browser you are using as well as the JavaScript version that runs on your browser. The site can be found through your Navigator browser's **Help|Handbook** selection or at http://home.netscape.com/eng/mozilla/ver/handbook/. Note that the word *ver* stands for the version of the browser. For example: http://home.netscape.com/eng/mozilla/4.0/handbook/ refers to Navigator 4.0.

JavaScript Resources a2z

This site is the ultimate JavaScript resource on the net. Here you will find all the Web sites that have used JavaScript in their sites. The site includes tutorials, JavaScript and LiveConnect examples, and links to other resources. The site can be found at http://www.tradepub.com/javascript, http://www.ibic.com/java, or http://knowledgebase.net/doc/kb_main.html.

Java World and *Netscape World*

Both *Java World* and *Netscape World* present one article on JavaScript every month. These articles are dedicated to the current implementations and benefits of the language and include some cut-and-paste scripts for your Web page. Their pages are located at http://www.javaworld.com and http://www.netscapeworld.com.

With many people's help and contributions, we've done our best to present a useful JavaScript resource guide. We hope you will follow some of our guidelines. Don't forget to write us and let us know how you are doing. Good luck!

APPENDIX A

COLOR VALUES

The color values listed here are used in HTML documents for the colors of text, backgrounds, links, active links, and visited links. As you probably know, any color is made from three other colors: red, green, and blue. The hexadecimal values of these colors are given in the Red, Green, and Blue columns.

Color Name	Red	Green	Blue
aliceblue	F0	F8	FF
antiquewhite	FA	EB	D7
aqua	00	FF	FF
aquamarine	7F	FF	D4
azure	F0	FF	FF
beige	F5	F5	DC
bisque	FF	E4	C4
black	00	00	00
blanchedalmond	FF	EB	CD
blue	00	00	FF
blueviolet	8A	2B	E2
brown	A5	2A	2A
burlywood	DE	B8	87
cadetblue	5F	9E	A0
chartreuse	7F	FF	00

Color Name	Red	Green	Blue
chocolate	D2	69	1E
coral	FF	7F	50
cornflowerblue	64	95	ED
cornsilk	FF	F8	DC
crimson	DC	14	3C
cyan	00	FF	FF
darkblue	00	00	8B
darkcyan	00	8B	8B
darkgoldenrod	B8	86	0B
darkgray	A9	A9	A9
darkgreen	00	64	00
darkkhaki	BD	B7	6B
darkmagenta	8B	00	8B
darkolivegreen	55	6B	2F
darkorange	FF	8C	00
darkorchid	99	32	CC
darkred	8B	00	00
darksalmon	E9	96	7A
darkseagreen	8F	BC	8F
darkslateblue	48	3D	8B
darkslategray	2F	4F	4F
darkturquoise	00	CE	D1
darkviolet	94	00	D3
deeppink	FF	14	93
deepskyblue	00	BF	FF
dimgray	69	69	69
dodgerblue	1E	90	FF
firebrick	B2	22	22
floralwhite	FF	FA	F0
forestgreen	22	8B	22
fuchsia	FF	00	FF
gainsboro	DC	DC	DC
ghostwhite	F8	F8	FF
gold	FF	D7	00

Color Name	Red	Green	Blue
goldenrod	DA	A5	20
gray	80	80	80
green	00	80	00
greenyellow	AD	FF	2F
honeydew	F0	FF	F0
hotpink	FF	69	B4
indianred	CD	5C	5C
indigo	4B	00	82
ivory	FF	FF	F0
khaki	F0	E6	8C
lavender	E6	E6	FA
lavenderblush	FF	F0	F5
lawngreen	7C	FC	00
lemonchiffon	FF	FA	CD
lightblue	AD	D8	E6
lightcoral	F0	80	80
lightcyan	E0	FF	FF
lightgoldenrodyellow	FA	FA	D2
lightgreen	90	EE	90
lightgray	D3	D3	D3
lightpink	FF	B6	C1
lightsalmon	FF	A0	7A
lightseagreen	20	B2	AA
lightskyblue	87	CE	FA
lightslategray	77	88	99
lightsteelblue	B0	C4	DE
lightyellow	FF	FF	E0
lime	00	FF	00
limegreen	32	CD	32
linen	FA	F0	E6
magenta	FF	00	FF
maroon	80	00	00
mediumaquamarine	66	CD	AA
mediumblue	00	00	CD

Color Name	Red	Green	Blue
mediumorchid	BA	55	D3
mediumpurple	93	70	DB
mediumseagreen	3C	B3	71
mediumslateblue	7B	68	EE
mediumspringgreen	00	FA	9A
mediumturquoise	48	D1	CC
mediumvioletred	C7	15	85
midnightblue	19	19	70
mintcream	F5	FF	FA
mistyrose	FF	E4	E1
moccasin	FF	E4	B5
navajowhite	FF	DE	AD
navy	00	00	80
oldlace	FD	F5	E6
olive	80	80	00
olivedrab	6B	8E	23
orange	FF	A5	00
orangered	FF	45	00
orchid	DA	70	D6
palegoldenrod	EE	E8	AA
palegreen	98	FB	98
paleturquoise	AF	EE	EE
palevioletred	DB	70	93
papayawhip	FF	EF	D5
peachpuff	FF	DA	B9
peru	CD	85	3F
pink	FF	C0	CB
plum	DD	A0	DD
powderblue	B0	E0	E6
purple	80	00	80
red	FF	00	00
rosybrown	BC	8F	8F
royalblue	41	69	E1
saddlebrown	8B	45	13

Color Name	Red	Green	Blue
salmon	FA	80	72
sandybrown	F4	A4	60
seagreen	2E	8B	57
seashell	FF	F5	EE
sienna	A0	52	2D
silver	C0	C0	C0
skyblue	87	CE	EB
slateblue	6A	5A	CD
slategray	70	80	90
snow	FF	FA	FA
springgreen	00	FF	7F
steelblue	46	82	B4
tan	D2	B4	8C
teal	00	80	80
thistle	D8	BF	D8
tomato	FF	63	47
turquoise	40	E0	D0
violet	EE	82	EE
wheat	F5	DE	B3
white	FF	FF	FF
whitesmoke	F5	F5	F5
yellow	FF	FF	00
yellowgreen	9A	CD	32

APPENDIX B

WHAT'S ON THE CD-ROM

The CD-ROM that comes with this book is an HTML-based CD-ROM, and you will need a Netscape 3.0+ browser to view its contents. All the code is tested on this browser, so we recommend that you do not use browsers other than Netscape 3.0+. After you put the CD in your CD-ROM drive, you'll find two files. One is called `book_index.htm` for Windows 95 users and the other called `book_id.htm` is for Windows 3.1 users. These are the main files. Once you open the appropriate file for your platform, you'll find yourself in an eady-to-navigate HTML page. This HTML page is divided into four parts:

- **Book Examples**: Contains all the working examples you have seen in the book.

- **Code Samples**: Contains JavaScript code samples, courtesy of many JavaScript programmers around the world. Please note that this code is copyrighted by the respective owners. There are over 100 code samples in this area (Figure B.1).

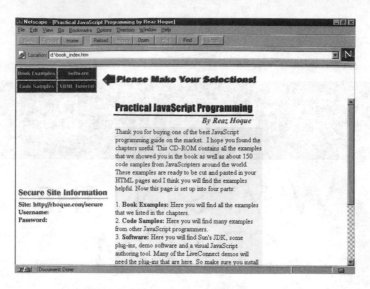

Figure B.1 The accompanying CD-ROM.

- **VRML Tutorial**: Contains an HTML-based VRML tutorial in which you can learn how to create simple VRML models. All the models are included on the CD-ROM.
- **Sample Software**: Contains Sun's JDK, Acadia Software's Visual JavaScript environment, plug-ins, LiveSite 2.0 beta, and more.

And, of course, the CD-ROM contains information to let you access the secure site at http://rhoque.com/secure. This site is designed only for you, the buyer of this book, so that you can check out examples, updates, and information on the ever-changing JavaScript technology.

INDEX

Appendix B located on page 489,
contains information about the
contents of the CD-ROM.